The Metaphysics of Dante's *Comedy*

Ben,

Congratulations & Best Wishes as you enter your senior year at Cedarville.

Thought you might like to reflect a little more on Dante in your spare time — admittedly a heavy lift — best chewed in small bites.

If you have significant questions I bet my friend Christian would be happy to engage @ christian.Moeves.1@nd.edu

Ciao,

Mark Cirkovic MD

AMERICAN ACADEMY OF RELIGION

The Metaphysics of Dante's *Comedy*

CHRISTIAN MOEVS

OXFORD
UNIVERSITY PRESS

2005

OXFORD
UNIVERSITY PRESS

Oxford University Press, Inc., publishes works that further
Oxford University's objective of excellence
in research, scholarship, and education.

Oxford   New York
Auckland   Cape Town   Dar es Salaam   Hong Kong   Karachi
Kuala Lumpur   Madrid   Melbourne   Mexico City   Nairobi
New Delhi   Shanghai   Taipei   Toronto

With offices in
Argentina   Austria   Brazil   Chile   Czech Republic   France   Greece
Guatemala   Hungary   Italy   Japan   Poland   Portugal   Singapore
South Korea   Switzerland   Thailand   Turkey   Ukraine   Vietnam

Published by Oxford University Press, Inc.
198 Madison Avenue, New York, New York 10016

www.oup.com

Oxford is a registered trademark of Oxford University Press

Library of Congress Cataloging-in-Publication Data
Moevs, Christian.
The metaphysics of Dante's *Comedy* / Christian Moevs
p.   cm.—(Reflection and theory in the study of religion)
Includes bibliographical references and index.
ISBN 978-0-19-537258-8

1. Dante Alighieri, 1265–1321. *Divina commedia*.   2. Metaphysics in literature.
I. Title.   II. Series.
PQ4432.M56M64 2005
851'.1—dc22   2004052088

Printed in the United States of America
on acid-free paper

O ben creato spirito, che a' rai
di vita etterna la dolcezza senti
che, non gustata, non s'intende mai . . .
                              (Pd 3.37–39)

Acknowledgments

Long journeys incur debts paid with love and gratitude. I offer both to my teachers, especially to Warren Goldfarb and Tom Ricketts for their unfailing mentoring and friendship; to Stanley Cavell for first showing me that every great literary text is a philosophical text, and every great philosophical text a literary text; to Martha Nussbaum, with whom I first read the *Comedy* in the context of ancient and medieval philosophy; and to the late Burton Dreben, whose undergraduate tutorial on J. L. Austin was one of the great intellectual experiences of my life. At Columbia I shall never forget the generous and extraordinarily perceptive guidance of Teodolinda Barolini, who made me a Dantist; Luciano Rebay's lucid meditation on the nature of poetry, which triggered my first reflections on Dante's poetics; Olga Ragusa's high seriousness in the study of literature; and Maristella Lorch, who planted the first seeds of this project, as she has so many others.

For detailed criticisms and suggestions on the entire manuscript at various stages, I am grateful to Teodolinda Barolini, Zygmunt Barański, Giuseppe Mazzotta, Robert Hollander, John Scott, Simone Marchesi, Steven Botterill, William Franke, Lino Pertile, Rachel Jacoff, Sandra Stow, and my sister, Marina Moevs, who proved to be an exceptional editor. Christopher Kleinhenz, Amilcare Iannucci, Franco Ferrucci, Frederick Crosson, Tom Flint, Mark Jordan, Henry Weinfield, Kevin Hart, Allen Mandelbaum, John Freccero, Francesco Sberlati, Manuele Gragnolati, Otfried Lieberknecht, Andreas Speer, Tamara Pollack, Tom Werge, and Jan Emerson all read and commented on all or parts of the manuscript. For opportunities to present parts of this work publicly, I am especially grateful to the Dante Society of America, Lino Pertile, Marty Cohen, Matthew Treherne and Vittorio Montemaggi, Alison Cornish, Michael Sherberg, Manuele Gragnolati, Andreas Speer, and Gloria Allaire. To David Burrell, C.S.C., I owe an incalculable debt, for the opportunity to teach a doctoral seminar with him on the metaphysics of creation, for guiding my thinking at every stage as this project developed, for reading several versions of the entire manuscript, and for his unshakable confidence in the outcome. My colleagues in Italian at Notre Dame—Theodore Cachey, Jr., John Welle, and Colleen Ryan-Scheutz—have fostered my work at every stage, both directly and by developing the place of Dante and Italian literature in the university's intellectual life. Jim Wetzel, Cynthia Read, Christine Dahlin, and Oxford University Press have made the process of publishing this book a pleasure.

I am grateful to the National Endowment for the Humanities for a year's support, and indebted to the extraordinary resources and generosity of the University of Notre Dame, especially the William and Katherine Devers Program in Dante Studies, the Zahm Dante Collection, the Medieval Institute, the Center for Philosophy of Religion, the Department of Special Collections, and the Institute for Scholarship in the Liberal Arts: they have made Notre Dame for me an unparalleled *studium* in which to read Dante.

The section "Time" of chapter 4 appeared in *Romance Notes* as "The *Primo Mobile* as a Pot of Time: *Paradiso* 27.115–120"; versions of brief passages of the conclusion appeared in *MLN* ("God's Feet and Hands [*Paradiso* 4.40–48]: Non-Duality and Non-False Errors") and *Lectura Dantis* ("Is Dante Telling the Truth?"); a slightly shorter version of the last section of chapter 3 appeared as "Pyramus at the Mulberry Tree: De-Petrifying Dante's Tinted Mind" in *Imagining Heaven in the Middle Ages*, edited by Jan Emerson and Hugh Feiss, O.S.B.

I dedicate this book to my parents, to my sister, and to my beloved Luke, who together have shown me the horizon of the world.

Contents

Abbreviations, Editions, Translations

Short form citations are used throughout the notes. The following abbreviations are used throughout the text:

CCSL	*Corpus Christianorum, Series Latina*
CSEL	*Corpus Scriptorum Ecclesiasticorum Latinorum*
Cv	*Convivio*
DDP	*Dartmouth Dante Project*
DVE	*De vulgari eloquentia*
EC	*Epistola a Cangrande*
ED	*Enciclopedia Dantesca*
If	*Inferno*
Mn	*Monarchia*
Pd	*Paradiso*
Pg	*Purgatorio*
PL	*Patrologiae cursus completus . . . Series Latina*
SCG	*Summa contra gentiles*
ST	*Summa Theologiae*
VN	*Vita Nova*

Dante's works are cited from the following editions, listed in the bibliography: *Commedia*, Petrocchi; *Convivio*, Ageno; *Vita Nova*, Gorni; *De vulgari eloquentia*, Mengaldo; *Epistola a Cangrande*, Cecchini; *Monarchia*, Nardi; *Questio de aqua et terra*, Mazzoni; and *Rime*, Contini. I cite the *Vita Nova* by the traditional chapter divisions, which Gorni gives in the notes on each page, and in a table on page 296, of his edition. Translations of Dante are my own unless otherwise noted, but I am heavily indebted to the English translations listed in the bibliography, especially Singleton (who closely follows

Sinclair), Mandelbaum, and Musa for the *Comedy*; and Lansing and Ryan for the *Convivio*. Translations of other authors are from the editions listed in the bibliography unless otherwise noted. The Bible is quoted in Latin from the Vulgate (*Biblia sacra*), in English from the Douay-Rheims version (*Holy Bible*). Quotations from Aristotle are from the revised Oxford translation (*Complete Works*); I cite the books of the *Metaphysics* by number (1 = A, 2 = α, 5 = Δ, 6 = E, 7 = Z, 8 = H, 9 = Θ, 10 = I, 11 = K, 12 = Λ, 13 = M). In referring to Aquinas's *Summa theologiae*, I omit *q* and *a* if the reference is to an entire article: 1a.12.4 = *Prima*, question 12, article 4; 1a2ae.q3.a8.ad2 = *Prima Secundae*, question 3, article 8, reply to second objection.

The Metaphysics of Dante's *Comedy*

Introduction

Non-Duality and Self-Knowledge

Good books have been written about Dante's passionate engagement with the world in space and time: history, politics, human action and emotion, the unfolding of divine providence. Good books
have been written about details of Dante's thought: his philosophical
sources, his moral and political ideas, his views on particular philosophical or theological questions, his views on poetry. What has
been missing is a book about Dante's metaphysics, about the understanding of reality, or more precisely about the understanding of the
relation between the world and the ground of its being, that constitutes the philosophical-theological foundation, and to a large degree
the motivation of all Dante's concerns, whether historical, political,
religious, or poetic. The center of these concerns is revelation: the
progressive unveiling of truth or being, in or through finite reality,
that constitutes salvation history, both of the individual and of humanity. Since Dante conceives his *Comedy* as both an account and
an instrument of individual and universal salvation history, one
could say that his central concern is the (revelatory) poetics of his
own poem. Thus the subject of this book will be the metaphysical
picture that grounds and motivates the *Comedy*, and the relation between those metaphysics and Dante's poetics.

   A book on Dante's metaphysics is necessary because his understanding of reality is so foreign to our own. To present Dante's ideas
about the cosmos, God, salvation, history, or poetry within the unquestioned context of widely diffused post-Enlightenment presuppo-
sitions (as is usually done) can be self-defeating: those ideas will
emerge distorted or diminished, deprived of their force, of the penetrating understanding that formed them. Dante's philosophical or
theological ideas in particular often become dead chess pieces,

moved by arbitrary rules, with no purchase on the world or on our own minds. The distortion of medieval metaphysical reflection common among modern nonspecialists is such that they often do not recognize that thought as medieval when it is presented to them in a more accurate form: it seems too daring, too sophisticated, too ideologically unfettered, too nonmedieval. It can even, to those who understand it, come to seem at least as compelling as our own examined or unexamined assumptions about the world.

The recovery of Dante's metaphysics is essential also if we are to resolve what has been called "the one fundamental question for all readers of Dante's poem" or "the central problem in the interpretation of the *Commedia*." That question or problem—which is ultimately about the poem's poetics—is what to make of the *Comedy*'s "exceptional and exceptionally insistent claims for its status as revelation, vision, or experiential record," its imposing itself, "like perhaps no other literary work, as somehow more than imaginative literature . . . as in some way religious truth, divine revelation." This is the crux the *Comedy* forces on readers of every era: how to cope with the paradox of a self-consciously fictive text that claims to be true, that confrontationally demands a response to its outrageous pretensions. The question becomes intractable, and the poem's truth-claims perhaps even incoherent, when divorced from the metaphysical understanding that underlies and motivates the poem. It has been argued that through the centuries readers have either encompassed the *Comedy*'s truth-claims within its fiction (whether as "poetic posturing," best formulated in Singleton's claim that "the fiction of the *Comedy* is that it is not fiction," or as a feature of its "Christian realism"), or else upheld those claims by saying that Dante "really believed" he was a prophet, or that he sought to impart theological or philosophical truths through poetry (Dante is *theologus* as well as, or at the expense of, *poeta*). All these responses are foreign to Dante's own understanding of his poem, because they do not address what metaphysically anchors the notion of truth for Dante. For Dante, truth cannot be a set of beliefs or ideas; nor can it ultimately be a claim about how things are in this world, or in another. In Dante's understanding, truth must transcend language, concepts, history, facts, all finite being, or else it would be contingent and relative: not truth. The *Comedy*'s truth-claims about the contingent—and thus about itself—are grounded in the *Comedy*'s metaphysics, in the relation of what is contingent to what is self-subsistent.[1]

Dante's metaphysics, and the cosmology that embodies them, are of course not just his: with their roots in Plato and Aristotle, they undergird much of the Western philosophical-theological tradition to his time and frame all later medieval Christian thought. I shall treat five principles that are fundamental to grasping the world-picture Dante shared with the profound thinkers of his age and that form the basis for understanding the *Comedy*'s purposes and poetics as Dante might have. In roughly the order of the chapters that discuss them in most detail, these principles are that (1) the world of space and time does not itself exist in space and time: it exists in Intellect (the Empyrean, pure conscious being); (2) matter, in medieval hylomorphism, is not something "material": it is a principle of unintelligibility, of alienation from conscious being; (3) all finite form, that is, all creation, is a self-qualification of Intellect or Being, and only exists insofar as it participates in it; (4) Creator and creation are not two, since the latter has no existence independent of the former; but of course creator and creation are not the same; and (5) God, as the ultimate subject of all experience, cannot be an object of experience: to know God is to know oneself as God, or (if the expression seems troubling) as one "with" God or "in" God.

Let me spell out these principles at greater length. In medieval hylomorphism (the matter-form analysis of reality), pure Intellect (consciousness or awareness) is pure actuality, or form, or Being, or God: it is the self-subsistent principle that spawns or "contains" all finite being and experience. Intellect-Being is *what is*, unqualified, self-subsistent, attributeless, dimensionless. It has no extension in space or time; rather, it projects space-time "within" itself, as, analogously, a dreaming intelligence projects a dream-world, or a mind gives being to a thought. The analogy holds in at least three respects: (1) like dreams or thoughts, created things are radically contingent, and dependent at every instant of their existence on what gives them being; (2) as there is nothing thoughts are "made of," so there is nothing the world is "made of": being is not a "something" to make things out of; and (3) dreams and thoughts have no existence apart from the intelligence in which they arise, but one cannot point to that intelligence because it is not a thing. In the same way, one cannot point to the Empyrean, the tenth heaven that the *Comedy* presents as the infinite intelligence/reality "within" which all things exist; remove it and the universe would instantly vanish. Note that the analogy in no way implies that the world is "unreal" or a "dream" (except in contrast to its ontological ground); rather, it expresses the radical non-self-subsistence of finite reality. This understanding of the radical contingency of "created" things is the wellspring of medieval Christian thought, without which the rest of medieval thought makes little sense.

Conscious being spawns experience by giving itself to it, by qualifying itself as this-or-that, and thus in one sense becoming other than itself. This is how the world comes into being: it is one valence of the Incarnation and the Trinity. However, just as a dreaming intelligence is immune to what happens in the worlds it projects, so conscious being cannot be affected by any world it creates and has no need to produce it at all: it always remains itself, knowing itself as the untouchable, dimensionless power that spawns and "contains" all finite experience. Since creation exists only as a facet, or qualification, of the self-experience of the creator, the two are not two, and yet the distinction between them could not be sharper: the creator is self-subsistent, attributeless, dimensionless, out of time; its creation is contingent, dependent, limited by attributes, ephemeral. As Beatrice puts it in *Paradiso* 29: conceived in itself, the ultimate ontological principle is a *splendore*, the reflexive self-awareness of pure consciousness; creation is its re-reflection as an apparently self-subsistent entity, a limitation of its unqualified self-experience *as* something, as a determinate thing. This voluntary self-experience of self as "other" is love; thus Dante can say that creation is an unfolding of divine love.

To the extent that finite creatures are "transparent" to pure form or Intellect, they are not other than the self-subsistent reality within which they arise (the Empyrean) and are thus not bound by space-time. Such creatures are immaterial and intelligent, nearly unqualified existence: they are angels. To the extent that finite things have spatiotemporal characteristics, they are other than conscious being, (apparently) alienated from or opaque to the reality that gives them existence. Such things are material. The being of the most material things, such as rocks, is so qualified, ephemeral, and contingent that they border on non-being. Humans are the horizon between the immaterial and the material, the infinite and the finite, the timeless and the temporal. In humans the ultimate ontological principle becomes aware of itself, *sé in sé rigira* (*Pg* 25.75): this is human consciousness or self-awareness, the divine and immortal element of the human being, manifest in space-time through the human form. If, hypnotized by their spatiotemporal form, humans experience themselves only as ephemeral bodies and identities, they are lost in eternal night and desire; if, following Christ, they turn their mind or awareness back on itself, surrendering all worldly attachment and greed (*cupidigia*), they can come to experience themselves as (one with) the reality that spawns all possible experience, immune to birth and death. Awakening to the morning of an eternal springtime, they return to their true home, the light-being-bliss-awareness-love that is the Empyrean, where all saved souls "reside."

The point, as I have said, is that that home (the Empyrean) is nowhere at all. It does not exist in space or time; thus neither does the spatiotemporal world it "contains." The Empyrean is the *subject* of all experience, it is what does the experiencing. As pure awareness or conscious being, its relation to creation, that is, to everything that can be described or talked about, may be metaphorically conceived in one of two ways: It may be imagined as an infinite reality containing the entire universe of every possible object of experience (this cosmological picture is the framework of the *Paradiso*) or it may be conceived as a point with no extension in either space or time, which projects the world of space and time around itself, as a light paints a halo onto mist. In the *Primo Mobile*, the ninth sphere, which is the nexus between the Empyrean and the world of multiplicity, between the subject of experience and every possible object of experience, Dante takes both these tacks.

In the *Primo Mobile*, Beatrice deconstructs Dante's notions of space and of time. She shows him that they are not self-subsistent realities; they do not consist in anything, in any smallest units or building blocks. In this profound sense, they are appearance, or *sembianza*, nothing but a self-experience of Intellect-Being. More specifically, Beatrice "explains" the nature and origin of time, in analogy with the generation of number in mathematics, upon entering the *Primo Mobile* in *Paradiso* 27. In *Paradiso* 28, Dante sees the inverse image of creation described above, in which the Empyrean is a dimensionless point projecting the rings of creation about itself, and Beatrice tells Dante that when he realizes that all spatial extension is *parvenza* (appearance, not a self-subsistent reality), he will see that the two opposing pictures of creation are perfectly equivalent. What is expressed spatially in either model is *virtù*, the self-knowledge of intellect: as intellect en-trues itself in itself (*s'invera*) more and more, it comes to know itself as encompassing, or spawning, more and more of the contingent universe. In perfect self-knowledge, it knows itself as a dimensionless point of awareness spawning all experience, or as an infinite, spaceless, timeless reality encompassing all space and time. When the pilgrim receives this elucidation in *Paradiso* 28, he is himself in the *Primo Mobile*, the ring closest to the point, or the ninth and last sphere of the spatiotemporal world. Beatrice's explanation sweeps away the last debris in Dante's mind, leaving his intellect as pure as the Northern Hemisphere after a north wind, so that *come stella in ciel il ver si vide* (87): like a star in the sky, truth (*what is*) saw itself. To achieve this pure reflexivity of conscious being is to become (one with) the ultimate ontological principle, what alone cannot not be: it is to find oneself in the Empyrean, as Dante does, one canto later, in *Paradiso* 30.

Textually, the precise pivot or nexus between creation and creator, time and eternity, death and immortality, in the bridge between the manifest and the unmanifest that is the *Primo Mobile*, is the enigmatic astronomical image of Latona's children, which opens the intervening canto, *Paradiso* 29, at the textual midpoint of Dante's sojourn in the ninth sphere. That image introduces the *Comedy*'s culminating full-scale account of the "act" of creation, or rather of the metaphysical relation between God and creation, which Dante-as-pilgrim is finally in a position to understand. To understand is not to grasp ideas or concepts: it is for Intellect, reflected in or as the human mind, to see and know itself as the basis of creation, which is to see truth, what alone *is*. It is to see that there is no where, no when, and no how in the creation of the world, no place, no time, and no manner in which the non-contingent One either does or does not experience itself as the contingent Many. Incarnation is one with Crucifixion: *what is* eclipses itself at the very moment that it reveals itself in/ as space-time by giving itself to finite experience. Crucifixion is one with salvation: the divine reveals, and awakens to, its own transcendence by its perfect self-sacrifice and surrender to and of the finite. This is the creation and redemption of the world, enacted within history as the Passion, Christ's and our own; it is enacted in a text as Dante's journey.

To experience and live the improbable postulate that even though consciousness (as in humans) appears to exist in, and depend on, the spatiotemporal world, the truth is the opposite (all space-time is a creation or projection of conscious being): it is to free oneself from the obsessive lure of the ephemeral (*cupidigia*) through faith (action and experience, not just words and ideas) and take one's rightful place in the Empyrean. It is to know oneself not only as a thing in space-time, but also as one with the source of space-time. It is to awaken to oneself Christically as the *subject*, and not only an object, of experience, by voluntarily sacrificing the attachment to, or obsessive identification with, the finite. It is to experience oneself as attributeless, extensionless, immune to all contingency: one with the ontological ground that spawns and knows all possible objects of experience as itself. It is to know oneself as everything, and as nothing, which is to love all things literally, and not just metaphorically, as oneself. It is to achieve salvation, or eternal life.

In this brief sketch of our itinerary, I have suggested that the *Primo Mobile* as a whole, and the opening simile of *Paradiso* 29 in particular, represent the fulcrum balancing the manifest universe against the ground of its being, multiplicity against unity. The cantos of the *Primo Mobile* are thus also the textual fulcrum of the *Comedy*, balancing the ineffable, experienceless self-experience of the experiencer itself (the closing cantos) against the inexhaustible totality of its self-expression as space and time, from the center of the universe to its outside edge, from the creation of Adam to Francesca's lapse and to the end of the world: in other words, the rest of the *Comedy*. The sojourn in the ninth sphere is also the crux of the pilgrim's journey: without the nexus or bridge of the *Primo Mobile*, there could be no "transhumanizing" (*trasumanar*), no Incarnation, no revelation, no redemption, no journey. There could be no translation of being into contingent or finite experience, and hence no space-time and no *Comedy*. This extraordinary metaphysical burden makes the cantos of the *Primo Mobile* the focus of this study; indeed, one might say that this book is an effort to understand the function and import of the opening simile of *Paradiso* 29 and culminates in the treatment of those lines in chapter 5, after of course laying the groundwork necessary to that end. The groundwork will have its own rewards, since it will require us to discuss, and I hope bring to life, many of the more difficult passages of the *Comedy* and of the *Convivio*.

I have said that a grasp of the metaphysical underpinnings of the *Comedy*, as I have sketched them, is the basis for understanding the *Comedy*'s purposes and poetics in a way more consonant with Dante's own understanding. The immediate consequences will be discussed principally in three expositions of Dante's poetics "in action," in sections titled "Pyramus and Thisbe" (*Purgatorio* 27) in chapter 3, "Unity in Diversity: Moonspots" (*Paradiso* 2) in chapter 4, and "Latona's Children" (*Paradiso* 29) in chapter 5, as well as in the conclusion. We may summarize some of these consequences under the following points:

(1) The kind of enlightenment or revelation this self-professedly salvific text is meant to trigger cannot be reduced to "doctrine," to a creed or set of ideas (already familiar to most in any case). To profess a religious or philosophical creed is not to achieve salvation; else many residents of Dante's Hell would live in Paradise, and some who live in Paradise, such as Ripheus, would live in Hell. In the *Comedy* salvation is rather a self-awakening of the Real to itself in us, the surrender or sacrifice of what we take ourselves and the world to be, a changed experience that is one with a moral transformation. We cannot know what we are until we surrender what we think we are, with all its attendant desires. Dante could say with Wittgenstein that he aims to prevent understanding unaccompanied by inner change, and that there can be no true understanding without moral perfection (perfect selflessness, the dissolution of the ego). For both, philosophical arguments that lead only to more philosophical arguments are a travesty of philosophy, an illness Dante calls *ingegno di sofista*, the mind-set of a sophist. The linear discourse of Dante's *Convivio* gives way to the *Comedy* for some of the same reasons, perhaps, that Wittgenstein's *Tractatus* gives way to the *Investigations*.

(2) By Dante's own definition of philosophy (the reflexive love of intellect for itself), a philosopher whose contribution can be reduced to doctrine, to a new set of ideas, has either been misunderstood or is not very good. Just as in the *Convivio* (3.14.15) true philosophy is said to lead to a celestial Athens in which different philosophical systems concur in the light of eternal truth, so "doctrine" in the *Comedy* points beyond itself: as in Beatrice's deconstruction of space and time, or final creation discourse of *Paradiso* 29, it leads the intellect toward knowledge of itself and dissolves. In this profound sense, there is no doctrine in the *Comedy*, no creed or set of ideas it wishes to inculcate. The *Comedy*'s aim is self-knowledge, the self-experience of *what is*.

(3) Dante's poetry has no content either (although it of course has a subject matter), because *what is*, its ultimate content and revelation, is not a thing. This truth was already implicit in Dante's definition of poetry in the *De vulgari eloquentia*, a definition that never mentions content. Needless to say, although the *Comedy* has no content that can be put into words (except as the *Comedy* itself), it has a purpose: as Dante Della Terza once remarked, in Dante's time people did not travel without a purpose. That purpose is, again, to trigger the awakening of the ultimate ontological principle to itself in us, which is revelation, or, in Christian terms, to know or receive Christ.

(4) Since in its own metaphysical framework the *Comedy* has neither doctrine nor content, a crux of Dante studies in much of this last century (and the preceding six), the apparent tension between *poeta* and *theologus*, between the *Comedy*'s poetic purposes and "what it aims to teach," is illusory, at least from a philosophical point of view. The most "doctrinal" passages of the *Comedy*, its greatest feats of narrative realism, its most ethereal lyrical flights, all have one aim: to reveal being, even though every sign, every signifier, every form, and every concept that Dante can use must necessarily also eclipse what it reveals.

(5) In Dante's metaphysical context, a text will reveal being only if it is in some sense transparent to (embodies) *what is*, pure love/awareness: the text in this sense will not be other than the reality that spawns (dictates) it. This is simply to say that in such a text the intelligence that reads recognizes itself, its own potential transcendence of all determinate form. This experience is *dolcezza*, the sweetness of infinity and unity tasted in the finite and particular: it is Dante's hallmark for poetic truth. Such a text is inspired, and it is an incarnation, or Christic revelation: it is what it reveals. When the *Comedy* grants itself scriptural authority, it is claiming to be such a text. In Dante's framework, such a text can arise only as creation does, directly from pure being or awareness (*Amor*), not from the personal agency of a finite intellect or ego (*Pg* 24.52–54): it is the Logos, the Word, arising from the Empyrean in the *Primo Mobile*, in the receptive and identity-emancipated awareness of the prophet/seer. A finite form through which *what is* glimpses itself gains authority and endures; hence the longevity of Scripture, mythological imagery, the *Comedy* itself.

(6) Only in the context of the *Comedy*'s metaphysics are two central cruxes of the last half century of Dante studies resolvable, or perhaps even coherent: whether the *Comedy* is meant to bear fourfold scriptural exegesis in general, and anagogical (figural) interpretation in particular; and whether the literal

sense of the *Comedy* is to be taken as true, as scriptural exegesis, and the *Comedy*'s own insistent claims, require. These questions have been so perplexing because they have no clear sense in the context of a materialist psychophysical dualism, the implicit world-picture of our time. In Dante's metaphysical framework, these questions, consciously pressed by the text, are meant to create the tension that triggers revelation: to understand how this self-consciously fictive text is literally true is to have understood its scriptural or revelatory status, which is to have received its anagogical or prophetic import. The *Comedy* claims to be literally true because, as I have said, it is claiming to embody or incarnate (give finite form to) Truth/Being, like Scripture, or Christ. Like the world, or the visions of Purgatory, it is a *non-falso errore*, a non-false error, contingent form disguising the reality it makes manifest by giving it finite attributes. Like Scripture, or Christ, the *Comedy* understands itself to be a finite form "transparent" to the reality it embodies, a reality that, in those who have eyes to see, can come to recognize and awaken to itself by reading this text.

(7) The *Comedy*'s unprecedented realism, its irresistible continuity with spatiotemporal experience, is thus intrinsic to its purpose: to understand how this fictive textual world becomes inescapably real is to awaken to the sense in which the spatiotemporal world is fictive (contingent or relatively "unreal"). By Dante's metaphysics, both worlds seem to be noncontingent realities because both force our suspension of disbelief, and by the same device: by drawing us inside their frame of reference so deeply that all our questions presuppose that frame of reference. Like a dreamer who has forgotten she is dreaming and has become simply a character in her dream, so we come to live only "inside" the physical universe, and not in the Empyrean which sustains it.

(8) In the *Comedy*, to journey toward self-knowledge is to assimilate as oneself, through direct poetic experience, the entire breadth of human experience in history, in its concrete and particular reality. Hence the *Comedy* is all-encompassing; it is built on human encounters; it is one man's *experience*, the assimilation of everyone's experience. Through this identification with the totality of possible experience, the obsessive point of view (*veduta*) and attachments of the individual ego begin to dissolve, and the subject of all experience, reflected as the individual mind, begins to awaken to itself, ultimately to discover itself, on the threshold of the Empyrean, as an extensionless metaphysical point, the light that spawns and is all things. Of that point, nothing can be said: it is not a thing, there is nothing to know. One can only be it; that is to know it.

(9) The discussions about whether Dante is a mystic or a rationalist, a Bonaventurian or a Thomist, a Neoplatonist or an Aristotelian, have been so fervent perhaps in part because the intuitive response in each case is that he is neither one nor the other, but both. This study may help confirm that intuition, by seeking to show that, from a metaphysical point of view, there is no fundamental incompatibility between these positions as they were held in Dante's time. As we have said, Dante himself aimed at a Truth in which all differences are reconciled. There is nothing more intellectually rigorous than

Dante's "mysticism"; there is nothing more "mystical" than his understanding of Intellect.

Is Dante's understanding of reality, as I have sketched it, radical? If it seems so, it is perhaps a sign of how far we are from it. Yet it could be argued that (with brief exceptions) the intuition that Intellect, as Being-in-itself, is the ultimate ontological principle, upon which all else depends, is implicit in some form in virtually the whole breadth of the Western spiritual and philosophical tradition, from Plato up to the Enlightenment (with many offshoots beyond); it is also implicit or explicit in most Indian and Asian philosophy. (That the contemporary Western world is an exception does not prove that we have understood what others have not; it could as well prove the contrary.) On the other hand, Dante would not have written the great wake-up call that is the *Comedy* if its message or revelation had not been as radical in his time as it is in ours, even though that revelation informs the very fabric of medieval Christian thought.

The point is, again, that to promulgate a set of ideas, a creed, a philosophy, a metaphysical world-picture, to praise or expound or teach Truth, is for Dante not the same as to see Truth, to awaken to the irreversible dissolution of the ego in the overpowering immediacy of the real. Nor is this awakening "to believe in God" as that is commonly understood: as David Burrell has remarked,[2] because God is not a thing, but the beginning and end of all things (Aquinas, *ST* 1a.2.Proem), any "believer" who assumes that he or she believes in the existence of one more entity than the nonbeliever (i.e., the world "plus something"—and quite an intrusive something!) is in fact an atheist or idol worshipper; one who considers himself an atheist because he rejects the God of such a believer may well be responding to Truth, and be a "believer." Revelation (the "unveiling of Christ") is by definition radical, and perhaps most radical to those most committed to promulgating it, because as Dante himself seems to have discovered, to promulgate it can be to defuse a world-shattering bomb into a set of ideas, concepts for the speculative understanding to grasp, beliefs to assert and define, formulas to entomb truth. Such promulgation is stillborn, with little power of persuasion, compatible with a life whose actions betray it, and unlikely to awaken sleepers. Its spiritual inefficacy could not be more evident than among Dante's greedy, quarrelsome, and murderous contemporaries, most of whom would have blithely professed allegiance to all the articles of Christian belief. In such hands creeds become simply another expression of individual and collective ego, of human political life. Hence Dante's obsession with separating church and state is also grounded in his metaphysics: it is precisely to keep revelation from becoming an ideology, or worse.

That Dante had been able to write the expository paean to Truth that is the *Convivio* (or, if we respect the fictional date of the *Comedy*'s events, the mystical invocation of Truth that is the *Vita Nova*) without experiencing inner change, with no real awakening or conversion, is the gist of Beatrice's attack when he meets her in Earthly Paradise, and it points to the watershed that is to divide the *Vita Nova* and *Convivio* from the *Comedy*. The radical revelatory poetics of the *Comedy* interrupt the rational narrative of the *Convivio*, as the poem itself warns us. Francesca, reading the Lancelot romance in *Inferno* 5, is damned because she fails to see in the literal sense of the story (what is there) its deeper message or purpose (what is not there), and thus misreads a text meant to warn her against adultery,[3] precisely the sin she says the text led her to commit. Statius, reading Vergil's *Aeneid* 3.56–57 and fourth Eclogue (*Pg* 22.37–42,64–73), is saved because he misreads the texts to see in their literal sense (what is there) what is not there: in the case of the *Aeneid*, a condemnation of his own sin of prodigality, and in the case of the Eclogue, the Incarnation itself. The lesson in reading is clear: not to misread the *Comedy* can only be to misread it. To find salvation in this text is to see in what is there (the literal sense) what alone cannot be there, because it is not a thing: it is to see truth, being, *what is*, which is for the intellect to awaken to its own emancipation and transcendence. A human intellect that gazes on a finite form (a text) and glimpses the ultimate ontological principle has, like Statius, recognized the Incarnation, Christ, the infinite in and as the finite: such an intellect has recognized itself. This self-revelation of the Real to itself is grace; it is the seed of what the *Comedy* aims to bring into the world: salvation, spontaneous morality, selflessness, enduring peace, a renewed political and social order reflecting the unity that underlies and is multiplicity. Dante probably hoped that the deliverance from evil the *Comedy* prophesies would come to pass if the *Comedy* itself could awaken its readers from their dreams, from a distorted vision of themselves and the world.

My concern with Dante's metaphysics of course in no way implies that Dante's passionate engagement with the fully present world in space and time, and with politics and history in particular, is unimportant or marginal. The opposite is true. As I have sought to show in an essay, a grasp of Dante's metaphysics may provide the foundation for a deeper understanding of Dante's political obsessions and providential vision of history. This book seeks to address a neglected sphere of inquiry in order to balance, complement, and enrich, not set aside, what has been amply treated in Dante studies. It should also be evident that it is not the purpose of this study, except incidentally, to trace a genealogy of ideas, to determine "where Dante got" this or that detail of "doctrine," an enterprise the great philosopher-Dantist Bruno Nardi termed both "perfectly useless" and usually impossible. Dante himself was not overly concerned with where he got what: he drew particular ideas with great freedom from different (often irreconcilable) sources, precisely because his purposes transcended differences of doctrine, differences that he considered a consequence of the inevitable ignorance and falsely motivated philosophizing of individual egos. I shall be concerned with a fundamental metaphysical understanding that informs the inherited and shared world-picture of Dante's time and that grounds the poem's revelatory poetics, the sense in which it transcends all doctrine. For this reason, for example, I shall not cite Aristotle only in the Latin translations available to Dante (e.g., in the commentaries of Aquinas, Albert, or Averroës), because I am interested in how the basic principles of Aristotle's thought inform all of Dante's philosophical tradition, from the Greek Neoplatonists to the Arab commentators, and not only thirteenth-century Latin Scholasticism. For the same reason, I shall often draw examples from Aquinas, Bonaventure, and others of Dante's near-contemporaries, not because I claim that one or the other is necessarily his source for specific details of his poem, but because they are clear references for how a diverse but ultimately congruous metaphysical tradition is received in Dante's time. It is that metaphysical understanding that generated, like deep and fertile ground, the great flowering of the late Middle Ages, and, as its sweetest and most nourishing fruit, Dante's *Comedy*.[4]

I

The Empyrean

Dante and Beatrice arrive in the *Primo Mobile* around line 100 of
Paradiso 27, and abandon it for the Empyrean at approximately *Paradiso* 30.37. In the cosmology accepted by Dante and most of his
contemporaries, summarized by Dante in the *Convivio* (2.3.3–7), the
Primo Mobile is the ninth of ten (sometimes eleven) heavens, or concentric spheres of creation. In this model, the earth is taken to be
the fixed center of the cosmos, and the eighth sphere, containing
the constellations of the stars, is the outer limit of the visible universe. Each of the wandering stars ("planets") is assigned its own
sphere, the innermost being the moon, followed by Mercury, Venus,
the sun, Mars, Jupiter, and Saturn. This system (with a different order of planets) was worked out by Eudoxus of Cnidus in response to
Plato's challenge to develop a mathematical analysis that would account for observed astronomical movements. In what has been
sternly termed "perhaps the most retrograde step ever taken in the
history of a science," Aristotle translated this mathematical model
into physical description. He considered each planet to be embed-
ded in a material sphere made of an invisible and incorruptible
ether, or "fifth essence," which manifests its perfection by uniform
circular motion. It has been often observed that Aristotle's cosmology superimposes mechanical explanation on an inherited Platonism. Thus, for example, the spheres impart motion to each other
through physical contact as efficient causes, yet the stars they contain partake in action and life, and the final cause of their movement is their love for the Unmoved Mover.[1]

Aristotle

For Aristotle, beyond the convex outer surface of the sphere of fixed stars, there was nothing, or rather there was God, the Unmoved Mover or First Cause, conceived as the metaphysical starting point for the chain of natural causality: "there is neither place nor void nor time outside the heaven. Hence whatever is there, is of such a nature as not to occupy any place, nor does time age it." Aristotle's Prime Mover, the foundational principle of the entire physical universe, was pure actuality, divine, perfect, eternal, changeless, absolutely necessary, good, indivisible, and dimensionless; as the goal of desire, it triggered eternal circular movement, the primary motion; as pure thought and life, its state was the joy of uninterrupted self-contemplation, the highest goal of life. The immediate subject of its influence, the eighth sphere, of the constellations, was then the "first moved," the *primum mobile*. Its regular rotation upon the axis of the earth once every twenty-four hours imparted motion to the spheres it contained, and thus to the cosmos as a whole. The observed irregularity of planetary movements was accounted for by complex combinations of the regular motions of multiple concentric spheres for each of the heavens (there were fifty-five orbs in all in Aristotle's system).[2]

Hipparchus's discovery of the precession of the equinoxes about 129 B.C. implied that the motion of the sphere of fixed stars too was complex (there was a slight west–east slippage in its daily east–west rotation), and so an invisible ninth heaven, "which many call Crystalline, that is, diaphanous or completely transparent" (*Cv* 2.3.7), was posited; Dante attributes both the discovery of the problem and its solution to Ptolemy (*Cv* 2.3.3,5; *VN* 29.2). This sphere contained no heavenly body: its function was simply to impart diurnal motion to the universe as a whole. Thus the *Primo Mobile* came to be a sphere distinct from the sphere of fixed stars. With the introduction of a ninth sphere responsible for the daily east–west movement of the heavens, the eighth sphere was no longer the fastest; indeed in its own particular motion it became the slowest, the *cerchio che più tardi in cielo è torto* ("the circle which is slowest turned in heaven" [*Pg* 11.108]): it completed one west–east rotation in 36,000 years, one degree per century (*Cv* 2.14.11, 2.5.16; *VN* 2.2), according to Ptolemy's calculations, or about 26,000, by ours. As the First Moved sphere was moved directly by God, so the particular motions of the other spheres were thought to be governed by immaterial Aristotelian "movers" or "substances," which in the Christian world usually came to be identified with angelic intelligences, instruments of the First Mover. This cosmological, "fundamentally religious" Aristotelian system eventually overlapped (never too comfortably) with the geometric calculating techniques of Ptolemy, whose epicycles, eccentrics, and equants reduced the number of concentric spheres to the nine mobile heavens inherited by Dante.[3]

Dante's Predecessors

The Empyrean, or tenth heaven, was a Christian addition to the Aristotelian-Ptolemaic universe, as Dante explicitly declares: "to be sure, beyond all these [mobile heavens] Catholics place the Empyrean heaven, that is to say, the heaven of flame or luminous heaven."[4] Indeed, its essential characteristic was to be "outside" or beyond the rotating spheres of the universe, occupying the same metaphysical position as, and absorbing the functions of, Aristotle's Unmoved Mover. Aristotle had insisted that since the eighth sphere, as the outer limit of the universe, contained all things, the universe was nowhere: there could be nothing, neither void nor space, "outside" the last moving sphere. To speak of an "outside" could only be to speak of a metaphysical principle of Being, "the thought that thinks itself," on which "depend the heavens and the world of nature." The problem was that, by Aristotle's physics, all motion must be referred to place, and all place to an immobile "container" or encompassing spatial referent. If the last sphere was not in a place, how could it be said to turn once a day?[5]

An unexpected nonastronomical contribution to the problem arose among the Catholics, who needed a place, that was not quite a place, to put the angels, Christ, and the resurrected blessed. This was the Empyrean, which arose as a purely intellectual or luminous realm, yet came to be thought of, among Dante's predecessors and contemporaries, as an immobile, almost-immaterial heaven containing the rest of the universe. In one of his most famous essays, Bruno Nardi traced the evolution of the concept of the Empyrean from its roots in Eastern and Near Eastern identifications of the conscious essential principle of the universe (God or Brahma), with light and fire (*agni*). Absorbed into the cosmogony of the Greeks, these ideas issued into the Neoplatonic doctrine that the One, identified with the principle of light, radiates from itself as *nous* (the "Intellectual-Principle" or "Intelligence" that is the foundation of the sensible world), in the same way that the sun radiates light. Re-reflecting as the world-soul, the One-as-*nous* both contains and penetrates the physical world (an idea echoed in the opening verses of the *Paradiso*: *La gloria di colui che tutto move / per l'universo penetra* ["The glory of him who moves all things / penetrates through the universe"]). Simultaneously one and many, the universal *anima* bridges the duality of spirit and matter: the world exists only as the manifestation of the world-soul. The supernatural splendor of that soul is the luminous Empyrean: it is both *tupos* (the ideal exemplar of the material world) and *topos* (the "where" of the universe), insofar as the world is situated nowhere except "within" it. As Nardi emphasizes, in Neoplatonic (and Platonic) thought the world-soul, or supernatural light, links the eternal to the temporal, the realm of intellect to the realm of sense it "contains."[6]

This Neoplatonic heritage informs the scattered references to the Empyrean in the early medieval period. Saint Basil (fourth century) postulates an invisible, timeless, changeless world of intelligible light, prior to the sensible universe, to host immaterial intelligences. Martianus Capella (fifth century) speaks of a luminous "Empyrean realm of pure understanding" beyond the swiftly turning periphery of the sensible world, a world "contained by the depth of the infinite Father." Isidore of Seville (seventh century) and the Venerable Bede (eighth century) mention an angel-containing heaven separated from the world by the turning firmament and cooled by the supracelestial waters of Genesis 1.6–7; Bede adds that this heaven is absolutely immobile. The doctrine of the Empyrean gained currency only in the twelfth century, when the widely diffused *Glossa ordinaria* explain the first verse of Genesis (*In principio creavit Deus caelum et terram*) by saying, "Not the visible firmament, but the Empyrean, that is, the fiery or intellectual heaven, which is so called not because of its burning but because of its splendor, since it was immediately filled with angels." Echoed by Peter Lombard in the *Sentences* (2.2.4), the *Glossa ordinaria's* definition of the Empyrean was absorbed into Scholastic philosophy, albeit as a more or less malleable concept based, as Aquinas remarks in the *Summa theologiae* (1a.61.4), on theological tradition rather than on scriptural authority. With the sudden infusion of Greco-Arabic learning into Christian thought at the end of the twelfth century (Ptolemy's *Almagest* was translated from Greek in Sicily in 1160, and from Arabic by Gherardo da Cremona in 1175; the *Liber de motus celorum* of Alpetragius [al-Bitruji], which defended the original Aristotelian system, was translated by Michael Scot in 1217), the seven heavens (air, ether, olympus, *spacium igneum*, firmament, acqueous [crystalline] heaven, and Empyrean or heaven of angels) common in pre-Scholastic cosmologies were replaced by the ten known to Dante: the nine mobile heavens of the Aristotelian-Ptolemaic system, plus the Empyrean.[7]

As Nardi demonstrates, not only the origin, but also the entire history, of the Empyrean is intertwined with that of Neoplatonism, both in Islamic and Christian thought. The *Liber Scalae Machometi*, a thirteenth-century Latin version of a long tradition of Muhammadan ascension narratives, speaks of a theological heaven that is a vast ocean of light. Sufic speculation, culminating in Ibn 'Arabī (1165–1240), conceives paradise as a world-encompassing angel-filled fire of eternal light; this is the One, and from it emanate as hypostases spiritual matter, universal intellect, and universal soul, which give being to all finite things. Among Christians, Michael Scot (c. 1170–c. 1235), in discussing the Empyrean, is concerned with the primacy of unity to multiplicity, that the Many are contained within the One. About fifty years later, Pseudo-Grosseteste observes that the Empyrean, as the *locus naturalis* of the universe, contains the cosmos not only spatially but also virtually: the *virtus* or causal-formative influence of all things contained within the Empyrean ultimately derives from the Empyrean itself, the foundation and first cause. More committed Aristotelians, like Albert the Great and Aquinas, as well as thinkers strongly influenced by the empiricism of Averroës, had little use for the Empyrean, except as the hypothesized supernatural home of the blessed. Their Empyrean had little or undetermined connection with, or influence on, the sensory world.[8]

Though this abode of God was said to be a purely intellectual realm, Dante's contemporaries conceived it as a spherical, corporeal, and immobile body containing the *Primo Mobile*. Despite their reluctance to say too much about what can so little be known (Bonaventure remarks that "of this heaven hidden to our senses, the holy doctors say little, and the philosophers even less"), they agreed that it had to be material, because it made little sense to speak of a place that was not a place, or of glorified bodies being nowhere. Albert the Great sums up the picture: "the heaven [caelum] is a pure body, in nature most simple, in essence most subtle, in incorruptibility most solid, greatest in size [quantitate], most pure in matter." Alexander of Hales, Richard of Middleton, Bonaventure, and Aquinas all speak of the Empyrean as material, as the greatest or highest body enclosing all other bodies; Aquinas specifies its matter as the supralunar quintessence or aither. In 1241 and 1244 the theological faculty at Paris decreed, "We firmly believe, that this corporeal place, that is, the empyrean heaven, will be [the abode of] the angels and holy souls and glorified bodies."[9]

That the Empyrean was immobile had always been assumed; since it encompassed the sphere of the Primo Mobile, it was natural to think of it as spherical. Based on the first verse of Genesis, as well as on Bede, the Glossa ordinaria, and Peter Lombard, the established view, as Aquinas observes, was that the Empyrean was created "in the beginning," together with the angels and matter. Since the Empyrean was not created to serve a purpose in the order of nature, opinion was tentative and divided about whether it exerted any influence or causality on the rest of the material world: Pseudo-Grosseteste and Richard of Middleton thought it did; Albert the Great thought not; Bonaventure thought maybe; Aquinas thought probably not, then changed his mind. He came to think that though both positions are probable, it was most likely that the Empyrean produced in the first moving heaven (and lower spheres) not transient effects of motion, but a fixed and stable "power of conservation or causation," or something of equal dignity; his final position was even more affirmative.[10]

All were unanimous on one thing: the Empyrean was luminous, though this was understood in various senses. As the home of the blessed, who shone brilliantly as they gazed, "face to face," on God, uncreated source of all light, with nothing interposed, the Empyrean was at least full of light, if indeed it was not light itself. For Bonaventure, for example, it was both "the most luminous of bodies" and "pure light," in the sense that it had no determining substantial form or essence except light. In the latter assertion Bonaventure, like many theologians of the Augustinian-Franciscan tradition, shows the influence of the so-called metaphysics of light. The complex of ideas now loosely termed the "metaphysics of light" descended from the Neoplatonic tendency, absorbed by the Christian patristic tradition, to identify God with light in a strict sense, and to think of created things as the reflection or radiation of that light. We may summarize the central strands of this variegated tradition in six points: (1) as self-subsistent Intellect-Being, God is self-radiant, intelligible, uncreated light, pure light in a proper sense; (2) created things are a reflection of the divine light, and participate in being and causality to the extent that they share in the nature of divine or created (reflected) light; (3) as the common substantial form of everything that exists, and the universal principle of causality, light (in whatever precise sense) informs and determines each finite thing in a hierarchy of being, from the most luminous, existent, and active (the outermost spheres) to the most inert, dark limit of non-being, the earth; (4) as a reflection of divine reality, the first and most immaterial of material things, physical light reveals the world to the senses; (5) in a subtle form, light bridges matter and spirit, linking body and soul and constituting the spirits of movement and sensation that animate living things; and (6) the human intellect is itself an active, radiant, spiritual light-energy, illuminating the objects of perception and receptive to the direct infusion of divine illumination. Indeed, in this picture the human soul is a great concentration of matter-informing light, akin in nature to the pure reflected *lumen* of the spheres and angelic intelligences, and even to originary *lux* itself. In varied guises and contexts, explicitly or implicitly, these ideas all become part of the fabric of medieval Christian thought, and of the *Comedy*.[11]

The essence of the "metaphysics of light" is that the assertion that God is light is not simply a metaphor. On the other hand, neither is it to be understood as reducing God to a sensory quality, or to any common notion of light. The thrust of this tradition is to bridge (not eliminate) the duality between creator and creation: light is in some sense both the self-subsistent transcendent reality and the first common principle of all finite things; it is in some sense both *lumen gloriae*, spiritual light apprehended directly by the intellect, and the reflected experience of that self-subsistent principle as a sensory quality. The second is the first as known ("reflected") within the sensible world; in this way earthly sensory experience is continuous with, a manifestation of, spiritual reality. Hence the paradigmatic expression of the "metaphysics of light," the early-thirteenth-century treatise *De intelligentiis* attributed to Adam de Belle-Mère, asserts that since light is a divine entity and the first of all substances, all things participate in the nature of light, which is to participate in divine being; light contains and sustains all things. In Robert Grosseteste's *De luce*, from the same years, a created point of pure light (*lux*, or simple being) radiates to distend matter (and space) to its most subtle, almost spiritual extension, forming the outermost sphere (for him the ninth sphere, or *Primum Mobile*); this then diffuses its reflected light (*lumen*, or spiritual body) back toward the center, concentrating matter into a hierarchy of spheres. Bonaventure too regards corporeal (created) light as a substance, the "common form" of all beings; it is more or less manifest in things insofar as they participate in being (are non-contingent or immaterial). The limit case in the created world is the Empyrean, which is pure light (the pure, created, substantial form of light), as in a different but analogous sense God can be said to be pure light (pure immaterial form).[12]

These ideas about light as a metaphysical and cosmological principle are easily corrupted into three rather primitive notions: (1) that light as a quality experienced by the senses could be self-subsistent, even God Himself; (2) if God is light and the world consists in light, then the world is "made of" God, thus collapsing the distinction between creator and creature; (3) if God is a self-radiating light, and creation that radiation, then the world emanates or pours out necessarily from God, thus annihilating the principle of a free act of creation by a creator. Aquinas in particular undercut these ambiguities at their source by insisting that light was an accident of a substance, and therefore not self-subsistent. So understood, light for Aquinas could be identified with God only metaphorically, and was simply a quality, not the substance, of the Empyrean. It is worth noting, however, that none of the Christian philosophers in the tradition of light metaphysics, not even the author of the *De intelligentiis*, made the mistakes mentioned. For example, what Bonaventure meant by "light," the "common form or nature of all bodies," is probably very close to what Aquinas meant by "act" or "being," and Bonaventure himself warns against ambiguities. Indeed, most of the characteristic features of the "light metaphysics" tradition were recuperated in various forms by Aquinas himself.[13]

Dante

This background is sufficient to clarify both the context and the originality of Dante's Empyrean, as developed in the *Comedy*. Its principal characteristics may be summarized under three points, which I shall treat under separate headings.

The Uncreated Edifice

In radical distinction from the Empyrean of the Scholastics, the Empyrean of the Comedy *is absolutely immaterial and uncreated: it does not exist in space or time.*

Apart from the *Comedy*, which is our primary concern, the Empyrean makes an appearance in the *Convivio* (2.3.8–12) and in the *Letter to Cangrande*, and we must briefly consider these. Dante's conception of the Empyrean shows some evolution from the *Convivio* to the *Comedy*: in fact, the standard view, as expressed by Attilio Mellone, is that the Empyrean of the *Convivio non esorbita dal suo tempo* ("does not depart from its time"), while that of the *Comedy* does. Although this is essentially true, it may not do justice to the tensions that already appear in the *Convivio*.[14]

In the *Convivio* (2.3.11), Dante says of the Empyrean: *Questo è lo soprano edificio del mondo, nel quale tutto lo mondo s'inchiude, e di fuori dal quale nulla è; ed esso non è in luogo ma formato fu solo nella Prima Mente, la quale li Greci dicono Protonoè.*[15] The Empyrean contains the entire universe, and it itself "is not in place." While we have seen that this is a proper Aristotelian assertion to make about the largest sphere of the physical universe (the "supreme edifice"), beyond which there is no place or void, the statement "it does not exist in place" could ambiguously suggest that the Empyrean does not itself *occupy* place (it encloses everything that does, "all the world"), and thus belongs to a metaphysical order of reality. The suggestion is reinforced by its being "formed only in the first Mind," and by the statements about the Empyrean that immediately precede and follow this passage:

> E quieto e pacifico è lo luogo di quella somma Deitate che sola [sé] compiutamente vede. Questo loco è di spiriti beati, secondo che la Santa Chiesa vuole, che non può dire menzogna; e Aristotile pare ciò sentire, a chi bene lo 'ntende, nel primo Di Cielo e Mondo. . . . Questa è quella magnificenza della quale parlò il Salmista, quando dice a Dio: "Levata è la magnificenza tua sopra li cieli."[16]

The Empyrean is the "abode" of God and of the blessed; however, as Étienne Gilson observes, "how can God and incorporeal spirits be *someplace*?" The Psalmist implies (Psalms 8.2) that the Empyrean is a divine magnificence or splendor raised *above* the skies. In fact, Dante seems to identify his Empyrean with what Aristotle placed beyond the physical universe, and Aristotle had certainly not placed an immobile astronomical heaven there, but rather nothing.[17] Aristotle had said,

> In the absence of natural body there is no movement, and outside the heaven [Primum Mobile] . . . body neither exists nor can come to exist. . . . Hence whatever is there, is of such a nature as not to occupy any place, nor does time age it; nor is there any change in any of the things which lie beyond the outermost motion; they continue through their entire duration unalterable and unmodified, living the best and most self-sufficient of lives.[18]

It seems likely that in referring to Book I of the *De Caelo* Dante had in mind this passage, implying that these beings are to be identified with Dante's "blessed spirits," by whoever properly understands Aristotle.

Ultimately what Aristotle had placed "beyond" the *Primum Mobile*, his sphere of fixed stars, was the Unmoved Mover, the thought that thinks only itself. The latter phrase is perhaps echoed by Dante's "that most high Godhead that alone fully sees itself," while the notion of Unmoved Mover is precisely how Dante begins his entire discussion of the Empyrean:

> Veramente, fuori di tutti questi [*cieli mobili*], li catolici pongono lo cielo Empireo, che è a dire cielo di fiamma o vero luminoso; e pongono esso essere immobile per avere in sè, secondo ciascuna [sua] parte, ciò che la sua materia vuole. E questo è cagione al Primo Mobile per avere velocissimo movimento; chè per lo ferventissimo appetito ch'è ['n] ciascuna parte di quello nono cielo, che è [im]mediato a quello, d'essere congiunta con ciascuna parte di quello divinissimo ciel quieto, in quello si rivolve con tanto desiderio, che la sua velocitade è quasi incomprensibile.[19]

The Empyrean is "immobile," "at rest and peaceful," because, unlike the *Primo Mobile*, it lacks nothing and hence has no desire; as the ultimate object of movement and desire, it is in effect identified with the *ens primum quietum et sempiternum*, the motionless and eternal First Being. By Aristotelian doctrine, all motion derives from desire or incompleteness; all motion is the actualizing or fulfillment of potentiality. The Unmoved Mover does not move because it alone is pure actuality; as the object of the desire that causes all motion, it must be eternal, without parts, and without magnitude. It is clear that if Dante is associating his Empyrean with what Aristotle places beyond the mobile spheres, he is implicitly dematerializing it.[20] On the other hand, we have seen that in these same passages Dante speaks of the Empyrean as *formed*, an *edifice* with *matter* and *flame*, whose *parts* are conjoined to the parts of the rotating Primo Mobile, to which it is *contiguous*.

There is in fact an obvious tension in this chapter from the *Convivio* between what Gilson terms astronomical and theological conceptions of the Empyrean: as a "tenth heaven" the Empyrean must be located beyond the *Primo Mobile*, containing it, but as "the seat of Divinity and the Blessed, it was impossible to consider it a material and astronomical heaven." Gilson observes that in passing from the ninth to the tenth heaven we are passing from a physical to a theological order of ideas, a fact implicit in Dante's introductory expression, "Catholics place . . . ," but obscured by placing the Empyrean in the sequence of astronomical spheres. The Empyrean understood as paradise ("spiritual fire, which is holy love or charity," as the *Letter to Cangrande* explains [24.68]) does not function well as an Aristotelian sphere.[21]

The treatment of the Empyrean in the *Comedy* is much more sophisticated: the tension is no longer between theology and astronomy, but between the One and the Many, how it is that contingent differentiation arises from, and yet is "contained within," simple Being. Along with this development, the word *empireo* itself disappears from the *Comedy* after being used only once (in *If* 2.21), as Gilson observes ("Recherche de l'Empyrée" 160): "the Empyrean has lost its name because its nature has changed. It became anonymous at the same time that it lost its reality as a distinct astronomical entity. What is this 'heaven' that has no place and no duration? Physically speaking, it is a myth; theologically speaking, it is a metaphor." In the *Comedy* the word *empireo* is replaced by a breathtaking array of metaphors for the omnipresent light-sweetness-love in which Being consists. As Gilson remarks (161), what all these phrases have in common is that they eliminate "the proper name of the thing that has ceased to be a thing," and thus avoid all the physical or limiting connotations of the word *empireo*. It is precisely when the all-permeating, all-encompassing beginning and end of all things becomes Dante's central focus that he no longer calls it *empireo*.

Thus in the *Comedy* the Empyrean is explicitly immaterial. When Dante leaves the *Primo Mobile*, Beatrice explains:

> Noi siamo usciti fore
> del maggior corpo al ciel ch'è pura luce:
>   luce intellettüal, piena d'amore;
>   amor di vero ben, pien di letizia;
>   letizia che trascende ogne dolzore.[22]   (*Pd* 30.38–42)

The *Primo Mobile* is the "greatest body," the Empyrean is pure intellectual light, awareness-love-bliss-sweetness. The same dichotomy is stressed elsewhere: the *Primo Mobile* is *lo real manto di tutti i volumi / del mondo, che più ferve e più s'avviva / ne l'alito di Dio e nei costumi* ("the royal cloak of all the world's revolving spheres, the heaven most alive and burning in the breath of God and in His ways" [*Pd* 23.112–114]); it is the *miro e angelico templo / che solo amore e luce ha per confine* ("the wondrous and angelic temple bounded only by love and light" [*Pd* 28.53–54]). The Empyrean is the "breath of God," love, light. In fact, as Mellone points out (*Dottrina* 32), Dante refers to the heavens as the "sensible world" or "body" (*mondo sensibile, corpo*) only when he means the nine spheres without the Empyrean.

Although in the *Comedy* (and the *Letter to Cangrande*, if it is his) Dante still occasionally speaks of the Empyrean as an encompassing sphere with "parts," he is more careful to correct misimpressions.[23] Thus Saint Benedict tells the pilgrim,

> il tuo alto disio
> s'adempierà in su l'ultima spera,
> ove s'adempion tutti li altri e 'l mio.
>   Ivi è perfetta, matura e intera
> ciascuna disïanza; in quella sola
> è ogne parte là ove sempr' era,
>   perché non è in loco e non s'impola.[24]   (*Pd* 22.61–67)

If we wish to conceive the reality in which all desire ends as the "last sphere," it is a sphere that "is not in place and has no poles." If we wish to picture it (for example, as a gigantic rose full of seats, children and sages), we must be aware that all that is appearance (*parvenza*), and the reality is light, however understood:

> Lume è là sù che visibile face
> lo creatore a quella creatura
> che solo in lui vedere ha la sua pace.
>   E' si distende in circular figura,
> in tanto che la sua circunferenza
> sarebbe al sol troppo larga cintura.
>   Fassi di raggio tutta sua parvenza
> reflesso al sommo del mobile primo,
> che prende quindi vivere e potenza.[25]   (*Pd* 30.100–108)

The light through which the creator becomes manifest to the creature can be none other than the *lumen gloriae*, the essence of beatific vision. The *lumen gloriae* is pure intellectual light, supernaturally infused into the created intellect, making that intellect deiform, conformed to the essence of God, Intellect itself. This intellectual light is won through love and desire; the beatific vision that results is marked by the three attributes of understanding, love, and bliss, which, as Giovanni Fallani and Simon Gilson point out, is precisely how Beatrice describes the Empyrean when she and Dante enter it: *luce intellettüal, amor di vero ben, letizia*. Dante is explicitly identifying the beatific vision with the Empyrean itself, a move that may make Dante unique among the theologians of his time.[26]

It is consistent with the *Comedy*'s understanding of the Empyrean that it, unlike the mobile heavens, is uncreated. In fact Dante does not list it among the first created things, which he identifies as the angels (*puro atto*), matter (*pura potenza*), and the material heavens between the two (*Pd* 29.22–36); nor does he ever say that it was created later. This too distinguishes Dante's understanding sharply from contemporary doctrines, which asserted, on the authority of the *Glossa ordinaria*, Bede, and Peter Lombard, that the Empyrean was created together with the angels and matter.[27]

One serious attempt has been made to demonstrate that Dante's Empyrean is corporeal. In a ninety-page essay, Bortolo Martinelli marshalls an overwhelming battery of references to argue, in effect, that since thirteenth- and fourteenth-century thought unanimously considers the Empyrean material and created, Dante must too (112, 142). The argument is unconvincing and requires elaborate and forced interpretations of Dante's text. Perhaps the easiest rebuttal is to note that in the inverse image of creation that appears in *Paradiso* 28, the burning point, "from which heaven and all nature depend," as Beatrice explains (*Da quel punto/depende il cielo e tutta la natura* [41–42]), projects around itself nine (not ten) rings of fire, which correspond to the nine moving spheres alone, the first of which is clearly the *Primo Mobile* (43–45, 70–72). Beatrice has identified the *punto* by translating Aristotle's phrase for the Unmoved Mover: *ex tali igitur principio dependet caelum et natura . . . hoc enim est Deus*, in the Latin version of Dante's time. Aristotle also explains that the Unmoved Mover is indivisible and has no parts or size, and in fact Dante states in the *Convivio* (2.13.27) that a point is unmeasurable and indivisible. The inference is clear: the dimensionless point, corresponding to the Empyrean and identified with the ultimate ontological principle, Aristotle's Unmoved Mover—which, Aristotle explicitly demonstrates, can have no size—is self-subsistent, uncreated, and immaterial, occupies no place, and is divinity itself, the source of the creation it projects. Martinelli's essay is precious, however, for its scholarship, and as the best demonstration of the audacity of Dante's departure from his contemporaries.[28]

The Divine Mind

In the Comedy *Dante identifies the Empyrean with the divine mind; the splendor of that mind is the luminosity of the "tenth heaven."*

Dante could not be more explicit. Beatrice says of the *Primo Mobile*:

> La natura del mondo, che quïeta
> il mezzo e tutto l'altro intorno move,

> quinci comincia come da sua meta;
>   e questo cielo non ha altro dove
> che la mente divina, in che s'accende
> l'amor che 'l volge e la virtù ch'ei piove.
>   Luce e amor d'un cerchio lui comprende,
> sì come questo li altri; e quel precinto
> colui che 'l cinge solamente intende.[29]   (*Pd* 27.106–114)

The *Primo Mobile* has no "where" except the divine mind, which of course is itself nowhere: the Empyrean is pure Intellect. As Gilson remarks, "It is absolutely certain that Dante is here speaking of the Crystalline heaven [the *Primo Mobile*] as encompassed by divine thought, the only place that one could attribute to it, even though that thought itself has no place."[30]

Mellone, up to his time alone (as he himself noted) among the interpreters of the passage, but later followed by others, argued that Dante was to be understood as saying: "the *Primo Mobile* has no other *place in which* are kindled the love that turns it and the virtue it rains down, *except* the divine mind." Then the following lines would be saying that as the *Primo Mobile* is encompassed by the Empyrean, so the Empyrean is encompassed by God (*colui che 'l cinge*).[31] Apart from the unnatural reading of lines 109–111 (a reading that moreover reduces them to a banality) and the conflict with *Paradiso* 28.16–78 outlined earlier, Mellone forgot his own demonstration (29) that the Empyrean is not a sphere: it does not exist in space-time. Indeed it does not exist at all, if to "exist" is to have any kind of determinate being. To "circumscribe the Empyrean" is simply to circumscribe the boundary of the *Primo Mobile*, a limit defined by love and light. Dante is saying that only the intelligence that can encompass the "outer boundary" (*precinto*) of the sensible world, that is, only the intelligence that can find all of reality within itself (*colui che 'l cinge*), can understand *that* or *how* the world is encompassed in, created by, Intellect (the divine mind). (It is to encompass the encompassing itself, so to speak.)[32] Such an intelligence can only be God or one assimilated to God (deiform): in other words, one that has reached the Empyrean, and thus passed beyond the "boundary" of the sensible world to the changeless reality (love-intellect-being) in which it consists. The *precinto* is the dividing line between the natural world, as known to the mind and senses, and its metaphysical (spiritual) foundation. Dante, by his own account in the *Comedy*, is one who has passed that boundary. That makes him, in his own estimation, one whose words reach beyond the "dividing line" to reveal the light-love-bliss in which all spatiotemporal experience ultimately consists.

In fact Dante consistently calls the Empyrean the "residence" of God, as well as of the blessed. We saw that the *Convivio* refers to the Empyrean as "the dwelling-place of that most high Godhead who alone fully sees Himself." In the *Comedy*, God, "that infinite and ineffable good that is there above" (*quello infinito e ineffabil bene / che là sù è* [*Pg* 15.67–68]), dwells "in the heavens, but not circumscribed" (*ne' cieli, non circunscritto* [*Pg* 11.1–2]): "there is his city and high throne: oh happy those whom he elects to be there!" (*quivi è la sua città e l'alto seggio: / oh felice colui cu' ivi elegge!* [*If* 1.128]). Denoting God as the Trinity, Dante "locates" Him in the same way:

> Quell'uno e due e tre che sempre vive
> e regna sempre in tre e 'n due e 'n uno,
> non circunscritto, e tutto circunscrive.[33]   (*Pd* 14.28–30)

Mellone, followed by others, argued, however, that Dante places yet another heaven, identified with God Himself, beyond the Empyrean. This extra heaven would be the *coelum Trinitatis*, a heaven occasionally added to the seven spheres of pre-Scholastic cosmologies. Among Scholastic philosophers, the *coelum Trinitatis* became a metaphor for the all-encompassing Trinity; precisely for this reason it was often interchanged with the Empyrean. Indeed, if the *coelum Trinitatis* was distinguished from the Empyrean in Scholastic thought, it was only because the Empyrean was conceived as created and material, and hence among the created things contained within the all-containing deity. It seems evident that Dante has fused Empyrean and *coelum Trinitatis* in his uncreated and transcendent tenth heaven, which he identifies with the radiance of *la mente divina*. Indeed the blessed, and the pilgrim himself, contemplate Christ and the Trinity from their "places" within the Empyrean, and it is within the Empyrean that the mystery of the Trinity is revealed to Dante.[34]

Dante has called the supranatural realm of the Empyrean "pure light, intellectual light," the light through which the creator becomes visible to the creature. To paraphrase *Paradiso* 13.52–63, God is the *lucente* (effulgent light), the Word is *viva luce* (living light), both are one with *Amor* (Love). Creation is the *splendore* (reflection) of that Intellect-Light, a "raying" (*raggiare*) into determinate identities while remaining always one (*etternalmente rimanendosi una*). Elsewhere Dante says, "The divine goodness, which spurns all envy from itself, burning in itself, so scintillates that it displays the eternal beauties" (*La divina bontà, che da sé sperne / ogne livore, ardendo in sé, sfavilla / sì che dispiega le bellezze etterne* [*Pd* 7.64–66]). We have seen that nothing was more natural to Christian thinkers than to speak of God as light, and that in the Augustinian tradition this manner of speaking was not considered strictly metaphorical, on Augustine's own authority.[35] Nardi's insistence, beginning in 1912, that Dante should be understood against the background of the "metaphysics of light" has been generally accepted, contested in the past only by a few Thomistic interpreters. The point of contention was not so much the identification of the Empyrean with God as pure intellectual light, as the supposed consequence that this would commit Dante to a doctrine of Neoplatonic emanation, as opposed to Thomistic creation. The real question then is, In what sense is the luminous Empyrean the cause or source of spatiotemporal reality? This question will be considered next; for now we can say that in the face of the multitude of explicit assertions in the *Comedy*, it is an uphill battle to argue that Dante considers light simply a metaphor for spiritual reality.[36] Nor is it easy in the context of medieval philosophy to give a precise meaning to "light taken in a strict sense," as opposed to common usage: all philosophical language is to varying degrees metaphorical, or "analogical." We can only conclude that in some sense spatiotemporal reality consists in (is "contained within") a self-subsistent light, "the lofty light which in itself is true" (*L'alta luce che da sé è vera*) [*Pd* 33.54, and see 124]), however understood. That light (*etterno lume, somma luce, vivo raggio, luce etterna, vivo lume, alto lume, fulgore*, to cite only from *Paradiso* 33.43–141) is identified with the supranatural conscious reality that "encompasses," sustains, and pervades creation.[37]

The Ground of Being

The Empyrean is the "cause" of the phenomenal world only in the sense that it is its "foundation," the ground of its being.

As the changeless substratum of sensible reality, Dante's Empyrean does not operate on the cosmos. The "tenth heaven" is the reality in which the universe consists (participates). As the ground of being of the sensible world, however—its source and end—the Empyrean may be conceived as the ultimate "cause" or basis of creation. It is in this sense that God is spoken of as First Cause throughout both the Neoplatonic and Aristotelian traditions.

We must guard against attributing our post-empiricist notion of causality to medieval philosophers. Neither Neoplatonists nor Peripatetics thought of the First Cause as the starting point of a temporal sequence of causes and effects; rather, they considered it the supreme principle in an ontological order of dependence. It is a vertical hierarchy: a relation of subsuming under more fundamental principles. Causality for the medieval world is less a temporal association between *events* than an ontological relation between *things*: an effect depends on its cause to the extent that it owes its existence to it. In other words, once a thing exists, it no longer "depends" in any sense on the preceding cause in a temporal series, but owes its continuing existence "here and now" to a cause above it in the hierarchy of being. Aquinas, for example, thought that a temporal series of causes and effects could stretch back to infinity, while the ontological series necessarily had to end in Being itself, God.[38]

The verticality of causality as a hierarchy of being is typically associated with Neoplatonism. A particularly vivid example is the *Book of Causes* (*Liber de causis*), a short treatise of great influence and authority (frequently cited by Dante) that circulated under the name of Aristotle in the Islamic and Christian world, was required reading at the Faculty of Arts in Paris in the thirteenth century, and was eventually correctly identified by Aquinas as a synthesis of Proclus's *Elements of Theology*. But the verticality of causality is also one of the most Platonic features of Aristotle's philosophy. Aristotle's *aition*, normally translated as "cause" in English, but perhaps better rendered as "explanatory principle" or "ground," answers the question, "What is responsible for the fact that such and such a state of things now exists?" What Aristotle means by "cause" cannot be reduced to an event that uniformly precedes another; when Aristotle says that we know a thing through its causes, he means (Platonically) that we understand it through its relation to more fundamental principles, the "first things" or *aitia*.[39]

The point may be rephrased by saying that cause and effect in a temporal sense are terms that apply only within creation. It is clear that between what exists out of time and without attributes, and what exists in time, there can be no causality in the sense of relations between events, or even between things. More generally, we shall see that the "secondary causes" that make a finite thing a this-or-that at any moment in time, as opposed to giving it being, cannot be attributed to Dante's Empyrean. The Empyrean does not determine identity; it is the reality within which the determination of identity occurs. God *does* nothing; God *is*.

These facts are obscured by any attempt to speak of the relation between God and creation, which always amounts to forming a mental picture. The picture offered to Dante was that of Aristotelian and medieval cosmology, in which God contains (and penetrates) a universe of rotating concentric spheres. The outermost of these, the *Primo Mobile*, is spun by its love for that Unmoved Mover, thus imparting motion to the eighth sphere and that sphere to the next. The formative influence (*virtù*) of all these rotating spheres generates the kaleidoscope at the center that is the sublunar realm of ephemeral sensory experience, of "brief contingencies" or *brevi contingenze* (*Pd* 13.63). By being the ultimate object of love, God "sets in motion" the entire chain of natural causality, or generation and corruption, which begins with the *Primo Mobile*.

The *Convivio*'s gloss on this picture, from the passage discussed earlier (2.3.8–12), is perhaps a little crude. After observing that "Catholics hold that beyond all these [moving heavens] lies the Empyrean Heaven . . . and they hold that this is motionless because it possesses in its every part the perfection required by its matter," Dante explains that the *Primo Mobile* spins "with the utmost speed, because in every part of that ninth heaven bordering the Empyrean there burns an ardent longing to be united to every part of that most divine heaven which is at rest." The Empyrean is immobile insofar as none of its "parts" would have any reason to occupy the position of any other of its parts, because they are all perfect and interchangeable. This is to say in effect that it has no parts and is thus uniform and indivisible. Nardi traces this argument to Michael Scot, who derived it from the opening proposition of Aristotle's *Physics* 6.4: "everything that changes must be divisible." The argument does not differ appreciably from saying, as Michael Scot also does, that a being does not move (change) insofar as it is perfect, that is, has no potential that remains unactualized.[40]

Then how is the "fastest heaven" (*ciel velocissimo*) different from the "immobile heaven" (*cielo immobile*)? To say that "each part" of the *Primo Mobile* wishes to join "each part" of the Empyrean is to say that, while the *Primo Mobile* is fully actualized in "substance" or in its totality, it is in potential as far as location. In other words, each of its parts is not, but could be, in the position occupied by each of its other parts. Since it cannot occupy each position with each part simultaneously, but only one at a time, it must move, which is in effect a desire on the part of the *Primo Mobile* to be assimilated to, one with, the First Cause. Nardi traces this argument to the great eleventh-century Islamic philosophers Avicenna (Ibn Sīnā) and Algazel (al-Ghazālī), who of course put no Empyrean beyond the ninth sphere, only the Unmoved Mover. The Unmoved Mover is *totum simul*, everything all at once: the *Primo Mobile* mimics the Unmoved Mover in space-time by all-encompassing and "incomprehensible" speed. As Nardi points out, in adopting this argument through Michael Scot, Dante has in effect substituted the Empyrean for the Unmoved Mover. Again the implication, not yet in focus in the *Convivio*, is that the *Primo Mobile* exists in space-time (although without any other limiting attributes), and the Empyrean does not. Spatiotemporal being can "assimilate itself" to what it consists in, the act-of-being itself, only by featurelessness, all-inclusiveness, and the omnipresence of infinite speed. In this sense, the *Primo Mobile* is moved from "within": there is nothing "without," beyond itself.[41]

In chapters 24–26 of the *Letter to Cangrande*, the same metaphysical picture is glossed in terms of light, in order to explain Dante's assertion that he was in "the heaven that most receives of His [God's] light" (*Pd* 1.4–5). The explanation rests on identifying the divine light with perfection (the actualization of all potentiality) and with the principle of ontological causality, the ultimate source of all finite being. There are two arguments. The first is that what contains something else as its natural place is also its formative cause, the source of its finite being: "containing" serves as a cosmological analog or metaphor for ontological causality. As the ultimate natural place, "which contains all bodies and is contained by none" (*continens corpora universa et a nullo contentum* [67]), the Empyrean is the ultimate ground of the being of the universe. Since ontological causality is nothing but divine light, in virtue of which all things are, the Empyrean is the most luminous heaven. As Mazzeo observes, this argument constitutes a fusion of Neoplatonic light theory with Aristotelian natural place; Martinelli traces the Neoplatonism to the *De intelligentiis* and the *Liber de causis*. The second argument resembles the *Convivio*'s argument for the Empyrean's immobility. The Empyrean alone does not move, because it always has perfectly in every part everything it could have: its "parts" do not suffer the limitation of being in one place instead of another (which is to say in effect that it does not suffer the privation of spatiotemporal extension). Since perfection is divine light, and the Empyrean is fully perfect, it is more luminous than all the other heavens. The two arguments together may be summed up in one sentence: the Empyrean is the light (however understood) in which reality ultimately consists.[42]

The sharp distinction traced here, between the totality of the natural order on the one hand and the metaphysical basis of its existence on the other, is a feature of Aristotle's philosophy, which, transformed by Christianity and Neoplatonism, persists as a central trait of Thomistic, indeed of Christian, thought. Aristotle's Unmoved Mover stands "outside" an eternally existing world that it perhaps did not create, and that it moves and sustains simply by existing, by being its good. The identification of God with pure existence, already penetratingly developed in an Islamic context by Avicenna and the Jewish philosopher Moses Maimonides, culminates in Aquinas, who, as the great Étienne Gilson never tired of reminding the world, conceived being not as "that crust of essences which is but the outer coating of reality," but rather as "the primitive

existential act which causes [a thing] both to be and to be precisely that which
it is." In short, for Aquinas, "existence is an act, not a thing." The distinction
between creator and creation thus becomes the distinction between "to be" and
"to-be-this-or-that." The essence of a creature is to-be-a-certain-thing. God's
essence is simply to be: this is why essence and existence are identical only in
God. It is the distinction between what lies "beyond" the all-encompassing
boundary of the *Primo Mobile* and everything that it "contains."[43]

The point is that nothing lies "outside" the *precinto* of creation, except,
if you will, an uninflected active verb, "to be." So in what sense do all
"saved" beings in the *Comedy* "reside" in the Empyrean? What does it mean,
metaphysically speaking, for the pilgrim to cross the boundary of the *Primo
Mobile*? In terms of Aquinian metaphysics, perhaps we could say a rational
being is "in the Empyrean" if, when it says "I am," "am" is an active verb.
Summed up in one sentence, Dante's journey of salvation would be to move
from *I* am to I *am*. I am not (primarily) a thing, but (one with) the act of
existing itself, however qualified. The act of existence of course cannot be
described in itself, because it is all there is. In this flash of insight, all "I"s
are one: each is everything and nothing. This was the revelation experienced
by Moses on Mount Sinai, which prompted him to tell the Israelites: "*I AM*
sent me to you."[44]

Here we can see to what point the Neoplatonic and Aristotelian pictures
of reality become indistinguishable in Aquinas, and in later medieval thought
in general, in that great period of "Neoplatonizing Aristotelianism" that had,
we should remember, absorbed as Aristotelian both the Proclean *Liber de causis*
and (through Avicenna and others) the so-called *Theology of Aristotle*, an epit-
ome of the *Enneads* of Plotinus himself. Aquinas's sharp distinction between
essence and existence, between non-self-subsistent being-this-or-that and the
timeless, dimensionless act of being itself, is heir to both the Aristotelian and
the Judaeo-Christian conceptions of God as an untouchable and attributeless
transcendence over empirical reality. It is also, Platonically and Neoplatonically,
the principle that "spiritualizes" material reality and establishes continuity between God and creation. In Aquinian terms, finite things share in the act of
existence. This sharing in being is one way of conceiving ontological causality,
whereby divine reality (light) permeates all things. As the *Letter to Cangrande*
explains, citing Aristotle's *Metaphysics* and the *Liber de causis* together, in the
whole hierarchy of being, "mediately or immediately, everything that has being,
derives being from [God]," and this first cause, Light or Intellect itself, is more
the cause of each thing than any secondary cause (54–61). It is through this
sharing or causality that God is One and yet (omnipresent in the) Many, or
"all-pervading," a truth for which the *Letter* cites many biblical authorities, as
well as Lucan (62–63).[45]

To put it another way: God is no more a carpenter within the Aristotelian
tradition than He is in the Neoplatonic tradition. To cite Aquinas citing Augustine, the universe is not a house God built and left standing. The act by
which God "first gave being" cannot be essentially distinguished from the act
by which God sustains being, nor is that act an event in space-time. The uni-

verse is something the divine act-of-existence is doing or making or lending itself to, moment to moment: should it cease to do so at any instant, there would be instantaneous nothingness. The divine is in every place because it gives being intimately, "from the inside," so to speak, to whatever exists in place, as the being of its being. In Augustine's words: "my God, I would have no being, I would not have any existence, unless you were in me. Or rather, I would have no being if I were not in you 'of whom are all things, through whom are all things, in whom are all things.' " A sentence from the *Book of Causes* (1.7) could serve as a gloss on Augustine: "A thing must be 'being' first of all, then 'living,' and after 'man.' " Or as Patrick Boyde elegantly (and Neoplatonically) summarizes the point: "if the source of light were ever to be switched off, the sphere of radiance that is the universe would immediately cease to exist." To understand medieval Christian thought is above all to grasp the radical contingency of the sensible world, which is to awaken to the notion of a creature and a Creator.[46]

These observations may help to clarify the *Letter to Cangrande*'s famous gloss (23.64) on the opening lines of the *Paradiso*: "the divine ray or divine glory 'penetrates and reflects throughout the universe': penetrates in regard to essence, reflects in regard to being." The act of being is "reflected" (*resplendet*) in the existence of finite beings as their substantiality, which is their luminosity. The determinate identity (attributes) that makes being finite (this-or-that), through or by which a thing is a certain kind or qualification of the act-of-existence, is essence. The divine light "penetrates through" the universe as essence in the sense that all attribute or identity is simply a mode of being, characteristics through which things exist, through which they share more or less in being: essence is nothing without existence. The distinction between essence and existence is thus more philosophical than empirical (existence in itself is no thing, and essence in itself is nonexistent), whether it applies to the self-subsistent divine light (in which they are identical) or to the reflection of that light as creation (in which they are not). Essence is no more a "thing" than existence.[47]

Given the pilgrim's claim to have "visited" the realm of transcendent being, it is not surprising that in the *Comedy* Dante is particularly careful to distinguish the Empyrean from the natural order, which alone is limited by identity, change, and causality. Representing the absence of all motion and desire, the essential traits of creation, the Empyrean is the heaven that the light of Providence "makes ever quiet, within which turns the one in the greatest hurry" (*fa 'l ciel sempre quieto / nel qual si volge quel c'ha maggior fretta* [Pd 1.122–123]). The "heaven in a hurry" is of course the *Primo Mobile*, "the one that sweeps the rest of the world along with it" (*costui che tutto quanto rape / l'altro universo seco* [Pd 28.70–71]). All formative-generative influence (*virtute*) in the physical world begins with this motion.[48]

> Dentro dal ciel de la divina pace
> si gira un corpo ne la cui virtute

l'esser di tutto suo contento giace.
   Lo ciel seguente, c'ha tante vedute,
quell' esser parte per diverse essenze,
da lui distratte e da lui contenute.⁴⁹   (*Pd* 2.112–117)

The "heaven of divine peace" is the Empyrean; the "turning body in whose power lies the being of all that it contains" is the *Primo Mobile*; the "following heaven, which has so many eyes/visible things," that is, stars, and "distributes that being into diverse essences, distinguished from, and yet contained within, that being," is the eighth sphere, the sphere of fixed stars or constellations. The *Primo Mobile* is thus the nexus between pure being and the differentiation of being into identity (essence). We have seen that finite being (to-be-a-certain-thing) may be thought of as a subcategory of being (to be), the ground represented by the Empyrean. The *Primo Mobile* "translates" the one into the other: it is not only the sharp dividing line between creator and creation, it is also the nexus between them. The great Christian Neoplatonist Pseudo-Dionysius, to whom we shall return, put it this way: the Preexistent, or Source and End of all things, "is the boundary to all things and is the unbounded infinity about them in a fashion which rises above the contradiction between finite and infinite. . . . He proceeds to everything while yet remaining within himself." For Dante, the *Primo Mobile* is what Nardi called the *anello di congiunzione*, the connecting ring or intermediary linking the temporal to the timeless, the finite to the dimensionless, the determinate to the featureless, the Many to the One. It is the link that for Nardi was lacking in Aristotle, and that was philosophically supplied by the Neoplatonists as the notion of a world-soul that contains, forms, and animates spatiotemporal reality.⁵⁰

Nardi, however, tended to over-Neoplatonize Dante, sometimes interpreting his metaphysics in a "pagan" mode insufficiently tempered by Thomas or Augustine. The principal distinction is that in "pagan" Neoplatonism the One, or supreme deity, is above being or existence in any sense, and therefore also above the divine mind or supreme intelligence, while Christian thought, both Augustinian and Aristotelian, tends to identify the divine mind with pure being, the divine itself. Thus in "Dottrina dell'Empireo" Nardi is led to equate Dante's Empyrean with Plotinus's world-soul, and the *mente divina* with *nous*, the luminous radiation of the One as awareness or Intellect. In this view the Empyrean, and not the *Primo Mobile*, would be the link between the sensible world and transcendent reality. It would be more accurate to say, however, that Dante's Empyrean *is* transcendent reality (the Christian equivalence God-Trinity-Logos), and the "vivifying container" of the world, which would perhaps correspond to the Neoplatonic world-soul (which cannot exist except in a body it animates), is the *Primo Mobile*, the "translator" of being into spatiotemporal manifestation. The radiant hypostasis of the One as *nous* is, if anything, what the Empyrean represents: it is the motionless radiance of the *mente divina*, the *luce intellettüal* beyond the *precinto* of sensible reality. In the "simple light" (*semplice lume*) of the Empyrean Dante sees the One that "binds" within itself "that which in the universe is scattered, dispersed in leaves" (*ciò che per l'universo si squaderna* [*Pd* 33.85–90]). In fact, in other essays Nardi makes no distinction between the Empyrean and the divine mind.[51]

That the Empyrean does not "act upon" creation is more explicit in *Paradiso* 27.106–111, where Beatrice says of the *Primo Mobile* that "the nature of the universe . . . begins from here as from its goal and starting-point" (*la natura del mondo . . . quinci comincia come da sua meta*). *Meta* can be glossed as the Aristotelian final cause, here the perfect motion all the other spheres seek to imitate by their nature and desire, and which prompts and regulates their movement. All finite being (*natura del mondo*) begins from the *Primo Mobile* and tends toward the *Primo Mobile*, the limit beyond which there is nothing except existence itself. In this sense, *meta* also preserves its etymological meaning of "turning-post" (as in a Roman hippodrome), here the ultimate limit of the world of determinate identity. As the source of finite being within being itself, the *Primo Mobile* is the link on which the pilgrim's journey, and the *Comedy*'s salvific mission, depends: there can be no "transhumanizing" or "inGoding" (*trasumanar, indiare*) if God is not "Creator" and the universe is not "creation," if determinate identity is not a sharing in, not in a profound sense one with, self-subsistent being. The Christian religion calls the bridge or union between finite being and sheer unqualified existence "Christ" or Logos, names that designate the identity/continuity between spatiotemporal reality and conscious self-subsistence.[52]

The *Comedy*, we have seen, represents that conscious self-subsistence as the Empyrean, which is divine being, pure intellectual light, the divine mind, love, joy, and sweetness (*luce intellettüal, la mente divina, amore, letizia, dolzore*). In the next two chapters I shall try to give a more precise sense to this string of identifications and to make clearer what it could mean to say that a mortal, finite, corporeal, spatiotemporal creature, such as the pilgrim Dante, could travel beyond the world to become one with the divine, with Intellect-Being itself. For now it is enough to observe that the "boundary" that "limits" creation is the act of being in which creation consists: in Aquinian terms it is to move from the realm of essence to that of existence, which is to move nowhere at all. What divides the natural from the metaphysical is the point where they are seen to coincide: "the love that turns" the *Primo Mobile* "and the generative power it rains down" (*l'amore che volge e la virtù ch'ei piove*), arise or ignite (*s'accende*) in that nothingness, the divine mind (*la mente divina*), in which all being consists (*Pd* 27.109–111). The *Primo Mobile* represents that "ignition": it draws life and power (*vivere e potenza*) from the ray (*raggio*) that constitutes the appearance (*parvenza*) of the Empyrean (*Pd* 30.107–108). In this sense the "nothingness" of the Empyrean may be thought of as a "something" that spawns and "moves" creation, and is the final cause, in a supernatural order, of the movement of the *Primo Mobile*. It is also in this sense that God is spoken of, for example in the opening and closing verses of the *Paradiso*, as the reality that moves and animates all things.

It should now also be evident why Beatrice picks Dante's sojourn in the *Primo Mobile* as the moment to teach him how time (*Pd* 27.115–120) and space

(*Pd* 28.16–78) "sprout" from the featureless "pot" of the ninth heaven—lectures that culminate in a full-fledged account of how the cosmos as a whole came into being (*Pd* 29.1–36). As we shall see in chapter 4, it is only when all this is clear to Dante that he will find himself beyond the *precinto* of space-time, in the omnipresent conscious nowhere that is the Empyrean.

2

Matter

We must now dispatch the notion that matter, for Dante and the tradition he inherited, is something "material," in the senses the word might evoke for a post-Cartesian (and perhaps pre-quantum) reader. The essential point is that we must not attribute to Dante an irreducible Cartesian duality between matter and mind, or think of matter as a self-subsistent explanatory principle: matter, for Dante, can have no ontological ground or source other than Intellect-Being. Dante's world is not made of fundamental building blocks, atomic or subatomic billiard balls, as it were; rather all sensible reality is a contingent (but otherwise absolutely "real") projection of self-subsistent Being, identified with pure Intellect or Awareness (which is not a thing). In rough terms this means, for example, that ontologically the brain depends upon consciousness, and not vice versa. It also implies that there is a way to travel in the physical world, and even beyond it, that leaves aside the laws of physics and material bodies. It is the route the pilgrim exploits, or rather the route that happens to the pilgrim: to identify more and more perfectly with the dimensionless conscious reality to which all spatiotemporal experience is immediately present, as in an extensionless point. To locate oneself in space and time is to locate oneself in conscious being, which is, as one who reaches the *Primo Mobile* discovers, "where" they exist.

Aristotle

We have seen that the *Primo Mobile* is a curious sphere: it is material, in fact the last material sphere of the universe (the "greatest body" or *maggior corpo*), but it contains no star or planet, and hence has no perceptible attributes except speed: it is the "fastest heaven" (*ciel velocissimo*). Thus Dante observes, upon his arrival in it: "Its parts, most living and exalted, are so uniform that I cannot tell which of them Beatrice chose as a place for me" (*Le parti sue vivissime ed eccelse / sì uniforme son, ch'i' non so dire / qual Bëatrice per loco mi scelse* [*Pd* 27.100–102]). In what sense does something have parts if those parts are indistinguishable? Speed implies motion, but the motion of what has no distinguishable attributes cannot be detected: what is moving, and in what sense can it be said to move?

What Dante is underscoring in the *Primo Mobile* is the concept of motion itself. Motion is *ubi*, where, plotted against *quando*, when. Dante has in effect already introduced the two great themes, *quando* and *ubi*, time and space, that will occupy this canto and the next, to culminate in *Paradiso* 29: the *Primo Mobile* represents the matrix space-time. Local motion is characteristic only of material things, as Dante, citing Aristotle, observes in the *Vita Nova*, because to exist as a material thing is to be located in space, which is to be located in time, and vice versa: it is again to plot *ubi* against *quando*. The point is still deeper: by Aristotelian (and modern) physics, in contrast to the Cartesian-Newtonian picture, space-time is a relative and dependent attribute, which has no existence independent of bodies in motion. The *Primo Mobile* could thus be said to represent matter itself, analyzed to its fundamental principles: extension in space and time, which is unfulfilled potentiality, which is motion or change.[1]

As the nexus between creator and creation, Dante's *Primo Mobile* "translates" self-subsistent being into contingent spatiotemporal manifestation. If Dante's aim is not only to guarantee the transcendence of the divine, but also, as Nardi suggests, "to heal [*saldare*] the fracture of theological dualism, between the spiritual world and the sensible universe, into a perfect and continuous unity," it is the *Primo Mobile* that must do the healing or welding.[2] Thus the *Primo Mobile* embodies an apparent metaphysical paradox: it is self-sufficient divine awareness and power projected into pure motion and desire, and material reality become featureless extension (*what* is extended?) and exalted, living potentiality. As we saw in chapter 1, it is the nexus between the One and the Many, between pure being and finite identity, between existence and essence.

So what is matter, as it "arises" from being in the *Primo Mobile?* We could say: material things are intelligible identities (forms) determined within the matrix space-time. Since it is form that gives being to matter, matter (and space-time) is nothing in itself: it is the character common to all spatiotemporal (changeable) form. This is the basic conception of matter in the later Middle Ages, and it derives, not surprisingly, from Aristotle.

Form and matter in Aristotle are concepts that have meaning only in relation to each other. This is to say that they do not refer to things; they are terms used in the philosophical analysis of things. Form denotes the identities assumed by *what is*, through which being is knowable; matter denotes the (apparent) autonomy or self-subsistence, as individual corporeal substances, of changeable spatiotemporal identities (forms). The matter of a thing is the "substratum" determined by the thing's form: it is the potential of that thing to change, that is, to be (further) determined by identity. If it had to be defined in itself, matter would have no attributes at all: "by matter I mean that which in itself is neither a something nor a quantity nor any of those other things by which being is determined."[3]

This analysis is intuitive at its simplest level: if a copper bowl is made into a statue, the same matter has had two successive forms. The copper that now has the identity of a bowl can potentially become a statue. Its becoming a statue would be the actualization of that potential. The bowl is in potentiality insofar as it is material, that is, insofar as it consists in copper that could become a statue. The (Platonic) implication is that what has no matter (potential for change) is eternal and unchanging: it is, at least loosely speaking, pure form or actuality. "Hylomorphism," the technical term for the form-matter analysis of reality, in fact refers to the (changing) forms, *morphai*, taken by *hyle*, the "stuff" or matter of the world. (*Hyle* literally means "wood" or "timber," corresponding to the Latin *silva*; thus the *selva oscura*, the dark wood from which the pilgrim's journey begins, philosophically evokes the flux of the material world.)[4]

Since the matter of a thing is designated only in relation to the form that determines it, copper itself can be thought of as some underlying matter determined by the form that makes it copper. What is that matter? For Aristotle it would be water, one of the four Empedoclean elements out of which all sublunar things are composed. Since water (or air, or fire, or earth) can be mentally conceived and talked about, it too is a determinate form of being; indeed the transmutation of the elements into each other is a fundamental principle of Aristotle's physics. What is the potentiality or substratum (matter) that takes on these successive identities? "What is ultimate is in itself neither a thing nor a quantity nor anything else" (*Metaphysics* 7.3.1029a25). Aristotle calls it prime or primary matter (*prote hule*), and hastens to clarify that it is simply a product of thought and never exists without some determining form by which it can be known, namely the elements and their compounds. This assertion, as well as Aristotle's statements about the indeterminacy of matter, led Aquinas and most Aristotelian Scholastic philosophers to think of prime matter, defined in itself apart from any form, as pure potentiality, an utter absence of any actuality or determinate being. This is to say that the ultimate stuff of the universe, in which all things consist, has no consistency at all, indeed does not exist, apart from its determination as identity.[5]

Aristotle's penetrating insight is that no materialistic doctrine ("the world is made of . . .") can sustain analysis: in defining matter, the ultimate stuff of the world, we are never saying what it is, but simply describing a form that it has assumed. By making Plato's transcendent forms immanent to, or constitutive of, material reality, Aristotle effectively "deconstructed" or dissolved the common notion of matter as something, however vague. One might say that for Aristotle "matter" refers to the continuity of objective experience in all its transmutations. It is perhaps an irony that Aristotle, not Plato, provided me-

dieval philosophy with the insight that allowed it to overcome the duality between the material and the spiritual or intelligible, the great reconciliation
denoted by "Christ" or logos that is so central to Christian Neoplatonism. (Medieval philosophers, most of whom viewed Aristotle as perfecting Plato, would
have seen no irony at all.) The dissolution of dualism is particularly evident in
the metaphysics of the soul: while Augustine (*De moribus* 1.27.52), echoing
Plotinus (*Enneads* 1.1.3), echoing Plato (*Alcibiades I* 129e), could define man as
"a soul that uses a body," Aristotle instead saw the soul as the *form* of the body,
apart from which the body has no existence at all. Christian theology of the
thirteenth century is in large measure a flowering of this prodigious insight.[6]

Dante's Predecessors

Although Aristotle may never have entertained a notion of prime matter as
"what matter is in itself," precisely because it could not be anything, the idea
of matter as a pure receptive potentiality, an unknowable substratum of all
things (sometimes viewed as if this were the description of something), did
become common currency in medieval thought. William Charlton, who does
not attribute such an idea to Aristotle, gives a persuasive account of how it was
consolidated: in short, by fusing Plato with Aristotle. Plato's *Timaeus* (49–52)
speaks of an ultimate, undefinable, virtually unknowable receptacle of all
things, "an invisible and shapeless kind of thing," an eternal space "that provides a seat for all things which come to be" and is thus a principle of multiplicity in contrast to the One. Quite naturally, subsequent thinkers, beginning
with the Stoics, identified this receptacle with Aristotle's *prote hule*, prime matter. This Aristotelian-Platonic conflation was then identified in turn with the
earth created as a formless void (*terra . . . inanis et vacua*) in the first verses of
Genesis, an identification promulgated repeatedly by Augustine. The groundwork for the later Middle Ages was completed by Chalcidius (fourth or fifth
century), who explains the *Timaeus* by quoting Aristotle, whom he considers
a Platonist, and by Simplicius (sixth century), who explains Aristotle's view of
matter in the *Physics* by quoting the *Timaeus*, which he considers to be in
fundamental agreement with Aristotle. As we have seen, by the Scholastic
period, in the absence of new Platonic texts, most Platonic influence had already been absorbed by Aristotelianism (largely through Islamic philosophers),
and went by Aristotle's name.[7]

　　By glossing the first verse of Genesis as the *hule* of the Greek philosophers,
Augustine (perhaps inadvertently) spawned the notion of "formless matter"
(*materia informis*) as a "something" separately created by God in the beginning,
even though he may never have held such an idea himself. The key issue,
which I will discuss in chapter 4, is whether creation can be conceived as a
process in time. Aquinas, for example, does not think Augustine thought there
was ever a moment when matter existed without form: it was separately created
by God not in the order of time, but in the order of nature or origin. In other
words, Augustine understands the days of creation in Genesis to reflect only

the logical order of dependence in nature; creation itself is instantaneous, in no time. Even if for Augustine *materia informis* was thus in effect equivalent to Aristotelian *prima materia*, Aquinas observes that for some of his successors (Basil, Ambrose, and Chrysostom) it was not: for them the informity of matter meant that matter had some rudimentary form (actuality) in itself, which was perfected in beauty or completion when it subsequently (i.e., in time) took on (some precise) form, in the "work of distinction."[8]

With the resurgence of Aristotelianism, philosophers found themselves with two (more or less) distinct notions of "first matter": the *materia informis* (or *incomposita*) of the Patristic tradition, and the technical Aristotelian term *materia prima*. Thus some Scholastic philosophers, especially in the Augustinian-Franciscan tradition, thought that "first matter" could exist separately in time, either through having some slight actuality or determination (e.g., Bonaventure) or, since God could do all things, as pure potentiality (e.g., Duns Scotus). This claim is often connected with Augustine's notion of *rationes seminales*, the idea that the first matter created by God "contains" the "seeds" of all the finite beings that "germinate" in time. This metaphorical notion is more exegetical than philosophical, meant to reconcile the simultaneity of creation (Ecclesiasticus 18.1) with its implied unfolding in time in Genesis; under analysis the doctrine may not be distinguishable from that of Aquinas, who attributed such "germination" in the potentiality of matter to the direct or indirect influence of the motion of the stars on particular material substances. In any case it is clear that neither Augustine nor his followers were "materialists" in any sense. As David Knowles points out, Augustine would never call the sensible world the *material* world: being a good student of Plotinus, he knew that the ultimate reality is spiritual, not corporeal, substance. Thinkers directly influenced by Aristotle's conception of matter (such as Albert, Aquinas, Siger of Brabant, and Giles of Rome) denied that matter is anything at all in itself. All medieval philosophers agreed with Dante (e.g., *Pd* 29.32–34) that matter, as (pure) potentiality, is at the opposite extreme from being or actuality (God): *pura potenza tenne la parte ima* ("pure potentiality held the lowest place" [34]).[9]

A few other strands in the medieval understanding of matter should be mentioned. An indirect but pervasive influence (especially through Pseudo-Dionysius) is Plotinus, who viewed matter as the element of non-being or "otherness" that limits the being of things, a kind of privation that distinguishes them from being itself, making them tend toward unreality and unintelligibility.[10] For the Islamic philosopher Avicenna (Ibn Sīnā), matter was responsible for contingency and multiplicity, a negation or darkness absorbing the light of form radiated by intellect. Averroës (Ibn Rushd), the great twelfth-century Islamic commentator of Aristotle, maintained, and showed convincingly that Aristotle maintained, not only that matter is nothing in itself, but that, as actualized by the world, matter is co-eternal with the Prime Mover and thus uncreated. These ideas were to provoke some philosophical stress in the later thirteenth century.

Saint Bonaventure, agreeing with Aristotle that matter has no being apart from form, completely identified matter with potentiality and form with actuality. Since God alone is pure actuality, this led him to consider matter as a principle of dependent but autonomous existence ("otherness") present in all things except God: as an attribute of contingency common to all determinate (and not simply spatiotemporal) identities, matter was corporeal (spatiotemporal and changeable) in physical objects and spiritual in angels. Aquinas rejected the idea of noncorporeal matter: angels are pure form, distinguished from God only by the fact that *what* they are (their essence or particular understanding) is not identical with the act of existence itself (*that* they are). Aquinas followed Aristotle closely but of course rejected the idea that matter was uncreated and eternal: given being by form, it can be said to have been "concreated" with form. In itself matter is not responsible for the existence of things, but once created as a universal principle of nature, it is not in itself subject to generation or corruption and in this sense endures forever.[11] Aquinas also dispensed with *rationes seminales* as superfluous.

The sum of this survey is simple: matter, in medieval thought, is nothing, or at best, very nearly nothing. The world does not consist in anything, in any thing: there is nothing it is "made out of." The failure to feel the power of this understanding is perhaps the greatest barrier in any effort to engage the *Comedy* on its own terms.

Dante

From what we have said, one could perhaps think of Dante's *Primo Mobile* as, among other things, the "birth" of matter: as an otherness or duality that arises from or within being-in-itself. This otherness is characterized by incompleteness (the capacity for motion or change, and thus desire) and by extension in space and time. It can be thought of as a substratum in which all noneternal things consist, as long as we remember it is nothing in itself apart from those things: it is only, so to speak, the "common form" of all spatiotemporal being. Dante's *Primo Mobile* suggests that the world is energy-consciousness-being reflected or manifest as spatiotemporal extension, an idea that might not shock contemporary physicists, though they might use different words.[12]

Matter, for Dante, is indeed nothing in itself. In the *Monarchia* (1.3.8–9) Dante asserts categorically that prime matter is pure potentiality and thus cannot exist apart from form. Indeed he goes further: he says that the multitude or totality of generated things is necessary in order to actualize at all times the full potentiality of prime matter; otherwise we would have to presume that unactualized potentiality could exist in itself, which is impossible. According to *Monarchia* 2.2.2–3, the world exists in the mind of God, and is extended or unfolded in fluctuating matter (*in fluitantem materiam explicatur*) through the instrument of the spheres; since matter itself "exists only as potentiality," it contributes nothing positive to the divine ideas, but can only detract from them. The *Questio de aqua et terra*, the little scientific treatise on the elements that Dante wrote at the end of his life, explains that all things composed of matter and form are contingent (*possunt esse et non esse*), but their forms exist eternally as act in divine intelligence and as potential in matter (44–46). The purpose of universal nature therefore is to realize the full potential of matter to manifest as form. This is to say that through the movement of the spheres every possible material form is simultaneously realized in matter, if matter is taken as a totality; but of course, by being actualized as one particular form, the matter of each corporeal body remains in potentiality to all the other forms it could (and will) take on. In relation to all the forms it does not have at the moment, but could, it is in privation, which functions as a third principle (with form and matter) of natural things.[13]

It can be seen, then, that sublunary matter is indeed *fluitans*, the realm of "brief contingencies" or "last potentialities" (*brevi contingenze, ultime potenze* [*Pd* 13.61, 63]): possessing no given form in itself, but successively taking on all forms, it is "pure potentiality" (*pura potenza* [*Pd* 29.34]).[14] It is also clear from these passages that Dante believes that prime matter cannot exist in itself apart from some form. These statements in Dante's later works are consistent with his assertion in the *Convivio* (3.8.15) that God, the angels, and *prima materia* can be known only through their effects, and not in themselves; again in the *Convivio* (3.15.6) he says that prime matter, like God and eternity, cannot be grasped by the intellect for what it is, but only approached by specifying everything it is not (*se non cose negando si può apressare alla sua conoscenza, e non altrimenti*).

Nevertheless the issue of prime matter in Dante has generated some controversy. The source of the trouble has been Beatrice's assertion, in *Paradiso* 29.22–36, that in the act of creation *forma e materia, congiunte e purette / usciro ad esser che non avia fallo* ("form and matter, conjoined and separate, came into being which had no defect"); of the substances (things) created,

> quelle furon cima
> nel mondo in che puro atto fu produtto;
>   pura potenza tenne la parte ima;
> nel mezzo strinse potenza con atto
> tal vime, che già mai non si divima.[15]   (*Pd* 29.32–36)

In these lines it is clear that Dante is using technical terms loosely to make a threefold contrast in creation, which he in fact calls a *triforme effetto* (28). In the sense that they have no matter, and are thus immortal, immune to change, space, and time (they are at the "top of the world" in the Empyrean), angelic intelligences can be said to be pure form or pure act, although speaking technically this would make them identical with, and nothing but, God. In the sense that the material and ephemeral sublunar world of the four elements has no particular form of its own but is constantly transmuting from one form into another with no stability or end, it can be said to be pure matter or pure potency (though of course if it were that in a technical sense it would not exist at all). Between the sublunar world and the Empyrean, the perfect and unchanging celestial spheres, material but stable, can be thought of as a permanent fusion of matter (as the special stable "fifth element," or ether) with their particular forms.

Most, however, have taken Beatrice's statement to mean that matter was created as a separate "thing" in time, and there was thus a "moment" when it existed either as a Bonaventurian *materia informis* with some inchoate form or actuality, or else as a (somehow) self-subsistent pure potentiality (what Scotus said God could, but probably did not, do). Nardi argued first for the former view, and then the latter; in both he was joined by other scholars and roundly attacked by neo-Thomists, joined in their turn by others. The first position contradicts Beatrice's identification of *materia puretta* with *pura potenza*, as well as the passages from the *Monarchia* and the *Questio*; the second, which has more recently been maintained by Mellone and Bemrose, contradicts the explicit assertions of the *Monarchia*, *Questio*, and *Convivio*; and both positions contradict other passages in the *Comedy*.[16]

The dispute is groundless, because, as we shall see in more detail in chapter 4, the entire thrust of Beatrice's account of creation in *Paradiso* 29 is that the "act of creation" is not a sequence of events in time: the world is a "triform effect" that flashes into being in its entirety instantaneously, literally in no time. At the center of the lines just quoted, Beatrice says (25–32):

> E come in vetro, in ambra o cristallo
> raggio resplende sì, che dal venire
> a l'esser tutto non è intervallo,
>   così 'l triforme effetto del suo sire
> ne l'esser suo raggiò insieme tutto
> sanza distinzïone in essordire.
>   Concreato fu ordine e costrutto
> a le sustanze; e quelle furon cima . . .[17]   (*Pd* 29.25–32)

The light metaphor is more precise for Dante than it is for modern readers: by Aristotelian authority, light propagates to infinity in no time, which is to say it is motionless.[18] As Beatrice explains, there is no interval between the emanation of light and its reflection: they are simultaneous. In the same way, all of creation (the "triform effect") "flashed into being all at once, with no distinction in beginning." Therefore matter came into being not merely in some inchoate form awaiting perfection, nor as ordered simply into the elements: there was never a moment when matter existed unactualized by all the forms that constitute creation, which is what the *Monarchia* and *Quaestio* also say. "Substances" (i.e., created things, not form and matter, which are not substances) "were con-created with their order and structure," which follows intrinsically from their particular balance of act and potency, form and matter.

As this passage makes clear, what is created is not form here and matter there (a nonsensical notion in any case), but rather *things*, the world. To have created anything is to have created (determinate) form or act; to have created any potential for change and multiplicity in form is to have created matter or potentiality; to have created the spheres is to have created forms that exhaust completely the potentiality of their particular substrate, the ether, and thus do not change (unlike the four elements, ether does not mix with or turn into any other element). In other words, to have created the world is to have created nothing but (determinate) form and matter, act and potency, which is not to have created something the world "is made of," but rather to have inflected or restricted the verb "to be," so to speak, giving rise to what is "other" than light-being-awareness-love itself.

Arising directly from the ground of being and dependent on nothing created, the principles of matter and form (*virtù informante*) are not in themselves subject to generation and corruption, and thus may be considered to have a beginning (with the world), but no end (*Pd* 7.64–72,124–138). The same applies to the angels, the human soul, and the spheres. These observations, which we will discuss in more detail in chapter 4, also accord with Dante's other assertions about matter. We need not conclude, with Nardi and others, that Dante changed his mind about matter just for the *Comedy* (and then changed it back again!).[19]

Matter-in-itself, conceived in the abstract as an analog to form-in-itself, is not usually what Dante means when he refers to the matter of a particular existing thing, of a "substantial form" (*forma sustanzïal, formas particulares*). That is, rather, proximate or relative matter, the immediately "underlying" substratum (*suggetto, subietto, subiectum*), or complex mixture of the elements (*complession potenzïata, subiectum mixtum et complexionatum*) that serves as matter for the form, as iron might for an ax, or wood for a bed.[20] (All corruptible things are formed from differing compounds of the four elements; how these elements could "leave their natural place" to be so mixed is the subject of the *Questio.*) An ax or bed or human considered apart from any particular material substrate is a "universal form," sometimes variously thought of as an exemplar, divine idea, or Platonic form. What detracts from these divine ideas or exemplars as they are realized in the world is not prime matter, which is nothing in itself, but ill-disposed *complession potenzïata*, the preexisting forms of matter, compounded from the elements, in which the new "image" (always perfect in itself) is to arise, or be "stamped." That matter, which Dante often calls worldly, mortal, or worked "wax," can be "deaf" or "disobedient" to the form it is to assume, just as certain materials are more suitable for a particular use than others. The height of material perfection is reached when the spheres (or the Creator Himself) order and predispose the "wax" most suitably for the new form to be assumed, as at the creation of Adam or the birth of Christ.[21]

Not only is (proximate) matter responsible for all imperfection in nature, it is also the principle of non-intelligence or non-intelligibility in reality: a thing can know and is knowable only insofar as it is form, not matter—actual, not potential. As we shall see in the next chapter, any immaterial substantial form (that is, any substance "separated from," not dependent upon, matter) is in fact an intelligence, commonly known as an angel.[22] To the angels we can add God, who as pure form or actuality is sheer intelligence-intelligibility (but not a thing in any sense), and the human soul, a substantial form separated from matter (not dependent upon it) and yet united with it (*setta / è da matera ed è con lei unita* [*Pg* 18.49–50]). Considered in its own essence ("denuded of matter"), the human soul is an incorruptible intelligence, like an angel (*Cv* 3.2.14); unlike animal souls (*Cv* 3.7.5), it does not require any matter or substratum to exist, but body is its natural manifestation or completion (e.g., *Pg* 25.88–108; *Pd* 14.43–66). The human soul is thus the "horizon" between the material and the immaterial, the corruptible and incorruptible (*Mn* 3.15.3).

Since prime matter is the paradigm of unintelligibility and (relative) nothingness, the question arose among Scholastic philosophers whether, as Dante puts it (*Cv* 4.1.8), *la prima materia delli elementi era da Dio intesa* ("whether the prime matter of the elements was an object of God's intention or understanding"). An avalanche of discussion has shown that the question cannot be answered, because it is hopelessly complex and confused: one cannot even be sure what Dante meant by it. *Intendere* could mean, as Nardi argued, "to will its existence," implying the question whether God (rather than finite intelligences) created it, or even whether it was something that could be created at all. These questions are really asking: what is prime matter, and in what sense can it be said to exist? This problem is intimately connected with the other senses of *intendere*: to know, or to conceive as an idea (*intelligere*). If prime matter is nothing, a pure potentiality, how can it be conceived (or said to exist)? What does the word refer to? Anything that can exist in itself as a determinate entity can also be known (through its form): if matter were something "material," so to speak, the question would not arise. The notion of matter is grounded in the duality between the subject (immaterial form or intelligence) and object (spatiotemporal form) of experience. This duality does not exist for God: God knows creation as His own ideas, which are identical with Himself. From a divine perspective (that is, from no perspective), there is no element of otherness (self-subsistence) in creation: it is not "real" in the sense of being a thing-in-itself. Then in what sense does matter exist? What is it? How did duality come into being?[23]

The questions are complex and confused enough to bring on discouragement. This seems to have happened to Dante: when he became entangled in the problem, his lady, Philosophy, ceased her benevolent diffusion of understanding, which so dampened his enthusiasm for her that he abandoned philosophy altogether for a time: *con ciò fosse cosa che questa mia donna un poco li suoi dolci sembianti transmutasse a me . . . un poco dal frequentare lo suo aspetto mi sostenni* ("since this lady of mine ceased to look at me with quite her usual sweetness . . . I kept away from her countenance a little while" [(*Cv* 4.1.8)]). Nardi and others have argued that Lady Philosophy's changed countenance implies that at some point Dante lapsed into emanatistic (Avicennian) doctrines incompatible with Christian faith.[24] This may be creating a mystery story where it does not exist. There is no need to posit dramatic lapses into exotic heresies on Dante's part: Dante is merely describing how he learned that prime matter is one of "those things that vanquish our intellect" (*quelle cose che lo 'ntelletto nostro vincono*), which we can know not in themselves, but only through their effects (*Cv* 3.8.15). It is one of those things, like God and eternity, that "dazzle our intellect," "upon which our intellect cannot look," and which we cannot begin to understand except by way of negation.[25] If there is a deeper lesson, or a hint of a crisis, it may be that Dante is first beginning to realize, on the threshold of abandoning the *Convivio*, that philosophy, and one's own efforts, cannot penetrate the mystery of being and creation. That understanding can only come from the self-revelation of the Real, that is, from grace, for which the only preparation within human power is purity and selflessness, the dissolution of ego and proud autonomy. Only moral perfection can bring understanding: when that truth comes into full focus, in a mature Dante, the *Convivio* dies, and the *Comedy* is born.

3

Form

The *Comedy* assures us that the pilgrim Dante transcends the physical world and penetrates the Empyrean. Because—as we saw in the first chapter—the *Comedy* equates the Empyrean with the all-encompassing divine mind, the poem is telling us that the pilgrim becomes, at least fleetingly, (one with) God, the ultimate ontological principle, and that he thus (at least fleetingly) encompasses all of space and time within himself. By showing, in the second chapter, that, for medieval thought, matter is not something "material," but a principle dependent on mind, we took a first step toward understanding what the pilgrim's claims to transcendence or "divinization" might mean. In this chapter I shall seek to recover the medieval understanding of the fundamental relations that link the human mind, the world, and God, relations that make the pilgrim's journey possible. The first section will engage Aristotle's penetrating analysis of the metaphysical notion of form and its relation to mind, an analysis that provides the philosophical foundation for medieval reflections on how human intelligence can transcend space and time, in both the Neoplatonic tradition and the late-medieval Aristotelian revival. This section will necessarily be a little more philosophically sustained and involved than the rest of the book, but I hope it will be engaging nonetheless, and shed some light. The second section will trace the Neoplatonic (and Christianized) heritage of Aristotle's analysis in a few essential features, focusing on the relation, and ascent, of the human mind to its "source." The third section will trace this inherited philosophical understanding in Dante as the framework for the *Comedy*'s salvific mission and poetics, which will concern us in the last subsection of this chapter, and in the remaining chapters of the book.

Aristotle

Matter or potentiality is a principle limiting the participation of things in being and awareness: to the extent that a thing is material, it does not exist, is not knowable, and is not conscious. It follows that form or actuality is the principle through which finite things do participate in Intellect-Being: through form, things exist, are knowable, and can be conscious. Nevertheless, for Dante and his tradition, form, like matter, is not a thing: there is no thing that makes the world, nothing that the things of the world are "made of." As Aristotle saw clearly, any "reductivist" account of reality (to one pre-Socratic principle, say, or to self-subsisting entities, such as Platonic Forms) ultimately explains nothing: it fails to confront the world itself, *that* it exists.[1] To confront the world as it is, and not seek to explain it away as an "appearance" of something else (unless of course that "something else" is nothing, not a thing), is to acknowledge the mystery of its being, which is to awaken to the divine. Hence the unlimited spiritual fecundity of Aristotelian metaphysics, both in its Neoplatonic (Plotinian) guise and in medieval Scholasticism. The fecundity is even greater because of the Aristotelian understanding of *nous* (intellect or awareness) as the ultimate divine reality or being of finite form, a reality in which human intelligence participates.

"Matter is in a way easy; form is frightfully puzzling." Peter Geach underscores Aristotle's remark with the often-quoted observation that "there is hardly a statement about form in the *Metaphysics* that is not (at least verbally) contradicted by some other statement." The millennial controversies over Aristotle's understanding of form have recently intensified, but we need not engage them to set out some basic principles. It is not easy to say how Aristotle's understanding of form differs from Plato's. The essential distinction should be that, for Aristotle, forms are not self-subsistent explanatory principles and have no existence apart from things: form is immanent in (constitutive of) the world, not transcendent. Aristotle begins to shade into Plato when he says that it is form that makes a thing what it is, and thus more than (or rather than) matter constitutes a thing's "essence" and makes it a substance (a thing that can exist "on its own," so to speak); that the form is the actuality, perfection, and formal cause of a substance; that a substance can be conceived (known) only in virtue of its form, since matter is in itself unknowable; that a form, as the intelligible what-it-is of a thing, can in some sense be common to more than one particular substance; that some immaterial forms (intelligences) are themselves substances, so that at least some forms do subsist on their own apart from matter; that in one precise sense (as known by mind) all forms can exist apart from matter. I shall discuss some of these points further; in general, we can say that in contrast to Plato, Aristotle stresses the ontological primacy, or at least dignity, of the particular, and starts from it, always seeking an elegant economy in his ontology. This in no way—at least to his Neoplatonic and medieval heirs—despiritualizes his metaphysics: Aristotle's physical world is nothing but the individual "instantiation" of being as intelligible spatiotemporal attributes, but those attributes themselves do not exist apart from that "instantiation," except in *nous*, in cognition or awareness.[2]

In Aristotle, as Aquinas too will reiterate, forms are not things to be "added to matter," or "latent within matter" to be educed from it; things exist through form, through the fact that in a particular case being is qualified as this-or-that. As identity, or the power to determine identity, form is the principle through which all finite beings have being: "a form is what it is to be some substance" and also "what it is for some substance to be." Here two features of Aristotle's conception of form must be clear. The first is that the things that constitute the world can be arranged in a hierarchy, a *scala naturae* that in its broadest form is also a scale of being, of perfection or actuality or fullness of existence. This idea, perhaps the most salient feature of the medieval under-standing of reality, was latent or implicit in Plato, but Aristotle made it explicit and theorized it, thus bequeathing it to his Neoplatonic posterity. For Aristotle, the position of each thing in the hierarchy, from minerals to the Unmoved Mover, is determined by its attributes, that is, by its form or actuality—or, rather, by the degree to which pure form or actuality is "infected with poten-tiality" in the case of any particular being. Apart from the detailed graded classifications Aristotle produced in particular disciplines, such as biology, the greater hierarchy ascends from inanimate things to living or ensouled things; of these, plants, lowest of the living, are capable only of nutrition; animals, of nutrition and sensation; and humans, supreme among material substances, of nutrition, sensation, and thought (*nous*), which is not dependent upon body. Above humans are divine unembodied intelligences, and finally, because "where there is a better there is also a best," the perfect actuality of the Un-moved Mover, the thought that thinks itself. This hierarchy, in which the higher "rules" the lower, and the lower in some sense aspires to the actuality or ful-fillment of the higher, integrates all Aristotelian thought, from biology and ethics to cosmology and metaphysics.[3]

The point is that the one principle common to all things is form: form makes a thing a pebble, but form also makes a god a pure intelligence, capable of becoming all things through thought. Things can be known only through their form, but all things exist only insofar as they are form, and things can think only by being pure form, which is *nous*. Material forms can in turn become the matter or potential actualized by higher forms, a hierarchy that culminates in a transcendent Form, *nous*-in-itself, that ultimately determines all and is determined by nothing. In sum, form can be understood not only as the principle of being and intelligibility, but also as the principle of intelligence itself. Thus the second feature of Aristotle's conception of form is that form can be conceived in two ways that are ultimately equivalent: as the actuality through which all things have being and are knowable, and as the power of self-subsistent awareness or intelligence (*nous*) to become finite attribute, through which all things have being and are known. How to conceive this dual nature of form, or the relation of form to mind, is the most obscure point of

Aristotle's philosophy. The few lines in which he treats the problem, in *De anima* 3.5, are probably the most analyzed, and the most variously interpreted, text in the history of Western philosophy.[4]

The nutritive or vegetative soul, or lowest form of life, is capable of taking material substances into itself, "matter and all": this is nutrition and eating, common to all life forms. Assimilated in this way into the creature that eats it, the original material substance or substantial form ceases to exist in itself. The sensitive soul, common to all animals, takes only the forms of things, "without their matter," into itself through the bodily senses: each of the senses is a capacity, limited in range by its material nature, to be informed by, or become, specific attributes of things; these disparate sensory attributes are consolidated in the "common sense" (the "root" of the various senses) to produce an image or phantasm of the material substance, while the substance continues to subsist in itself. Like the sensitive soul itself, sensations and sense images are material, entirely dependent upon body and therefore perishable. *Nous*, unique to humans among animals, is radically different. It is a part or potentiality of the human soul that is nothing in itself, "not actually any real thing" (*De anima* 3.4.429a24), absolutely immaterial and dependent on no organ, with no intrinsic nature or attributes, and hence absolutely unrestricted in its capacity to take on the forms of everything that exists: it is a power to be everything ("the soul is in a way all existing things" [3.8.431b21]). Because of this similarity to the "Receptacle" of *Timaeus* or to prime matter (3.4.429a27), this "potential," "passive," "possible" aspect of intellect was sometimes called the "material" intellect, though it is of course absolutely immaterial. In fact Aristotle specifies (3.4, 3.5.430a18) that *nous* is *apathes*, unaffected or unconditioned by any of the things it becomes; it is *amiges*, "unmixed" with any organ or character or structure that could limit or taint its transparent power to be all things; it is *choristos*, "separable," capable in principle of existing apart from all things, immune to bodily processes, self-subsistent, not part of the world and its flux.[5]

The fundamental point is simple and radical: *nous*, awareness or mind, is nothing until it thinks, and when it thinks, it is what it thinks (3.4.429a24, 429b32). Actualized by the actuality of a substantial form, it comes into existence as that form itself: the thought, the act of thinking, what thinks, and the object of thought are all identical (3.4.429a17, 3.5.430a20, 3.7.431a1). Of course, unlike the vegetative soul, intellect takes on only the form of a material thing, not its matter: what that distinction comes to is problematic, but it means in any case that the thing continues to subsist in itself as a substance (it is not consumed or "eaten," so to speak). In humans, *nous* is a faculty of soul, a potentiality only intermittently actualized by thought. As a potentiality, it is entirely dependent for its actualization on the phantasms fed to it by the body and its powers of sensation (e.g., 3.8.432a7). Thus in humans, as a "potential" or "passive" intellect, *nous* is in a sense perishable and body dependent: without the body, it is nothing (3.5.430a25). But if we reflect on the profound consequences of the identity of thought with its object, that cannot be the whole story (3.4.429b23–430a9). Anything that has form, that is, anything, can be thought of: as an object of thought; it is at that moment mind or intelligence, an act of thinking. Indeed any form without matter is a thought, an act of thinking or *nous*: if the form can subsist that way (without matter), it is itself an intelligence; if it cannot, it is only potentially and intermittently an intelligence (when it is thought of). So then how can we distinguish the human potential intellect from anything else? Why is not every object *nous*, intelligence, if it can exist intermittently as mind? Or, from the other side: how can form be only intermittently an intelligence? What makes it so, if it is not always so?

These are the questions left lingering at the end of *De anima* 3.4 and summarily addressed in the notoriously cryptic remarks of 3.5. What we find in all nature, Aristotle explains, we must find in the soul: a passive potentiality or matter and a causal actuality or form. Thus there is not only a sense in which thought "is what it is by virtue of becoming all things," but also a sense in which thought "is what it is by virtue of making all things" (430a14–17). The latter is *nous poietikos*, "maker mind," which "is in its essential nature activity" (430a18), and thus has been variously called active, agent or productive intellect. It is "a sort of positive state like light; for in a sense light makes potential colors into actual colors" (430a16); it is like an art to its material (430a13). It is thought in *this* sense that is *apathes*, *amiges*, and *choristos*, unaffected, unmixed, and separable; it is an "originating force" (430a19). In an absolute sense, actual knowledge, identity with the object of knowledge, is logically and temporally prior to potential knowledge; only in the case of the individual is potential knowledge "prior in time to actual knowledge" (430a20–22, 3.7.431a1–3). "When separated," this uninterruptedly actualized intellect or act of knowing "is alone just what it is, and this alone is immortal and eternal (we do not remember because, while this is impassible, passive thought is perishable); and without this nothing thinks" (3.5.430a23–26).

Nowhere except in this passage does Aristotle distinguish between productive and passive intellect: in the *Generation of Animals* (2.3.736b14–28), Aristotle says that the rational (aspect of) soul alone is separable from body, enters "from outside," and is divine; elsewhere in *De anima* he says that in comparison to the perishable, bodily affections of memory, love, and hate, "thought is, no doubt, something more divine and impassible" (1.4.408b27–33); "thought or the power of reflexion . . . seems to be a different kind of soul, differing as what is eternal from what is perishable; it alone is capable of being separated" (2.2.413b25–27). In the fragments that survive of the *Protrepticus*, Aristotle says again that *nous* is what is immortal and divine in us (B108–109); it is the god in us (B110), through which we become like God (B28).[6]

To shed light on *De anima* 3.5, we must place next to it, as Aristotle's ancient and medieval interpreters did, *Metaphysics* 12.7. The first principle or first mover, upon which "depend the heavens and the world of nature" (1072b14), is always in the state in which we can share only intermittently: it is pure uninterrupted thought or contemplation. In particular, it is thought as the active possession of its object, not simply as the capacity to become the object, because the former "is the divine element which thought seems to contain, and the act of contemplation is what is most pleasant and best" (1072b22–23). As pure immaterial intelligence and actuality, "eternal and un-movable and separate from sensible things" (the traits of *nous*, and of active *nous* in particular), the first mover is without magnitude, without parts, and indivisible (1073a4–6). What does it think? Of course mind thinks only itself, because when it thinks it is identical with what it thinks: there is no duality between subject and object. More precisely, as Aristotle explains in 12.9, be-cause *nous*, conceived as a divine principle in itself, is dependent on absolutely nothing but itself, divine thought does not think itself in an incidental way (by thinking things), but rather by contemplating precisely itself: "it must be itself that thought thinks (since it is the most excellent of things), and its thinking is a thinking on thinking," or rather it is thinking thinking thinking, *noesis noeseos noesis* (1074b33–34, 1075a10). In other words, divinity, conceived in it-self, is the perfect reflexive actuality (self-awareness) of pure awareness, which of course is nothing at all, the power to be everything. As Aristotle was to discover in his afterlife, it is the I AM that grounded the authority of Moses.[7]

Taking these Aristotelian passages together, and without entering into vexed details, we may draw some basic conclusions. We must again remember that all things, whether pebbles or minds, exist through form: form is the actuality, existence, and intelligibility of things. Some forms (immaterial ones) are a power to be other forms: an intelligence is a variable form, so to speak, the power to be everything and nothing. This power is *nous*: it can—indeed, since actuality is ontologically prior to potentiality, it must—be thought of not only as a potentiality, a nothingness, but also as an active power, the principle of form or actuality itself, through which all things have being. To describe *nous*, one could describe any or all of the things that constitute the world; defined in itself apart from all the things it can be, isolated as the transcendent and immanent principle of all finite being, it is the actuality of pure awareness, which is self-awareness. In fact, whenever form is "separated from matter," it becomes conscious of itself as intelligence, the intelligibility and being of the world: it is at that moment *nous*. Any form that subsists in itself "without matter" is always *nous*. Conceived in itself, *nous* is not only a power to become, but also to make, all things: this is why in humans *nous* (unlike prime matter) is not just one of the objects it becomes, even though it is only intermittently actualized. Human *nous* is a participation in the foundational principle of the universe, in the world's being and intelligibility, which are one. As Aristotle observes (*Metaphysics* 12.8.1074b1–3), thus is the ancient myth validated, that "the divine encloses the whole of nature."

Here we see that various aspects of Aristotle's philosophy fit together, as they are wont to do. Aristotle's stress on the fact that the rational soul "comes from outside," is divine, in some respect immortal, and that it presupposes no organ or body, is all to say that it is not subject to generation, corruption, or any natural process. The intellective soul does not rely on body or the world because it is ontologically prior to it, which is to say it is related to the ultimate reality (pure form or actuality) in which all things consist. The Christians were to express the same point by saying that the rational soul depends on (is produced by) only God, and is thus immortal. Moreover, it no longer seems arbitrary for Aristotle to claim that the Unmoved Mover moves all things as final cause, as their goal or object of desire and love; or that all things have "something divine in them" (*Nicomachean Ethics* 7.14.1153b32) that consciously or unconsciously moves them toward happiness or fulfillment, an impulse that grounds the human notion of the good, and whose ultimate goal is the Unmoved Mover (*Metaphysics* 12.7.1072b1–15). The Prime Mover is pure form, the principle of intelligence-intelligibility-being through which every being is; it is the principle that becomes manifest, and conscious of itself, as form becomes immaterial. To aspire upward in the hierarchy of being is to aspire to a greater range of existence, and ultimately to be unbound by any particular mode of existence: to be the power to be anything. It is, ultimately, for things to aspire to be what gives them being: form itself, which is *nous*. This is the ultimate consequence of Aristotle's rejection of Platonic Forms and dualism: intelligence-intelligibility-being must then be intrinsic to things, the being of their being, which is why the world is knowable.

A material thing is other than *nous*, other than self-subsistent actuality. That is, it is only potentially *nous*, and is actually *nous* only when it is thought of (but then of course it will be dematerialized); on the other hand *nous* is only potentially a material thing, and actually becomes the thing only by dematerializing it in an act of thought. To "dematerialize" the thing means to know it only through its form, what makes it what it is and gives it being. Matter in an absolute sense refers to nothing except the "otherness" or duality between finite being and mind: that "otherness" is the non-self-subsistence of spatiotemporal attribute. In other words, a form is material insofar as it has features, chief among them spatiotemporal extension and change or corruptibility, that distinguish it from *nous* itself. It is in this sense that material forms "give being to matter," and yet have no being apart from matter. Matter is, so to speak, what all material forms have in common; it is nothing in itself. In a profound sense, even a material thing is not other than *nous*, conceived as making all things, as the principle of form-in-itself: if it were, the thing could not be known, and would not exist. How material a form is depends on how entirely it is limited by spatiotemporal attributes, which roughly coincide with sensory qualitites. Already in Aristotle's world one can distinguish an ascending hierarchy from the elements to mixed bodies to plants to animals to humans. In Neoplatonic thought the hierarchy is more explicit: to the extent that being is other than, or distant from, *nous*, it is contingent and ephemeral, potentiality and matter and nonexistence, light lost in darkness.

Expressed in strictly Aristotelian terms, "salvation" would be to share in the reflexive self-awareness of *nous* without interruption, whereupon one could describe oneself as (one with) anything or everything that exists, or as (one with) the principle through which all things exist. For the Christians this would of course entail an apparently non-Aristotelian possibility: the dissolution of the ego, of the sense of oneself as only a finite subject of experience, through humility, self-sacrifice, surrender, and selfless love. It would be actually to live in that realm of divinity "beyond" space-time, which the Christians were to make into the Empyrean, but which already for Aristotle represented the highest ideal of human aspiration.[8]

It has been said many times that the Platonism Aristotle kicked out the door came back in the window (Nardi), or that Aristotle simply systematized the Platonic heritage (Hicks), or, more fully, that Aristotle's "final conclusions on all points of importance are hardly distinguishable from those of Plato. . . . He is everywhere a Platonist *malgré lui*, and it is just the Platonic element in his thought to which it owes its hold over men's minds" (Taylor). The conclusion gains particular force because Aristotle admits a sense of form as unchanging universals. But for Aristotle these do not exist in themselves as necessary features of being: they result from the description of an actual world that exists through form. Aristotle's world is a radical modification or perfection of Plato's: for Plato, knowledge is won by freeing the intellect from the body and the illusions of the senses, so that mind may perceive or remember the ideas of things in its own being from before its incarnation, *despite* the world. For Aristotle the world *is* intelligibility and being; knowledge is the capacity of the rational soul to become the world. The two views express very different feelings about the world and human life: as Giovanni Gentile observes in exquisite pages, Aristotle dissolves the pessimism that motivates and underlies Plato's transcendent optimism. Although Aristotle grants transcendence only to Intellect, and denies it to Plato's Forms (and everything else), metaphysically Platonism and Aristotelianism ultimately coincide: for Plato as well as Aristotle the world exists through form, and form-in-itself is intelligence-intelligibility-being. The power of this understanding accounts for its dominance over two thousand years of Western thought and explains Aristotle's medieval reputation as, in Dante's words, "the master of all who know," of "nearly divine genius," whose "divine judgment" makes all other judgements superfluous, "master and guide of human reason," "supreme philosopher," "glorious philosopher," "master of philosophers," "our master," and "master of our life": in short, *the* Philosopher.[9]

To counter what to medieval philosophers would seem, and one modern philosopher has termed, "the errors of Descartes" as we approach Aristotle and Dante, it may be worth observing that the understanding I have described cannot be designated by the modern term "idealism," if that is taken to be opposed to "realism," or even to "materialism." Such terms, and a host of others that come in their train ("mental states," "extramental," "mind-body problem," "external world," "red patch now," "supervenience," and so on) would have been incomprehensible both to Aristotle and to medieval thinkers. These terms are post-Cartesian, and from a medieval point of view would probably seem to express a kind of skepticism or mannerism, a worldview in crisis through internal incoherence. Their germ is the Cartesian notion of mind as an individual, solipsistic, thinking subject, with immediate access only to itself, and for which everything else is external, indeed subject to existential doubt. Mind, as a thinking thing or identity, and matter, as spatial extension, thus become entirely distinct and incompatible substances. The paradoxes that result spawn an obsession with epistemology, with attempts to build bridges between matter and mind. (Skepticism may be not the failure cleverly to bridge the gap, but to have posited the gap.) The readiest solution to this mind/matter divide is to eliminate one end of the bridge or the other, monistically reducing everything to one of the two principles: hence materialism (or physicalism or naturalism) and idealism. If you keep the bridge, with both principles, you have dualism. The thrust of these terms as they are used today derives from the picture or angst that spawned them, which is why it is almost inaccurate to call the atomism of Democritus or Lucretius "materialism": it is too "innocent and cheerful." Like other modern "isms," the terms are inapplicable to Aristotle and his medieval legacy, whose shared understanding is that reality may be described in two interchangeable ways: as being, or as intelligence-intelligibility. Intellect is nothing, or the world, or God; it is not a "something" that filters reality (through "categories" or otherwise), or to which reality can be reduced. It is not "consciousness" in its post-seventeenth-century sense of a "private mental theater" divorced from "external reality," a sense that inverts the word's etymological meaning of "knowing together" (*cum-scire*). In modern times there have been calls to return to the earlier approach, especially among neo-Thomistic philosophers. Even the philosopher-Dantist Nardi—no friend of neo-Thomism—ultimately concluded, with his usual vividness: "To heal from the dementia there is only one remedy: . . . return to the Aristotelian principle of the coincidence between what is thought and the act of thinking, and kick out the illusions of Satan, of which Descartes was the victim, with the efficacious exorcism Saint Francis recommended to Brother Ruffino."[10]

Dante's Predecessors

Because it is the sacred duty, or affliction, of philosophers to talk when there is nothing to say, they are prone to make something out of nothing. In the case of Aristotelian noetics, this means turning what Aristotle had repeatedly said is not a thing (it is in different senses nothing, the world, or God, and is both immanent and transcendent to the embodied soul) into two things, a passive intellect here and an active intellect there, and then worrying over their relations for two thousand years. Thus while *nous* still seems to be one in Aristotle's younger colleague Theophrastus, it has already become two in his great commentator Alexander of Aphrodisias (c. 200 A.D.). The active intellect is now God (the Unmoved Mover); the potential (Alexander calls it "material") intellect is in the soul, and is actualized—in the right circumstances, even divinized—by the divine self-thinking *nous*. In various guises, and largely through Neoplatonism, this view, that the human mind relates to a divine intelligence above itself in order to know, becomes the dominant model of human intellection for a millennium, whether that intelligence is a single hypostasis of the divine reflected again in the soul (Plotinus); or a divine illuminating light through which the created light of each mind sees the true reality of things within itself (Augustine and Bonaventure); or a "giver of forms," last in the hierarchy of pure intelligences, that radiates the forms of things both into matter and into the human soul (Avicenna); or a single intelligence that "borrows" the imaginative faculty (phantasms) of individual human beings in order to think, lending them even their power to receive forms (the potential intellect), so that only the human race as a whole is immortal, and not the individual soul (Averroës). In an alternate model, Themistius (fourth century) makes the active intellect intrinsic to each soul, as what actualizes, and the actuality of, the potential intellect. Nine centuries later, when Albert the Great and Aquinas counter the views of Avicenna and Averroës, and restore the full Aristotelian faith in the inherent intelligibility of the world, this intrinsic active intellect becomes the power of the rational soul to "abstract" forms or essences from matter; it actualizes the potential intellect by illuminating it with the help of pure divine light (Albert), or by "storing" the abstracted essences (species) in it (Aquinas).[11]

Our concern is not the variation in these models, but rather the shared understanding that underlies them all, the heritage that is Plato reworked by Aristotle reworked by Plotinus, all reworked again by Aristotle *redivivus* in the thirteenth century, and all sharpened in the light of Christian meditation. From our discussion of Aristotle, we may distill that understanding into three fundamental principles, which were to become the foundation of the medieval understanding of reality.

1. God, as pure being or actuality or form, is the reflexivity of pure awareness (Intellect itself), which is nothing (not a thing), but the active power to be everything and nothing.

2. Each thing that exists, exists only as a qualification of or participation in Intellect-Being. As determinations or limitations of being, things are radically other than the principle of Being itself (Aquinas would say they participate only in "common" or "created" being), yet if they were not in, of, through, or from God, they would not be. In an absolute sense, only God is; all else shares.

3. Human awareness (the rational soul) is a special case, a special sharing in or affinity with the ultimate ontological principle. Hence its (at least potential) immortality, freedom in and from space and time, immunity to the power of any created thing (freedom of the will), and potential for what was variously called contemplative rapture (*alienatio mentis, ek-stasis*), deification (*deificatio*), or divine union (*unio mystica*).

Our particular concern is the third principle, because it in fact subsumes the first two, and because it is the principle that underlies the pilgrim Dante's journey, his claims to have visited the Empyrean. The question, in short, is: how does the human soul or intelligence come to experience itself as divine, all-encompassing, and (one with) the ultimate principle of all being? Aristotle supplied the metaphysical foundation to answer the question (in sum, that being and intellect are interchangeable), but the elaboration of the answer was to be the work of his Neoplatonic heirs, and especially of the Christian Neoplatonic tradition, which *was* the Christian tradition until the rediscovery of

Aristotle himself. As in all major spiritual and philosophical traditions, the Neoplatonic-Christian answer to the question, "How may the soul know God?" is, in a word: by knowing itself. If Intellect is the principle of Being-in-itself, then human intellect comes to know God, and all things, by truly knowing itself, or knowing its true self, the ground it shares with *what is*. This revelation can come only through surrendering or sacrificing everything it thinks it is or needs or wants: that is, every thing. Focusing on the principle of self-knowledge, let us briefly trace the history of this self-surrender or divinization, and the path to it, in a few key figures of the Neoplatonic-Christian tradition. This little survey will restore the context in which the pilgrim makes his flight to the Empyrean, introduce a number of concepts crucial to our discussion in the next chapters, and sketch the process the *Comedy* aims to set in motion in the pilgrim's alter ego: in the reader, whose own incipient awakening is to be triggered by the "shock of beauty" the *Comedy* aims to deliver.[12]

Plato had of course already mapped an ascent of the mind beyond all things and concepts to the Form of Forms, through contemplation, love, and purification; human *nous*, being of divine origin, may be divinized, becoming in some sense one with the Absolute. Because the ultimate principle (the Beautiful or the Good or the One) may be defined in itself only by distinguishing it from all things (i.e., by saying what it is not), it follows that understanding can neither be put into words nor achieved through words: after continued application and communion it is born suddenly, "like a blaze kindled by a leaping spark." Plato also taught that the human soul is a "middle being" in the cosmos that can descend toward matter or rise toward spirit (the ultimate germ of the *Comedy*'s travelogue). Above all, Plato transmitted the great ancient motto inscribed on the temple of Apollo at Delphi and promulgated by Socrates as a religious and philosophical injunction: *Gnothi seauton*, the Ciceronian *Nosce teipsum, Know yourself*. As the *Alcibiades I* (and later Cicero) explained, to know yourself is to know your soul, which is to know the divine, the foundation of being, reflected within you. Thus in Plato we already have three key ideas: deification as the ultimate and spontaneous fruit of self-knowledge; the incommunicability and transcendence of true understanding; and the human soul as a "middle being" in the cosmos. All these ideas will be integral to the subsequent tradition.[13]

The "founder" or dominant figure of Neoplatonism is Plotinus, who lived in the third century A.D. His student Porphyry tells us that Plotinus lived in order to achieve union or identity with the divine, and often did achieve it; Plotinus's own writings stress that true philosophy must lead to experience, without which what he is saying cannot be understood. As the ultimate, omnipresent, grounding principle of reality, the One is prior to determinate form, and thus beyond all attribute and multiplicity, even beyond the logical duality between subject and object that characterizes ordinary consciousness (i.e., it is beyond self-consciousness, the sense of "I" as a "something" that knows). That duality or "I awareness" arises within the One as *nous* (Intellect), which is both transcendent and simultaneously One-Many (each thing in it simultaneously includes and is the whole); its thought constitutes the forms or determinate being of the world. Intellect is the home of soul, which arises within *nous* to become the life and structuring organization of body, whether of living things, humans, celestial spheres, or the world as a whole. In humans, part of the soul remains always home with Intellect, simultaneously One-Many; the rest, distracted by the claims of the body and forgetful of itself and its source, alienates itself from *nous* and forgets that it encompasses and is all things. This descending series of emanations or hypostases, which Plotinus often compares to the diffusion of light (hence the medieval "metaphysics of light"), is not a process in time, but rather creates time by generating the world. Each hypostasis is a kind of turning back on itself toward its source, through a wish to belong only to itself; by this "turning" it gains awareness of itself, and constitutes itself, so to speak, as a subsistent reflection of that source. This turning or reflexivity is a Platonic theme that will find frequent echoes in Dante.[14]

The falling away from the One into the Many is balanced by the restlessness and longing of the Many to return again into the One: this is the sublime Plotinian equilibrium that (through Augustine, the church fathers, and Pseudo-Dionysius) came to govern Christian thought, ultimately to provide the organizing principle for Aquinas's *Summa theologiae*, as well as for Dante's *Comedy*. In particular the human soul is a frontier or border (*methorion*), both separating and uniting spirit and matter, eternity and time, rising or descending into the one or the other (an idea that will flower in Dante's *Primo Mobile*, as we shall see). Since the soul's true self or home is Intellect, the injunction to know oneself means to come back into the awareness of self as *nous*, and through *nous* ultimately to experience oneself as—that is, to lose oneself as, or to be—the One, the ultimate attributeless subject of all experience, from which or within which all experience arises. The ascent begins through the "shock of beauty," which reorients the mind away from the senses and into the depths of itself toward its source (one might say that this is the shock the pilgrim Dante will call "Beatrice"). It is a spontaneous movement toward absolute purity and renunciation, a knowing that is a stirring of love so intense that the soul becomes love, willing to renounce everything, to surrender all self-definition, to retain nothing of itself, in its thirst to be all, to rest in the One. Each human being is thus "all and one"; humans contain every hypostasis of the divine within themselves but rarely turn inward to know themselves. Truly to know oneself is to know one's true self, so that "the man is changed, no longer himself nor self-belonging; he is merged with the Supreme, sunken into it, one with it: centre coincides with centre." Here we have the key elements of the later tradition: God's utter transcendence of all (conceptual) knowing and duality; the soul as horizon between spirit and matter; the intimate interiority of the divine as the source or ground of the soul, touched only as the purified intelligence ("I-awareness") reenters itself and transcends itself through love.[15]

It was only natural to absorb the power and subtlety of Plotinus's vision into the meditation on Christian revelation, a process well underway in the work of the church fathers, most of whom were saturated with Platonic and Neoplatonic philosophy. On the question of deification through self-knowledge and purity, the links seemed ready-made: Jesus had said, "The kingdom of God is within you," and He had said that only those who gave up everything for this treasure would find it; He promised that the pure in heart would see God, as Moses, Paul, Peter, James, and John all did in this life. The Gospels revealed that the path to God is purification ("Be perfect as your heavenly Father is perfect"), which is self-sacrifice and renunciation, epitomized in the Cross, a dying to this life: to seek one's life is to lose it, to lose one's life is to find it. By mirroring (contemplating) more and more brightly the brightness of the Lord, said Paul, "we are turned into the image we reflect; this is the work of the Lord who is Spirit." Identifying wholly with Christ, both God and man, we live in Christ, or rather Christ or the Spirit of God lives in us, and no longer we in ourselves: this is truly to love, which is to dwell in God, who is love. Christianity recasts the Neoplatonic tradition it adopts: Christ, the Word, designates the oneness of the human and the divine, a union lost in human experience but restored through sacrifice. Sacrifice is revelation: the loving surrender of the human mind to the ground of its being is one with, and consequent upon, the loving surrender of the transcendent to the finite, of God to and as man; this is the awakening of Truth (Intellect-Being) to itself in the world. The name for this awakening/self-manifestation is Christ, and there is no path to it that does not go through the Cross, through the crucifixion of self by which human beings recognize themselves as the loving self-sacrifice, the self-giving, of God, of Intellect-Being itself. This is to recognize oneself as, in, or through Christ, which is to know Christ, to live in Christ. In Christian thought, to know Christ is not, as many people think, simply to have heard of Him.[16]

Thus the fathers, absorbing Platonism and then Plotinus, stress that the soul is potentially, not innately, divine, and they stress the centrality of Christ and ecclesial community against the Plotinian, philosophical "flight of the alone to the Alone." The paradigm of Christian Platonism might be Saint Clement of Alexandria's famous maxim, from around 200 A.D. but repeated down the ages from Athanasius and Augustine through Aquinas: "God became man so that (you may learn from man how) man may become God." Perfected through purity, contemplation, and obedience to God, says Clement, we become gods, like God, participants in the divine, through the gift of God. The path, again, is self-knowledge, through Christ: "If a man knows himself he will know God, and by knowing God he will be made like God." In the third century, Origen, whose influence was later often nameless but pervasive, teaches that in reading Scripture, we must transcend "the letter that kills" (as Paul put it), in order to ascend toward spiritual (anagogical) understanding, that is, toward God; to approach God is for the virgin soul, like Mary, to give birth to Christ. By contemplating God, the purified intellect is deified; in Jesus, human and divine nature mingle, and through Jesus, medium and mediator between God and flesh, human nature in us becomes divine, one with God. Saint Athanasius (fourth century) tells us that God is not far off, but may be found in ourselves, which is why the Savior declared, "The kingdom of God is within you"; it is by the intelligence in us (undistracted by sensual pleasures) that we come to see God: "The soul of man, being intellectual, can know God of itself, if it be true to its own nature." In the same century Saint Gregory of Nyssa draws together many of these themes, and stresses that because God lives in us, we encompass all of creation within ourselves:

> Our greatest protection is self-knowledge, and to avoid the delusion that we are seeing ourselves when we are in reality looking at something else. . . . Now anyone who has any regard for the life of this world . . . does not know how to distinguish himself from what he is not. No passing thing is strictly ours. . . .
>
> You alone are made in the likeness of that nature which surpasses all understanding; you alone are a similitude of eternal beauty, a receptacle of happiness, an image of the true Light; and if you look up to Him you will become what He is, imitating Him Who shines within you, Whose glory is reflected in your purity. Nothing in all creation can equal your grandeur. All the heavens can fit into the palm of God's hand; the earth and the sea are measured in the hollow of His hand (Isaiah 40.12). And though He is so great that He can grasp all creation in His palm, you can wholly embrace Him; He dwells within you, nor is He cramped as He pervades your entire being.

The proper use of human intelligence is to distinguish oneself from everything that one is not, which is to distinguish oneself from every thing; this is to know oneself as (one with) what does not come and go, the no-thing that contains and spawns all things: pure awareness-being itself.[17]

It has been argued that since Saint Augustine, the most influential thinker in the history of Christianity, was already a Christian at the time of his conversion, he really was converted to Plotinus or his student Porphyry: to "the books of the Platonists" (*libri Platonicorum*), as he calls them. This of course is not quite true, but he would not have been converted without Plotinus, whom Augustine never ceased to revere, and whose philosophy, by Augustine's own account, opened his eyes to an understanding of reality that allowed him to respond to Christian revelation. Christianity, for Augustine, is the fulfillment and fruition of Platonic philosophy, which had already taught that reality is ultimately spiritual and that the soul comes to God by entering into itself through purification and illumination. Hence Augustine's great stress on redirecting the mind in toward itself ("by the Platonic books I was admonished to return into myself"; "see, You were within and I was in the external world and sought You there"), and his stress on the *Nosce teipsum*, epitomized in his "perfect prayer": *Deus semper idem, noverim me, noverim te* ("O God, always one and the same, grant that I may know myself, grant that I may know You"), in which the last clause is consequent on the second, and the second on the first, on divine grace. *Noli foras ire; in te ipsum redi*: withdraw from the senses, return into yourself, transcend mutability and thought, sharpen the mind to a point, to find the Truth that dwells within you, the Truth that leads us on by its indescribable sweetness. The mind's sight or eye touches God (fleetingly) through purity, by withdrawing what it has added to itself, which is attachment and the desire for mortal things. Our inner eternal light is a participation in Christ; our self-knowledge is an image of the Trinity active within us; incorporated into the church, we share in Christ's body, becoming not only Christians, but Christ. "The Light itself is one, and all those are one who see it and love it"; it "is seen by a power of sight which makes those who already see with it not human but superhuman." Augustine teaches his heirs that to enter into and know oneself is to surrender all that the intellectual soul is not in itself (including all thoughts and ideas); this is the path to God, and indeed to all true knowledge and understanding, because what encompasses all dwells within us as the ground of all thought and being.[18]

Around 500 A.D. a Syrian monk fused Proclean Neoplatonism with Christian theology in a few tracts and letters that he attributed to the philosophizing Dionysius the Areopagite, converted by Saint Paul in *Acts* 17.34. The authority of the Dionysian corpus (which was accepted as authentic) in later medieval thought is exceeded only by that of Augustine and of the Bible: the supposedly Aristotelian Aquinas, for example, cites it about 1700 times. In Pseudo-Dionysius, Christian Neoplatonism reaches some of its most dramatic expressions:

> Leave behind you everything perceived and understood, everything perceptible and understandable, all that is not and all that is, and, with your understanding laid aside. . . . strive upward as much as you can toward union with him who is beyond all being and knowledge. By an undivided and absolute abandonment of yourself and everything, shedding all and freed from all, you will be uplifted to the ray of the divine shadow which is above everything that is. . . .
>
>   Here, renouncing all that the mind may conceive, . . . he [Moses, figure of the contemplative] belongs completely to him who is beyond everything. Here, being neither oneself nor someone else, one is supremely united by a completely unknowing inactivity of all knowledge, and knows beyond the mind by knowing nothing.

The soul or intelligence is divinized by the absolute transcendence of self, of all thought and knowing, through a radical self-emptying, in order to come into the experience of that which is no thing, outside of which nothing is. This is for the soul to move in a circle, turning "within itself and away from what is outside," gathering itself in upon itself to reach "the Beautiful and the Good, which is beyond all things." Thus the One leads us "into a godlike oneness, into a unity reflecting God," uniting the divinized mind with the Light beyond all deity, in the cessation of all thought. Pseudo-Dionysius infuses a new drama into the expression of God's utter transcendence of the finite and of the conceptual and is the main Christian source of a tradition (including John Scotus Eriugena in the ninth century, and later Eckhart) that if we think—as we do—of being in terms of things (and of intellect in terms of thoughts), then it is truer of God to say that He does not exist (and does not think) than that He does: as pure awareness, He is the "nonexistent" source or ground of all thought and being.[19]

Tasting the sweetness of God, says Saint Bernard in the twelfth century, we come to love Him for no end except Himself. Only then can we truly love others and ourselves without self-interest; only then does the intellectual soul become "inebriated with divine love" and forget itself, becoming like an empty or broken vessel, and "hastening toward God and clinging to him" become "one with him in spirit." To surrender all self-will, self-interest, and concern for the body is to dissolve human desire into the divine will (like water in wine, iron in fire, air in sunshine); this is truly to love, which is to be deified, assimilated to the divine. Citing his own experience, Bernard insists that understanding can come only through such experience. The foundation, again, is self-knowledge; *Nosce [Scito] teipsum* is a precept descended from Heaven. The sage drinks at his own well, brings his attention back to himself; his meditation begins and ends with himself. To know oneself is to know that human beings occupy "the middle place between the highest and the lowest"; it is to know not only the misery of a humanity enslaved by the misuse of the senses, but also the glory of the divine nature in which the mind was made to share, into whose image we are called to be transformed, through a mingling of the enlightened mind with heavenly light. Through knowing ourselves we come to love Christ, the Word, who gives us back to ourselves: through Christ, God shares in humanity so that humanity may share in divinity. To his heirs (as in the *Comedy*), Bernard becomes the paradigm of the contemplative, the paradigm of the ancient Christian tradition of a "loving knowing," a knowing that becomes love, or a loving that becomes knowing, through a Christlike surrender into selflessness.[20]

In the same century Richard of St. Victor systematizes and theorizes the preceding tradition, placing even more emphasis on the *Gnothi seauton*, a *sententia* uttered by one "descended from heaven." God is an intoxicating inner sweetness through which we forget the body and the world and turn inward: the mind is "ravished into the abyss of divine light," shedding and forgetting itself and all outward things, to pass into God, becoming all things to all men to save all. He who does not enter into himself knows nothing, because only through knowledge of self may we know "everything celestial, terrestrial, and infernal." Talk and reasoning are useless for penetrating the divine light; rather, return to yourself, climb the mountain of self-knowledge, and ascend above yourself through yourself. On the mountain of self-knowledge you will transcend all worldly knowledge, all philosophy; on that mountain you will see Christ transfigured, and you will know God, the Creator whom Plato and Aristotle resisted only because they did not fully know themselves. Only through knowing your own spirit may you know God, because the soul is the mirror for seeing God. But that mirror must be wiped clean, and you must long gaze into it: this is for the mind to shed desires, gathering itself into unity to enter into itself, forgetting everything exterior and even interior, in order to remain in its innermost shrine, which is to fly in contemplation. This self-gathering can happen only when we love God alone, when the mind forgets even itself in contemplating its ground or source, the divine light, resting in Him to whom it is one and the same thing to be everything that is, and who alone can truly say, "I am who I am." The peak of the mountain of self-knowledge is where the mind comes to a supreme point; this is to reach the *sanctum sanctorum*, the innermost recess of the mind. Reaching this point through divine favor, the mind is enlarged to become more than human; it is transfigured, falling away from the human into the divine, through a dawning of divine light. Many of these images recur in the course of the pilgrim Dante's journey (including of course the mountain), and I shall return to some of them over the next chapters; for now we need only observe Richard's emphasis that *all* true knowledge (including worldly knowledge) depends upon self-inquiry. To bring the mind to a point in its source, before every concept and idea, transcending all philosophy, is to see the reality that both spawns and is all things, to see God, or Christ transfigured: it is to lose oneself in an all-encompassing enlargement of mind, in divine Intellect itself.[21]

In the thirteenth century Saint Bonaventure stresses again that the highest part of the soul is the most interior: beyond the senses, imagination, reason, understanding, and even intelligence lies the *apex mentis seu synderesis scintilla*: the peak or point of the mind, which is also the peak or point of love or attraction (*apex affectionis*) and the spark of conscience in us, the ground of morality. Through this point or spark the mind that has entered itself, turning away from creatures and leaving behind "everything sensible, imaginable, and intelligible," focuses itself in single-pointed attention on its ground or source, on the eternal Light that formed the mind itself, until as pure intelligence it passes beyond itself into that source, which is for the mind or love to pass over (*transire*) into Truth, pure Being, what alone is, "totally transferred and transformed into God." The lure of the senses is the obstacle to self-knowledge:

> It seems amazing when it has been shown that God is so close to
> our souls that so few should be aware of the First Principle within
> themselves. Yet the reason is close at hand: for the human mind,
> distracted by cares, does not enter into itself through memory;
> clouded by sense images, it does not turn back to itself through in-
> telligence; allured away by concupiscence, it does not turn back to
> itself through desire for inner sweetness and spiritual joy.

The direct experience of God is a kind of death to this life; it alone—not talking or thinking or writing—constitutes wisdom. The path to this experience, as in the whole Christian tradition back to Origen, is through purgation leading to illumination leading to union. Union is possible only through the nexus between God and creation that is Christ: the Word is the metaphysical medium through which the divine expresses itself *as* the world, and it is also the medium through which—by taking human form and sacrificing itself on the Cross—the divine reveals itself to man *in* the world. God leads man to God by revealing Himself as man; the mind goes beyond itself only by contemplating Christ as both God and human, by identifying itself with Christ. Bonaventure, as heir to Joachim of Fiore, and like Dante after Bonaventure, thought the coming of Saint Francis—the perfect exemplar of renunciation (poverty) and identification with Christ, sealed by the stigmata—was an epochal event, destined to inaugurate a time in which people would again understand the Bible spiritually and turn toward selflessness and contemplative life. Like Joachim and Dante, Bonaventure did his best to usher in that new age, although seven centuries later it seems still to be heralded around the corner.[22]

During Bonaventure's time, the great Neoplatonic (Augustinian) tradition he represented met Aristotle and, in Thomas Aquinas, fused again with Aristotle for the second time, or rather for the third, if we count Aristotle's Neoplatonizing experience at the hands of the Islamic philosophers who gave him back to the West. Aquinas's reconciliation of Augustinian "fideism" and Aristotelian "rationalism" was so harmonious and penetrating, so true to the essential principles of both in showing their compatibility with each other, that it of course irritated the intransigent extremists on both sides and did not attain anything like its current reputation and authority until the sixteenth, and then again in the nineteenth, century. For Aquinas, all of creation is a (Neoplatonic) hierarchy determined by the degree to which each thing participates in the act-of-being (*esse*), which is the degree to which it participates in intelligence (awareness or knowing), in intelligibility (knowability), in truth, in unity, in interiority, in causal power, in actuality, and in love: in God. In a sense, everything that exists, by virtue of the fact that it exists, already participates to some degree in the divine, a view that makes Aquinas one of the most "Neoplatonic" of medieval philosophers. Intelligences, embodied or not, are a special case ("God is the beginning and end of all things, and especially of rational creatures," we learn at the outset of the great *Summa*): they are much more like, share much more in, the self-subsistent reality (Intellect itself, whose first name, for Aquinas, is *esse*, "to be") that gives things being, which is why even embodied intelligences are not ephemeral and not subject to any thing. As the highest of animals and lowest of intelligences, humans are the frontier or border (*confinium*) "between spiritual and corporeal nature, as a kind of medium between the two"; the human soul "is on the horizon of eternity and time." The human soul, as the form or being of the body, is the culmination of the physical world, which it radically transcends through its power, as intellect, to take into itself (to be) the form of anything that has being: thus the human soul in a sense encompasses or is all things (*quodammodo omnia*); it is a "little world." The human being is the medium or mediator between God and the physical world: as Norris Clarke has put it, "lowest of the spirits," the human soul "reaches down into matter to take on a body for itself, thereby lifting up matter into the light of consciousness and enabling the material world to return to God in the great circle of being"; in Luigi Bogliolo's words (inspired by Aquinas), "In man, all is saved by returning to God; all is lost, if man is lost." Thus the purpose of human life is deification, a full participation in the divine nature, which is to know God by becoming like God (deiform), so that "the essence of God itself becomes the intelligible form of the intellect," and the divine essence is "both what is seen and what is doing the seeing."

This surrender of self can occur only through grace, the self-giving of the ground of self (God), and it never abolishes the "ontological divide" between self-subsistent and created being.[23]

Because Aquinas thought that embodied intelligence "knows itself, and all within itself" not through a direct Neoplatonic introspection transcending thought, but only through an "Aristotelian" activity of knowing and abstracting universals from particular material things (that is, by thinking thoughts), he was exceptional among medieval theologians and philosophers (even among the so-called Averroists or radical Aristotelians, who in their noetics and "mysticism" were more "Neoplatonic" than Aquinas himself) in categorically denying the human capacity to know God "in this life." He may have discovered that here he was mistaken: toward the end of his life, while celebrating Mass, he underwent a revelatory experience so cataclysmic it put a sudden stop to the *Summa Theologiae* and all his writing. He told his secretary Reginald, "I cannot do any more. Everything I have written seems to me as straw in comparison with what I have seen." The incident is important because it suggests again that, in a medieval framework, philosophy and theology seek and prepare a revelation that transcends thought and language: if they achieve their goal, they end in silence. It also implies that Evelyn Underhill's famous remark that philosophizing or theologizing intellectuals are "no more mystics than the milestones on the Dover Road are travellers to Calais" ("mystics" being those who speak from direct experience of the transcendent, rather than from speculation or the authority of someone else's experience) is not necessarily true, at least in a medieval context.[24]

The last stop in our little survey, and its culmination, is Dante's exact contemporary, and in many ways direct counterpart, north of the Alps: Meister Eckhart. In seeking to trigger an awakening, to put Truth into words, Eckhart's daring equals Dante's. Eckhart's fundamental message is that the "spark" or ground of the soul, pure Intellect, is identical with God ("God's ground and the soul's ground are one ground"), so that to "break through" and experience that ground is to be God (while also remaining oneself). There can be no duality between God and soul in "experiencing God," because God, as pure Intellect itself and the ground of being, is not an object, but rather the ultimate subject, of all experience: it is what is doing the experiencing ("My eye and God's eye are one eye and one seeing, one knowing, and one loving"). Therefore to know God can only be to know oneself as God, to lose one's "I" in the nothingness of an all-encompassing "I," so to speak: only (what has become) God can know (be) God. "Some simple people think that they will see God as if he were standing there and they here. It is not so. God and I, we are one. I accept God into me in knowing; I go into God in loving." The truth is that man and God are one, without distinction or multiplicity, "nothing but one." God's being is the soul's being: for the soul to awaken to this truth is for it to give birth to Christ, the Word; or rather, it is for the soul to realize that it itself is Christ, the only-begotten Son of God, as well as the Father who begets it. "The Father gives birth to his Son without ceasing; and I say more: He gives me birth, me his Son and the same Son. I say more: He gives birth not only to me his Son, but he gives birth to me as himself and himself as me and to me as his being and nature." In other words, there is an "uncreated" spark in the soul that does not touch time or place. Through this spark, beyond the duality of "creature" and "God," the soul is God and God is the soul; this spark is, like Mary, both virgin and wife, ready to give birth to Christ. This is the soul's inmost ground or silence, a divine abyss or light, in which alone we can know and conceive things as they are. We come to it only by turning away from ourselves and created things, accepting or seeking nothing outside ourselves, diving into the bottomless well within us through absolute detachment and renunciation, annihilating or abandoning ourselves, wanting nothing, knowing nothing, having nothing, being as free and empty as before we came from God. "God is free of all things, and therefore he is all things": since God is not a thing, we make ourselves equal to God only by making ourselves equal to nothing.[25]

Let us sum up this brief history. The human soul or intelligence is divinized or "united with God" by entering into or rising above itself through perfect self-knowledge: it truly knows itself by knowing its true self, which is to know (experience) what Intellect is in itself, which is to lose oneself in the ground of one's being, of all being. The human intelligence may come to this experience only by giving up its exclusive self-identification with any finite thing or mode of existence. As Christianity emphasizes, this is to sacrifice all attachment, even to physical life, to surrender and crucify the ego in perfect selflessness. Self-sacrifice constitutes the perfection of love and wisdom, the experience of self as—like God, Intellect-Being itself—everything and nothing. This unconditional sacrifice, or revelation, happens on its own: it is divine grace, the awakening of the divine to itself in us; we can do no more than prepare for it, making straight the way of the Lord, so to speak. In Christianity, the paradigm and name of this sacrifice-revelation is Christ; but Christ reveals and restores the true nature of man, of Adam as God made him: the summation and microcosm of the world, containing all within himself, the horizon and link between spirit and matter, eternity and time, God and creation.[26]

We could thus sum up the Neoplatonic Christian tradition (indeed all major spiritual traditions) by saying: self-sacrifice is self-knowledge; self-knowledge is wisdom; wisdom is love; love is God; God is sweetness or bliss. Unity is divinity, purity is enlightenment: we can know what we inalienably are, or are from, only by surrendering what we contingently are, with all its concomitant desire and fear. Wisdom or understanding expands with love: a mind willing to be nothing, no longer petrified by its obsessive self-identification with the body, memories, expectations, family, and other attachments, is freed to experience itself as all, to recognize itself in, and as, each thing that exists; such an intelligence awakens to its own immortality and transcendence. Knowing itself as (one with) all things, as nothing in itself, it craves nothing, seeks nothing, rejects nothing, fears nothing: it loves unconditionally and absolutely. The Christian path to this love is epitomized in the Passion: hear all and say nothing; bear all and do nothing; give all and take nothing; serve all and be nothing. That the path is anything but passive has been demonstrated by its difficulty, and by its effect when practiced.[27]

Within the spatiotemporal world, the precise nexus between creator and creation is the focal point of self-awareness, the innermost or highest peak or point or spark of the human mind, in or through which human beings, by shedding the self-identification with any thing, come to know themselves as (one with) God, which is really for divine self-subsistent Intellect to know itself as or through the human. Through this point—at the midpoint of the onto-logical hierarchy of being that constitutes reality—the ground of being comes to consciousness of itself in, and as, creation. To experience this spark or nexus as oneself is to experience oneself as Christ, both God and man, bridging the infinite and the finite: it is to give birth to Christ, to see Christ transfigured on the mountaintop of self-knowledge, to know Christ, to be Christ, to live in Christ and no longer in oneself. The mark of this experience is an unutterable sweetness that eclipses the lure of the senses and reverses the natural orien-tation of the mind from outward to inward, resulting in spontaneous renun-ciation, detachment, and selfless love, a feeding on the source of all being within oneself. To reverse the natural orientation of the mind is for the human soul, the horizon or border between the One and the Many, between eternity and time, between matter and God, to witness the setting of greed, ignorance, and desire, and the dawning of understanding, freedom, and immortality.

As Bonaventure said, the innermost spark or peak of the mind, through which it—by grace—touches and knows the ground of all being as itself (i.e., experiences truth), is thus the source of all morality and conscience. Morality flows from understanding, which is love, the experience or recognition of the other as oneself. To the extent that a word, thought, or action reflects, and tends toward, the experience of all as oneself (the dissolution of the ego), it is moral, that is, in harmony with truth or reality; to the extent that it does the opposite, it is immoral, and in its disharmony with reality contains the seeds of its own destruction. Briefly put, as truth is love in speech, so morality is love in action. In the *Comedy*, the growth in love or understanding (moral perfection) is vividly represented by the pilgrim's journey from the center of the earth to the Em-pyrean, through which he literally encompasses (experiences) more and more of the world as himself. To understand Dante in his own context, it is important to grasp this "grounded" and "intrinsic" understanding of morality, which is not based simply on authoritative injunctions or "moral reasoning." From a medieval point of view, no action grounded in mere "reasoning" can be moral, even if it is "correct," because its motivation will not be moral: it will not be grounded in, and thus will not foster or reveal, love or selflessness or under-standing or truth.[28]

The understanding of the human person or intelligence as the nexus, or potential mediator, between the ephemeral world and the divine, between mat-ter and self-subsistent Intellect-Being, shows that the three principles distilled from Aristotle at the beginning of this section may be reduced to one. This one foundational principle grounds all spirituality and revelation and underlies the greater Platonic-Aristotelian tradition as a whole: as the reality in and through which all things exist, Intellect or consciousness (Being) alone may be—in some sense—simultaneously many and one, both immanent and transcendent, each thing, everything, and nothing. That is, the One and the Many, while radically distinct, are not ultimately two: they coincide, as the intelligence that comes to know itself discovers. No spiritual or philosophical tradition is more determined to capture this inexpressible truth precisely than the Christian, in which the principle, incarnated and revealed in Christ, is the focus of the religion itself. Already in Plato the ultimate ontological ground may be distinguished from all things and concepts, and thus defined in itself, only by saying what it is not; this practice launched the Western tradition of negative (apophatic) theology. Like Neoplatonism itself, Christianity expresses itself variously between the poles of immanence (God is, or is in, all things) and transcendence (God is nothing, or creatures are nothing). Hence Plotinus: "the One is all things and not a single one of them," it is "absent from nothing and from everything"; Augustine: "Only of the Immortal can one really say that He is"; Pseudo-Dionysius: the Godhead "is multiplied and yet remains singular," it "is all things" and it "is no thing"; Richard of St. Victor: "Nothing is more present than that most absent One. . . . Nothing is more absent than that most present One"; Aquinas: God is "in all things . . . by his very self . . . as containing them," yet God is also "above all things," and multiplicity itself "would not be contained under being, unless it were in some way contained under one"; Eckhart: "All creatures are a pure nothing," but all creatures are (in) God, apart from whom nothing is.[29]

Eckhart expresses the foundational principle most precisely (i.e., "orthodoxly") when he says, "If someone were to have the whole world and God, he would not have more than if he had God alone." In other words, a material thing (or individual mind) is not "something added" to or "outside" Intellect, the ground of its being: the thing and its ground are not two, though they are not the same. Things are "made of" nothing; they exist only in and through God, Intellect-Being, but that is not "something" to make things out of. A close analogy, used by Richard of St. Victor and others, is how thoughts are "made by," or "exist in," mind.[30] Mind is certainly not just one of its thoughts: it is, rather, the power to spawn or be any thought, the actuality from or within which thoughts arise. Although thoughts "exist only in mind," the actuality or power that sustains them is nothing, not a "something" thoughts are "made of." As we shall see in the next chapter, this principle of nonduality between the world and the ground of its being underlies the concept of creation ex nihilo. In the Christian religion this principle—revealed as truth, not speculation; as history, not philosophy; as experience, not words; as incarnational reality, not a concept or idea; and as accessible to all, not just to a philosophizing elite: revealed as constitutive of oneself and all things—is named "Logos" or "Christ." The name denotes the self-manifestation of that principle within and as the world, and it designates the principle's coming to consciousness of itself in and through the human form.

This foundational Christ-principle, through which the temporal may reveal the eternal and finite contingency (oneself) may be unveiled as ultimately one with (not other than, "redeemed by") infinite self-subsistence, constitutes the key or drive-spring of the *Comedy*'s metaphysics and poetics. Not by chance, the principle (applied to angels) crowns *Paradiso* 29, the canto that, as we shall see, constitutes the pivot between space-time and its dimensionless ground within the heaven of the *Primo Mobile*, itself the nexus between the One and the Many:

> Vedi l'eccelso omai e la larghezza
> de l'etterno valor, poscia che tanti
> speculi fatti s'ha in che si spezza,
>   uno manendo in sé come davanti.[31]   (*Pd* 29.142–145)

Reflected or refracted into the mirrors of itself that are finite intelligences, conscious being remains simply itself, the one all-sustaining reality, outside of which nothing is.

Dante

We have seen that the central principle of Platonic-Aristotelian metaphysics is that form, through which the world has being, is the more or less qualified self-experience of Intellect (pure form, being, or actuality) and has no existence apart from it. It is in this sense that nothing exists apart from God, yet insofar as anything has attributes or identity, it cannot be said to be identical with God, conceived as the awareness (nothingness) in which all things consist. Dante grasped this principle with great lucidity already in the *Convivio*, but its full experiential or "incarnational" (concept-transcending) import will unfold only in the *Comedy*.

Intellect

In the *Convivio* (3.7.2–8) Dante stresses the continuity in the scale of being as degrees in the "transparency" of form to the pure intellectual light that is God; the hierarchy of form is the "intellectual order of the universe" (6). Dante compares this varying capacity of form to receive and manifest "the divine goodness" to the way different substances block, limit, or concentrate the simple light of the sun (i.e., are opaque, translucent, or transparent or reflective [2–4]). The difference of course is that while objects do not depend on sensible light to exist, intellectual light-love (*la divina bontade*) constitutes the being of things: "otherwise they could not be" (*altrimenti esser non potrebbero* [2]). Dante goes on to explain (5–6) that the "opacity" or "transparency" of form to the divine intelligence that gives it being depends upon how limited (material) the form is:

> Thus God's goodness is received in one way by separate substances,
> that is, by the Angels, who have no material dimension and are, as

it were, transparent by virtue of the purity of their form; and in another way by the human soul which, although it is partly free from
matter, is also partly impeded by it, like a man who is entirely in the
water except for his head, of whom it cannot be said that he is entirely in the water or entirely out of it; and in another way by animals, whose souls are entirely confined to matter, although they are,
I grant, endowed with some nobility; and in another way by plants;
and in another way by minerals; and by the earth in a way different
from the others, since the earth, being the most material of all, is
the most remote from and the most dissimilar to the first utterly
simple and perfectly noble power which is purely intellectual, that
is, God.[32]   (*Cv* 3.7.5)

Although particularly associated with Neoplatonism (Dante introduces this
passage with references to the *Liber de causis* and Albert the Great's highly
Neoplatonic *De intellectu*), we have seen that the ontological hierarchy of form
is also integral to Aristotle's metaphysics and was emphasized by both his
Arabic and his Scholastic commentators. In this hierarchy, Dante says that
angels are "transparent" (*diafani*) to, in some sense not other than, what gives
them being, pure *virtute intellettuale* itself. Humans alone are like angels
through their heads (their intelligence, or self-awareness), which are out of
matter (not dependent on space and time), but humans are in matter through
their bodies: the human soul is the bridge or nexus between intellect and
spatiotemporal extension. The implication of the swimmer analogy cannot be
lost on any reader of the *Comedy*: a creature that has only its head out of water
may easily drown. To drown is to experience oneself as entirely subject to
spatiotemporal contingency, having lost sight of the ultimate ontological principle (*il ben de l'intelletto*) in oneself (*If* 3.18). This death by drowning in the sea
of multiplicity and ephemerality is the peril from which the pilgrim is rescued
in the first lines of the *Comedy* (*If* 1.22–27); as we shall see, it is the peril
Ulysses, for all his reasoning and eloquence, fails to detect. Farther down the
scale of being, completely subject to spatiotemporal contingency, are brute
animals (what—ironically—Ulysses said humans were not made to be [*If*
26.119], although he ultimately failed to distinguish himself from them); the
lowest point on the hierarchy, at the farthest extreme from Intellect-Being,
comprises minerals and earth, entirely "opaque" to ("other than") the self-
subsistent principle which gives them being, pure awareness itself.

Because in the "intellectual order of the universe" there are "almost continuous gradations" from the lowest to the highest form, human nature, as
manifest in different individuals, is continuous with animals on one side and
with incorporeal intelligences on the other:

Although so far I have set down only the general gradations, we
could nevertheless set down the particular gradations: that is, that
among human souls one receives the divine goodness differently
from another. Thus in the intellectual order of the universe there is
a scale of ascent and descent along almost continuous gradations

from the lowest form to the highest and from the highest to the lowest, as we see in the order of beings capable of sensation. Further,
between the angelic nature, which is purely intellectual, and the human soul there is no intervening grade, but rather the one is, as it
were, continuous with the other in the scale of gradation. Again, between the human soul and the most perfect soul among brute animals there is also no gap: so it is that we see many men who are so
base and have sunk so low that they seem scarcely distinguishable
from beasts. Consequently it must be stated and firmly believed that
there are some so noble and of such lofty nature, that they are almost nothing but angels; otherwise the human species would not be
continuous in both directions, which is inconceivable. Aristotle, in
the Seventh Book of the *Ethics*, calls such beings divine.[33]

(Cv 3.7.6–7)

Again, in the range of its possibilities human nature links the sublunar realm
of contingency, whose peak is the sensitive soul, or animal nature, to the pure
intelligences whose "home" is the Empyrean, outside of, and encompassing,
the spatiotemporal world. As Dante explains in the *Monarchia*, through the
human being's double nature as both an ephemeral body-soul composite and
an intelligence separable from (not dependent upon) anything corruptible
(here Dante cites Aristotle, *De anima* 2.2.413b25–28), he "alone among things
is the medium or link between the corruptible and the incorruptible; hence
philosophers compare him to the horizon, which is the medium or link between two hemispheres." We have already seen that this idea, as well as the
comparison to the horizon (which may have been diffused by the *Liber de
causis*), has a long tradition in medieval philosophy.[34]

The "first utterly simple and perfectly noble power which is purely intellectual, that is, God," is not a thing that can be "subdivided" among finite forms
of being; rather, it is like a light in which all forms participate without in any
way affecting it or lessening it:

Since every effect retains something of the nature of its cause . . .
every form partakes in some way of the divine nature. This is not to
say that the divine nature is divided and distributed among the
forms, but that it is participated in by them in almost the same way
the nature of the sun is participated in by the other stars. The nobler
the form, the more it retains of this nature; consequently the human
soul, which is the noblest form of all those that are generated beneath the heavens, receives more of the divine nature than any
other.[35]   (Cv 3.2.5–6)

The divine nature is being, life, awareness-love; the more a creature is assimilated to the ground and source of its being, the more it manifests of (is "transparent" to) this nature. Thus all things manifest something of God as Being
by simply existing; by living, plants and animals manifest something of God
as the power of action and life; in humans the divine principle is manifest,

and becomes aware of itself, as intellect (consciousness), one with life and being, revealed as ontologically prior to, and thus not dependent upon, nature or any spatiotemporal thing. In the simple terms of folk wisdom: God sleeps in rocks, stirs in plants, awakens in animals, and becomes aware of Himself in humans. The analogy to the way the stars (which for Dante would include the planets, or "wandering stars") participate in the nature of the sun is based on the widespread medieval conviction, derived from Aristotle and vigorously defended by Albert the Great, Averroës, and others, that the sun is the sole source of celestial light, and that the heavenly bodies, transparent in themselves, become luminous (indeed luminescent) by absorbing or embodying that light to their core, and then reflecting or re-radiating it. Different heavenly bodies have different luminosities and colors because they have different natures (forms) or degrees of nobility, which determine their capacity to receive or incorporate the celestial light; the moon even exhibits a varying nature, and hence varying receptivity, in its own substance, as Beatrice explains to Dante in *Paradiso* 2. A perfectly noble body fully and perfectly embodies the celestial light of the sun through its entire substance, and re-radiates it fully; in the same way, Dante is saying, of all sublunar forms human nature most perfectly embodies, and manifests, the divine ground of its being.[36]

Dante goes on to explain that spiritual thirst is the instinct to "strengthen one's being": "Since it is most natural to God to will to be—because, as we read in the book mentioned above, 'being is first of all, and before that there is nothing'—the human soul naturally wills with all its desire to be; and since its existence depends upon God and is maintained by Him, it naturally longs and wills to unite itself to God in order to strengthen its being" (*Cv* 3.2.7).[37] The human desire to be is a reflection of the divine nature, Being itself, in the soul. To "fortify one's being" is to "aspire upward" in the hierarchy of form, which is to experience oneself ever less as a contingent object of experience, and ever more as pure Intellect-Being, the non-contingent subject of all experience.

That the being, essence, and formative-causal influence of all things find their ultimate ground in Intellect is reiterated in the *Letter to Cangrande*:

> Every essence, except the first, is caused. . . . Every essence that is
> caused, is caused either by nature or by intellect [*intellectu*], and if by
> nature, it is caused by intellect, since nature is the product of intelli-
> gence. Therefore everything which is caused, is caused by some in-
> tellect, either indirectly or directly. . . . And so, as before we came to
> the first cause of being itself, so now we come to the first cause of
> essence and formative power [*virtutis*]. It is clear, then, that every es-
> sence and formative power proceeds from the first, and that lower
> intelligences receive as from a source of light, and transmit like mir-
> rors to the intelligence below them, the rays of the being above
> them. This seems to be clearly treated by Dionysius when he speaks
> of the *Celestial Hierarchy*. Because of this the *Book of Causes* says
> that "every intelligence is full of forms." And thus it is clear how

reason demonstrates that the divine light, that is, the divine goodness, wisdom, and formative power, shines everywhere.[38]   (*EC* 21)

We must remember that causation here refers not to a temporal sequence of
events, but to the causal-formative power implicit in ontological dependence,
through which being is further and further qualified as diverse essences. The
idea of "relayed" or hierarchical ontological dependencies within creation, in
analogy with reflected light (again, not in time, as light too occupies no time)
is Neoplatonic, as the *Letter's* references indicate; the idea that the entire hierarchy of finite form is a function of, and ultimately consists in or is contained
by, Intellect (pure awareness or being) underlies the entire medieval philosophical tradition.

The *Letter* goes on to quote a number of biblical texts asserting that God
fills Heaven and earth and all things, texts that culminate in the pagan poet
Lucan (*Pharsalia* 9.580): "Jupiter is whatever you see, wherever you move" (22).
The *Letter* is commenting on the first lines of the *Paradiso*:

> La gloria di colui che tutto move
> per l'universo penetra, e risplende
> in una parte più e meno altrove.
>   Nel ciel che più de la sua luce prende
> fu' io, e vidi cose che ridire
> né sa né può chi di là sù discende;
>   perché appressando sé al suo disire,
> nostro intelletto si profonda tanto,
> che dietro la memoria non può ire.[39]   (*Pd* 1.1–9)

As we saw in the first chapter, and as the *Letter* explains (23), the divine light
(formative power-being-intellect) penetrates all things as their essence (their
this-or-thatness, or way of existing), and "shines" in things as their being, one
(in the most noble forms) with their luminosity. The "more or less" is obvious,
says the *Letter*, since there is a hierarchy in the scale of being or perfection,
ranging from the incorruptible (heaven) to the corruptible (the elements). As
we have seen, to be in the heaven most saturated with the all-penetrating light
is to be in the Empyrean, which is to be nowhere; the light is God, the awareness that projects or contains creation. The human intellect, in approaching
that light, is approaching itself, entering into itself in order to lose itself ("im-
merse itself," *profondarsi*) in its ground and source, self-subsistent (unqualified)
Intellect-Being. In that place, there is nothing to remember, because there is
nothing to forget: memory, which records the traces of finite form and contingency (the "this-or-that" which is the stuff of sensory image, imagination, and
thought), "cannot follow" intellect in its plunge into itself, in its experience of
itself as the source and totality of all finite being. All created intellect thirsts
for this experience: *già mai non si sazia / nostro intelletto, se 'l ver non lo illustra
/ di fuor dal qual nessun vero si spazia* ("our intellect is never sated if it is not
illuminated by the truth outside of which no truth finds place" [*Pd* 4.124–126]).

Dissociated from memory, imagination, and the other contingency-based faculties of embodied intellect, human intellect manifests its "connaturality with separated substances," that is, with intelligences not dependent upon body, intelligences whose "home" is the Empyrean, "outside" space and time.[40]

For Dante, human knowledge usually begins from the senses, as it always does for Aristotle. The end-result of sensation is the phantasm, or sensory image, presented to the intellect either by the cogitative (estimative) faculty (the power of the sensitive faculty to judge the veracity of the image it collates from the various senses), or else by the imaginative faculty (fantasy). The latter is distinguished from the estimative faculty by its power to produce or store phantasms from previous acts of sensation, or even directly under the influence of the spheres and the divine mind itself:

> O imaginativa che ne rube
> talvolta sì di fuor, ch'om non s'accorge
> perché dintorno suonin mille tube,
>   chi move te, se 'l senso non ti porge?
> Moveti lume che nel ciel s'informa,
> per sé o per voler che giù lo scorge.[41]   (*Pg* 17.13–18)

A light or intelligence that "takes on form in heaven," either spontaneously or through divine will, "moves" the imaginative faculty, focusing the mind so inward on the images arising within it that the senses become completely inoperative. This happens when the mind is so freed from flesh and from thought (*peregrina / più da la carne e men da' pensier presa*) that it "divines its own visions" (*a le sue visïon quasi è divina* [*Pg* 9.13–18]). In other words, when the human intellect is dissociated from spatiotemporal form, finite forms arise spontaneously within it as they arise in angelic intelligences, or in the divine mind itself: the human mind "takes dictation," so to speak. Such images or intuitions, undistorted by a finite point of view (*veduta*) or by sensation, are self-revelations of reality, with the same actuality, truth, or being as the sensory world. This phenomenon, which grounds prophecy and divinely inspired art— and thus (according to the *Comedy*) the *Comedy* itself—can occur only because of the affinity (*proporzione*) between human intellect and angelic intelligence (*Cv* 2.8.13): when the human intelligence is freed from body, sensation, and thought, it is assimilated to a "separated substance," an angel.[42]

Although individual and finite, all angelic and beatified human intelligences are also one, each knowing all the others as immediately as it knows itself, because they all consciously participate in the one reality of Intellect-Being. This unity and "in-him-ing" (*inluiarsi* [*Pd* 9.73,81; 22.127]) is a constant theme of the *Paradiso*, perhaps most powerfully expressed in the "skywriting" through which souls gather spontaneously to form emblems and words that point to the ground of their being, and through which that ground speaks, saying "I" instead of "we" (*Pd* 18.71,109, 19.10–12). An analogous principle underlies Dante's Averroistically inflected observation, in *Monarchia* 1.3.7–8, that the possible intellect is continuously and fully actualized only by humanity collectively, a remark that in no way implies that human intellects are not also individual; on this point Dante never wavers.[43]

Without the phantasm there is no thought: thought feeds on spatiotemporal form or on concepts abstracted from it, which is why an angelic intelligence, for example, cannot be an object of thought. It is also why thought or reason (as opposed to intellect or intuition) is so limited and can shed so little light on the world as a whole: as the *Monarchia* explains (3.15.7–9), through reason (*phylosophica documenta*) man, as a corruptible being, can seek only earthly happiness; to reach eternal life, his goal as an incorruptible being, he must gaze on the divine light itself, a path prepared through the *documenta spiritualia*, the teaching of writers, prophets, and saints inspired by God. That teaching or revelation too, however, must be "translated" into concept and image, through the manipulation of finite spatiotemporal contingency that is thought and language:[44]

> Così parlar conviensi al vostro ingegno,
> però che solo da sensato apprende
> ciò che fa poscia d'intelletto degno.
>   Per questo la Scrittura condescende
> a vostra facultate, e piedi e mano
> attribuisce a Dio e altro intende;
>   e Santa Chiesa con aspetto umano
> Gabrïel e Michel vi rappresenta,
> e l'altro che Tobia rifece sano.[45]   (*Pd* 4.40–48)

Since the *Monarchia* explains that worldly happiness is not really an ultimate end in itself, but is ordered to beatitude (3.15.17), we may conclude that philosophy too—for the mature Dante—is not an end in itself, but is ordered toward (is propaedeutic to) the revelation communicated by prophets and divinely inspired texts, such as (according to the *Comedy*) the *Comedy* itself. This is precisely the use the *Comedy* makes of philosophy, as this book aims to demonstrate.

Intellect (the power of "sight") and love are one, but intellect is logically prior to love. This truth is reflected in the Trinity, as we shall see in the next chapter, and in the Empyrean: the tenth heaven *is* pure intellectual light, *full* of love (*al ciel ch'è pura luce: / luce intellettüal, piena d'amore* [*Pd* 30.39–40]). An intelligence loves only in the degree to which it experiences the "other" as itself, which is the degree to which it knows itself as (one with) the ground of finite being, which is the degree to which it sees or understands. The power of sight itself is based on moral perfection (*buona voglia*), and on grace, the self-revelation of Intellect-Being in or as the finite intelligence:

> tutti hanno diletto
> quanto la sua veduta si profonda
> nel vero in che si queta ogne intelletto.
>   Quinci si può veder come si fonda
> l'esser beato ne l'atto che vede,

> non in quel ch'ama, che poscia seconda;
>   e del vedere è misura mercede,
> che grazia partorisce e buona voglia:
> così di grado in grado si procede.[46]   (*Pd* 28.106–114)

Beatitude is based on love, which is based on the power of sight or understanding, which is based on merit, which is based on grace and moral perfection. King Solomon lays out the same chain of logical (not temporal) dependence in *Paradiso* 14.40–42, 46–51, a passage chiastically structured so that grace, at the center, radiates outward into vision, then love, and then beatitude.[47]

As the form of forms, or universal form of being, God is the pure light of awareness in which all experience arises, a light that can be seen, or, rather, that sees itself through us, only when we consume or consummate in it our particular perspective, sight, or viewpoint (*aspetto, veduta*):

> E' mi ricorda ch'io fui più ardito
> per questo a sostener, tanto ch'i' giunsi
> l'aspetto mio col valore infinito.
>   Oh abbondante grazia ond' io presunsi
> ficcar lo viso per la luce etterna,
> tanto che la veduta vi consunsi![48]   (*Pd* 33.79–84)

To shed a point of view, joining one's sight with the eternal sight, is to shed the last traces of exclusive identification with a particular identity: it is again, as Richard of St. Victor said, to leave oneself and all things behind, in order to come to an all-encompassing enlargement of awareness, an *alienatio mentis* or *deificatio*. What Dante saw, strictly speaking, was nothing: in him, Intellect (the power of sight itself) came to know itself as the being and substance of all things. This is to experience all things as one, as oneself:

> Nel suo profondo vidi che s'interna,
> legato con amore in un volume,
> ciò che per l'universo si squaderna:
>   sustanze e accidenti e lor costume
> quasi conflati insieme, per tal modo
> che ciò ch'i' dico è un semplice lume.
>   La forma universal di questo nodo
> credo ch'i' vidi, perché più di largo,
> dicendo questo, mi sento ch'i' godo.[49]   (*Pd* 33.85–93)

Dante has experienced the revelation that all perceivers and things perceived ultimately are the qualified projections or reflections of one limitless and dimensionless reality. Intellect-Being writes the scattered pages of creation by identifying itself with (as) them, giving itself to the multiplicity of finite experience; it "binds" those pages into one volume in the sense that (to any intelligence that knows how to read, that has eyes to see) all of creation manifests the single simple reality that grounds it and contains it. Conversely,

Intellect-Being, reflected in and as the finite mind, seeks to "read" those scattered pages that it itself has written: this is the innate human desire to know, to understand, to seek Truth. To succeed in reading them is to understand them (all of creation) as a coherent book (bind them into one volume), which is to read and receive the message of their author. For a created intellect to receive that message is for Intellect-Being to awaken to itself within the world, as or through a finite intelligence: this is Christian revelation, or salvation. The book of creation is written, bound, and read by love, by the power of consciousness to experience itself as, or give itself to, finite experience, and to reawaken (as a finite intelligence) to the experience of all things as itself: love is the universal form of the "knot" that writes and binds the scattered pages of finite experience. This knot is therefore—Christically—the nexus between self-subsistent divine unity, denoted by the word *interna*, which evokes the Trinity (or the rational faculties of intellect, memory, and will), and ephemeral matter or multiplicity, denoted by the word *squaderna*, which evokes the number four, the number of matter, composed of four elements. The "knot" is the revelation (as *experience*) of the non-duality between the world and the ground of its being: it is Christ, the experience of self-sacrificial, self-giving love as the ultimate reality of all things. The knot of Love that writes and binds the book of creation is the *nodo* of the Incarnation of the Word, a knot that—in *Paradiso* 7.52–57— the pilgrim cannot untie by thinking, by "restricting" his mind *di pensier in pensier*, from thought to thought, as here too reason will fail. We shall see that this knot of Love is the heart of the *Comedy*'s poetics: as the poet Dante has the poet Bonagiunta say in *Purgatorio* 24.52–62, the power faithfully to transcribe the direct inner dictation of Love, so that Love fully determines one's "signifying" (which means in effect that the "signifying" ultimately reveals or signifies Love itself), is the *nodo* that separates Dante from other poets. The *Comedy* is telling us that this poem can be salvific, can trigger an awakening, because it arises directly from the ground of being (is written by Love) as creation itself does, or as Scripture does.[50]

The phrase *sustanze e accidenti* encompasses all finite being. *Sustanze* are substantial forms, many of which are material (*Pg* 18.49–50); they are the invariant (apparently self-subsistent) things of which changing attributes (accidents) are predicated, as "fat" or "old" is predicated of Socrates, who can be more or less fat, but not more or less Socrates. An accidental form exists only as a modification of a substantial form, and is thus variable and contingent. By saying that substances and accidents and *lor costume* (their behavior or nature) were *conflati insieme* (literally, "breathed into one"), Dante is underlining the contingency of *all* finite form in relation to Intellect-Being: exposed as contingency dependent on a truly self-subsistent reality, the apparent self-subsistence of substances cannot be distinguished from the ephemerality of accidents.[51]

"Substances and accidents, and their relations, were conflated together in such a way that what I say is (but) a simple light." All of the universe consists in one utterly simple light; Dante's words, which seek to convey that revelation, are themselves that light, the revelation of what alone *is* ("what I say is a simple light"), but insofar as they must communicate it through concept and image (finite form), they reveal only a simple glimmer of that light: finite form simultaneously disguises and reveals truth. The tercet, like others in the compressed last cantos of the *Comedy*, is not unlike a Zen "direct pointing," a perspective-shaking play on word or image that seeks to awaken us to what we cannot see because it is all there is.

The light Dante is describing is the light of the Empyrean, the actuality of all finite being. Dante describes the same light with similar compression when he begins the description of the Empyrean, at verse 100 of *Paradiso* 30—numbers that (as Singleton observes) are not likely to be a coincidence:

> Lume è la sù che visibile face
> lo creatore a quella creatura
> che solo in lui vedere ha la sua pace.   (*Pd* 30.100–102)

"There is a light up there that makes the Creator visible to that creature who finds peace only in seeing Him." Strictly speaking, only God can see God: the light, or power of sight, by which Being-Awareness is seen can only be the light, or power of sight, that is Being-Awareness itself. The subject of all experience (what is doing the experiencing) cannot be an object of experience: to see God is to experience oneself as, to lose oneself in, God. *In lumine tuo videbimus lumen* ("In your light we shall see the light" [Ps. 35.10]): this light, or power of vision, is the supernatural *lumen gloriae*, "lent" to a finite intelligence by grace, through which God becomes the intelligible form of the intellect itself, as Aquinas explains. In one sense, the light of being "becomes visible" by spawning the universe, through its projection or reflection as creatures; but of course it has then become invisible, becoming "other" than itself, ephemeral finite things. Only that creature—that finite love and intelligence—in or through which the ultimate reality longs to awaken to itself, so that that intelligence seeks only itself, its source and ground, and finds no rest or peace in any ephemeral thing—only that creature will see the light that projects and is all things, by coming to know itself as that light, that light as itself.[52]

The final revelation or understanding of this non-duality between God and self, as a truth immune to all concept and thought, a truth revealed only in the Incarnation and in experience, ends the *Paradiso*:

> Quella circulazion che sì concetta
> pareva in te come lume reflesso,
> da li occhi miei alquanto circunspetta,
> dentro da sé, del suo colore stesso,
> mi parve pinta de la nostra effige:
> per che 'l mio viso in lei tutto era messo.
> Qual è 'l geomètra che tutto s'affige
> per misurar lo cerchio, e non ritrova,
> pensando, quel principio ond' elli indige,
> tal era io a quella vista nova:
> veder voleva come si convenne

> l'imago al cerchio e come vi s'indova;
>   ma non eran da ciò le proprie penne:
> se non che la mia mente fu percossa
> da un fulgore in che sua voglia venne.
>   A l'alta fantasia qui mancò possa;
> ma già volgeva il mio disio e 'l *velle*,
> sì come rota ch'igualmente è mossa,
>   l'amor che move il sole e l'altre stelle.[53]   (*Pd* 33.127–145)

As the pilgrim's power of sight/understanding increases (*Pd* 33.109–113), pure Light-Intellect-Being, *la profonda e chiara sussistenza* ("the deep and luminous subsistence"), unchanging in itself, seems to project itself in three circles, representing the Trinity; in the second circle (reflected from the first, as light from light), the pilgrim makes out "our image" (*la nostra effige, imago*) and focuses his full attention (*viso*, "sight") on that, seeking to grasp how that image can "take its place in," "adapt or assimilate itself to" (*convenirsi a*) the circle that is the Second Person of the Trinity. The pilgrim is seeking to understand how man—the human form, he himself—can be *imago et gloria Dei* (I Cor. 11.7), Christ, God made visible. It is to "love oneself in God," as in Saint Bernard's fourth and culminating way of love. It is also to seek to understand the non-duality between two incommensurables, between on the one hand the circle of eternity or unity, of angelic self-knowledge, and of perfect heavenly motion, and on the other the square of time, rectilinear sublunar motion, animal nature, and the four elements of corruptible multiplicity. What defeats the geometer, thinking (*pensando*) how to square the circle, is that π is an irrational number, a principle or origin (*principio*) never to be found; what defeats the pilgrim is that the understanding he seeks is not conceptual: there is no "how" involved. The understanding comes in a flash of illumination or experience, canceling concept and image (*l'alta fantasia*) and with them the last trace of autonomous desire and will, which are now integrated into the harmony of creation, into the experience of self and all things as the self-expression of divine love. This firsthand knowledge of Truth or reality, of all as oneself, alone quenches the thirst for understanding.[54]

Throughout the Empyrean, the dissolution of duality is already explicit in how the pilgrim sees the *umbriferi prefazi* ("shadowy prefaces" or imagery) through which divine being gradually unveils itself to his understanding. The Empyrean is revealed to the pilgrim as an ocean of light with himself at the center (this is the vision that begins in *Paradiso* 30.100, introduced by the triple *vidi . . . vidi . . . vidi* of 95–99) only when he makes "better mirrors of his eyes" by "drinking" with them, literally immersing them into, what he had first observed as a river of light distinct from himself (61–90). This overcoming of duality between what sees and what is seen dissolves the *sembianza non sua* ("semblance not its own") of the light, to reveal the *regno verace* ("the true kingdom" [93–99]). Though this latter vision, as image, is still *parvenza* ("appearance" [106]), it is now "not other" than the pilgrim's power of sight itself: the *mezzo* or medium of perception that divides all perceivers from what they perceive has disappeared. A medium is essential to physical perception in Aristotelian theory: as Dante explains in the *Convivio* (3.9.7–12), it is the substance through which the form detected by the senses is conveyed. Without a medium, accurate sensation is impossible, as when an object touches the eye or ear (for the senses of touch and taste, flesh is the medium). In the Empyrean, the disappearance of the *mezzo*, and thus of all dualistic sensation, is immediately underlined:

> La vista mia ne l'ampio e ne l'altezza
> non si smarriva, ma tutto prendeva
> il quanto e 'l quale di quella allegrezza.
>   Presso e lontano, lì, né pon né leva:
> ché dove Dio sanza mezzo governa,
> la legge natural nulla rileva.[55]   (*Pd* 30.118–123)

The Empyrean is out of space-time, untouched by physical laws; it is a dimensionless point, in which all is immediately present, a "space" of consciousness, in which the "sight" of awareness "takes" (*prendeva*) as itself all it sees, all that exists. Note that within the *Primo Mobile*, that is, in space-time, the pilgrim's vision was still governed and limited by a *mezzo* (e.g., *Pd* 27.73–75), while in *Paradiso* 31, in the Empyrean, Beatrice's image (*effige*), though immeasurably "distant," *non discendëa a me per mezzo mista* ("did not descend to me mixed with a medium" [73–78]). The duality or otherness between subject and object, perceiver and perceived, is part of the hypnotic beauty, longing, and poignancy of life in space and time, as evoked in the pilgrim's first dawn in Purgatory, where the *mezzo* is identified with the atmosphere itself (*Pg* 1.13–18). In the passage from *Paradiso* 30, Dante is playing on the double sense of *mezzo* as "medium" and "intermediary": where "God governs" without an intermediary, that is, for what is dependent only on Being-Awareness, and not on any created thing, there is no medium of perception, no duality. As Beatrice explains in *Paradiso* 7, where the word *mezzo* in the sense of "intermediary" occurs three times (67, 70, 142), what is independent of all created things is immortal, and in a deep sense not "other than," not divided from, the ground of its being: it is, Beatrice says, and as Aristotle had explained, what comes from "outside" the world, the "rational soul" or *nous*, human (and angelic) self-awareness.

Philosophy

In the *Convivio*, the connaturality between human intelligence and divine Intellect triggers an effusive enthusiasm for philosophy as a salvific path to fulfillment and contemplative transcendence. Thus Dante explains that as the ontological principle through which things have being, form is synonymous with existence, actuality, perfection, life, movement, and cause. The soul (vegetative, sensitive, or rational) is the act or form or cause of any living body, and is defined by its highest faculty, which in man is the intellect. Our bodies, essence, and very being therefore depend on our intellect (consciousness), which is a participation in divinity itself:[56] "The soul . . . that is the most perfect of all, is the human soul, which through the nobility of its highest power, reason, participates in the divine nature as an everlasting intelligence. For in that supreme power the soul is so ennobled and stripped of matter that the divine light shines in it as in an angel; thus philosophers call man a divine living being" (*Cv* 3.2.14).[57] Human intelligence is continuous with angelic intelligence and with the divine mind itself:

> This mind is predicated only of man and of the divine substances,
> as may be seen clearly from Boethius, who predicates it first of men,
> when he says to Philosophy: "You and God, who placed you in the
> minds of men"; then he predicates it of God, when he says to God:
> "You produce all things from the heavenly exemplar, you, most
> beautiful, who bear the beautiful world within your mind." . . . So
> now we can see what mind is: it is that subtle and most precious
> part of the soul which is divinity.[58]   (*Cv* 3.2.17–19)

Since, as we saw in chapter 2, form itself cannot be defective but is limited only by the particular complex of elements in which it arises, there is no intrinsic limitation to human perfection: when matter is most suitably disposed to receive the human form, the result is divinity incarnate, the perfect knowledge or *ingegno* of Christ, and of Adam. Thus Dante says, in both the *Paradiso* (13.73–84) and the *Convivio* (4.21.10), that if the spheres were perfectly aligned to transmit their full formative-causal influence (itself derived from the Empyrean, pure Awareness-Being), and the preexisting compound of elements (the "wax") were most perfectly prepared to receive it, the eternal light that spawns all things (*la luce del suggel* or *deitade*) would be perfectly manifest in human form: another Christ or God incarnate would be born.[59]

Throughout his works Dante stresses this "natural affinity" between the human intellect and the pure thought that, according to Aristotle, constitutes divine actuality. God is "the spiritual and intelligible sun," which "illuminates first itself with intellectual light, and then the heavenly creatures and the other intelligible creatures" (*Cv* 3.12.6–7); God is the "divine intellect" that is "cause of all, especially of the human intellect" (*Cv* 2.4.14). In the *Convivio*, salvation itself seems to be won by exercising this supreme faculty, which man has in common with God. The idea so enthused the younger Dante that he equated philosophy, Wisdom, and divine intellect:

> Finally, as the highest praise of Wisdom, I say she is the mother of
> all, and before any other principle, by saying that with her God be-
> gan the world and especially the movement of the heavens, which
> generates all things and from which every movement has its origin
> and impetus. . . . she [Wisdom] was in the divine thought, which is
> Intellect itself, when it made the universe, from which it follows that
> she made it. . . . O worse than dead, you who flee her friendship,
> open your eyes and gaze! For she loved you before you existed, pre-

paring and planning your coming; and after you were made, to lead you straight she came to you in your own likeness.[60]   (*Cv* 3.15.15–17)

To flee the "friendship" of Wisdom is to reject Philosophy, the contemplative or speculative life through which that "friendship" is cultivated. To neglect Wisdom is to be more dead than dead, not only because it is to neglect the intellective faculty that must govern all our other faculties if we are to achieve happiness (*Mn* 1.5.4), but because it is an implicit rejection of eternal life: to flee Wisdom, the source and sustainer of our own being and of all things, amounts to fleeing Christ, who is Wisdom come in our own likeness.

Indeed through philosophy the soul marries God:

> Philosophy is a loving exercise of wisdom; it is found in the greatest measure in God—since supreme wisdom and supreme love and supreme actuality are in Him—and it cannot exist anywhere else except insofar as it proceeds from Him. Divine philosophy therefore pertains to the divine essence, because in God nothing can be added to His essence; in God philosophy is most noble, because the divine essence is most noble, and in Him philosophy exists in a true and perfect manner, as in an eternal marriage. In the other intelligences philosophy exists in a lesser way, like a mistress of whom no lover has complete enjoyment, but must rather satisfy his longing by gazing on her. . . . O most noble and excellent is that heart which is intent upon the bride of the Emperor of heaven—and not only bride, but sister and most beloved daughter![61]   (*Cv* 3.12.12–14)

Pure speculative contemplation of the ultimate cause of finite being is, for Dante as for Aristotle, a divine and superhuman activity. For the Dante of the *Convivio*, it is also a contemplation of the Word or Logos, and of the Wisdom of the Solomonic Proverbs: it is to feed on Christ, "the bread of the angels" (*lo pane delli angeli*), who, by taking human form, became the bread of man. Indeed, considered in its own essence, philosophy is the reflexive love of intellect, the ultimate and foundational ontological principle, for itself: the philosophizing soul "contemplates its own contemplating . . . turning back upon itself and falling in love with itself" (*Cv* 4.2.18). The perfection and source of philosophy is thus one with the essence of God; philosophy is *quella la cui propia ragione è nel secretissimo della divina mente* ("she whose true being and source is in the innermost depths of the divine mind"), as the last sentence of the *Convivio* asserts (4.30.6). This self-contemplation of the ultimate ontological reality (its identification with itself) constitutes understanding, the perception and foundation of truth. In *Convivio* 3.14.13–15 Dante explains that philosophy grounds faith, and thus hope and charity, the three virtues through which we "rise to philosophize in that celestial Athens where, by the light of eternal truth, Stoics and Peripatetics and Epicureans harmoniously join together in a single will." As Dante suggests in *Convivio* 4.22.14–18, the three sects will not find Christ (felicity) in the tomb of earthly and mortal things, but, directed by the angel of nobility or infused moral perfection, they will find the resurrected Christ in the Galilee of contemplation. The various philosophical doctrines, properly pursued, dissolve and merge in the contemplation of the self-subsistent light of self-awareness from which they begin and in which they end.[62]

Philosophy is thus spawned by truth, and aims at the uninterrupted contemplation of truth, which is bliss:

> Philosophy, considered in itself and apart from the soul, has understanding as its matter (*subietto*), and as its form an almost divine love for the intellect. . . . the efficient cause of philosophy is truth. . . . the goal of philosophy is that most excellent delight which suffers no interruption or imperfection, namely, the true happiness which is acquired through the contemplation of truth.[63]
>
> (*Cv* 3.11.13–14)

This is "original and true philosophy . . . in its being" (*la primaia e vera filosofia . . . in suo essere*); all the subjects (*scienze*) philosophy addresses are called philosophy only by extension (*Cv* 3.11.16–18). The love (power of self-identification) that constitutes philosophy/wisdom is divine (all-encompassing) and eternal; it therefore eclipses all finite attachments. This transcendence of attachment and egotism in itself constitutes moral perfection; indeed devils cannot philosophize, lacking love. Understanding is the highest perfection of the human soul and constitutes man's ultimate happiness, to which all men by nature strive; only by gazing on the eyes of philosophy can humans attain human perfection and the end of all desire, namely, the perfection of reason, the foundational principle of their being (3.15.4–5).[64]

This exalted conception of philosophy, as a path to attain fulfillment, happiness, moral perfection, and—through the assimilation of the human intellect to an angelic intelligence—the vision of God, transcends its Boethian antecedents and has evident affinities to philosophical currents associated with lay culture and the "Averroistic" or "radical Aristotelian" tendencies (themselves quite Neoplatonized) of the university arts faculties in the second half of the thirteenth century. The theological tradition since Augustine had reserved to revealed Christian wisdom alone the claims now being made for philosophy in the enthusiasm triggered by the recovery of Aristotle. The theological reaction to this development culminates in the Condemnations of 1277, which denounce, for example, the idea that "there is no more excellent kind of life than to give oneself to philosophy" (Proposition 40), or that "we can have felicity in this life, and not in another" (176). But the lines of division are not so clear: the *Convivio*'s Lady Philosophy is imbued with Solomonic, Johannean, and Eucharistic mysticism (and numerous biblical intertexts), all of which link her to the Beatrice she has only temporarily displaced. Moreover, Saint Albert the Great himself affirms the central tenet of the "Averroists": that the human intellect can have direct intuition of separated substances (angelic intelligences) in this life, thus conjoining itself with the divine agent intellect and achieving the direct vision of God, the fulfillment of contemplative happiness while still in the body. Though Aquinas attacked this view, he too conceived beatitude on the model of the philosophical contemplation that anticipates and participates in it in an ultimate fulfillment certainly attainable by man, although not in this life, and not apart from the perfection of love.[65]

The overlapping complexities of these issues, and endless discussion, have shown that it is probably always an oversimplification to seek a definitive "intellectual itinerary" for Dante, such as an "Averroistic" *traviamento* in the *Convivio*, followed by a return to theological "orthodoxy" in the *Comedy* (which—among many other moves that defy all critical simplification—places the emblematically "Averroistic" Siger of Brabant next to Aquinas in Paradise). For our purposes, we need not engage this discussion, because the fundamental metaphysical picture we have been tracing in this book is common to all these positions and underlies every stage of Dante's intellectual and spiritual life. Nevertheless, the *Convivio* is indeed interrupted and abandoned for the radically new enterprise of the *Comedy*, and the very opening of the poem, as well as the pilgrim's first encounter with Beatrice at the end of the *Purgatorio*, is the account (not necessarily biographical) of a close escape from a nearly fatal moral, spiritual, and intellectual dead end. It is Beatrice who rescues Dante in the *Comedy*, and not the *donna gentile*, whom the *Convivio* had identified with Lady Philosophy and sought to put in Beatrice's place.[66]

The engine of salvation in the *Comedy*, embodied in Beatrice, is not the *Convivio*'s enthusiastic praise of salvation and truth, nor sophisticated speculation about the transcendent, nor encyclopedic explanations of the world, nor philosophical and contemplative self-help. None of these can change our experience of ourselves; thus none can permanently change our actions and behavior; thus none can change the world. From the *De vulgari eloquentia* and the *Convivio* to the *Comedy* and the *Monarchia* and the *Letter to Cangrande*, Dante defines himself as the poet of change, rectitude, and moral reform. Indeed, the *Convivio* (and the *Comedy*) identify morality or ethics (*scienza morale*) with the *Primo Mobile*, the ninth sphere, just below the Empyrean itself (theology or *scienza divina*), and above physics and metaphysics, which are associated with the eighth sphere, and which depend on morality as the eighth sphere depends on the ninth. This dependence is complex: on the one hand, even though contemplation is the ultimate aim of man, it is moral philosophy that directs us to it, by ordering human objectives; on the other, contemplation or speculative thought that has no (moral) consequences, that does not result in changed action and experience, is pseudo-contemplation, self-deception, sophistry, or pseudo-philosophy. As the *Letter to Cangrande* emphatically puts it, the *Comedy* ultimately falls under moral or ethical philosophy, because its ultimate aim, even when it treats speculative matters, is not speculation, but action (namely, to lead humans to happiness). Salvation, after all, is a practical affair: *something* has to change.[67]

What drove Dante from the *Convivio* to the *Comedy* was, in part, what six centuries later drove Wittgenstein from the *Tractatus* to the *Investigations*: the imperative "to prevent understanding unaccompanied by inner change," the realization that understanding is not a set of ideas. The *Comedy* is grounded on the principle that there is no true understanding without (moral) transformation. Understanding, selfless love, and moral perfection are one: all three are spontaneously born together when the very concept of "other" (*altrui*) dies, killing its root and progeny, ego and greed (*cupidigia*), and with them, illusion, immorality, and political disunity. For the Dante of the *Comedy*, what alone can change us is not the praise of beauty or truth, not the endless ratiocinations of the mind, but only beauty-truth itself: Beatrice, the self-unveiling or self-giving of the Real, the *riso de l'universo* ("the smile of the universe"), a cosmic power of attraction or love so intense that it steals the mind and heart from themselves, teaching them the unutterable sweetness that is self-sacrifice, love, the surrender to the ground of one's being, of all being. How is beauty communicated or unveiled? How is the infinite revealed in the particular? Through ("divinely inspired") art or poetry: through forms transparent to the reality that gives them being, the reality in which all things consist. Perhaps Dante became fully conscious of the world-changing power of poetry as an agent of transformation, and thus as a vehicle of understanding deeper and truer than philosophy and all rational thought, by reading Vergil while writing the fourth book of the *Convivio*. It is indeed the *poet* Vergil (and not a cipher for Reason or anything else) who guides the pilgrim's first faltering steps toward understanding, and whose power to trigger conversion or awakening (even beyond his own understanding) is figured and celebrated in the Statius of the *Purgatorio*.[68]

The *Convivio* already betrays tensions in its account of philosophical "salvation." The philosophical enthusiasm of the *Convivio* is undercut by reminders that the human soul is not a pure intelligence (*sustanza separata* or *partita*), but an embodied finite identity whose highest faculty is intellect. Thus a living human being cannot attain the perfection of philosophy, or *somma beatitudine* (*Cv* 4.22.18); "in the other intelligences philosophy exists in a lesser way" (3.12.13). For a finite intelligence to be also embodied (and thus to have fully identified itself with particular spatiotemporal attributes) means that unlike angelic intelligences it perceives the forms of reality as "other," as autonomous from itself: it is a potential intellect. This is to say that it gains knowledge only through sensation, and not through uninterrupted, unlimited, and unmediated intellectual cognition (2.4.17). Such an intellect even loses direct awareness of its own immortality, "which we cannot perfectly see while what is immortal in us is mixed with what is mortal" (2.8.15).[69]

Thus in *Convivio* 3.15.6-10 Dante explains that there are things that "in some way dazzle our intellect, ... on which our intellect cannot look, namely God, eternity, and prime matter" (6),[70] although Dante argues that this fact does not limit the potential beatitude of each finite intelligence, for nothing desires what it cannot attain. As we have seen, what limits human intelligence is the complex of secondary attributes in which it arises, which in most humans more or less obscures intellect. In the *Convivio* Dante thinks of these limitations as virtually universal defects (*malizia*) of mind and body (4.15.11-17, 3.2.18). In 1.1.2-7 Dante lists the human impediments to philosophy: sensory handicaps, addiction to harmful pleasures, pressing responsibilities, and lack of access to learning. The second merits *biasimo* and *abominazione*, blame and abhorrence; so to some degree does the fourth. It is easy to see that for Dante these defects together affect almost all human beings: "Anyone who considers this matter well can clearly see that only a few can attain what all desire to possess, and that those who are hindered from so doing, and pass their entire lives starved of this food, are almost beyond number. Blessed indeed are those few who sit at the table where they feed on the bread of angels! And pitiful are those who share the food of sheep!" (*Cv* 1.1.6–7).[71]

From a philosophical point of view, the *Convivio* gives way to the *Comedy* when Dante recognizes that moral imperfections are not simply one impediment to human understanding and happiness, but constitute the limitation itself, and that moral perfection is the result not of self-help, but of all-encompassing love, the spontaneous surrender to the ground of one's own being. What obscures the human intellect is matter: the mind's obsessive and habitual self-identification with the contingent, finite objects of its own experience, which it does not recognize as its own substance. This constitutes the web of desires, attachments, emotions, passions, and fears that are the fabric of human life, and the habit of a mind that does not know itself. The *Comedy* is born when Dante realizes that the banquet of Christian wisdom, though freely offered, is expensive, and the cost is nothing less than surrender, the sacrifice of one's cherished and familiar "I" and "mine." The premise of the *Comedy* is that surrender-love-understanding is prepared for only by self-purification, and remains a gift beyond the province of the self; it is a spontaneous annihilation of self-deception, the self-knowledge of the intelligence freed from thinking it is merely this-or-that and therefore from pursuing any other this-or-that. This self-knowledge is the vision of God, the actuality through which all things are.

It is thus no coincidence that the *Comedy* defines its own poetics in Purgatory, in an encounter with the glutton Bonagiunta, on the ledge of gluttony, at the heart of a sustained thematic tension between using the mouth to consume and using the mouth to praise. The mouth of one who does not know himself is rapacious, devouring the world through greed and need (*cupidigia*), which is ultimately to starve and devour oneself, like Erysichthon (23.25–27), or the purging souls consumed by their desire for an apple on a tree (23.1–6, 34–35), or the counter-Mary who devours her own son in an inversion of the Eucharist (23.28–30). The mouth of one awakened to truth and Christ, one who feeds on the ground of all finite being within and as oneself (and note that the terrace of gluttony immediately follows the liberation of Statius, with all of its echoes of Christ born and resurrected), opens only to praise, to give from one's own fullness in gratitude, like Mary, who uses her mouth not to feed herself at Canae but to intercede for mankind (22.142–144), or like the purging souls who now sing the Fiftieth Psalm: *Domine, labia mea aperies, et os meum adnuntiabit laudem tuam* ("Lord, open my lips, and my mouth shall proclaim your praise") [23.11]). By having Bonagiunta designate him as the poet "who brought forth the new rhymes, beginning 'Ladies who have an understanding of love'" (*colui che fore / trasse le nove rime, cominciando / "Donne ch'avete intelletto d'amore"* [*Pg* 24.49–51]), Dante defines himself as one who uses the mouth to praise, not to consume—as one awakened to the divine within him: *I' mi son un che, quando / Amor mi spira, noto, e a quel modo / ch'e' ditta dentro vo significando* ("I am one who, when Love inspires me, takes note, and as He dictates within, so I go signifying" [*Pg* 24.52–54]). The poem Bonagiunta cites is the first *canzone* and the turning point of the *Vita Nova*. In chapter 18 of the *libello*, Dante has just told a group of ladies that earlier he had sought beatitude in Beatrice's greeting (*saluto*, which was for him health-happiness-salvation, *salute*); when Beatrice denied him her *saluto*, Dante's Lord Love (*Amore*) placed all Dante's beatitude in what could not fail him (*in quello che non mi puote venire meno*), namely, in pure selfless praise of Beatrice, praise that sought nothing, that was its own reward (18.4–7). Dante had discovered, or so he thought, that selfless love is itself beatitude and fulfillment, alone immune to contingency, and the end of all desire; but as the insightful ladies point out (18.7), if he knows this, then why doesn't he show it when he writes poetry—that is, why does he talk about himself and complain? Chastened and determined to put into effect the new "poetry of praise," but intimidated by the *alta matera* (18.9), Dante stalls, until one day his tongue speaks "almost as if moved by itself" (*quasi come per se stessa mossa*), and says: *Donne ch'avete intelletto d'amore* (19.1–3). Cited by Bonagiunta in *Purgatorio* 24, this *incipit* thus emblematically represents the poetry of selfless love (even if realized only in the *Comedy*), of praise and surrender to the divine, the response to a divine inspiration (*Amor*) that transcends the individual and all self-interest: in sum, the response the Fiftieth Psalm invokes. Indeed, it has been noticed that Dante uses the word *cominciando* or *incominciando* ("beginning") only twice in the *Comedy*, and both times in the same position, with strong enjambment at the end of a line. The first time, in the context of defining Dante's poetics here in *Purgatorio* 24, Dante is the subject of *cominciando*, and his poem *Donne ch'avete* the object; the second time, *incominciando / l'alto preconio* ("beginning / the sublime annunciation"), the subject is Saint John the Evangelist, and the object is the opening of his Gospel, "In the beginning was the Word." Yet again, the *Comedy* presents itself as a re-revelation of the revelation that is Christ, whose import and source is selfless love (*Amor*), the ultimate ground of all being.[72]

The Beatrice of the *Comedy* is not impressed with the intellectual efforts of the *Convivio*; nor, perhaps (if we respect the fictional date of the poem, which antedates the *Convivio*), with the inconstant and uncomprehending adulation of the *Vita Nova*. Those effusions, and thirty months of devoted philosophical study (*Cv* 2.12.7), did not prevent Dante from continuing to pursue *le presenti cose / col falso lor piacer* ("present things, with their false pleasure" [*Pg* 31.34–35]), desiring mortal things as if they were not mortal (*Pg* 31.52–54) and pursuing false images of the good (*imagini di ben seguendo false* [*Pg* 30.131]). Dante's celebration of philosophy (and of Beatrice) was nothing more than lip service to the *Vita Nova*'s discovery that all trust should be placed in *quello che non puote venir meno*, in what cannot fail; it was not reflected in how Dante actually lived and experienced himself and the world. Dante did not understand what he was saying; he was not speaking from direct experience of truth and reality, from the spontaneous crucifixion of the self. In a sense, the young Dante (as the author of the *Comedy* presents him) was in the position of Augustine after he converted to the books of Plotinus, and before his irrevocable conversion to Christ (which required moral transformation and a new way of life). Meeting Dante in Purgatory, Beatrice reprimands him sarcastically (30.121–138; 31.22–75) for the mental confusion his actions showed, inconsistencies a child could detect, but which escaped the bearded philosopher. She underlines the futility and self-deception of any intellectual speculation that does not result in changed perception and behavior. When Dante asks her, "But why do your longed-for words soar so far beyond my sight, that the more it strains the more it loses them?" (*Ma perché tanto sovra mia veduta / vostra parola disïata vola, / che più la perde quanto più s'aiuta?*), Beatrice answers:

> Perché conoschi . . . quella scuola
> c'hai seguitata, e veggi sua dottrina
> come può seguitar la mia parola;
>   e veggi vostra via da la divina
> distar cotanto, quanto si discorda
> da terra il ciel che più alto festina.[73]   (*Pg* 33.82–90)

Whether the "school" and "doctrine" refer to the *Convivio*'s philosophical pursuits or to an obsession with the ephemeral that belied the *Vita Nova*'s mystical incantations (and that philosophy then failed to dissolve), Dante's obstacle to understanding has been precisely his particular *veduta*, the perspective of a finite mind and ego, and his struggle to understand not by surrendering it, but by strengthening it (*quanto più s'aiuta*). Philosophical contemplation, Aquinas observes, is not Christian contemplation: it is born in self-love, not in charity, which is selfless love; even philosophical asceticism is not renunciation for Christ. Our way (*vostra via*) is not God's way: where there is "I" and "mine," there God is not, and where God is not, there is no understanding, and no peace. The pilgrim Dante is finally learning, instead of just saying, that love is selflessness, and self is lovelessness.[74]

Pyramus and Thisbe

To see how the themes of this chapter play out and fuse in a concrete example, let us look closely at a precise image in the *Comedy*, the poem's two explicit evocations of the tale of Pyramus and Thisbe. These evocations, in *Purgatorio* 27 and 33, occur at a critical textual locus: they bracket Dante's reunion with Beatrice in Earthly Paradise, after he has climbed the mountain of Purgatory; the first evocation in fact marks the threshold of Eden itself, in what Steven Botterill has called "perhaps the most supremely and literally liminal canto in the whole *Commedia*" (although I would reserve that rubric for *Paradiso* 29). These evocations point to how Eden is lost and recovered, and to the relationship that links spontaneous self-sacrifice, self-knowledge, and Christian revelation. They will serve as the first of three examples of the *Comedy*'s revelatory poetics "in action," examples of how poetry transcends philosophy, of how the *Comedy* supersedes the *Convivio*.[75]

In *Purgatorio* 27, the pilgrim Dante is on the seventh and last ledge of the mountain of Purgatory. This ledge corrects the tendency to follow "bestial appetite" (*Pg* 26.84–85), the carnal love that condemns Francesca to the second circle of Hell. The pilgrim has finished his poetic purgation on all the other ledges of the mountain, and is ready to enter into the garden of Earthly Paradise; all that separates him now from Eden, and from Beatrice, is a wall of purifying fire. That wall of fire serves two functions: in relation to the seventh ledge in particular, it is the purification of the tendency toward carnal love, the least culpable of sinful dispositions, because (as the mark of fallen humanity) the least avoidable; and as the line that divides Purgatory from Earthly Paradise, the fire represents the final purification of human love; it is a purification of *concupiscentia*, emblematic of *cupidigia*, through which all purging souls must pass, and not just the lustful. This is because, as Vergil has explained, all sin is a distortion or limitation of love.[76]

Indeed the first and most universal limitation of human love, through which human beings alienate themselves from God or truth, is their exclusive self-identification with the ephemeral, finite attributes that qualify their particular act of existence: the body. The obsessive identification with the body makes human love carnal and spawns insatiable desire, *concupiscentia*: to experience oneself only as a body in space and time is to conceive all things as other than oneself, and to seek to overcome this limit and isolation by consuming or possessing the world (the "other") through the senses, like Francesca, Ulysses, and every other sinner in Hell. Thus the two functions of the curtain of fire confronted by the pilgrim ultimately coincide: lust is itself an emblem of the experience of self as limited to finite body (as "other" than the world, than God), which is original sin, whose result is *cupiditas* or *cupidigia*, the starving wolf (*antica lupa*) that rules the world, *il mal che tutto 'l mondo occupa*, the source of all human misery. Since in the *Comedy* Hell proper (after Limbo) begins with sensual love (Francesca) and Purgatory ends with it, *concupiscentia* could be said to bracket all human temporal experience.[77]

Francesca in fact identifies herself (*If* 5.97–99) by conjuring the merging of rivers into one, through which, she says, they find peace: *Siede la terra dove nata fui / su la marina dove 'l Po discende / per aver pace co' seguaci sui* ("The land where I was born lies on that shore where the Po descends to be at peace with its followers"). Peace is her leitmotif (92, 99), what she longs for and will never have (31–33, 42–45, 113): it is a craving for union enacted, but never fulfilled, in her clinging to Paolo (74, 102, 105, 135), whom she thinks of principally as a beautiful body (101–102, 104, 135). Love, in Francesca's world, leads to death, not life (61, 69, 106–07, 141–142), to torment and uncertainty, not peace. What could the union, peace and life that Francesca longs for be, in a medieval context? It could only be to discover that she and Paolo are already inalienably and eternally one. In the terms of Francesca's river imagery, this would be to experience oneself not only as an autonomous river, a separate name, form, and identity that longs to merge with another river, but to recognize that as a river one's being is entirely constituted by water: one has no being apart from water. To know oneself as water (in river form) is to recognize all water, all rivers and the sea itself, as *already* oneself, one with one's own being. Indeed, if I, as water, were not, then no river, no sea, could be. This realization is revelation, peace, union, the consummation of the desire that first leads one being to seek (itself in) another, in which it glimpses, as beauty, what it itself is. Dante's life journey, as presented in his poem, begins with Francesca's love, but unlike hers, it does not stop there. The river, in longing for another river, is driven to come to know itself as water: the individual "I (am-this-or-that)," growing in love and surrender, becomes Christ's "I," the "I AM" revealed to Moses. To know oneself only as a named river, and not as water, is to be alienated from the ground of one's own being: it is to think of God as "not a friend" (Francesca's phrase in *If* 5.91), as irrevocably "other" (Ulysses' *altrui*: *If* 26.141), or as altogether absent, as all the residents of Hell do.[78]

Vergil is hard pressed to convince the pilgrim to enter the fire. To pass through the fire is to be willing to sacrifice the body, to give up the instinctive, exclusive self-identification with it, to trust that one is more than body, that one's existence does not depend on it. Dante refuses categorically. He gazes at the flames, *imaginando forte / umani corpi già veduti accesi.*[79] The vivid memory of human bodies burned alive in public squares makes physical death seem anything but unreal to him. Vergil reasons with Dante (*Pg* 27.20–32), telling him the fire cannot damage him or kill him, but reason is no use: Dante remains *fermo e duro*, unmoved and hard (34). The identification with the body cannot be overcome by thinking. Reason is a limitation of awareness through concepts: it depends upon the realm of finite attributes. Thought feeds on finite form; to ask thought to free one from the attachment to finite being is like trying to catch the thief by dressing him as a policeman.

Then Vergil has a brainstorm: he tells Dante, *Or vedi, figlio: / tra Bëatrice e te è questo muro* ("Now see, son, between Beatrice and you is this wall" [*Pg* 27.35–36]). This approach works magically:

> Come al nome di Tisbe aperse il ciglio
> Piramo in su la morte, e riguardolla,
> allor che 'l gelso diventò vermiglio;
>   così, la mia durezza fatta solla,
> mi volsi al savio duca, udendo il nome
> che ne la mente sempre mi rampolla.
>   Ond' ei crollò la fronte e disse: "Come!
> volenci star di qua?"; indi sorrise
> come al fanciul si fa ch'è vinto al pome.[80]   (*Pg* 27.37–45)

The tale of Pyramus and Thisbe is told by Ovid in the fourth book of the *Metamorphoses* (55–166). Pyramus and Thisbe lived in ancient Babylon, a city built by Semiramis, whose husband was King Ninus (Dante mentions both in his only explicit reference to Pyramus outside the *Comedy*, in *Monarchia* 2.8.3–4). Pyramus and Thisbe lived in adjoining houses; in their passion-bound hearts or minds they burned with love for each other (*captis ardebant mentibus ambo*), but their fathers would not allow them to meet or marry. The more they hid their love, the more the fire burned (*tectus magis aestuat ignis*). As luck would have it, there was a crack in the wall between their two houses, which allowed them to make "a path for words" (*vocis fecistis iter*), to have a kind of verbal love and union (*blanditiae . . . transire solebant*), though they were physically separated by the wall. They complained to the wall:

> "invide" dicebant "paries, quid amantibus obstas?
> quantum erat, ut sineres toto nos corpore iungi,
> aut, hoc si nimium est, vel ad oscula danda pateres?
> nec sumus ingrati, tibi nos debere fatemur,
> quod datus est verbis ad amicas transitus aures."[81]
>> (*Metamorphoses* 4.73–77)

Frustrated, they agreed to slip out of town and meet at night, by the edge of the forest, at the tomb of Ninus, beside a spring where a mulberry tree grew, laden with white fruit (*arbor . . . niveis uberrima pomis, / ardua morus*). Thisbe arrived first, but a lioness, fresh from the kill, came to drink at the spring. Terrified, Thisbe ran and hid in a cave, dropping her veil. As the lioness left the spring, she found the veil and tore it with her bloody jaws. Then Pyramus came, and found no Thisbe, only her blood-stained veil (*vestem . . . sanguine tinctam*) and the paw-prints of the lioness. Misled into thinking Thisbe had been killed, Pyramus blamed himself for her death (*ego te, miseranda, peremi*) and, kissing her garment, stabbed himself with his sword (*accipe . . . nostri quoque sanguinis haustus!*). The spurting blood stained (*tingit*) the mulberry's fruit dark purple.

Thisbe then returns and finds Pyramus near death. She embraces the body (*amplexaque corpus amatum*) and calls his name:

> "Pyrame," clamavit "quis te mihi casus ademit?
> Pyrame, responde! tua te, carissime, Thisbe
> nominat: exaudi vultusque attolle iacentes."
> ad nomen Thisbes oculos iam morte gravatos
> Pyramus erexit visaque recondidit illa.[82]
>> (*Metamorphoses* 4.142–146)

This is the moment that Dante captures to evoke the whole tale, almost translating Ovid: *Come al nome di Tisbe aperse il ciglio / Piramo in su la morte, e riguardolla, / allor che 'l gelso diventò vermiglio* ("As at the name of Thisbe, Pyramus, at the point of death, opened his eyelids and looked at her, when the mulberry turned bloodred" [*Pg* 27.37–39]).[83] Noticing Pyramus's empty scabbard, in a gesture of heroic tragedy Thisbe seizes Pyramus's sword and falls upon it, with these words to him:

> "tua te manus" inquit "amorque
> perdidit, infelix! est et mihi fortis in unum

hoc manus, est et amor: dabit hic in vulnera vires.
persequar extinctum letique miserrima dicar
causa comesque tui; quique a me morte revelli,
heu sola poteras, poteris nec morte revelli."[84]

(*Metamorphoses* 4.148–153)

Her last prayer (which is fulfilled) is that, having been joined by their "sure love" (*certus amor*) in their last hour, they share a burial mound, and that the tree "keep the marks of the killing and always have sombre / fruits fit for griefs, memorials of a double act of bloodshed" (*signa tene caedis pullosque et luctibus aptos / semper habe fetus, gemini monimenta cruoris*).

Let us observe some of the striking features of Ovid's account, which may have triggered Dante's evocation and response. The mute and ever-present witness to the Ovidian tragedy is the tree: not only does Ovid devote three lines (4.125–128) to its changing from white to red with blood, but it is in the shadow of the tree (*sub umbra arboris*) that the lovers hope to meet, that Pyramus kills himself (*ad pactae arboris umbram*), that Thisbe looks for him, uncertain if this is the right tree since its fruit is now red (131–132), and then kills herself, begging the tree to keep its red fruit as a memorial to the "double bloodshed" (158–161). This Ovidian emphasis alone shows that Dante's *allor che 'l gelso diventò vermiglio* is not a *fredda reminiscenza dotta* ("a cold learned reminiscence"), as Momigliano suggested, but a loaded reference. In Ovid, the tree itself becomes the emblem of love that ends in tragedy.[85]

Ovid's two references to the lovers' passion as a hidden inner blaze dovetail nicely with Dante's *contrapasso*, in which the lustful pass through an external fire. Ovid's description of the crack in the wall (*fissus erat tenui rima . . . paries*) that separates the lovers physically, but unites them verbally by making "a path for words," finds a parallel in Dante's situation, in which a wall of fire separates him from Beatrice but words—her name—make a path through it. Indeed Dante has already evoked Ovid in *Purgatorio* 9, where he describes a split in a wall, which turns out to be the entrance to Purgatory (*là dove pareami prima rotto, / pur come un fesso che muro diparte, / vidi una porta, e tre gradi di sotto*) ["where at first there appeared to be merely a break, like a fissure that divides a wall, I saw a gate, with three steps beneath"]; *Pg* 9.74–76). Dante's *fesso*, in what might otherwise seem to be a gratuitous line, echoes Ovid's *fissus*; for a medieval reader the image of a crack in a wall probably would instantly evoke Pyramus. Ovid's tale of Pyramus and Thisbe thus brackets all of Purgatory: it is evoked at its threshold and at its summit, the threshold to the Earthly Paradise. Dante creates another verbal link between the two passages by using the word *muro* for both the wall of Purgatory and the wall of fire (*Purg.* 9.75, 27.36). Ovid's tale of a love leading to death frames the purgatorial ascent, the tale of how a love is acquired that leads to life.[86]

We should also observe the explicitly sexual nature of Pyramus's and Thisbe's love. They want to be joined with their whole bodies (*toto nos corpore iungi*), or at least to kiss. The sterility or unconsummated nature of their love is underlined by sexual imagery: Pyramus's blood spurts high like a jet of water

from a hole in a pipe (*tenui stridente foramine longas eiaculatur aquas*); Thisbe
sees the scabbard empty of the sword (*ense / vidit ebur vacuum*), which was still
warm from being in Pyramus (*adhuc a caede tepebat*), puts its point under her
breast, and falls on it.[87] Their love is almost fetishistic: thinking Thisbe dead,
Pyramus kisses her bloody veil (*dedit oscula vesti*); Thisbe "filled his wounds
with tears and mixed her weeping / with his blood." Although Dante does not
play on it explicitly, the mixing of water and Pyramus's blood could conjure
Christ's Passion and the Eucharist, which may not be irrelevant, as we
shall see.

Thisbe thinks Pyramus has been taken from her and attributes the loss to
blind fate or misfortune (*quis te mihi casus ademit?*). Love causes death: Pyramus was destroyed by his hand, and by love, but Thisbe too has a strong hand,
and love, which will give her the strength to wound, and follow him in extinction. This is the (suicidal) heroic love of the high tragic style: it is Dido's love.
Dido, *colei che s'ancise amorosa* ("she who slew herself for love") is in fact Francesca's companion in the second circle of Hell; Francesca comes from *la schiera
ov' è Dido* ("the troop where Dido is" [*If* 5.61, 85]). These links are not fortuitous,
because Francesca introduces herself to Dante as *noi che tignemmo il mondo di
sanguigno* ("we who stained the world with blood" [90]), just as Pyramus
stained the mulberry; the word *tignemmo* is picked up in the *Comedy*'s second
Pyramus passage (*Pg* 33.67–75) as *tinto* and echoes Ovid's *sanguine tinctam* and
tingit. Moreover, Thisbe notes, with bitter irony, that Pyramus could only have
been torn from her by death, but now that she is dying, he cannot be torn from
her even by death (*poteris nec morte revelli*). Francesca too is joined forever with
Paolo in death; she too tells us that Love brought them to one death (*If* 5.103–
106).

If the heroic sensual love of Pyramus and Thisbe, of Dido, and of Francesca
leads to death and constitutes tragedy, then eros metamorphosed into the love
named Beatrice, the love that is Christian revelation and that leads to union
and to life out of time, is comedy, the style of Dante's poem and of the Bible.
Here too Dante plays on Ovid: while Ovid's tree will always bear dark fruits
(offspring) fit for mourning (*pullosque et luctibus aptos / semper habe fetus*) as a
memorial of doubled gore (*gemini cruoris*), Dante says that Beatrice's name *ne
la mente sempre mi rampolla* ("ever buds [or springs forth] in my mind"). Ovid's
tree of death becomes, through Beatrice, a tree of life.[88]

In calling Pyramus, Thisbe says her name (*tua te . . . Thisbe / nominat. . . .
ad nomen Tisbes*). That *nomen* brings Pyramus back from death in a pseudo-
resurrection and unfulfilled union: he sees her only to close his eyes again and
die without a word. Beatrice has been dead ten years, but her name, conquering
all death like the incarnate Logos, reunites Dante with her, and he can speak
with her. Again, Dante plays on Ovid: Beatrice's *nome* conquers his resistance
to the fire and brings him into Eden, as a *pome* ("fruit") wins over a child;
Dante stresses the link by placing the words in rhyme.[89] But Ovid uses *pomum*
twice to refer to the fruit of the mulberry, the first time (4.89) to how white it
is, and the second to its changed color (4.132). Ovid's symbol of love leading
to death is transformed by Dante into a promise of life and fulfillment. As we

shall see, Dante's use of *pome* is even more loaded: we need only remember that, conquered by the lure of a *pome*, Adam and Eve were ejected from, not ushered into, the garden of Eden, and tasted death, not life.

The web of meaning around Dante's *gelso* ("mulberry") becomes still denser if we consider that in the Christian exegetical tradition the mulberry has its own set of associations, derived principally from Luke 17.6 ("And the Lord said: If you had faith like to a grain of mustard seed, you might say to this mulberry tree, Be thou rooted up, and be thou transplanted into the sea: and it would obey you"), but also from Psalm 77.47 ("And he destroyed their vineyards with hail, and their mulberry trees with hoarfrost"). Commenting on Luke, Saint Ambrose explains that the mulberry tree represents the devil, because at first it is white, when the tree flowers, but reddens when the fruit forms, and finally turns black, just as the devil, losing the white flower and power of his angelic nature, cast down through his reddening betrayal, shuddered with the dark odor of sin. This association of the mulberry with the devil was widely echoed in the exegetical tradition: the *Glossa ordinaria* cite it, Hugh of St. Cher gives six reasons for it (none of them exactly Ambrose's), Saint Bonaventure calls it the tropological sense of the passage, and Aquinas in the *Catena aurea* quotes the fourth-century Saint John Chrysostom as an additional reference for it.[90]

Read *in malo*, then, Dante's *gelso* conjures not only the Ovidian account of sexual passion leading to sterility and death, but also the devil himself: the darkening of the fruit is the fall from innocence to rebellion and damnation. This interpretation of the mulberry is however balanced by another *in bono*, which most commentaries stress more, and give first. As John Freccero has observed, this gloss derives from Augustine, who explains that the mulberry tree is the Gospel of Christ's cross, which, with its bloody fruits hanging like wounds on the tree/cross (*in ligno*), will offer nourishment to the multitudes. This mulberry tree/cross, or Gospel, will be uprooted from the perfidy of the Jews and planted in the sea of the gentiles by the mustard-seed faith of the apostles. The Venerable Bede agrees, adding the note that mulberry leaves thrown onto a serpent kill it, and that this fact supports his gloss, because the Word of the cross, as it confers all wholesome things, removes everything noxious. The *Glossa ordinaria* quote Bede as the first gloss on *moro*, along with his note on the serpent. The early-fourteenth-century *Postilla* of Nicholas of Lyre stress this "moral sense" of *moro*: mulberries produce a liquid that resembles blood; hence the mulberry tree signifies the cross, and its fruit is Christ Himself, reddened (*rubricatus*) on that tree/cross by His own blood. Again, this is the tree that the apostles transplanted from the land of the Jews into the sea of the gentiles. Bonaventure quotes this *in bono* interpretation from the *Glossa ordinaria*, calling it the allegorical sense of the passage, and adds that this blood inflames (*accendit*) us to oppose vice.[91]

Read against this background, *in bono*, Dante's mulberry tree evokes the cross, Christ's Word and Passion, uprooted from those who would not receive it and planted in the receptive heart. To receive the mulberry is to be inflamed not by sensual desire but by the blood of self-sacrifice, by death to the self in

Christ. It is to kill the serpent of *concupiscentia* with a leaf from the sacred tree/
cross, and to reenter the garden of eternal life. It is faith that plants the cross
in the heart (*in bono*), or casts out the devil (*in malo*): like a mustard seed, it is
powerful even when very small.[92] For Dante the memory of a *nome*, the sacred
name of Beatrice, is enough.

The polarity between Christlike selfless love and selfish desire emerges
also in medieval glosses to Psalm 77.47 (*occidit ... moros eorum in pruina*).
Quoting Augustine, the *Glossa ordinaria* explain that the mulberry is warm by
nature, and hence signifies charity, which is killed by frost. A commentary
attributed to Manegold de Lautenbach explains that the frost signifies hidden
hatred, that is, the shadows of foolishness that kill our love for our neighbor.
The mulberry's red fruit denotes the love of others, which should be so strong
in us that we give our lives for our brothers, and pour out our blood (*sanguinem
effundamus*).[93] Pyramus pours out his blood, but his is a suicide from frustrated
desire, not a life-giving sacrifice born of selfless love.

A last feature of medieval exegesis on mulberries, which Freccero points
out in another context, may also be relevant. Dante's word for *morus* is *gelso*.
Gelso is the Latin *celsa*, which usually means "sycamore." Mulberries and syc-
amores are inextricably conflated in the Middle Ages: for *arbori moro*, the *Glossa
ordinaria* give a marginal reference to *sycamino, sycomoro* (5:927a). In Greek,
the first is a mulberry, the second a sycamore. Isidore of Seville suggested that
sicomorus derived from *sicut* and *morus*, because its leaves are like a mulberry,
but it is called *celsa* in Latin because it is tall. In any case, in the Middle Ages,
to evoke the one tree was to evoke the other. As Freccero notes, both trees
suggested the cross, because *moros* means "foolish," and Saint Paul had written
that Christ crucified is foolishness to the gentiles. This connection is significant, because the sycamore was the tree Zachaeus climbed (Luke 19.2–10) to
see Christ, from which Christ called him to conversion and salvation, though
he had been a tax collector and sinner. Freccero quotes Albert the Great's gloss
on the passage: "It took no less power and mercy to call Lazarus back to life,
from hell to the upper world, than to call Zachaeus back from the abyss of vice
to the grace of repentance and justification." Dante, poised like Pyramus on
the brink of sensual attachment and death, is called back to freedom and life
by Beatrice's name: for the pilgrim, Ovid's mulberry becomes Zachaeus's sycamore; pagan tragedy becomes Christian redemption.[94]

Similar allegories inform the medieval reading of the Pyramus tale itself.
The early-fourteenth-century *Ovide moralisé* incorporates and allegorizes a
nine-hundred-line twelfth-century elaboration of Ovid's tale known as *Piramus
et Tisbé*.[95] The *Ovide moralisé* explains that the mulberry's change from white
to red indicates the Crucifixion on the holy and glorious tree, tinted with the
precious holy blood (1185–1190), an example the saints and martyrs of old times
followed out of their faith and love for God, thus acquiring Paradise (1207–
1225). But today no one would suffer martyrdom for Christ or for His name
(*son non*), since all seek only worldly joys (1228); no one is willing to suffer
death or give their bodies (*cors*) to martyrdom (*martire*) for love of God. How
do they think they will be cooked (*cuite*), when the Son of Man comes again,

who delivered Himself to death to deliver them from death (1236–1246)? The lion with bloody jaws is the devil who devours souls and will be put to flight at the Second Coming (1247–1267). Again, many of these details resonate with Dante's context: by entering the fire the pilgrim is surrendering his attachment to the body and worldly joys, accepting a martyrdom for the sake of a holy name, through which he will escape death forever. This is to follow Christ on the cross, turning the mulberry red.

Another early-fourteenth-century moralized Ovid, though slightly later than Dante, is that of Pierre Bersuire (Petrus Berchorius).[96] Bersuire considers the Pyramus tale an allegory of the Passion and Incarnation of Christ. Pyramus is the Son of God, Thisbe the human soul; the two are bound in love but separated by the wall of sin. The mulberry tree is the cross under which the two meet, the spring the baptismal font. Stolen away by the devil (the lion), the soul (Thisbe) misses the coming of Christ (Pyramus), who out of love for the strayed soul gives Himself to death, staining the cross (mulberry) with His blood. Returning to Christ, the faithful soul stabs itself mentally with compassion for His Passion. Although Bersuire takes Pyramus *in bono* as a figure of Christ, the central allegory is the same: the mulberry is the cross stained by Christ's Passion.

Dante too makes a subtle link between Christ's self-sacrifice and the Pyramus simile of *Purgatorio* 27: the canto opens by saying the sun was *là dove il suo fattor lo sangue sparse* ("there where its Maker shed His blood"), in an astronomical periphrasis that may trace a cross.[97] It may be significant for Dante that in Ovid, Pyramus's last words are, "Drink now my blood too!" (*accipe nunc . . . nostri quoque sanguis haustus* [4.118]): a Christlike or eucharistic exclamation, except that it is addressed to Thisbe's blood-soaked veil. How do all these suggestions relate to the pilgrim Dante at the wall of fire?

The only union Pyramus ever had with Thisbe was through words, which reached through matter, so to speak, to unite them. In the grip of bodily attachment and *concupiscentia*, however, he arranged the meeting in the forest. Note the irony: it is Pyramus's sensuality, his quest for carnal union, that leads to his irrevocable separation from Thisbe and his death. It is a double irony: his obsession is such that he jumps to the mistaken conclusion that Thisbe is dead, and then commits suicide. Through his sensuality or complete self-identification with the body, Pyramus in effect steals Thisbe, and his own body, from himself. This is a paradigmatic example of what Dante, in connection with the second reference to Pyramus, calls *il viver ch'è un correre a la morte*, the kind of life that is a race toward death, that cannot transcend death.[98] It is being that is lost in becoming, consciousness consumed by contingency.

The mulberry stained by Pyramus's blood is in tension with, or is transfigured into, the cross stained by Christ's. In metaphysical terms, the first denotes the act of existence eclipsed by its qualification as this-or-that: a suicide. The second denotes the freedom of conscious being from and in all contingency: spawning finite experience by giving itself to it, it reveals its own transcendence, its oneness with all possible experience, by self-sacrifice, the relinquishment of the finite. To identify exclusively with the ephemeral is to suffer the fate of the ephemeral; to identify also with the limitless reality that grounds the ephemeral is to live in space and time unbound by space and time. Christ's death is a voluntary self-sacrifice born of self-knowledge, a death to all possible death. One could say, inverting Dante's phrase, that it is a *morir ch'è un correre a la vita*.

Balking at the curtain of fire, Dante is poised between Pyramus and Christ. Both when Beatrice was alive and when she was dead, Dante separated himself from her, as the pilgrim Dante does now, by not knowing himself: by identifying himself, and thus her, principally with ephemeral material forms, by failing to rise above the lure of the contingent (*le cose fallaci*). This is the gist of Beatrice's scolding when Dante finally crosses the fire and meets her face to face in Eden. She tells the angels,

> Sì tosto come in su la soglia fui
> di mia seconda etade e mutai vita,
> questi si tolse a me, e diessi altrui.
> Quando di carne a spirto era salita,
> e bellezza e virtù cresciuta m'era,
> fu' io a lui men cara e men gradita;
> e volse i passi suoi per via non vera,
> imagini di ben seguendo false,
> che nulla promession rendono intera.[99]   (*Pg* 30.124–132)

and she tells Dante,

> Mai non t'appresentò natura o arte
> piacer, quanto le belle membra in ch'io
> rinchiusa fui, e che so' 'n terra sparte;
> e se 'l sommo piacer sì ti fallio
> per la mia morte, qual cosa mortale
> dovea poi trarre te nel suo disio?
> Ben ti dovevi, per lo primo strale
> de le cose fallaci, levar suso
> di retro a me che non era più tale.[100]   (*Pg* 31.49–57)

Note that Beatrice's *belle membra* are, like Christ's blood, *sparte*, scattered, shed, on earth. Her indifference to them is one with the self-knowledge or surrender that opened her to eternal life. The pilgrim, on the other hand, had so identified with Francesca and her type of love that he had fainted at her story, falling like a dead body: *caddi come corpo morto cade* (*If* 5.142). In this Dante is not alone: the fire of the seventh ledge is peopled with his predecessors, love poets purging their sensuality.

Beatrice's name calls the pilgrim Dante through the fire, out of the consuming grip of the things that beguile and do not endure. Names penetrate matter, as language penetrated a wall to unite Pyramus with Thisbe. Language reflects shared experience, the imperfect recognition of other as self, of the world as one: language is the mark of the human, of consciousness, the ground of reality in which things are one, coming to awareness of itself as the human. When a human being fails to recognize another as himself, Intellect or Being has been eclipsed by the seductive multiplicity of creation; this eclipse is the Fall from Eden, the birth of ego and alienation, the loss of political and linguistic unity. It is the loss of what distinguishes the human from the animal: self-awareness, and what is one with it, speech.[101] Hence the progressive failure of language and communication in the *Inferno*, and the silence of the dying Pyramus. Beatrice's name is salvific because for the pilgrim it ultimately denotes the ground of all finite being, revealed to him in, through, or as the finite form aptly named Beatrice. This is simply to say that in Dante, conscious being, the ultimate ontological reality, began to awaken to itself when it recognized itself in/as that form. Having glimpsed itself, the Real is obsessed with itself: Beatrice's name constantly springs up/buds forth/bears fruit in Dante's mind. This is the operation of grace.

The name Beatrice thus denotes for Dante the self-revelation (as personal *experience*) of Being itself, the subject of all experience: beauty is the self-revelation of the infinite in the particular, of the ground of being through the forms that qualify it. Beatrice's name denotes Amor, selfless love itself: it is the Word, the Logos. Beatrice's name thus denotes the essence of poetry: words that reach through the dividing wall of material forms, of identity, to reveal all reality as continuous with oneself. In fact it is poetry that reunites Dante with Beatrice: he has had to write sixty-three cantos of the *Comedy* in order to come into her presence again, in *Purgatorio* 30.

Dante is won over by Beatrice's name the way a child is cajoled into obedience by the promise of a *pome*, a fruit or apple (*indi sorrise / come al fanciul si fa ch'è vinto al pome*). The pilgrim's conversion or capitulation, whereby he recovers Eden and finds life, is not a process of adult reasoning, argumentation, acquiring doctrine, or philosophizing. It is a childlike act of surrender to a reality only glimpsed and not seen, of faith in a revelation that belies appearances, of childlike trust.[102]

Ever since a fruit eaten introduced death, lust, exile, and pain into the world, the word *pomum* has been heavily freighted in the Christian tradition, and the *Comedy* is no exception. The fruit desired and lost by Adam is sacrificed and recovered in Christ, the second Adam. Dante describes his entire journey as a quest for *dolci pomi*. In *Inferno* 16 (61–62), the pilgrim tells the three Florentines, *Lascio lo fele e vo per dolci pomi / promessi a me per lo verace duca* ("I am leaving the gall, and I go for sweet fruits promised me by my truthful leader"). Soon after Dante's *pome*-induced conversion in *Purgatorio* 27, Virgil tells Dante that when he enters Eden, he will at last find the *dolce pome* that he, like all mortals, craves:

> Quel dolce pome che per tanti rami
> cercando va la cura de' mortali,
> oggi porrà in pace le tue fami.[103]   (*Pg* 27.115–117)

In *Purgatorio* 32 Dante compares the Transfiguration to a foretaste (the blossoms) of the apple tree that makes the angels gluttons for its fruit (*pome*): *Quali a veder de' fioretti del melo / che del suo pome li angeli fa ghiotti* ("As when brought to see some of the blossoms of the apple tree that makes the angels greedy of its fruit" [73–74]). Dante is evoking the Song of Songs 2.3: "As the apple tree among the trees of the woods, so is my beloved among the sons. I sat down under his shadow, whom I desired: and his fruit was sweet to my palate." Saint Ambrose explains that here the church is speaking to Christ: this fruit tree's fragrance is so pleasing that it surpasses all other trees, signifying that Christ fixed to the cross, like an apple hung on a tree, spread the fragrance of the world's redemption. Indeed, Ambrose says, there is not only fragrance, but sweet food in the apple: this sweet food is Christ. The church preaches the fruit of the Passion, the fruit that is the Lord Jesus Christ: what food can be sweeter in our mouths than the remission of sins? The *pomum* is that Christ hung for us; this *pomum* is the Lord.[104]

The net of associations tightens: Ambrose remarks in his commentary on Luke that Zachaeus on the sycamore is clearly a new *pomum* of a new era, because Christ came for this, so that from trees men would be born instead of fruits. Albertus Magnus likens Zachaeus to the sycamore itself, noting that man is born to conceive divine sweetness and to bear the fruit of sweetness (*ad divinam concipiendam dulcedinem, et fructum dulcedinis ferendum*); but, enervated by the heat of worldly cupidity (*calore cupiditatis mundi*), the foolish man bears no fruit. The pilgrim Dante, searching through the branches of creation for the sweet fruit, is seeking Christ, the Passion, the fruition of redemption. But the pilgrim is also Zachaeus, the fruit redeemed by Christ, called by Christ's revelation to feed on the sweet fruit that feeds the angels. The *pomum* is both the redeemer and the redeemed, because redemption is the revelation that the two are one. The *pomo*, conjured for Dante by Beatrice's name, is the power of love (self-identification) intrinsic to conscious being: it is the seeker, the subject of all experience, the substance of all things. In seeking Christ through the fronds of creation, the pilgrim is seeking himself.[105]

Dante drives home this ultimate revelation with his last use of the word *pome* in the *Comedy* (*Pd* 26.91–92). Finally meeting Adam face to face, Dante exclaims to him, *O pomo, che maturo / solo prodotto fosti* ("O fruit that were alone produced mature"). That Adam is himself the *pomo* that he sought as if it were something other than himself is underscored by Adam's explanation of his fall in the same canto: *Or, figliuol mio, non il gustar del legno / fu per sé cagion di tanto essilio, / ma solamente il trapassar del segno* ("Now know, my son, that the tasting of the tree was not in itself the cause of so long an exile, but solely the overpassing of the bound" [*Pd* 26.115–117]). The *segno* is not an arbitrary limit set by a jealous god: indeed for medieval thought the goal of all human life is deification or union with God. To overstep the *segno* is rather to seek more from the ego and the senses, from finite being, than what they can provide. What the senses can provide is the sustenance of physical life, and the first promptings to inquiry; they cannot provide ultimate answers or satisfy the quest for happiness and understanding. The illusion that the final fulfill-ment of desire and understanding can be wrung from the world, from ephem-eral finite being, is the failure of intellect or self-knowledge that undoes Dante's Ulysses, in his mad quest to gain experience of the world in the few days left to his senses (*If* 26.97–99, 114–120). Ulysses is blind to the mystery of exis-tence itself ("*that* things are"), a mystery immune to all thought, fact collection, and explanation ("*how* things are").[106] It is the mystery Christianity designates by Creation and Incarnation. One might say that in Christian thought, the world, taken in itself, is an endless string of zeroes: nothing. Indeed, in itself it would have no existence at all. Like that string of zeroes, the world becomes infinitely valuable and full of meaning—and exists—when a "1" is put in front of it: that "1" is the ground of its being, the mystery of existence itself. For Dante the loss of the "1" is also the root of insatiable desire (*cupidigia*); it is itself a symptom of self-alienation, of having lost sight of one's own reality, of the ground of being in/as oneself. To seek the *pomo* as other than oneself, to have posited an irreducible *altrui*, like Ulysses (*If* 26.141) or Francesca, is to have posited an irreducible ego, or isolated self: it is *already* to have lost Eden. In effect, it is to substitute the "1" with the ego, a finite identity, and seek to turn that into God.

Adam underscores the fact that he is the *pomo* by substituting *legno* for *pomo* in his answer ("it was not the tasting of the wood [the tree]"). In scriptural contexts *lignum* is often used in a double metonymy to denote the tree, and thus its fruit. We should note, however, that Dante uses only *legno*, and never *pomo*, in referring to efforts to consume the fruit of the biblical tree. The *pomo* is what humans desire (indeed, the *Convivio* presents it as the child's first desire); *legno* (wood) is what they get when they try to ingest the *pomo* through the senses. To seek through the *rami* and *fronde* (branches and leaves) of cre-ation for oneself is to bite into bitter, hard wood, into death and disappoint-ment, and to lose the expected reward of tender sweetness, the sweet fruit. It is the fate of Pyramus.[107]

In *Purgatorio* 27 Dante indicates his capitulation to the purifying fire, his moving toward Christ and away from Pyramus, with the phrase *la mia durezza fatta solla* ("my hardness now made soft" [40]) he had been *fermo e duro* ("fixed and hard" [34]). This is an obvious metaphor for the dissolution of stubborn-ness. Since in this particular context that stubbornness is Dante's attachment to his own body, this softening is to bite into the *pomo* instead of the *legno*, to feed on love/being rather than on the finite forms it spawns.

This gloss is underlined by the *Comedy*'s other explicit reference to Pyra-mus, in *Purgatorio* 33. The pilgrim is in Earthly Paradise, where he has wit-nessed the pageant which emblematically portrays human spiritual history: the fall of Adam, his redemption through the revelation of Christ and the church, and his second fall, so to speak, through the corruption of the church. The centerpiece of the drama is the tree of the garden of Eden, the twice-robbed plant (56–57), the *legno . . . che fu morso da Eva* ("the wood [tree] that was bitten by Eve" [*Pg* 24.116]). That tree is very tall, and its foliage is inverted: its branches taper toward the bottom and expand toward the top. In the pageant Christ's revelation is represented by the dual nature of a gryphon, symbolizing the conjunction of the human and the divine, the power to live simultaneously both within and beyond the realm of creation.[108] Unlike fallen man, the Christlike man does not bite into the *legno*:

> Beato se', grifon, che non discindi
> col becco d'esto legno dolce al gusto,
> poscia che mal si torce il ventre quindi.[109]   (*Pg* 32.43–45)

The gryphon responds, *Sì si conserva il seme d'ogne giusto* ("So is preserved the seed [progeny] of all righteousness [of every non-sinner].") The redeemed are not blinded to Being by being-this-or-that: in precise terms, for them the act of existence is not eclipsed by its qualification as spatiotemporal form. Thus Christ, the second Adam, defeating the devil's temptations in the desert, undoes the Fall and exile of the first Adam; thus the converted escape famine and death. Note that just as Pyramus lost Thisbe in death at the moment he seemed closest to possessing her, so here the attempt to consume, to tear away (*discindere*) and swallow a part of the world in order to possess the sweetness and fullness of being in which all things consist is really to have ingested the poison of mortality and disappointment. It is not a coincidence that while the gryphon's eagle-parts are gold, its other parts are *bianche . . . di vermiglio miste* ("white mixed with red" [*Pg* 29.113–114]), and Pyramus's white mulberry became *vermiglio*: the color evokes Christ's sacrifice and *caritas*, selfless love, as well as violent bloodshed. Self-sacrifice, the dissolution of *cupidigia*, is the mission and import of the *Comedy*, and it is the opposite of the alluring tree: as Cacciaguida tells Dante (*Pd* 17.130–132), his message is food bitter to the taste, but vital nourishment in the stomach.[110]

After noting that to rob or tear the inverted tree is to blaspheme against God, Beatrice makes the connections among the two trees, Dante's transgressions, and Pyramus explicit, in her enigmatic way:

> Dorme lo 'ngegno tuo, se non estima
> per singular cagione essere eccelsa
> lei tanto e sì travolta ne la cima.
>   E se stati non fossero acqua d'Elsa
> li pensier vani intorno a la tua mente,
> e 'l piacer loro un Piramo a la gelsa,
>   per tante circostanze solamente
> la giustizia di Dio, ne l'interdetto,
> conosceresti a l'arbor moralmente.
>   Ma perch' io veggio te ne lo 'ntelletto
> fatto di pietra, e impetrato, tinto,
> sì che t'abbaglia il lume del mio detto . . .[111]   (*Pg* 33.64–75)

Dante cannot understand why the tree is inverted, and how its being forbidden represents divine justice, because the *vani pensier* ("the vain thoughts") in his head have petrified his intelligence, turned it to stone, and tinted it. The Elsa is a calcifying river: any object left in it becomes encrusted with minerals. We know from context that the *vani pensier* are either philosophical concepts and doctrines, as *Purgatorio* 33.85–86 may suggest, or, more generally, the obsession with finite things that Dante's philosophical pursuits failed to dissolve (Beatrice's reprimand of *Pg* 30–31). The pleasure those thoughts gave Dante did to his mind what Pyramus did to the mulberry tree: stained it red with the blood of mortality, shed by insatiable desire. The pilgrim's intellect is stone, petrified, and stained with Pyramus's blood: this is the legacy of self-centered desire, redeemable only by Christ's blood, the self-sacrifice that brings understanding, peace, and life. The word *impetrato* is meant to trigger associations: in the *Comedy*, for example, it calls to mind Ugolino's failure to weep, speak, or respond, *sì dentro impetrai* ("I so turned to stone within" [*If* 33.49]), when his children, like Christ, offer their flesh to him as food; he offers in return not the bread (of life) they ask for, but stone. The word also evokes the futile erotic passion and "tragic" style of Dante's *Rime petrose*: in "Io son venuto" the speaker's obsessed mind is *più dura che petra* ("harder than stone"). The fetishistic object of passion becomes Medusa (*If* 9.61–63), who renders the mind impenetrable by the light of truth.[112]

The tension between Pyramus and Christ, between wood and fruit, between hardness and softness, is the tension that makes humans the horizon between the corruptible and the incorruptible, between the ephemeral and the eternal. In humans, Intellect or Being, the ultimate ontological reality, becomes aware of itself, *sé in sé rigira* (*Pg* 25.75). In this respect humans are divine: they transcend all finite forms, all events in time and space. But insofar as they identify themselves only with the body and determinate attributes and attempt to pursue and ingest other forms of being as autonomous realities, they are as mortal and finite as those forms themselves. The human intellect, that participant in unlimited being, has become petrified, fixed, by identifying itself exclusively with this-or-that. So fixed, *impetrato*, it is also *tinto*: it is stained with mortality, the death that comes from insatiable desire, from having forgotten one's own freedom and infinity, like Pyramus and Thisbe, or Adam and Eve.

Thus Beatrice says that the petrification of Dante's mind makes it impossible for him to understand why the branches of the tree are inverted so as to be inaccessible, and why it is forbidden to eat from that tree. Encrusted or hypnotized by the concepts and forms that constitute the world, the intellect cannot see itself, it cannot see that it itself is what it seeks, that it already is (one with) the totality of being. To be in Hell is in fact to have lost the *ben de l'intelletto* (*If* 3.16–18). The treasure of the intellect is the self-knowledge of the intellect itself. A mind that has lost that treasure cannot see that what the tree of life promises to the senses is inaccessible to the senses; it is a revelation whose tip, whose smallest branch, extends into the spatiotemporal world, but whose substance lies hidden in the depth of one's own being. As Augustine discovered, to know God is to know oneself; to seek God in the outer world is to lose both oneself and God. The petrified and tinted mind cannot see that to seek the *pomo* as other, by attempting to devour forms in space-time, is to have exiled oneself from oneself, to have banished oneself from one's own garden.

To soften this petrification is to taste the sweetness of the *dolce pomo*: as Richard of St. Victor had said, it is to taste an intoxicating inner sweetness, to transcend all philosophy on the mountaintop of self-knowledge, to fall away from the human into the divine.

It has been observed that in the closing cantos of the *Purgatorio*, Dante sets off his life-giving reunion with Beatrice against a background of Ovidian "tragic love-deaths"; through these allusions Dante is underlining the distance between his world and Ovid's, between natural passion and transfigured salvific love, between the endless cyclic metamorphosis of fallen nature and the unique liberating metamorphosis that transforms man into God. He is also emphasizing the distance between his "divinely inspired" poem and all other poetry, here represented by the great classical poet of love, Ovid. For Michelangelo Picone, *Purgatorio* 27 (in particular, the Pyramus episode) represents the passage of *auctoritas* from Ovid, the classical poet of love, to Dante, the modern Christian poet of love, crowned on the summit of Parnassus by Vergil.[113]

For Saint Augustine too, Ovidian tales of tragic love represent a barrier to the pursuit of a higher life-giving contemplation. In the *De ordine*, written in the year of his conversion to Christianity, Augustine beseeches the young poet Licentius, who had started to recite a poem about Pyramus and Thisbe, " 'I am vexed somewhat because, singing and crooning in all kinds of meter, you pursue that verse-making of yours which may be erecting between yourself and reality a wall more impenetrable than they are trying to rear between your lovers (Pyramus and Thisbe), for they used to sigh to each other through a tiny natural crevice.' "[114] If Dante knew the *De ordine*, it may not be a coincidence that Dante's *tra Beatrice e te è questo muro* (*Pg* 27.36) parallels Augustine's *inter te atque ueritatem inmaniorem murum*, immediately before the *Comedy*'s first explicit reference to Pyramus. Dante may be linking Pyramus's fate to that of the poets who celebrate his love; that is, of all love poets, the young Dante and his penitent friends on the seventh ledge included. In fact, in late-medieval poetry (as, for example, in Pier della Vigna and Chiaro Davanzati), Pyramus and Thisbe often symbolized faithful lovers and the most refined chivalric love. In at least one French romance (*Floris et Liriope*, c. 1250), passion is triggered by reading about Pyramus and Thisbe, as Paolo and Francesca's love is enflamed by reading about Lancelot and Guinevere.[115]

Gradually won over by Augustine, Licentius eventually agrees that philosophy "is more beautiful than Thisbe, than Pyramus, than Venus and Cupid, and all such loves of every kind," and gives thanks to Christ.[116] Relenting a little, Augustine tells Licentius that he can do a little versifying, since in moderation the liberal arts can encourage the pursuit of truth. But, he says,

> "At that point where Pyramus destroyed himself . . . and she
> slew herself over his half-dead body—as you were about to relate—
> there, in that very anguish where it is proper that your poem should
> reach its highest flight, you have a golden opportunity: satirize the
> curse of that unclean lust and those burning passions by which

those deplorable things come to pass. Then soar aloft with all your power in praise of pure and genuine love—love wherein souls endowed with knowledge and adorned with virtue are, through philosophy, united to understanding, and whereby they not only escape death, but moreover enjoy a life most happy."[117]

At the moment when Dante is about to see Beatrice, when his poem is about to take "its highest flight . . . in praise of pure and genuine love" in paradise, Dante evokes the "burning passions" that lead Pyramus to "deplorable" self-destruction. This is what Augustine suggested in the *De ordine*. But as we have seen, Dante's Pyramus also functions simultaneously as an image and counterimage, a nodal point or trigger, of Christ's Passion, of the redemptive cross, of purifying self-sacrifice, of Zachaeus's conversion, of the pilgrim Dante's conversion to Beatrice, of the reader's own awakening. All this is accomplished not in a philosophical treatise, but in a love poem: such density of meaning and experience, such a conversion or awakening, can be triggered only by poetry, or rather, Dante probably thinks, only by his own "divinely inspired" poem, the self-dissolving web he has woven around silence; to the rest of poets, Augustine's criticism applies. If Dante knew the *De ordine*, he may, in his inimitable way, have taken Augustine's cue, separated himself from other poets, and overturned Augustine's attack on poetry in the process.[118]

4

Creation

We must now understand that creation "out of nothing," in Christian thought, is not an event or a process: there is no how, when, or where in the creation of the world. How, when, and where are all internal to finite being, and more precisely to space and time: any account of creation that mentions events or things is not an account of creation, but a description of the world. Such an account says nothing (except analogically) about the relation of the world to the source and ground of its being. It is already implicit in Aristotle that there can be no explanation of the *being* of things, of "how" things depend on "the thought that thinks itself," because there is no how, no relation in any common sense (as between things or events), nothing to explain: self-subsistent Intellect is not in itself a thing, and *is* what it thinks. As we have already begun to see in the preceding chapters, to grasp the Christian understanding of creation is to grasp a non-reciprocal and non-dual "relation of dependence" between a radically contingent world (at every instant it exists) and the self-subsistent and dimensionless ground of its being (which can only be known as oneself, through a revelation prepared by the surrender of self). In this chapter we shall trace this understanding in Dante by discussing the tension between Neoplatonic emanation and "Thomistic" creation, the meditation on unity in diversity of *Paradiso* 2, the relation between body and soul, and the "birth" of time and of space in the *Primo Mobile*.[1]

Aristotelianism and Neoplatonism

The problem of creation in Dante's time involved interpreting, and synthesizing, Scripture, Aristotle, and the Neoplatonic tradition that fed on both. Much of the work of synthesis, especially in establishing the fundamental metaphysical compatibility between (Neo-)Platonism and Aristotle, had been done before the Middle Ages even began. Most of Aristotle's ancient commentators were in the Platonic-Neoplatonic tradition; indeed Philip Merlan has argued that Aristotle himself, as interpreted by his followers (especially Alexander of Aphrodisias, known in his time as "the second Aristotle"), may be thought of as the bridge between Platonism and Neoplatonism, between Plato and Plotinus. The New (Platonic) Academy, founded about 150 B.C. by Carneades, had already fostered what Cicero describes as "a philosophy that, though it had two appellations, was really a single uniform system, that of the Academic [Platonic] and the Peripatetic [Aristotelian] schools, which while agreeing in doctrine differed in name." The Neoplatonists assume that in most cases Aristotle and Plato are in agreement (for example, in the fifth century Proclus sought to systematize all Greek philosophy as a progressive penetration of divine revelation; in the sixth Simplicius called Aristotle Plato's "truest pupil" and "best interpreter"), and Aristotle served for centuries as the basis for studying Plato. The writings of Plotinus himself, according to his great student and biographer Porphyry, are "full of concealed . . . Peripatetic doctrines—Aristotle's *Metaphysics*, in particular, is concentrated in them," and indeed much of Plotinus's thought relies on or responds to Aristotle (and his commentators) more than Plato. The fusion of Aristotle and Neoplatonism is completed in the Islamic philosophers (e.g., al-Fārābī, Avicenna, and Averroës), who consider Greek philosophy from Aristotle to Proclus to be one integrated corpus, capped by the mystical *Theology of Aristotle* (i.e., Plotinus's *Enneads* 4–6). Aristotle enters the Latin West in the thirteenth century from the Islamic philosophers and is read through their commentaries, which means that much of Aquinas's "Neoplatonism" in effect comes from his Aristotle. One example of the intricacy of the Platonic-Aristotelian tradition will suffice: Bonaventure (an "Augustinian") and Aquinas (an "Aristotelian") both think Aristotle's God is the sustainer and (in some sense) "creator" of a beginningless universe, a view that derives from Proclus's pupil Ammonius (who was reconciling Aristotle with Plato's *Timaeus*) and from the Plotinian *Theology of Aristotle*; the view was consolidated in the tenth century by the Islamic philosopher al-Fārābī, in a work called *The Harmonization of the Opinions of the Two Sages, the Divine Plato and Aristotle*, whence it came to Avicenna and Maimonides, who bestowed it on thirteenth-century Latin philosophers. The point is that Aristotle, as he reentered the late-medieval world, was highly Neoplatonized (if he was not a Platonist himself), and Plato, as he reached Augustine and Christianity through Plotinus and Pseudo-Dionysius, had already once assimilated Aristotle. The great historian of medieval philosophy Van Steenberghen has said that we should not think of the conflict between Franciscans (Bonaventure and Pecham) and Dominicans (Aquinas) in later medieval thought as a conflict between an Augustinian system and an Aristotelian system, but as a tension between "two unequally developed forms of Latin Aristotelianism." When we impose "schools" on medieval thinkers, we need only remember that they thought, or could think, that Aristotle wrote the *Liber de causis*.[2]

It was Bruno Nardi's lifelong effort to "discredit [*sfatare*] the legend of Dante's Thomism," which first demonstrated the complexity of Dante's philosophical formation. Historically Nardi was reacting against the neo-Thomistic movement triggered by the encyclical *Aeterni Patris* of Pope Leo XIII (1879) and reaffirmed ever more stringently by subsequent papal documents: *Doctoris Angelici* (1914), *Studiorum Ducem* (1923), and *Humani Generis* (1950). Ironically, given the conservative backlash against Aquinas in his own time (nine propositions of the Condemnations of 1277 are from Aquinas, and thirty involve his teachings), the movement was itself a reaction to "modernist" philosophy. It prompted several Catholic theologians and scholars, the most important of whom were Busnelli and Mandonnet, to try to demonstrate that Dante nowhere diverged from Thomistic "doctrine" (see the preface to Busnelli's *Cosmogonia e antropogenesi*, a book dedicated to Pius XI, author of *Studiorum Ducem*). Nardi's exaggerations in the other direction (Dante's Avicennism, Averroism, emanationism, and heterodoxy) must be seen in light of this polemic. Kenelm Foster accurately summarizes the current view: Dante deeply admires Aquinas because Aquinas (especially through his Aristotelian commentaries) formed Dante as an "Aristotelian," but no one would claim today that Dante was ever a "Thomist" in Busnelli's sense; in any case Dante could not have distinguished the "schools" of his time as rigorously as modern scholars do. We might add that we should probably cease to accuse Aquinas (and Dante) of "Aristotelianism," or any other "-ism": as Mark Jordan has pointed out, Aquinas would be stunned to learn he was an "Aristotelian," or even a "philosopher," a term he reserves for non-Christians and often contrasts with Christian wisdom or beatitude. As we have already suggested, and as Jordan has argued in Aquinas's case, to reduce philosophy to "isms" is to reduce it to dogmas, ideologies, bodies of propositions: this is largely a post-Enlightenment phenomenon, and foreign to Dante and Aquinas, who considered philosophy (a preliminary training in) the pursuit, and love, of wisdom, truth, and understanding.[3]

Wishing to gloss Aristotle's profound silence about "how" the One "gives rise to" the Many, the Neoplatonic tradition, as we have already seen, spoke of an "emanation" in degrees or stages, an outpouring of light from Light in a series of reflexive turnings or hypostases, in which each level of reality causes (gives being to) the next, creating a chain of mediate links between attributeless self-subsistence and contingent finite being. In some ways, this hierarchy fit Aristotle well: it could be (and was, by the Arabic philosophers) identified with the descending sequence of his concentric cosmological spheres, each moved by an immaterial intelligence (soon to become angels), a hierarchy that begins with a transcendent Unmoved Mover "beyond" the world and ends at the center of the world in the realm of sublunar contingency, a kaleidoscope of ephemeral generation and corruption produced by the influence of the turning heavens.

Most of this picture poses little problem for the concept of Christian creation (and is in fact absorbed by Aquinas), on two conditions: (1) the "mediate links" are conceived as concurrent secondary or "nonessential" causes (in the production of differentiation or distinction) within the single primary "act" whereby self-subsistent Intellect-Being spawns and sustains the totality of finite being; and (2) there is no necessity, no "natural overflowing," in the emanation of the Many from the One (the One does not "need" to produce the Many). In other words, finite being is freely conferred by, or exists by participating in, only self-subsistent Being itself; it cannot be conferred by anything that Being has produced, or that is itself dependent and contingent. The world, *in each particular thing and in its entirety*, depends directly, immediately, non-dualistically, absolutely, and incessantly on the ground of its being: if the world were completely "other" than, not "one with" (i.e., did not "participate in") that ground, it would not be. To use the closing words of Plato's *Parmenides*: "if the One is not, nothing is."[4] To lose sight of this point is to lose the very concept of creation, the nexus of identity and opposition between the One and the Many, between the self-subsistent and the contingent, which for medieval Christian thought is the center of all meaning, and which the Christian religion calls "Christ" or the "Word." As we have seen, and shall see more clearly in this chapter and the next, it is the nexus the *Comedy* embodies in the *Primo Mobile*.

Neoplatonic emanation, with the conditions stipulated, is thus compatible with Christian creation, and in fact permeates Christian thought on creation. Augustine had already assimilated emanation (in its Plotinian guise) to Judeo-Christian creation, with the qualification (itself derived from Porphyry) that was to become the cornerstone of Christian medieval thought: God is not the Good or One *beyond* being, but true Being itself, both immanent and transcendent. Recent trends in the study of Aquinas have emphasized more and more the "Neoplatonic" character of his thought, stressing for example the principle of participation as the key to Aquinas's understanding of the relation of creatures (and humans in particular) to divine Being; since each distinction of finite form (essence) reflects a diverse participation in Being, and hence degree of perfection, Aquinas's cosmos is a great and continuous Neoplatonic hierarchy, in which all things freely emanate from, and are permeated by, God, and God "governs the lower things by means of the higher."[5]

Although Aquinas himself often speaks of creation as an "emanation," he is addressing (and overcoming) a persistent tension between the two notions. The Plotinian tradition that produced the *Liber de causis* and the *Theology of Aristotle* tended to speak of each cause in the Neoplatonic hierarchy as producing its effect (the cause beneath it) in its entirety, and attempted (as in Proposition 18 of the *Liber* itself) to reconcile this idea with creation by saying that the remote (first) cause "is more intensely the cause" of a thing than the thing's proximate cause, which serves as an instrument of the remote cause. Without precise glossing and interpretation, this tradition can suggest a notion of "mediate" creation (God "creates through" created things), blurring the distinction between contingency and self-subsistence, between the world and the ground of its being. The tendency is more pronounced in Neoplatonic currents that developed in an Islamic context. The paradigm is Avicenna: upon the premise that only one can come from One, God creates only the intelligence of the first sphere (the *Primo Mobile*); this intelligence then produces its sphere (both matter and form) out of nothing (*ex nihilo sui et subiecti*), as well as the intelligence of the second sphere, which produces its sphere and the intelligence of the third, and so on. The intelligence of the last sphere, of the moon, produces the matter of the sublunar world; variously disposed by the influence of all nine spheres, this matter is then "stamped" by the intelligence of the sphere of the moon (the *dator formarum* or agent intellect) with the forms of the elements and their compounds. The whole process has the "necessary" character of a natural mechanism or causal network.

There is no question that Dante is inspired by this "Avicennian" Neoplatonic picture, or even perhaps that (in some qualified sense) "the doctrine of mediate creation insinuated itself into Dante's mind," as Nardi maintained. Nardi relished scandals and polemics, and certainly triggered some by this suggestion, since as Aquinas blandly observes (speaking of Avicenna), that "the heavenly bodies are media in some way between God and things here below even as regards creation . . . is contrary to faith, which teaches that the whole of nature in its first beginning was created directly by God." But Nardi's suggestion must be highly qualified, because there is also no question that Dante understands and emphasizes the Christian concept of creation. As Nardi too admits, and as we have already seen in chapter 2, creation for Dante is a "triform effect" (*Pd* 29.28) in which the top, middle, and bottom of the world come into being simultaneously, instantaneously, immediately, and spontaneously. In the *Monarchia* Dante states clearly, in harmony with Aquinas against Peter Lombard, that "it is easy to demonstrate" that God cannot in any way delegate the power to create.[6]

Let us look at passages from three cantos (*Paradiso* 2, 7, and 13) in which the *Comedy* directly addresses the question of the metaphysical relation between the One and the Many, between self-subsistent and contingent being. All three cantos have been said to betray lingering traces of a tempered "Avicennism" (Nardi), or to adapt Avicennistic reminiscences to new meanings (Mellone). The passages from the first of the three cantos, *Paradiso* 2, will constitute the second of our three examples of Dante's poetics "in action."[7]

Unity in Diversity: Moonspots

Paradiso 2 begins with a warning to Dante's readers, in their little boats, to turn back to their familiar shores, not to try to follow Dante's singing ship in its great and unprecedented crossing of the deep. Only those few who have already fed on the bread of angels—on the Word, on revelation, on Christ—may attempt to follow in their sturdier vessels, clinging to Dante's wake before it is lost in the equal water of the great sea:

> O voi che siete in piccioletta barca,
>   desiderosi d'ascoltar, seguiti
> dietro al mio legno che cantando varca,
>   tornate a riveder li vostri liti:

> non vi mettete in pelago, ché forse,
> perdendo me, rimarreste smarriti.
>   L'acqua ch'io prendo già mai non si corse;
> Minerva spira, e conducemi Appollo,
> e nove Muse mi dimostran l'Orse.
>   Voialtri pochi che drizzaste il collo
> per tempo al pan de li angeli, del quale
>   vivesi qui ma non sen vien satollo,
>   metter potete ben per l'alto sale
> vostro navigio, servando mio solco
> dinanzi a l'acqua che ritorna equale.[8]   (*Pd* 2.1–15)

The divinely inspired poet gives a momentary trace of form—image, concept, word—to undifferentiated Intellect-Being, as he himself charts or experiences it, but that ephemeral wake or furrow (*solco*), like all finite being, is contingent, and inevitably dissolves in "the water that flows back smooth." Only those willing to abandon the familiar names and forms of their finite existence (*li vostri liti*) and willing to confront the ocean of Awareness or Being itself should dare to follow Dante, and they must stay in his wake, guided by one who can "translate" the ground of being into finite signs or forms, thus revealing it to the reader, or, rather, triggering its self-revelation in the reader. The warning is not gratuitous: what follows in the canto is meant to drive back those who, not used to feeding on the *pan de li angeli*—Christ, the source of all being within or as themselves—cannot fathom the real meaning of the bizarre, dry, and "scientific" lecture Beatrice is about to deliver. Those few who have eyes to see or ears to hear may instead hope for a profound experience of revelation or understanding, and be confirmed in their navigation of the deep, their journey in Paradise.[9]

The theme of the canto, unity in diversity, or the nexus One-Many, is introduced by the pilgrim's arrival in the sphere of the moon (30–36): he is "conjoined" with the solid, diamondlike substance of that sphere, "received into it" as water receives a ray of light while remaining one (*permanendo unita*). The analogy is loaded: the image of matter-penetrating light that does not corrupt or divide is a medieval metaphor for the virgin maternity of Mary, that is, for the virgin birth or Incarnation of Christ, of God revealed in and as man. Indeed, Dante says (37–42), if he was body (*s'io era corpo*), and on earth we cannot conceive the compenetration of bodies or dimensions, that should only intensify "the desire to see that essence in which one sees how our nature and God were united" (*il disio / di veder quella essenza in che si vede / come nostra natura e Dio s'unio*). The repeated emphasis is on *seeing*, which is not a matter of concepts or reasoning: "There [in the Empyrean] shall be seen what we hold by faith, not demonstrated, but self-evident, like the first truth man believes" (*Lì si vedrà ciò che tenem per fede, / non dimostrato, ma fia per sé noto / a guisa del ver primo che l'uom crede*) (42–45). To grasp the non-duality or nexus between contingent finite being and its ground is a question of sight or experience: as we saw in chapter 3, it is to see (be) Christ, to give birth to Christ. It is the human birthright, because—as Christ reveals—man is himself the link or bridge between the world and its source. To see Christ is to see all spatiotemporal substances as contingencies "transparent" to their ground and to each other, as thoroughly "compenetrable" and not "other" than oneself. What alone prevents this angelic mirroring or "entering of one into another" (*alterum alterum introire*) is the thickness and opacity of the mortal body, which blocks or hides the human spirit (*grossitie atque opacitate mortalis corporis humanus spiritus sit obtectus* [DVE 1.3.1]).[10]

"If I was body": this is indeed the question, because, as we saw in discussing Pyramus and Thisbe, human intellect is normally blinded by its self-identification with the body, leading it to experience itself as irreducibly "other" than the ultimate ontological principle, and thus other than all the objects of its experience. This blindness or self-alienation is the ground of sin, suffering, and violence. All three are promptly conjured by Dante's next question to Beatrice (49–51): *Ma ditemi: che son li segni bui / di questo corpo, che là giuso in terra / fan di Cain favoleggiare altrui?* ("But tell me: what are this body's dark marks, which down there on earth make people tell the tale of Cain?"). Popular belief "explained" the moon's spots by saying that Cain, upon murdering his brother, was banished to the moon, where he had to bear in eternity a bundle of thorns, visible as the *segni bui*, the dark spots. Dante is evoking the opening event in the long litany of human violence and suffering. That litany arises from the eclipse or obscuring of the light of the One by the marks or signs of the Many: the paradigm of this eclipse is a human intellect that cannot recognize itself in its own brother, its brother as itself. The word *altrui* ("other"), the marker of Ulysses' doom (*If* 26.141) and one of many Ulyssean echoes in the canto, may be charged here (it also recurs at line 88): the very notion of "else" or "other" is the root of all sin, of eviction from Eden. As Dante himself says in the *Monarchia* (1.15.2–3), "unity seems to be the root of what it is to be good, and multiplicity the root of what it is to be evil. . . . Hence we can see that to sin is nothing other than to despise the one and progress toward the many." Note that Dante is *not* saying that multiplicity is evil: rather, multiplicity, with its power to eclipse or hypnotize ("petrify") intelligence, makes evil possible—it is its root.[11]

To Dante's question about moonspots, Beatrice indulgently answers (52–57), in effect, that even in the realm of nature, where the senses can unlock some answers, reason, in its dependence upon sensory input, does not get very far (*dietro ai sensi / vedi che la ragion ha corte l'ali*); it is much more prone to error in a metaphysical question, for which the senses are useless (*dove chiave di senso non diserra*). It is not reason (*ratio*), a discursive analysis and synthesis (*divisio* and *compositio*) of concepts derived from finite experience, that will supply the answer Dante is looking for, which is ultimately "how" the Many arise from, or inhere in, the One: reasoning will only clear the ground and aim Dante's vision. The answer can come only from a simple and direct intuition or experience: through pure *intellectus*, proper to angelic intelligence, or rather, proper to all intelligence unlimited or unobscured by body, for which spatiotemporal reality is "transparent," not "other." Among human intelligences, normally bound by sense and reason (*Pd* 4.40–42), these can only be intelligences that have fed on the bread of angels, penetrating into themselves, into pure Intellect-Being, so far that memory cannot follow (*Pd* 1.7–9).[12]

In the center of the canto, Beatrice uses rational demonstration (*argomentar*), grounded on empirical evidence, to show Dante that his own understanding of the moonspots is "submerged in falsehood" (61–63). The "explanation" Beatrice rejects, that the undifferentiated substance of the moon has varying density, reduces diversity to the varying appearance of one material substance, which is in effect to evade the question of "how" the Many arise from, or inhere in, the One, by not addressing the essential differentiation within material substances. When the pilgrim Dante ingenuously says (59–60), in consonance with the *Convivio* (2.13.9), that "what appears to us diverse up here is caused, I think, by the density or rarity of bodies" (*Ciò che n'appar qua sù diverso / credo che fanno i corpi rari e densi*), Beatrice answers:

> Certo assai vedrai sommerso
> nel falso il creder tuo, se bene ascolti
> l'argomentar ch'io li farò avverso.
>   La spera ottava vi dimostra molti
> lumi, li quali e nel quale e nel quanto
> notar si posson di diversi volti.
>   Se raro e denso ciò facesser tanto,
> una sola virtù sarebbe in tutti,
> più e men distribuita e altrettanto.
>   Virtù diverse esser convegnon frutti
> di princìpi formali, e quei, for ch'uno,
> seguiterieno a tua ragion distrutti.[13]   (*Pd* 2.61–72)

Beatrice's point is that the *denso/raro* explanation, if extended to all the stars, would eliminate all real diversity of form or formal-causal influence (*virtù*), which leaves the kaleidoscope of sublunar experience unaccounted for. This shows that the "explanation" ultimately explains nothing: an understanding of multiplicity must address the source of determinate form, which by definition must be beyond determinate form, beyond the empirical, in the origin of diverse "formal principles" (71, 147). These, as we shall see, can arise only in Intellect itself, and there is no "how" to that arising.[14]

Beatrice proceeds to dismantle Dante's explanation on empirical grounds (73–93). If the appearance of dark spots results from patches of rare matter, then those patches must either extend entirely through the moon or alternate with denser matter. The first alternative is not the case, because if it were, then during a solar eclipse—and we must remember this evocation of eclipse—the light of the sun, "ingested" by the rare matter, should glimmer right through the moon, which it does not. If rare and dense matter alternate, then in some areas, where there is dense matter, the light would reflect off the surface, and these areas would appear bright; but the light would penetrate surface areas of rare matter and reflect from underlying strata of dense matter, as from a mirror: these reflections from farther in the moon, at a greater distance from the observer, would appear darker. At this point, if the reader has not already turned back, disillusioned by Paradise, Beatrice drives him back with a garage experiment (94–105): to dissolve the illusion that light reflected from a greater distance is dimmer, she tells Dante to take three mirrors, to place two on either side of him, one straight ahead of him and farther away, and a source of light behind his back, to illuminate all three mirrors. There you will see, she says (*lì vedrai*), if you actually try it (*se già mai la provi*), that, while the surface area of the light reflected in the central mirror is smaller, it has the same intensity as the light reflected from the closer mirrors.

Textually, as John Kleiner has underlined, this is an extraordinary moment. The fact is that in the central mirror Dante will see no light at all, but only the reflection of his own body, *unless his body is transparent to light.* Whether it is or not, whether the pilgrim experiences himself as transparent to, one with, the ground of his being ("if I was body"), is, as we have seen, a question of his vision, of his experience of himself, of his awakening to the Christic nexus between One and Many, between self-subsistence and contingency. The implication that the pilgrim's body is now "transparent" to light marks this passage as the culmination and resolution of a persistent theme in the *Purgatorio*: the "breaking" of light by Dante's mortal body (as in 5.9, where the "breaking" is linked to the pilgrim's ego or self-consciousness, or in 26.22–23, where Dante's body is a *parete al sol*, a wall to the sun, evoking the frustrated eros of Pyramus and Thisbe). In *Paradiso* 2 the question of the eclipse/manifestation of the light of Intellect-Being by the human body is—in one of the most breathtaking moves in the *Comedy*—encoded into the experiment itself: as Kleiner has pointed out, by precisely specifying the location of the mirrors and lamp (and doubling the closer mirror, when one would do), Dante has deliberately inscribed the pilgrim in a cross, in a crucifixion. To see only the body is to fail to see it as the self-manifestation, in the world, of the ground of all being: it is to fail to recognize Christ, resulting in crucifixion. But crucifixion, the voluntary sacrifice of (one's self-identification with) the body, is itself the self-revelation of the divine, of the ground of all being, in the world. The mirror experiment proves to be the key to the canto, a canto that itself provides the key, and serves as a selective gateway, to the *Paradiso*.[15]

At this culminating moment, Beatrice changes direction. Reason and demonstration are over; she has set up the trigger for awakening, understanding, *intellectus*, self-knowledge. The sublime discourse she now gives is not an explanation of "how" the Many arise from the One, the Other from the Same: there can be no such explanation. One must experience that nexus in and as oneself. Having stripped and purified Dante's intellect of concepts and misconceptions, like water denuded of any particular form, Beatrice wishes to "inform" it with pure light itself:

> Or, come ai colpi de li caldi rai
> de la neve riman nudo il suggetto

> e dal colore e dal freddo primai,
>   così rimaso te ne l'intelletto
> voglio informar di luce sì vivace,
> che ti tremolerà nel suo aspetto.[16]   (Pd 2.106–111)

The water imagery, so insistent in the Comedy, is not casual: as we have seen, water (the substrate or suggetto of snow or ice) takes on and sheds different forms and names, thus becoming in one sense other than itself, while always remaining itself, as, analogously, Intellect-Being "takes on" (but remember it is not a thing!) and sheds the finite forms of reality. Multiplicity, Beatrice observes, arises in the eighth sphere: it thus balances the One (the Empyrean) across the nexus or fulcrum that is the Primo Mobile.

> Dentro dal ciel de la divina pace
> si gira un corpo ne la cui virtute
> l'esser di tutto suo contento giace.
>   Lo ciel seguente, c'ha tante vedute,
> quell'esser parte per diverse essenze
> da lui distratte e da lui contenute.
>   Gli altri giron per varie differenze
> le distinzion che dentro da sé hanno,
> dispongono a' lor fini e lor semenze.
>   Questi organi del mondo così vanno,
> come tu vedi omai, di grado in grado,
> che di sù prendono e di sotto fanno.[17]   (Pd 2.112–123)

Although I discussed the first two tercets in chapter 1, I may recapitulate here: The "heaven of divine peace" is the Empyrean; the "turning body in whose causal-formative influence lies the being of all it contains" is the Primo Mobile; the heaven with many sights or eyes is the eighth sphere, that of of the fixed stars or constellations. The eighth sphere "distributes" the act of existence through diverse essences (the stars), essences that are distinct from, but nothing apart from or "outside" of, the act of existence they qualify. The seven planetary spheres absorb and dispose these distinct formal-causal influences in different ways, each receiving them from above and radiating them below, thus controlling ("seeding") the incessant generation and corruption of sublunar substances.

Although the picture and its expression are quite Avicennian, as Nardi emphasized, Dante is not saying that the Primo Mobile (or any subsequent sphere) confers being in an Avicennian sense, producing both the matter and form of what it contains, which would flatly contradict Paradiso 29.35–36 and 7.70–72: matter, angels, and spheres issued directly from God with no other agents. Essere here denotes spatiotemporal existence, the mode of being of all that the Primo Mobile contains. The qualification of being as spatiotemporal attribute arises in the Empyrean as the Primo Mobile, and begins from the Primo Mobile, the limit of nature. It cannot be attributed to Intellect-Being itself, and in this sense, as we saw in chapter 1, the Primo Mobile, not the Empyrean, may be thought of as the first cause or origin of finite being: "the nature of the world ... begins from here as from its goal" (la natura del mondo ... / quinci comincia come da sua meta" [Pd 27.106–108]).[18]

The reference to finite sublunar form—the content of human earthly experience—as a "seeding" (semenze) by the "organs of the world" (the heavens) picks up an evocation, earlier in the canto, of Jason as a farmer: those few who follow in Dante's wake will be more astonished than the followers of Jason, who saw armed men spring up when he planted serpents' teeth (Que' glorïosi che passaro al Colco / non s'ammiraron come voi farete, / quando Iasón vider fatto bifolco [16–18]). Jason—that great crosser of seas—grew men from teeth, but those few humans who stay in the furrow (solco [14]) made by Dante as he plows the ocean of being will be born—to their much greater astonishment— as gods, transhumanized, like Glaucus, who in the sea became "a consort of the other gods" (Pd 1.67–72). To be deified is to see, in Paradise, how creation, including oneself, is "seeded," born from, the ground of its being: this is Christ's revelation, itself a plant "seeded" only through the blood of self-sacrifice (Pd 29.92, 24.110, 23.132). It is the "seeding" Ulysses never saw, when—in a profound irony—he exhorted his own followers on the deep, Considerate la vostra semenza: / fatti non foste a viver come bruti ("Consider your seeding: you were not made to live as brutes" [If 26.118–119]). One who does not know one's "seeding" or source, or identifies that seeding with the seeding of sublunar ephemerality, is himself an eclipse of the light of Intellect or Being, a soul assimilated to a brute animal, and not to an angel. Such a one will drown in the sea of being, like Ulysses, instead of swimming in it as his home, like Glaucus.[19]

Beatrice tells Dante (124–126) that he can now see how she is heading for the vero, the truth, being, and understanding that he desires, so that now he can ford the waters alone (Riguarda bene omai sì com' io vado / per questo loco al vero che disiri, / sì che poi sappi sol tener lo guado). She is implicitly saying that the understanding Dante seeks cannot be communicated as words or concepts, but only pointed to through them: he must see or experience truth/being, and its relation to finite form, in or as himself. The single undifferentiated source or ground of diversity is Intellect itself:

> Lo moto e la virtù d'i santi giri,
> come dal fabbro l'arte del martello,
> da' beati motor convien che spiri;
>   e 'l ciel cui tanti lumi fanno bello,
> de la mente profonda che lui volve
> prende l'image e fassene suggello.
>   E come l'alma dentro a vostra polve
> per differenti membra e conformate
> a diverse potenze si risolve,
>   così l'intelligenza sua bontate
> multiplicata per le stelle spiega,
> girando sé sovra sua unitate.[20]   (Pd 2.127–138)

The "blessed movers" are angelic intelligences; *virtù* is the causal-formative influence intrinsic to intellect/will. A particular *virtù* arises from an intelligence as the "hammer's art" "breathes" from a smith: the intelligence is the smith, the stars are the hammer, the formative influence of the stars (ultimately displayed in sublunar matter) is the hammer's art (compare *Cv* 4.4.12, 1.13.4, *Mn* 3.6.5). The stars of the eighth sphere are the image (and, for what lies within the sphere, the impressing stamp or seal) of the ideas or formal principles that arise in the angelic intelligence (*mente profonda*) that moves the sphere. Thus, multiplying or unfolding its power or nature (*bontate*) in or through particular finite essences (the stars), that intelligence remains one and indivisible, like the divine mind it reflects, reflexively (like all unobstructed intellect) "circling upon its unity" in self-knowledge (compare *Cv* 2.4.18). In a similar way the human rational soul is one, despite the fact that it "resolves" or unfolds itself in or as the varied organs of the body, exercising ("conformed to") the different powers (*potenze*) of sensation, nutrition, and so forth. What bonds with and "vivifies" the stars or sphere is not the intelligence itself (angelic intelligences, unlike the human soul, are by definition substances "separated from matter," *sustanze separate da materia* [*Cv* 2.4.2]), but its influence (139–141): *Virtù diversa fa diversa lega / col prezïoso corpo ch'ella avviva, / nel qual, sì come vita in voi, si lega* ("Each formative influence makes a different compound with the precious body it vivifies, binding itself to it like life in you"). Mixed with, and variously shining through, the matter of the heavenly bodies, like the joy of a soul shining through a living eye, these influences appear as different luminosities, reflecting the joy of the angelic intelligences that are their source (142–148). Hence the dark and the bright (*lo turbo e 'l chiaro*): hence moonspots.

It may well be that the moonspots are apparent only to unperfected ("sublunar") human vision, which is more attuned to difference, to the obscuring of the light of being by "otherness," than to unity, the nonduality of all things with the light that gives them being. We saw that Dante introduces the spots as "what makes others [*altrui*] down there on earth speak of Cain" (50–51); the spots are "what appears to us [i.e., on earth] diverse up here" (*ciò che n'appar qua sù diverso* [59]). Arriving in the moon itself, on the other hand, he sees it as a pure diamond struck by sunlight, *lucida, spessa, solida e pulita* ("brilliant, dense, solid, and polished" [32–33]), and when he looks back at the moon with heavenly eyes, from *Paradiso* 22—that is, from the eighth sphere, the very source of multiplicity itself—he sees the moon ("Latona's daughter") "without that shadow" (*senza quell'ombra*) that had made him think it had varying density (139–141). The marks of difference, the root of Cain's sad legacy, no longer obscure unity, the light of the Empyrean, to a perfected understanding or love.[21]

As we saw in chapter 1, Dante and the Neoplatonic tradition tended to identify Intellect or Being with light taken in a strict sense (the so-called metaphysics of light): this is the light that penetrates and sustains the universe, reflecting more in one place and less in another (*Pd* 1.1–3). Dante's *Paradiso* is built on representing the light of Intellect-Being through its sensible reflection, through light as a sensory quality. One function of *Paradiso* 2 and its mirror experiment is to establish, at the outset of the *Paradiso*, the qualities of sensory light that allow it to represent the ultimate ontological principle. The most important of these is precisely what Beatrice says the mirror experiment will establish: the penetrative intensity, or apparent surface brightness, of a source of light is (at least in theory) invariant with distance: it is equal in intensity throughout the universe, though its source appears smaller when perceived or reflected from a greater distance, as Beatrice says. The principle is both startling and valid, and Dante may have discovered it. It is perhaps equally important that (as the experiment suggests) reflections of light may be endlessly multiplied without affecting the intensity or unity of their source; moreover we have seen that for Dante light propagates instantly, so that all reflections at any distance will be simultaneous. Like Intellect-Being itself, light is everywhere all at once, *totum simul*, all-encompassing, all-penetrating, and omnipresent. By raising and rejecting the *raro/denso* theory of moonspots, Beatrice also introduces the principle fundamental to the canto's (and the *Paradiso's*) meditation on revelation/crucifixion, intellect, and the body: the (varying) capacity of matter to "ingest," reflect, or eclipse light is an image of the varying degrees to which finite intelligences experience themselves (and spatiotemporal bodies) as "other" than (alienated from) or "transparent" to (one with) the ground of their being.[22]

Subsistences and Contingencies

A further indication that Dante is not speaking of (mediate) creation in *Paradiso* 2.112–123 is the word *fanno*, to "make" or "do": *Questi organi del mondo . . . di su prendono e di sotto fanno* ("These organs of the universe . . . take from above and make or do below" [123]). The distinction between "creating" (*creare*) and "making" or "doing" (*facere*) is fundamental in later medieval thought. The first is what God alone can do; the second, in its proper sense, is what things can do, or rather what God "does through things," and is more technically known as "generation" or "propagation" or the "work of distinction." Piccarda makes the distinction explicitly in *Paradiso* 3.86–87: the will of God is *quel mare al qual tutto si move / ciò ch'ella [divine will] crïa o che natura face* ("that sea toward which moves all that it [divine will] creates or that nature makes"). Although *facere* can be used in a broad sense to indicate creation out of nothing (as it is in the Nicene Creed), *creare* can never be used to indicate the generation of things from or by what is itself a contingent finite being. Creation is the "act" whereby a thing has being; generation is what determines it, at any instant (including the instant of first creation), as this-or-that. As the Nicene Creed makes clear, all things are created by God: whatever is, insofar as it is, "participates" in self-subsistent being, or it would not be. As Aquinas puts it, "a created thing is called created because it is a being, not because it is *this* being. . . . God is the cause, not of some particular kind of being, but of the whole universal being." On the other hand, the changing and ephemeral identities of things are governed by the processes of nature, and in this sense, almost everything is subject to generation and corruption. One might say: insofar as things exist, they "depend" directly on the Empyrean; insofar as they exist as this-or-that, most things *also* depend on nature (particularly on the spheres, beginning from the *Primo Mobile*).[23]

All things are therefore created, and most of them are also made. This does not imply that some things (such as the spheres or angels) were created first and then "made" others. It only means that some things are ontologically dependent on others: there is a hierarchy of being in the order of nature (distinction), in which some things cannot exist as what they are unless a whole series of other things exist as what *they* are. These other things may be said to be logically prior or "prior in nature," but they are not "prior in duration" or in time: nothing stands between any thing and the ground of its being. It is in this sense that Aquinas says, "The corporeal forms that bodies had when first produced came immediately from God"; as he explains, this simply means that "in the first production of corporeal creatures no transmutation from potentiality to act can have taken place." In other words, there was no becoming. This in no way implies that at the moment of first creation the hierarchy of ontological dependence inherent in the distinction of being did not exist, or that in the first production of things God "had to do something special," which "later" the spheres did. The moment of first creation is only conceptually, but not essentially, different from any other: the only difference is that before that moment there was nothing. Indeed, for Aquinas the created world could very well have always existed, with little consequence for the Christian understanding of creation; we only know that the world is not eternal because Scripture tells us so. The "act" of creation (the radical dependence of all things on the ground of their being at every instant they exist) logically implies, but must not be identified with, the hierarchical dependencies of determinate form within spatiotemporal being.[24]

Not unlike Aquinas, but more than Aquinas, Dante emphasizes the hierarchy of ontological dependence embodied in the spheres, reflecting a different balance in the fusion of the "Aristotelian" and "Neoplatonic" traditions. This fusion is strikingly apparent in one of the most beautiful passages of the *Comedy*, in *Paradiso* 13. It is no small tribute to Aquinas, and no accident, that Dante places these lines in his mouth:[25]

> Ciò che non more e ciò che può morire
> non è se non splendor di quella idea
> che partorisce, amando, il nostro Sire;
>   ché quella viva luce che sì mea
> dal suo lucente, che non si disuna
> da lui né da l'amor ch'a lor s'intrea,
>   per sua bontate il suo raggiare aduna,
> quasi specchiato, in nove sussistenze,
> etternalmente rimanendosi una.
>   Quindi discende a l'ultime potenze
> giù d'atto in atto, tanto divenendo,
> che più non fa che brevi contingenze;

> e queste contingenze essere intendo
> le cose generate, che produce
> con seme e sanza seme il ciel movendo.[26]   (*Pd* 13.52–66)

All things, mortal and immortal, are the (apparently self-subsistent) reflection (*splendore*) of the idea (the Word-Son-Christ) born from 'ntellect-Being (our Father, *il nostro Sire*) through an act of love (the Holy Spirit, *amando*). Since form is not a thing, but both the principle of being itself and the principle through which all things participate in being, metaphysically it corresponds to the Son or Word, the Second Person of the Trinity. Finite form arises through love (the Third Person): it is the power of self-subsistent awareness or being (the First Person) to experience itself as, or give itself to, finite attribute and identity. The Trinity evoked in the first tercet is evoked again in the second: the Word-Son is a living light (*viva luce*) which flows from the source of light (its *lucente*, the Father), but is not other than (does not "dis-one" itself from) its source: both are a power of love, of self-identification or self-giving, which "en-threes" itself with them. Metaphysically, Dante's persistent plays on the Trinity point to three perspectives on the ultimate ontological principle. Applying the Aristotelian analysis of causality to the indissoluble unity of the first principle, Dante repeatedly assimilates *what* creates (the "starting point" or efficient cause) to the First Person, *how* (by what law or pattern) it creates (the formal or exemplary cause) to the Second Person, and to what *end* it creates (the final cause) to the Third Person. Since the three are one, one could say that nothing exists in an absolute sense except love: love may be described either as pure awareness, the power of *what is* to be (know itself as) all things (this power is the Father); or else it may be described as the world, all the things conscious being gives being to by knowing them as itself (the Son). One could also say that ultimately nothing exists except the principle of form (the Word): the self-determination of the principle of form as this-or-that is love (the Holy Spirit); unqualified, form is pure intelligence or being (the Father).[27]

In the sense that angels are immaterial intelligences, not "other" than (not alienated from) the ground of their being, and ontologically not dependent on anything created, they are "subsistences" (*sussistenze*): not contingent or ephemeral. Because they are individual finite intelligences, awareness qualified by some trace of attribute or identity, they are *nove*: they are new (created), and they are nine (differentiated in perfection), resulting in a hierarchy of nine choirs, corresponding to the nine heavenly spheres. Note that this rise of individual "I am"s from the "I AM" of pure awareness is not an explanation, nor does it admit one. To "gather its rays" into finite intelligences that are mirrors of itself and in which it mirrors itself (*quasi specchiato*) is intrinsic to the nature of conscious being, to its actuality or goodness or fullness (*bontate*), and (as we saw in *Paradiso* 29.142–145)[28] it in no way affects its unity (*etternalmente rimanendosi una*). Conscious being (form or light) is (in some sense) both the One and the Many, and it is the nexus between them.

Opposed to the *nove sussistenze* ("nine/new subsistences") are the *brevi contingenze* or *ultime potenze* ("brief contingencies" or "last potentialities"), whose being in space at any moment in time hinges on a whole series of ontological dependencies within finite being, beginning with the angels (*quindi discende*). These "generated things" (*cose generate*) are the transitory names and forms of sublunar experience, which give way one to the other under the influence of the turning heavens (*il ciel movendo*), whether through inorganic change (*sanza seme*) or through reproduction (*con seme*). Nevertheless, these sublunar things too are nothing but the "shining" (*raggiare*) of the light source (*lucente*), a radiance now highly qualified, conditional, and ephemeral, being that is almost extinguished in darkness. Note that here, as in *Paradiso* 29,[29] Dante refers to the angels (the links in the ontological hierarchy) as "act" or "actuality" (*giù d'atto in atto*), and to sublunar material substances as "potentialities" or "contingencies" (*potenze, contingenze*). Since matter, as the potential for change exhibited by spatiotemporal form, is the principle of "non-subsistence" (except in the spheres, which are a special case), immaterial intelligences may be thought of as non-contingent actualities in their own nature; on the other hand, as substances whose transitory actuality in no way depends on themselves (they are a constant "becoming" governed by the turning spheres), sublunar material things may be thought of as pure potentiality or contingency.

Since Aquinas's speech follows the chiastic balancing of the Franciscan "Neoplatonic" and Dominican "Aristotelian" traditions in *Paradiso* 11 and 12 (among other chiasmi, the Dominican Aquinas praises Francis, and the Franciscan Bonaventure praises Dominic), it may not be far-fetched to observe, as a last remark on the passage from *Paradiso* 13, that the first half of the speech uses a Christianized Neoplatonic vocabulary (*idea, reflection, light, love, goodness, shining, reflected, remaining one*), although philosophically it implicitly rests on Aristotelian metaphysics, while the second half uses an Aristotelian vocabulary (*subsistences, potentialities, act, contingencies, generated, seed, moving heaven*) but philosophically describes a Neoplatonic "relayed" ontology.

The distinction between generation and creation is spelled out in *Paradiso* 7:

> La divina bontà, che da sé sperne
> ogne livore, ardendo in sé, sfavilla
> sì che dispiega le bellezze etterne.
> Ciò che da lei sanza mezzo distilla
> non ha poi fine, perché non si move
> la sua imprenta quand' ella sigilla.
> Ciò che da essa sanza mezzo piove
> libero è tutto, perché non soggiace
> a la virtute de le cose nove.[30]   (*Pd* 7.64–72)

The passage is saturated with "Neoplatonism," as Nardi repeatedly argued. Besides the evident echoes of the "metaphysics of light," it seems explicitly to distinguish "mediate" and "immediate" creation, with the corollary that only what is "immediately" created (*sanza mezzo*, without an intermediary) is eternal. Although almost universally diffused in commentaries, such a reading is a serious misunderstanding, because it undercuts what Beatrice is trying to make Dante see about the freedom of the will, Christian revelation and redemption, and the relation between the human rational soul and God, not to mention that it undercuts the fundamental Christian principle, which Beatrice will shortly reaffirm (although here too she has been misunderstood), that all things are created by God without any "help." Beatrice is saying that what scintillates, distills, or rains (*sfavilla, distilla, piove*) directly from the fullness of conscious being (*la divina bontà*) without the qualifying concurrence of natural processes (*sanza mezzo*) is immortal (*non ha poi fine*), because it is dependent on *nothing but* the ultimate ontological principle. In this sense, it is not "other than" the ground of its being: it is not "separable from" or other than the "seal" or "stamp" that determines its finite identity within Intellect-Being itself, so to speak. Any thing that is not dependent on anything created (that is, not subject to anything "new," to anything that now is but once was not, which means to any thing) is fully free: it is governed or controlled by nothing except the ground of all being (which is not a thing).[31]

Later in the canto, anxious that Dante should "see as she sees" (123), Beatrice clarifies further:

> Tu dici: "Io veggio l'acqua, io veggio il foco,
> l'aere e la terra e tutte lor misture
> venire a corruzione, e durar poco;
>   e queste cose pur furon creature;
> per che, se ciò ch'è detto è stato vero,
> esser dovrien da corruzion sicure."
>   Li angeli, frate, e 'l paese sincero
> nel qual tu se', dir si posson creati,
> sì come sono, in loro essere intero;
>   ma li alimenti che tu hai nomati
> e quelle cose che di lor si fanno
> da creata virtù sono informati.
>   Creata fu la materia ch'elli hanno;
> creata fu la virtù informante
> in queste stelle che 'ntorno a lor vanno.[32]   (*Pd* 7.124–138)

The endless arguments over this passage derive from conflating the ontological hierarchy intrinsic to the cosmos with the "act" of creation itself, and from thinking of creation as a process in time.[33] Beatrice imagines a confused Dante objecting, with respect to her earlier explanation, that since every thing, including the four sublunar elements (*acqua, foco, aere, and terra*) and all their compounds, is created by God, then everything must be immune to corruption (*da corruzion sicure*), which certainly does not seem to be the case. Again Beatrice explains that of all the things created, some are ontologically dependent on (*informati*, "informed by") others (which in no way implies that those other things were created first in time), while some things are dependent on nothing created, but only on Intellect-Being itself. Those that are not dependent on anything created (that is, on any thing) are "created just as they are, in their entire being" (*creati sì come sono, in loro essere intero*): these are the angels and the heavenly spheres (*il paese sincero*). What the four elements and all things made of them (in other words, all sublunar objects) are at any given instant (including the instant of first creation) depends on other created things, namely the causal-formative influence embodied in the stars and angels (note the word *fanno*: sublunar things are not "created in their entirety" because they are *also* made or generated). Hence one cannot have a sublunar object unless one also has angels, stars, heavenly spheres, and matter (which is not a thing, but may be variously conceived as the spatiotemporal "substrate" of the sensible universe, the potential for change and multiplicity in spatiotemporal form, or the "otherness" or duality between spatiotemporal form and Intellect-Being). This means, again, that sublunar things are radically ephemeral and contingent: their coming and going (generation and corruption) are completely subject to the processes of nature, internal to the mechanism of the world.

As we saw in discussing the creation passage of *Paradiso* 29 (in the "Dante" section of chapter 2), the spheres are a special case: even though they are spatiotemporal (material), Beatrice says that they too, like the angels, were "created as they are, in their entire being." This is because the spheres are made of ether, a fifth element (quintessence) that does not mix with or change into any other element: its potentiality is completely exhausted (actualized) by the forms of the spheres. Remember that form gives being to matter: to have created the spheres is to have created spatiotemporal bodies with no potential for change, but only for motion. Not dependent on any created thing, immune to any process of generation and corruption, the material spheres are in time, move in time, and in fact generate time, but they are immune to time: they are aeviternal.[34] They are both within and beyond the order of nature: in it, but not subject to it. Indeed by existing in space-time they themselves generate the processes of nature and its laws: they are the "instruments" of angelic intelligences, which "reside" beyond nature in the Empyrean. The spheres are thus the *mezzo* or medium between Intellect-Being and *fluitans materia*, sublunar contingency. In the *Comedy*, the spheres or stars become an emblem of salvation: salvation (Christ's revelation) is to be able to live within time, as a mortal creature subject to, and with a character and physical attributes completely determined by, the order of nature (the stars), and yet to transcend time and nature, by coming to know oneself as (one with) the ground and source of all finite being, as immune to the power of any created thing. This is one reason why the souls of the blessed appear to the pilgrim within the spheres that determined their character, dispositions, and earthly destiny, although they "live in" and are not "other than" the Empyrean.

Body and Soul

Both *Paradiso* 7 and *Paradiso* 13 emphasize the "mechanistic" causal subjection, ephemerality, and contingency of sublunar things for a specific purpose: in order to distinguish the human intelligence or rational soul from such things.

In *Paradiso* 7.70–72 Beatrice says that what rains from divine goodness without a medium (*mezzo*) is "fully free, because it is not subject to the influence of the new things," which means not subject to anything, since all things are "new" (created). The paradigm of this freedom is an angelic intelligence. Beatrice continues by saying that "the more conformed" an intelligence is to "the divine goodness" that is its source, the more it "pleases" that source, because the power of selfless love (*l'ardor santo*) is greatest (*più vivace*) in what is most like that source. All of this applies equally to human intelligence:

> Più l'è conforme, e però più le piace;
> ché l'ardor santo ch'ogne cosa raggia,
> ne la più somigliante è più vivace.
>   Di tutte queste dote s'avvantaggia
> l'umana creatura, e s'una manca,
> di sua nobilità convien che caggia.
>   Solo il peccato è quel che la disfranca
> e falla dissimile al sommo bene,
> per che del lume suo poco s'imbianca.[35]   (*Pd* 7.73–81)

What alone makes a human intelligence dissimilar (*dissimile*) to self-subsistent Intellect-Being (the *sommo bene* or God)—in other words, what alone makes it subject to things or "disfranchised"—is sin, which obscures the light of Intellect-Being in that intelligence (the intelligence is "little illumined" by that light). Sin, as we have seen,[36] is in fact an obsessive and self-limiting self-identification with ephemeral spatiotemporal form, paradigmatically the body: it is to experience oneself as enslaved and mortal by identifying oneself entirely with what is subject to natural causality and corruption, which is to petrify, obscure, or eclipse the light of intellect in oneself. Beatrice is saying that in its true, original, and redeemed nature, the human soul or intelligence is wholly free—in no way dependent on or governed by the order of nature, or any thing. Thus it is radically different from plant and animal life, which is entirely subject to natural causality and therefore contingent and ephemeral:

> L'anima d'ogne bruto e de le piante
> di complession potenzïata tira
> lo raggio e 'l moto de le luci sante;
>   ma vostra vita sanza mezzo spira
> la somma beninanza, e la innamora
> di sé sì che poi sempre la disira.[37]   (*Pd* 7.139–144)

The souls of all plants and animals are "drawn from" varying compounds of the sublunar elements (*complession potenzïata*) by the influence of the stars, but human life (the human intelligence or rational soul) "breathes directly" from the "supreme beneficence," from Intellect-Being itself. That is why the human mind or soul is always in love with, and never ceases to seek union with, the ground of its being, of all being.

Beatrice's distinction between plant and animal life on the one hand, and human intelligence on the other, is loaded, because a human being, as an earthly spatiotemporal creature, a mortal natural organism, is a complex of attributes, physical characteristics, tendencies, dispositions, emotions, abilities, mental patterns, vocations, and character, and all of these are very much part of the processes of nature, they are very much determined by the stars.[38] That is precisely why, by identifying ourselves exclusively with them, we "disfranchise" ourselves, alienating ourselves from the ground of all being, and assimilating ourselves to animals whose entire being is simply an ephemeral production of nature. It is, like Ulysses, not to know one's "seeding," or to confuse it with the "seeding" or generation of the body.

The body, or human animal organism itself (what Dante in the *Convivio* calls *l'anima in vita*), is produced by the processes of nature, just as animals are. We have seen that in Aristotelian thought soul is a "serial" concept:[39] in the progression from vegetative to sensitive to rational soul, each stage in the series presupposes, and in some sense assimilates, all the preceding stages. In the series nutrition, sensation, and intelligence, each power or life principle is subsumed by the next as a facet of its greater possibilities of being. Thus sensation, as we saw, is a kind of proto-intellect, a capacity to take on a limited range of being (specific qualities within a certain range of intensity), but it is completely dependent on bodily organs, and thus ephemeral. The sensitive soul, or living organism, is the "greatest work" that the processes of nature (things) can produce. Since the human potential intellect, or rational soul, is a power to take on or encompass the forms of all things, it certainly cannot be any of those things, or be produced by any thing: it radically transcends the order of nature. As Aristotle explained, it comes "from outside" and is immune to all natural processes; as Dante says, it "breathes" only from God, in whose unqualified existence it shares.

The generation or "seeding" of the human animal organism (the sensitive soul or *anima in vita*) through the processes of nature is spelled out in detail by Statius in *Purgatorio* 25.37–60. The active power of the semen first informs menstrual matter with a nutritive life principle corresponding to that of a plant; continuing its work, it becomes a sensitive life principle with powers of movement and sensation, and as such produces, through the processes of nature (*natura* [60]), all the members and organs of the fetus. Now, says Statius, comes the critical point or nexus (*tal punto* [62]), which has misled even the wise, namely Averroës: how the fetus is transformed from a mere living thing or animal (*animal*) into a "speaker" or human child (*fante*), a rational soul, a user of language (61–66). Why is this point so critical? Because not to see this point clearly is to be blind to the Christic nexus between the natural and the transcendent, the human and the divine: it is either to "disjoin" (64) the possible intellect from the living organism (like Averroës) or to conflate the two. In either case, it is to consider oneself an ephemeral product of nature, which is to eclipse the light of being in oneself, which is to crucify Christ (to fail to recognize Christ). Note that this lesson is given by Statius, who has himself just been liberated from any self-subjection to the finite through a Christlike resurrection or revelation (*Pg* 20–21), and that he gives it on the threshold of the seventh ledge, the ledge of lust or body identification, just after the culmination of the *Comedy*'s meditation on its own revelatory poetics in *Purgatorio* 24.[40] Statius now dramatically reveals truth:

> Apri a la verità che viene il petto;
> e sappi che, sì tosto come al feto
> l'articular del cerebro è perfetto,
>   lo motor primo a lui si volge lieto
> sovra tant' arte di natura, e spira
> spirito novo, di vertù repleto,
>   che ciò che trova attivo quivi, tira
> in sua sustanzia, e fassi un'alma sola,
> che vive e sente e sé in sé rigira.[41]   (*Pg* 25.67–75)

When nature has finished the production of the fetus or living organism, completing also its brain, its work in making a human being is done. The First Cause now turns to this "great work of nature" (*tant' arte di natura*), and breathes into it "a new spirit, full of power," which subsumes the active life principle of the fetus (corresponding to the sensitive soul) into its own substance, making one soul: this "new spirit" is the rational soul, created "directly" by God, and dependent on no thing. Thus this soul not only "lives and feels" (*vive e sente*), through the powers of nutrition and sensation it has subsumed; it also "turns itself upon itself" (*sé in sé rigira*): like the angels, and the ultimate ontological principle itself, it is a power of self-awareness or consciousness or self-knowledge, a power to know all things as itself, and to know itself as (one with) the ground of all things.[42]

That this self-knowledge or self-awareness is obscured more in one human being than another is the fault of nature, of the whole process of generating the human organism that Statius has just outlined. In simple terms, the ground of all being is more or less manifest in different human beings, depending on their physical characteristics, dispositions, and character, which are governed by nature and the stars. Thus the *Convivio* explains (4.21.5–8) that the "distance" of the human possible intellect from the pure Intelligence that is its source depends on the more or less limiting characteristics of the human organism into which it descends, and these depend on the semen and on the dispositions of the inseminator (*seminante*) and of the heavens or constellations. If the receiving (sensitive) soul is pure, then the intelligence will be "well abstracted and absolved from all bodily shadow" (*bene astratta e assoluta da ogni ombra corporea*) and the power of divine intelligence will multiply in it; this is the seed (*seme*) of happiness. The same point is made just after the passage discussed earlier from *Paradiso* 13: the compounds of elements (*cera* or "wax") from which the turning heavens (*il ciel movendo*) generate "brief contingencies" may be better or worse suited to receive that heavenly influence, which is why one tree gives more fruit than another, and why humans are born with different dispositions (*con diverso ingegno*) (67–72). If those compounds were worked to the perfect point (*se fosse a punto la cera dedutta*) and the heavens aligned to exert their greatest power, the light of the imprinting seal would be completely manifest (*la luce del suggel parrebbe tutta*): the Trinity or ground of being would be fully revealed in human form (73–75), as in another incarnation of God (*Cv* 4.21.10). (Note that yet again a point designates the nexus of human and divine.) Working like an artisan with a trembling hand, however, nature always transmits the light of being defectively (76–78), except at the creation of Adam (humanity in its original or natural state) and at the incarnation of Christ:

> Però se 'l caldo amor la chiara vista
> de la prima virtù dispone e segna,
> tutta la perfezion quivi s'acquista.
>   Così fu fatta già la terra degna
> di tutta l'animal perfezïone;
> così fu fatta la Vergine pregna.[43]   (*Pd* 13.79–84)

At the moment of first creation, and at the Incarnation, the "informing stamp" of the Trinity (the "first power," "clear sight," "warm love") perfectly disposed and aligned nature through the whole ontological hierarchy, so that the fullness of divine being was manifest in nature (*quivi*) through the human form, the greatest work of nature. Note the equivalence of Adam and Christ: in the case of Adam (at the moment of first creation) the compounds of elements (*la terra*, or *cera dedutta*) were perfectly disposed at their peak or *punto*, to be "worthy" of the perfection or summit of all organic life (*l'animal perfezïone*), which allowed the rational soul to fully manifest its divinity as, through, and in a perfect human being; in the second case (the Incarnation), the informing power of Intellect-Being directly impregnated the Virgin. In both cases the result was the same: the divine revealed itself in nature as or through the human form, thus revealing the true or original nature of the human being as divine. We might add that according to the *Vita Nova* (29.2–3), this perfect disposition of nature, or concurrence of secondary causes, also occurred at the birth of Beatrice, which is why she is a miracle (a nine), a self-revelation of the Trinity within the world.

It is essential to realize that no matter what one's nature-determined characteristics and character may be, they in no way preclude the human soul from coming to self-knowledge, from Christically awakening to its transcendence of nature, precisely because the human soul or intelligence is ontologically prior to nature, and thus not in its power, no matter how much it identifies itself with things that are. This is the truth Marco Lombardo unveils, with a sigh at the blindness of the world and the pilgrim ("*Frate, / lo mondo è cieco, e tu vien ben da lui*" [" 'Brother, the world is blind, and you clearly come from it' "]), when Dante asks him if the stars are the cause of human evil (*Pg* 16.58–66). Even if the stars initiated every one of your movements (as they do initiate almost all of them), Marco Lombardo says (73–74), you would still be perfectly free:

> A maggior forza e a miglior natura
> liberi soggiacete; e quella cria
> la mente in voi, che 'l ciel non ha in sua cura.[44]   (Pg 16.79–81)

The freedom of the human intellect/will is precisely that it lies subject to a higher power and greater nature than the natural world: because it is only created (cria) and not generated (it rains directly from the Empyrean, so to speak), the heavens have no power over it. Blindness to this truth led the ancients to make the planets that initiate human actions into gods (Pd 4.58–63): this blindness, or failure to see/recognize Christ, is the essence of paganism (26–27, 64–69).

As our discussion has shown, the freedom of the will, in Christian thought, is not a question of having many choices, as in a supermarket. To be free is not to be in the power of any thing that exists, to know oneself as ontologically prior to the order of nature, one with the Empyrean itself, even though as a spatiotemporal being one is also a product of nature. That is why the freedom of the will is at the core of Christian revelation, and why a meditation on broken vows, and on different degrees of beatitude (Pd 3–4), immediately follows the meditation on body, light, and crucifixion in Paradiso 2. The pilgrim wants to know why Piccarda should have a lesser degree of beatitude if she was forced to break her vow of renunciation against her will. Beatrice first clarifies that blessed souls reside not in the planets that determined their character, but all equally in the Empyrean (i.e., beyond the order of nature), though they participate in that "eternal breath" to different degrees (Pd 4.28–39). She then explains that in truth nothing could have constrained Piccarda to break her vow if her will had been "entire" (82), as the counterexamples of Saint Lawrence, who allowed himself to be grilled alive, or Gaius Scaevola, who burned off his own hand, clearly show (73–87). Beatrice's point is that what qualified or obscured Piccarda's intellect/will was some degree of attachment to, or limiting self-identification with, the natural world, namely her own body. This is a failure of perfect self-knowledge, some obscuring of the light of Intellect-Being by the body. Lume non è, se non vien dal sereno / che non si turba mai: anzi è tenebra / od ombra de la carne o suo veleno ("There is no light, if it come not from the serene that never is obscured: all else is darkness, the shadow or the poison of the flesh" [Pd 19.64–66]). This obscuring of the light of the Empyrean by body is manifest in Piccarda's own shadowy bodily form (Pd 3.10–30), which contrasts with the pure luminosity of the souls of upper Paradise. Some degree of body identification or worldly ambition is characteristic of all the blessed in the first nine cantos of the Paradiso, encompassing the first three spheres (up to the sphere of the sun); not coincidentally, these are the spheres that fall within the conical shadow cast by the earth (Pd 9.118–119).

After explaining that the human rational soul or intelligence is subject to no thing, *Paradiso* 7 concludes with some of the most misunderstood lines in the *Comedy*:

> E quinci puoi argomentare ancora
> vostra resurrezion, se tu ripensi
> come l'umana carne fessi allora
>   che li primi parenti intrambo fensi.[45]   (*Pd* 7.145–148)

In the standard view, which is virtually universal, Beatrice would be saying that God "directly created" the human body "in its entire being" (like the angels, the rational soul, and spheres) when God created the rational soul (our "first parents"), and the body is therefore in its "true nature" immortal. As David O'Keeffe pointed out in 1924 (to no avail), and as this discussion has already shown, it is highly unlikely that Beatrice is saying something so incoherent. First of all, we know from extensive empirical evidence that the body is indeed mortal: no one has ever lived who has not died, including Adam, Eve, and Christ Himself. In fact no spiritual tradition more than the Christian reminds man that the body is made from dust and returns to dust. Second, the body is not at all created "in its entire being," but is very much dependent on created things, on the processes of nature: Statius has indeed given a painstaking account of this dependence, and has called the body *tant'arte di natura* (such art of nature [*Pg* 25.71]). Third, if the body were not dependent on any thing, but only on Intellect-Being itself (like the spheres or rational soul), then its immortality (not its resurrection) would follow as an immediate logical consequence from what Beatrice has said: no arguments or reasoning would even be necessary. Fourth, developing the third point, and ignoring for the moment the confusion between immortality and resurrection, if the resurrection/immortality of the body could be proved (deduced), then Christ's resurrection, the central article of Christian faith, would be perfectly gratuitous: unnecessary, and not an article of faith.[46]

Beatrice is of course saying something different, more coherent, and more interesting. O'Keeffe observes (61–62) that the *argomentare* Beatrice suggests is an *argumentum convenientiae* ("of fittingness"), a set of considerations that allow one to make a case for the resurrection of the body, even on rational grounds. The principal ground (*quinci*) is that the rational soul transcends nature and always desires *la somma beninanza*, union with the beatitude that is its source (142–144); an added consideration (*se tu ripensi*) is that the human body and the human soul were created not as separate things, but as one: to create a human being is to create an embodied life principle or intelligence, not a Platonic soul on the one hand, and on the other a body in which to trap it. (In other words, not only was the "body" not created "in its entire being," it was never created at all as a "thing": what was created was a human being.) Besides the parabolic authority of Genesis (1.26–27, 2.21–22), Beatrice is drawing on the profound Aristotelian principle that the soul is the form of the body: it gives it being. The body is ontologically dependent on the soul and has no existence apart from it, as all creation depends on Intellect-Being, and matter on form. Now the rational soul is immortal, since it is not dependent on nature. Because the rational soul or intelligence subsumes as itself the nutritive and sensitive life principles of the body, the natural entelechy or perfection of the immortal human soul is embodiment: it is in a sense incomplete, not fully itself, if it does not exercise all its intrinsic powers as or through a body. Incomplete, it would never experience the perfection of beatitude toward which its very nature disposes it, which means it would desire what is unattainable, which is against philosophical and natural principles.[47] From all these considerations one might reasonably postulate the resurrection of the body. In fact, in Dante's otherworld, souls cannot even wait for the resurrection: Statius explains that upon death, human souls, carrying with them both "the human and the divine" (both the nutritive-sensitive and the intellective powers), unfold their powers of life and sensation as temporary aerial bodies, through which they act and feel (*Pg* 25.79–108).

How then did Adam and Eve, and all their progeny, come to suffer death, if the soul gives being to the body, and the rational soul is immortal? Beatrice answered this question earlier in her talk, in the passage with which this section opened (*Pd* 7.73–81): only sin disfranchises the human creature and makes it dissimilar to its source, the *sommo bene*. Sin, Beatrice says, is a *mal dilettar*, a faulty seeking of delight or pleasure, through which "our nature" removes or distances itself from Paradise (82–87). In the subsection on Pyramus and Thisbe (in chapter 3) I glossed this *mal dilettar* as the "hypnosis of the finite," the obscuring or petrification of the light of intellect by an obsessive self-identification with the body, a seeking of oneself as "other" through the senses. Remember that intellect, as nothing in itself, *is* what it identifies itself with; an embodied intellect that remains awake to its own transcendence (its "source") lives in time but not subject to time, in the eternity that is the now, the Christic point or nexus between space-time and its ground; nor perhaps does such an intellect lose the formative power over nature intrinsic to conscious being. If it forgets itself—forgets, like Adam, that it already is potentially all things in all time—it experiences itself merely as the greatest work of nature, a sensitive soul or organism, and thus experiences the natural fate of that organism; it also loses its power over nature.[48] In simple terms, to alienate oneself from the ground of all being, and identify oneself instead with what is contingent, ephemeral, and subject to nature, is to suffer the fate of such things, and to lose all power over them.

How is eternal life regained? Beatrice goes on to explain, in effect, that despite the penitential correctives through which an obscured intellect can, and must, retrain its search for happiness (i.e., from "outside" to "inside"), there is no way it can come to clarity and redemption on its own, overcoming its own Ulyssean madness (*follia* [93]), unless the Light itself clears it, so to speak (82–93). In the most exalted and magnificent manifestation of its own nature (both as self-giving and as justice) "between the last night and first day" (i.e., in all time, seen as a collapsed point), the "divine goodness" did this clearing by sacrificing itself to take on the human form as Christ and then sacrificing that form in Crucifixion, thus making humans themselves (those with eyes to see and understand [94–96]) capable of raising themselves (97–120). To "raise themselves" is to regain the Empyrean through their own awakening to the ground of all being, which is really the awakening of that ground to itself in them. Beatrice has re-expressed the great Clementine dictum that God became man so that man may learn from man how to become God.⁴⁹

Time

On the threshold of the *Primo Mobile*, and about to leave the eighth sphere, the source of spatiotemporal multiplicity, the pilgrim has his last look back into space and time. Beatrice tells him to turn his eyes from above to below, and to "see how he has turned" (*Adima / il viso e guarda come tu se' volto* [*Pd* 27.77–78]). The pilgrim obeys:

> Da l'ora ch'ïo avea guardato prima
> i' vidi mosso me per tutto l'arco
> che fa dal mezzo al fine il primo clima;
>   sì ch'io vedea di là da Gade il varco
> folle d'Ulisse, e di qua presso il lito
> nel qual si fece Europa dolce carco.
>   E più mi fora discoverto il sito
> di questa aiuola; ma 'l sol procedea
> sotto i mie' piedi un segno e più partito.⁵⁰   (*Pd* 27.79–87)

The "first clime" is one of seven parallel horizontal zones into which geographers divided the habitable earth. In breadth it spans the area from the equator to about eight degrees north; its full length (*tutto l'arco*) is 180 degrees, from the Ganges to Gibraltar (Cadiz, or *Gade*). When Dante last looked down, upon entering the eighth sphere in *Paradiso* 22 (133–154), he was at the midpoint of the arc, over Jerusalem. He has now traveled 90 degrees to the end of the arc: he is over the limit of the inhabited world, the strait of Gibraltar. Dante is on the threshold between the finite Mediterranean world of familiar names and forms and the open ocean of formless being: he can look either way, so to speak, as in the eighth sphere he can look down or up. The sun is moving ahead of Dante: it illumines only the part of the inhabited world touched by Christ's revelation—the span Dante has just traveled—from the coast of Asia Minor to Gibraltar, and it is lighting more and more of the open ocean beyond. In his sojourn in the sphere of fixed stars, moving from Jerusalem to Gibraltar, Dante has covered the entire "threshing ground" (the earth is called *aiuola* both times he looks back [*Pd* 22.151, 27.86]) in which the good grain sprouted from Christian revelation is divided from the weeds and chaff. The crop to be threshed is planted and harvested by the eighth sphere itself: it is ultimately what "seeds" all the dispositions, ambitions, and traits, the world of multiplicity and "otherness," that constitute human mortal life. The fruit planted usually rots inside as *bozzachioni*, rarely maturing into sweet plums (*sosine vere* [*Pd* 27.126]); the good harvest is gathered out of time and space into the Empyrean, as "all the fruit collected by the turning of these spheres" (*tutto 'l frutto / ricolto del girar di queste spere* [Pd 23.20–21]).

Ironically, and chiastically, the ocean of pure being toward which Dante is moving, and on whose threshold he stands, is denoted by a catastrophic failure to navigate it (*il varco / folle di Ulisse*, "the mad passage or crossing of Ulysses"); the world of finite form he is leaving is denoted by a pagan image of salvation and surrender (*il lito / nel qual si fece Europa dolce carco* ["the shore on which Europa made herself a sweet burden"]). We have seen that Ulysses sought understanding by "becoming a knower of the world" (*del mondo esperto* [If 26.98]), seeking to devour the world in the few days left to his senses (114–116), without sacrificing his own ego or sense of self (100–101); he pursues the sun (117) in a voyage governed by the ephemeral reflected light of the moon, the light of finite created intelligence, which waxes and wanes five times, corresponding perhaps to the senses (130–132). Ulysses is presumptuous not for *what* he sought—deification, in Dante's world, is the true goal of every human being—but for *how* he sought it: without turning within to know himself, without sacrificing his unquestioned identification with, and reliance on, a finite mind and body, without surrendering to the ground of his own being. The mind and senses he relied on could help him only with the familiar names and forms of the finite Mediterranean; they are of no use for navigating the deep (103–111). Europa is Ulysses' opposite: on the same shore where Christ was born, she experienced the sweetness of loving surrender to the divine (Jove) in incarnate form (a bull), making herself a sweet burden on the back of God, to be carried by Him as a prize onto the open sea (*mediique per aequora ponti / fert praedam* [Ovid, *Metamorphoses* 2.872]). Like the pilgrim, and unlike Ulysses, Europa does not transcend the finite by fleeing it; she surrenders instead, through love, to the divine manifest in it. The pilgrim has indeed turned since he began his journey: he has turned from the world to its ground, from self-sufficiency to surrender, from attachment to self-sacrifice, from outward to inward.[51]

After looking down, the pilgrim's mind and eyes spontaneously and obsessively turn back toward Beatrice, the form through which the divine reveals itself to them: no human form that nature or art can offer the eyes, as bait in order to beguile the mind, could rival the "divine pleasure/beauty" (*piacer divin*) that inundates him when he turns from the world to her *viso*, to her eyes or face (Pd 27.88–96). A human form in which the divine is perfectly manifest is simply a bait through which the divine, reflected as the human mind, beguiles and feeds on itself. In fact the power Beatrice's gaze bestows on the pilgrim "uproots" him from the "beautiful nest of Leda" and impels him into the swiftest sphere, the *Primo Mobile* (*la virtù che lo sguardo m'indulse, / del bel nido di Leda mi divelse / e nel ciel velocissimo m'impulse* [97–99]). Leda's story is parallel to Europa's: Dante conjures both within fifteen lines, at the very moment he transcends multiplicity (Leda's nest, the sphere of constellations) and reaches the source of space-time itself, the *Primo Mobile*. Ravished by Zeus, who had taken finite form as a swan, Leda, the most beautiful of mortals, bore an egg, from which the Twins (Gemini) were born. "Leda's nest" thus denotes the constellation of Gemini, the sign that governed Dante's birth, determined his attributes as an earthly creature, and bestowed on him his poetic genius; it is the sign Dante returned to when he entered the eighth sphere (*Pd* 22.110–123). Note that the pilgrim is "going back the way he came": having entered space-time with or through a set of characteristics bestowed by Gemini, he is returning to the source of those traits in Gemini and then passing beyond them into the source of space-time itself, the *Primo Mobile*. The pilgrim's understanding or self-knowledge now transcends his finite identity or attributes.

Dante's reference to "Leda's nest" probably runs deeper, however. By extension that "nest" is the eighth sphere itself, which diversifies being into material essences, into ephemeral sensory forms. When Intellect-Being (Zeus) gives itself to mortal beauty (Leda), the world of spatiotemporal multiplicity is born (which begins from the "nest" of the constellations). It is a two-way street: when the pilgrim's mind is ravished (like Leda) by the self-manifestation of the divine in the finite (Zeus as swan, or Beatrice), he is "uprooted" from the world of spatiotemporal multiplicity (and his own earthly attributes) and plunged into contemplating the source of space-time itself. Note again the Christian nature of this transcendence: it occurs through a ravishment or giving of self, a surrender to a self-revelation of the divine in or as the finite. *Paradiso* 27 (like *Purgatorio* 27) is clearly a canto of transition: the pilgrim's last look down exhausts the themes derived from earthly experience, and he will now contemplate the nature of space-time itself, "how" it arises from the ground of all being.[52]

Beatrice addresses the nature and origin of time immediately upon entering the *Primo Mobile*. Her explanation wastes no time: it is one tercet, with a second tercet to say how obvious (*manifesto*) the matter should now be to Dante. She says of the *Primo Mobile*:

> Non è suo moto per altro distinto,
> ma li altri son mensurati da questo,
> sì come diece da mezzo e da quinto;
>   e come il tempo tegna in cotal testo
> le sue radici e ne li altri le fronde,
> omai a te può esser manifesto.[53]   (*Pd* 27.115–120)

The motion of the *Primo Mobile* is not *distinto*, not divided, measured, marked, or determined, by any other motion (of any sphere); rather, all other motions, in particular those of the other spheres, are *mensurati*, measured, by this motion, as ten is measured (divided) by a half and a fifth, by five and two. Thus how time has its roots in this flowerpot (*testo*) of the *Primo Mobile*, and its fronds in the other spheres, may now be manifest to Dante and, presumably, to us.

On the simplest level, perhaps Beatrice is saying, as Jacopo della Lana, *L'ottimo commento*, Benvenuto da Imola, and many later commentators suggest, that the diurnal motion of the *Primo Mobile*, the complete revolution that constitutes one day, is the fundamental measure of time, generating the concept of day, and by subdivision the concept of hours, and by multiplication providing the measuring units for the months and years, which are based on the motions of the other spheres. Hence, as a half and a fifth precisely measure or divide ten, or, rather, as five and two produce ten, so one day gives rise to the proportions and measures of 24, 7, 28, 12, and 365, proper to the hours, days of the week, days of the month, months of the year, days of the year. As the *ciel velocissimo*, the fastest sphere, the *Primo Mobile* provides the natural base unit of temporal measure.

But the *Primo Mobile* is the origin and measure of time in a stronger sense as well: as the first-moved sphere, it imparts diurnal motion to all the other spheres, including the sun and moon, and is the ultimate source of all motion, change, and alteration in the physical world. As Portirelli, Lombardi, and many later commentators point out, since the *Primo Mobile* itself, and thus its motion, is invisible and insensible, the roots of time, its origins and intrinsic unit of measure, are indeed hidden as in a flowerpot, and we see only the fronds of time in the visible motions of the planets. Thus when we say, as Dante does in *Paradiso* 10.30, that the sun measures earthly time, we are referring to an appearance or effect, a frond, whose ultimate cause, principle, or root lies hidden in the invisible motion of the first-moved sphere. Indeed in this sense to say that the motions of the other spheres are *mensurati* by the motion of the *Primo Mobile* means not only that they are calculated by it, but that they are actually regulated by it, as Aquinas too says (e.g., *ST* 1a2a.90.4). Thus Dante observes in the *Convivio* (2.14.15–18) that the *Primo Mobile*

> regulates with its motion the daily revolution of all the other
> spheres, so that every day they all receive [and rain down] here be-
> low the influence of all their parts. . . . Thus supposing that it were
> possible for this ninth heaven not to move . . . truly here below there
> would be no generation nor plant or animal life; there would be nei-
> ther night nor day, nor week nor month nor year, and the whole
> universe would be disordered.[54]

In *Convivio* 3.15.15 Dante says that "with her [Wisdom] God began the world and especially the movement of the heavens, which generates all things and from which every movement has its origin and impulse."[55] In other words, all change and all physical life derive causally from the motion of the *Primo Mobile*: as the causal source of all change, the invisible *Primo Mobile* is the hidden source of time.

Time and change and variety, the multiplicity of motions and effects, are born from the unity and simple causal motion of the *Primo Mobile* as naturally and organically as fronds grow from the hidden roots of a plant. As Carroll points out in his commentary, since this "pot" (*testo*) has no other "where" (*dove*) than the "divine mind," than "light and love" (*mente divina, luce e amor* [*Pd* 27.109–112]), all motion and time and causal power arise from the divine mind in this sphere through the seraphim, who govern it: "Time, therefore, is infinitely more than a mere succession of corporeal movements. It is the procession of the Light and Love of Eternity into the temporal life of man." This potted plant, the *Primo Mobile* itself, represents the nexus between the Many and the One, between the changing sensible world and the dimensionless ground of its being.

In comparing the birth of time to motion measured as numbers measure each other, Beatrice however has more in mind: she is invoking Aristotle's analysis of time in *Physics* 4.10–14, which Dante had explicitly cited in *Convivio* 4.2.6: "Time, according to what Aristotle says in the fourth book of the *Physics*, is 'number of motion, with respect to before and after'; and 'number of celestial movement,' which disposes things here below to receive the informing powers in diverse ways."[56] Aristotle in fact had said,

> For time is just this—number of motion in respect of "before" and "after." . . . If, then, what is first is the measure of everything homogeneous with it, regular circular motion is above all else the measure, because the number of this is the best known. Now neither alteration nor increase nor coming into being can be regular, but locomotion can be. This also is why time is thought to be the movement of the sphere, viz. because the other movements are measured by this, and time by this movement.[57]

The fundamental point in the Aristotelian conception of time, implicit in hylomorphism, is that temporal extension, like spatial extension, has no fundamental unit or "building block." That is to say, time and space are both infinitely divisible and continuous; they do not consist in anything, in any irreducible seconds or atoms, as it were. In short, there is nothing that the spatiotemporal world is "made of": it is ultimately the self-experience of conscious being, the thought that thinks itself. Therefore the unit used to measure time (or space) is arbitrary: time is simply the number of whatever (repeating) units are used to measure it. That is why Aristotle says that time *is* number, but an ordinal, not cardinal number: it is *nothing but* a unit designated by number. Time is not the change of any particular thing, but a measure of the change in things. The unit of duration that measures time can only be determined by a "before" and "after," that is, by some kind of change ("movement" in the broad or philosophical sense) in some continuing substance. Since change occurs only in what has spatial extension, only material forms exist in time: what has no spatial extension has no temporal extension either, and vice versa. In the first section of chapter 2, we saw that this logical interdependence of space and time (space-time) is implicit in Dante's description of the *Primo Mobile* as pure motion, "where" (*ubi*) plotted against "when" (*quando*). Aristotle found the universal measure of time in the cyclic and eternal revolution of the spheres, and by implication in the perfectly simple motion of the first-moved sphere, or *Primum Mobile*, which for him was the sphere of fixed stars. To measure this motion is to measure time, the varying motion of all other things, and to measure time, or the change in anything, is to measure this motion.[58]

Augustin Mansion has shown that Averroës made explicit what was implicit in Aristotle: the multiplicity of movements in creation would imply a multiplicity of concurrently running times, unless they are all measured by a single concrete universal measure, which can only be the simple and all-inclusive movement of the first-moved sphere, the *Primo Mobile*. As Mansion demonstrates, this way of accounting for the "unicity" of time, by invoking the actual causal dependence of all change on the circular movement of the *Primo Mobile*, was adopted by both Albert the Great and Aquinas, and thus became the common ground of "Aristotelian" Scholasticism. In their commentaries on the *Physics*, both Albert and Aquinas stress that in perceiving any movement, one is recognizing the movement of the cause of all movement, the *Primo Mobile*. Thus the number that measures the movement of the *Primo Mobile* is the universal measure of all rates of change. This is to say, as Albert and Aquinas do, that time is in the movement of the *Primo Mobile* as in its *subject and* its number, while it is in all other things only as number.[59]

It is evident, then, that by Aristotelian metaphysics, if one posits the "creation of the world," as the Christians did, it cannot be an event in time; that creation is not an event in time was also stressed by Augustine and his followers. Time comes into being with creation, with the qualification of being as spatial attribute. In other words, it is born in the *Primo Mobile*, in the nexus between the Empyrean and the sphere of fixed stars. As the ultimate "source" of contingent spatial extension (material form) within conscious being, the *Primo Mobile* is the source of time. Thus Dante can exclaim, when he has reached the Empyrean, "I, who had come to the divine from the human, to the eternal from time" (*ïo, che al divino da l'umcno, / a l'etterno dal tempo era venuto* [*Pd* 31.37–38]). What is above time is conscious being, which is dimensionless: to see God is to see "contingent things before they exist in themselves, gazing on the point to which all times are present" (*le cose contingenti / anzi che sieno in sé, mirando il punto / a cui tutti li tempi son presenti* [*Pd* 17.16–18]).[60]

Beatrice's "explanation" goes still deeper, however. What Beatrice says, precisely, is that the motion of the other spheres (and thus ultimately of all their effects) is "measured" by the "unfactorable" motion of the *Primo Mobile* as ten is *mensurato* or *distinto* by *mezzo* and by *quinto*. To "measure" ten by a half and a fifth is to factor it into (distinguish within it) the prime numbers five and two. Prime numbers, as Martianus Capella explains, cannot be "measured" by any other numbers, but only by one and themselves. Rather, one could say they are the irreducible terms of analysis for an infinity of other numbers. In this sense prime numbers have no attributes except for those they display in generating other numbers, that is, except for the logical potential or implications intrinsic to their nature, to the concept of number itself. This is a variation on the ancient idea that the number one, by giving rise to the concept of number, can be said to contain or generate all of mathematics: *ipsum unum est principium numeri; unus semen numerorum* ("one itself is the beginning of number; one is the seed of numbers"), as Isidore says in the *Liber numerorum*. As Macrobius observes, one is the timeless, always in the present:

it is Mind or Soul, which is not a number, yet "produces from itself, and contains within itself, innumerable patterns of created things."[61]

So how does time arise from the *Primo Mobile*? Beatrice's point is that there is no how, no process: the spatiotemporal world of change and multiplicity arises in the Empyrean, in the reflexivity of conscious being, as mathematics arises from, or is implicit in, the number one, or as two by five make ten. As mathematics adds nothing to the concept of one but unfolds its intrinsic power and nature, so the spatiotemporal world adds nothing to the Empyrean but manifests its power and actuality. Since there is no how, no process, in the generation of numbers from one, or of space-time from conscious being, there is literally nothing to explain, and Beatrice is not giving an explanation. She is pointing toward an awakening, toward a coming to self-knowledge: for intellect to know itself is already to see all possible time and space within itself, as itself. The world of space and time is contained within the "I AM" of consciousness as mathematics is contained in the number one.

A question remains: why does Beatrice choose apparently arbitrary numbers, speaking of two and five, and not one, as the unmeasurable source of ten? Cacciaguida says that to know the number one is already to get five and six (*Pd* 15:55–63), and the birth of spatial extension, in *Paradiso* 28, is linked to the succession of integers from one. In the *Metaphysics*, Aristotle, followed by his commentator Aquinas, stresses that only the number one "measures" all numbers and is not "measured" by any other number: all numbers are known through the one, the starting point of number. Beatrice's choice of numbers annoyed Dante's commentators Buti and Porena, the latter to the point that he proposed amending the text to read *da mezzo di quinto* instead of *da mezzo e da quinto*: half of a fifth of ten would give the number one he wanted.[62]

It is not likely that Beatrice's choice of numbers is arbitrary. Let us survey some of the associations that two, five, and ten could have had for Dante. We have said that two and five are prime numbers, the quotients or factors (fractions) of ten. Thus in the *City of God* (11.30) Augustine observes, "Four is a part of ten, but it cannot be called a fraction [*quota*] of it. But one is a fraction of it, a tenth: and two is a fifth, and five a half." But why two, five, and ten? The commentator Mattalia is perhaps close to the mark when he observes that for Dante ten is the perfect number, completing the series of simple integers, and is the number of the Empyrean, the tenth heaven. Already in the *Metaphysics* (1.5 [968a.8]) Aristotle had remarked that because ten is "thought to be perfect and comprise the whole nature of numbers," the Pythagoreans had said that there must be ten heavens; in his commentary Albert stresses the parallel. In the *Vita Nova* (29.1) Dante, in line with a pervasive medieval tradition, refers to ten as "the perfect number" (*lo perfetto numero*); in the *Convivio* (2.14.3), echoing Isidore ("ten is perfect and final" [*denarius perfectus atque finalis est*]) and others, he explains that all numbers after ten are made by altering ten with the numbers one through ten; Martianus Capella remarks that ten contains within itself all numbers (7.742), and that five is the bisection of the perfect circle of ten (7.735).[63]

Two, Dante says in the *Convivio* (2.14.3), echoing Aristotle's *Physics* (5.1 [224b.1]), is the number of local movement, which by necessity must be from one point to another. In his commentary to the *Physics* (5.1 [641]), Aquinas stresses that the requisites Aristotle prescribes for all motion are five in number: that which causes motion, that which is moved, time in which the motion occurs, and the two points or states from which and to which the motion proceeds. Perhaps Beatrice is suggesting that ten, the atemporal, aspatial stillness and fullness of the Empyrean, can be factored into movement, that is, into the duality or difference of an original state and an altered state, which is already to have the other factor, five: the duality of mover and moved, the duality of before and after, and one with these, time.

Two is an even number; five is odd. In the *Convivio* (2.13.18) Dante cites Aristotle citing Pythagoras to say that the odd and the even are the principles of natural things, and that all things are number. Two and five make seven, and Macrobius, referring to the *Timaeus*, says that the truly perfect, that is, the all-encompassing World Soul, is a product of the seven odd and even numbers of the *tetraktys*, the Pythagorean sequence. Macrobius also explains that two represents the seven planetary spheres, including the sun and moon (since the motion of these seven spheres is contrary to, other than, the eighth sphere), while five represents the eighth sphere (of fixed stars), because it has five zones: the numbers two and five thus sum up the spheres contained in Dante's *Primo Mobile*. By representing the eighth sphere, five for Macrobius "designates at once all things in the higher and lower realms . . . the sum total of the universe"; Martianus Capella concurs, because five represents the four elements plus the ether of the spheres; as Curtius remarks in his excursus on numerical composition, for the Middle Ages five is the "symbolic number of the world" (503). But two, for Macrobius as for many patristic sources, also represents change and corruption (*corruptibilia et transitoria*, as Hugh of St. Victor puts it); Martianus Capella says two is the mother of the four corruptible elements (7.733). Perhaps Beatrice is suggesting that to factor ten, the Empyrean, into the odd and even numbers five and two is to give rise to all of creation, corruptible and incorruptible: this is what happens in the *Primo Mobile*, which in Dante's cosmology corresponds in a sense to the Neoplatonic world soul, the nexus between the One and the Many, the unmanifest and the manifest, represented by seven, the sum of five and two. The patristic tradition in fact associated seven with the Holy Spirit, as Macrobius had with the world soul, and of course seven designates the completion of the work of creation.[64]

Seven, for Macrobius, is also the number of man (1.6.62); a long patristic tradition agrees, because man, the bridge between creator and creation, is made of the four corruptible elements plus will, intellect, and memory, or the love of God through heart, soul, and mind (Augustine, *On Christian Doctrine* 2.16.25). Two and five, whose sum is man, both also evoke sin: two the falling from unity or perfection (i.e., from ten), and five the five senses which cause that fall. Thus there may be at least one more suggestion in Beatrice's numbers. The *Convivio* (2.14.14–15) tells us that the *Primo Mobile* represents Moral Philosophy, because as Thomas says commenting on the second book of the *Ethics*, Moral Philosophy disposes us for the other sciences. For as the Philosopher says in the fifth book of the *Ethics*, "legal justice puts in order the sciences to be learned, and commands that they be learned and taught, so that they are not abandoned"; and so the said heaven governs with its movement the daily revolution of all the others.[65]

Dante is saying that the second and fifth of the (ten) books of the *Ethics* demonstrate that moral philosophy, or *giustizia legale*, orders and directs the acquisition of all knowledge: there can be no understanding without moral virtue. Ten, as Augustine stresses (*City of God* 15.20), and by a universal medieval tradition, represents the Law, because of the Decalogue, the Ten Commandments, which were divided among two tablets (but by tradition as seven plus three, not five and five). Ten also represents, according to Augustine, the knowledge of Creator and creature (*On Christian Doctrine* 2.16.25), or the totality of human wisdom. In the sphere that corresponds to moral philosophy, Beatrice's *cotal testo* ("such a pot/text" [*Pd* 27.118]) may have a double sense, directing us back to the text of Aristotle's *Ethics*, the fifth and second of whose ten books make ten, that is, indicate in the moral law (itself a ten) the ground of the perfection of human wisdom (also ten): ten is thus measured and ordered by the second and the fifth.

In relation to time, says Augustine, the number ten admonishes us to live chastely, as the five books of the Law of Moses command. Rabanus Maurus, Isidore, and others also refer the parable of Matthew 25.1, which compares the reign of God to ten bridesmaids, of whom only half, a wise five, had extra oil for their lamps and could meet the delayed bridegroom in the night, while the foolish five were excluded, unrecognized by the groom. The moral is given explicitly in Matthew (25.12–13): "keep your eyes open, for you know not the day or the hour." These reflections on the moral implications of Beatrice's numbers may help shed light on what to many commentators has seemed an abrupt *non sequitur*: Beatrice's terse account of time in *Paradiso* 27 is preceded and immediately followed, without transition, by violent attacks on human corruption and *cupidigia*, whose waves submerge the eyes of mortals (121–123). Only small children (*parvoletti*) have faith and innocence; as they grow to adulthood (ironically, to full rational self-awareness and speech) they turn black with blindness and iniquity (124–141). Again, ten is measured by a half and a fifth: how we live in creation, in the fronds of time, will determine whether the Empyrean, the hidden root of time and of our own being, will indeed be *manifesto* to us.[66]

Space

Paradiso 28, in which the pilgrim will come to understand the nature and origin of space, opens with an enigmatic image of seeing and turning. After Beatrice, who "imparadises" Dante's mind, has "opened the truth against the current life of wretched mortals" (in *Paradiso* 27), Dante sees a brilliant point of light reflected in Beatrice's eyes, as one would see a double candlestick behind one by looking in a mirror, and he turns so that his eyes are "touched" directly by what had been behind him, which is what appears in that sphere (the *Primo Mobile*) whenever one "looks well" into its circular space or encompassing (*ciò che pare in quel volume, / quandunque nel suo giro ben s'adocchi* [*Pd* 28.1–18]). By turning to see directly what (or as) Beatrice sees, Dante is assimilating his sight, or point of view, to hers. In absolute terms, to turn from the reflection to the source is to turn from the world to its ground; it is to focus the light of awareness on itself in a single point. What is thus revealed is there to be seen whenever (*quandunque*) one turns upon oneself and looks well: as we saw in the second section of chapter 3, turning, in the Platonic and Neoplatonic traditions, represents the power of the mind to enter within itself and contemplate in or through itself the source of finite being.[67]

The reflected image, Dante explains, "says the truth" (*dice il vero*): it "accords with it [truth/being] as a note does with its meter" (*s'accorda / con esso come nota con suo metro*). Notes "accord perfectly" with their rhythm (*metro*) and cannot misrepresent it, because rhythm constitutes their being, so to speak: notes have no existence apart from rhythm, from some duration in time. In the same way, a reflected image has no being apart from what it reflects, and finite form—the world—has no existence apart from the light of Intellect-Being, here reflexively turned on itself as the focal point of the pilgrim's awareness. Dante's simile exactly represents the nondual relation between finite form and the ground of its being: just as rhythm cannot be heard except through pitch (*nota*), so the ground of being cannot be manifest to the senses except through its reflection as determinate form.[68] In order to produce reflections (finite forms) in the perceiver's mind, the source of light (awareness itself) must be behind him, where he does not yet have it in his sight or thought, as Dante's simile specifies (*prima che l'abbia in vista o in pensiero*). If he turns to that source and focuses on it consciously, it dazzles the power of sight and cancels images: awareness becomes absorbed in itself, focused on itself in a dimensionless point.

What the pilgrim sees when he turns is in fact an extensionless and overpowering point of pure luminosity, as much smaller than the tiniest star as that star is smaller than the moon (19–21): so much does the dimensionless light of pure awareness transcend the finite mind of image, sense, and reason. The point the pilgrim sees is the *punto* or nexus between spatiotemporal extension and self-subsistent conscious being, which has been the constant theme of this study since the second section of chapter 3: as Richard of St. Victor said, to bring the mind to a supreme point in its source, before all concept, idea, and philosophy, is to see the reality that both spawns and is all things; Bonaventure called that point the *apex mentis* or *apex affectionis*, through which the mind that has entered itself leaves behind every idea and thing, focusing itself in single-pointed attention on its ground, ultimately to pass beyond itself into pure Being, "totally transferred and transformed into God"; Eckhart called that point the "uncreated spark" through which the soul and

God are one. That point is thus also—to complete the circle of our study—the ultimate ontological principle as Aristotle defined it: the reflexivity of pure awareness, "the thought that thinks itself," upon which "depend the heavens and the world of nature" (*Metaphysics* 12.7.1072b14). In fact these words of Aristotle's are the first words Beatrice utters about the *punto: Da quel punto / depende il cielo e tutta la natura* ("From that point depend the heavens and all of nature" [41–42]).[69]

How does the entire universe depend upon that point, upon the reflexivity of conscious being? We should have understood by now that there can be no "how": in a sense, the universe *is* that point, that point *is* the universe. More precisely, that point projects the spatiotemporal world from itself as a source of light "paints" (*dipigne*) a halo onto mist (22–24); note that the halo is a reflected image (like the world) and has no being apart from the source of light. Thus arises the universe as extension in space:

> Forse cotanto quanto pare appresso
> alo cigner la luce che 'l dipigne
> quando 'l vapor che 'l porta più è spesso,
> distante intorno al punto un cerchio d'igne
> si girava sì ratto, ch'avria vinto
> quel moto che più tosto il mondo cigne;
> e questo era d'un altro circumcinto,
> e quel dal terzo, e 'l terzo poi dal quarto,
> dal quinto il quarto, e poi dal sesto il quinto.
> Sopra seguiva il settimo sì sparto
> già di larghezza, che 'l messo di Iuno
> intero a contenerlo sarebbe arto.
> Così l'ottavo e 'l nono; e ciascheduno
> più tardo si movea, secondo ch'era
> in numero distante più da l'uno;
> e quello avea la fiamma più sincera
> cui men distava la favilla pura,
> credo, però che più di lei s'invera.
> La donna mia, che mi vedëa in cura
> forte sospeso, disse: "Da quel punto
> depende il cielo e tutta la natura."[70]   (*Pd* 28.22–42)

Notice the stress on spatial extension: *appresso, distante, circumcinto, larghezza, contenerlo, arto, distante, distava*. Dante's relentless rehearsal of the sequence of rings as the ordinal numbers from two to nine makes explicit what was implicit in Beatrice's "numerical" account of the origin of time: it is telling us "how" space arises from conscious being. Just as the sequence of integers is an endless unfolding or manifestation of the concept of number implicit in unity (in the number one), so spatial extension is an unfolding or expression of the actuality of conscious being, of the reflexivity of awareness that is the *punto*. Again, the "unfolding" adds nothing to its source: it is contained within it, so to speak. The world does not consist in anything; in that sense, it can be said to be appearance, a reflection.

The closer a ring is to the *punto*, which corresponds to the Empyrean, the more it "en-trues" itself [*s'invera*] in it (the less it is other than Intellect-Being itself); an increasing numerical "distance" from the all-encompassing unity of Intellect corresponds to an increasing limitation of being by finite attribute. As Beatrice explains (101–102), the angels are assimilated to the point in the degree to which they can "see." The pilgrim's current "power of sight" or self-knowledge corresponds to the ring closest to the focal point, reflected in the sensible world as the *Primo Mobile*, which is in fact "where" he stands in his journey, as Beatrice tells him (43–45). That ring, she says, is so *punto* ("prod-ded," "pricked") by the fire of its selfless love (*affocato amore*) that it is the swiftest of all. Like the intelligences that govern the *Primo Mobile*, to which he is at least fleetingly assimilated, Dante is so *punto* by the *punto* as virtually to be the *punto*, the love or light in which all finite being consists. As we shall see, and as Dante will underline, this *punto* of self-sacrificial love that conquers the pilgrim is in ironic contrast to the *punto* of sensual love that conquered Paolo and Francesca (*solo un punto fu quel che ci vinse* ["one point alone it was that conquered us"; *If* 5.132]), a *punto* that divided them forever, condemning them to insatiable desire.[71]

The "relentless rehearsal" of integers is interrupted only once, by the sim-ile of "Juno's messenger" (32–33). This interruption divides the sequence at the seventh ring, corresponding to the third sphere: Venus. The interruption has been called "untimely," a feeling that should prompt us to ask why it is there. The messenger of Juno, which Dante is linking to Venus, the goddess of love and beauty, is Iris, the rainbow; Iris is the bridge of communication between Heaven and earth, between gods and humans. The rainbow is a re-flection of light as ephemeral beauty and thus is the "messenger" or revelation of the divine in or as the world. In fact the rainbow is the seal of the divine love for man (Genesis 9.12–17), and a witness to God, by its beauty calling men to the praise of the God who made it (Sirach 43.11–12). But the bridge linking God and man can also divide them: ephemeral beauty can hypnotize human intelligence-love, binding it to the finite and blinding it to itself (as in Francesca); this is the power of the goddess, and planet, Venus. In fact the planet Venus, representing earthbound love, is the last planet to fall within the shadow of the earth (*Pd* 9.118–119), one more reason the sequence is inter-rupted here.[72]

Although the pilgrim's intelligence is by now largely de-petrified, he still regards spatial extension as a subsistent reality. He says to Beatrice:

> Se 'l mondo fosse posto
> con l'ordine ch'io veggio in quelle rote,
> sazio m'avrebbe ciò che m'è proposto;
>   ma nel mondo sensibile si puote
> veder le volte tanto più divine,
> quant' elle son dal centro più remote.

> Onde, se 'l mio disir dee aver fine
> in questo miro e angelico templo
> che solo amore e luce ha per confine,
>   udir convienmi come l'essemplo
> e l'essemplare non vanno d'un modo,
> ché io per me indarno a ciò contemplo.[73]   (*Pd* 28.46–57)

The pilgrim has realized that the model (*essemplare*) he is seeing (the self-subsistent point projecting concentric reflected rings about itself) is the precise inverse of the copy (*essemplo*) that is the sensible world, in which the Empyrean contains the concentric spheres of creation; among rings (in the intelligible order) the "most divine" is the smallest, while among spheres (in the sensible or material order) it is the largest. The pilgrim has experienced a radical shift of perspective: from seeing the ontological hierarchy of being, through the reflected image that is space-time, as an ascent from the material (at the center) to the divine (at the periphery), he now sees it in its truth or source as beginning from the reflexivity of conscious being (at the center) and radiating out as spatial extension or "otherness" (as the periphery). By turning from the reflected image to its source, aligning his sight with Beatrice's, the pilgrim's point of view has shifted so that his center (where he looks from) is no longer matter (space-time) but the focal point of the mind: after his last look back into space-time, he has definitively turned his sight from "outside" to "inside."

The pilgrim cannot understand why the sensible world should be the inverse of the intelligible: his understanding still suffers from the illusion that space is absolute, a reality that exists in itself apart from the determination of Intellect-Being as spatiotemporal form. This is the last vestige, in the pilgrim, of the "petrification" of intellect by sensible form, the last barrier to his full self-knowledge as (one with) the source and ground of all finite being. The world the pilgrim inhabits at the moment, at his level of understanding, is a "wondrous and angelic temple": although it is "transparent" to its source, the love and light that constitutes its boundary (*confine*), it still has spatial structure (smaller and larger, up and down, before and behind). To bring the pilgrim's desire "to an end" within that temple is to dissolve the last traces of the illusion that the world is a self-subsistent reality autonomous from conscious being, from himself. It is in effect for the pilgrim to cross the boundary of the temple into the Empyrean, having assimilated as himself (having been "satiated" by) the model or revelation set before him (48, 62). Again, he cannot overcome the barrier by thinking or by his own efforts (57), because thought feeds on concepts and identity, which are themselves derived from the spatiotemporal world, and thus bound by the illusion he is seeking to overcome.

In fact the pilgrim is yet again grappling with the knot or nexus between self-subsistent Intellect-Being and spatiotemporal contingency, which is the knot of the Incarnation, of revelation, of Christ, and, I have argued, of the *Comedy*'s poetics. Beatrice tells the pilgrim (58–60) it is no wonder his fingers are not up to untying such a knot (*non sono a tal nodo sufficienti*): the reason it has become so tight and hard is that almost no one "attempts" it (*tanto, per non tentare, è fatto sodo*). Beatrice is alluding to how few turn from the world to its source to reach this nexus on the road to salvation and understanding. What she will say will satiate him; he can use it to sharpen himself into a point:

> Piglia
> quel ch'io ti dicerò, se vuo' saziarti;
> e intorno da esso t'assottiglia.
>   Li cerchi corporai sono ampi e arti
> secondo il più e 'l men de la virtute
> che si distende per tutte lor parti.
>   Maggior bontà vuol far maggior salute;
> maggior salute maggior corpo cape,
> s'elli ha le parti igualmente compiute.
>   Dunque costui che tutto quanto rape
> l'altro universo seco, corrisponde
> al cerchio che più ama e che più sape:
>   per che, se tu a la virtù circonde
> la tua misura, non a la parvenza
> de le sustanze che t'appaion tonde,
>   tu vederai mirabil consequenza
> di maggio a più e di minore a meno,
> in ciascun cielo, a süa intelligenza.[74]   (*Pd* 28.61–78)

What determines the size of the heavenly spheres is the causal-formative influence (*virtù*) they embody. The greater the power of a finite (created) intelligence to identify with and determine finite form, the greater its love and understanding: the closer it is to the perfect reflexivity or self-knowledge of the ultimate ontological principle. This hierarchy in the intelligible order is reflected in the sensible order as the capacity to encompass, and determine, more and more of the realm of spatiotemporal being. Standing in the *Primo Mobile*, Dante is in the swiftest and most-encompassing sphere, which turns and contains all the rest of the universe; this sphere is the image, in the sensible order, of the greatest finite (created) power of love and intelligence: the seraphim. In sum, Beatrice says, if you "measure" *virtù* and not "the appearance [*parvenza*] of the substances that appear as round to you" (whether circles of angels or spheres), you will see no contradiction between the source and its mirror-image, between the intelligible order and its spatiotemporal reflection. Spatial extension is nothing but an inverse or reflected manifestation of a hierarchy determined by the degree of self-knowledge of created intellect, or, more generally, by the degree to which finite form is "other than" (qualifies or limits) pure awareness; it is in this sense *parvenza*, not a self-subsistent reality.

    Dante emphasizes the importance of Beatrice's elucidation with a nine-line simile:

> Come rimane splendido e sereno
> l'emisperio de l'aere, quando soffia
> Borea da quella guancia ond' è più leno,
>   per che si purga e risolve la roffia
> che pria turbava, sì che 'l ciel ne ride
> con le bellezze d'ogne sua paroffia;
>   così fec'ïo, poi che mi provide
> la donna mia del suo risponder chiaro,
> e come stella in cielo il ver si vide.[75]   (*Pd* 28.79–87)

The revelation that spatial extension is appearance grounded in the self-knowledge of intellect, and not a "thing-in-itself," clears the pilgrim's understanding as the gentle northwest wind clears the entire sky (*l'emisperio de l'aere*) of the mist and cloud that obscured it (*la roffia / che pria turbava*). *Roffia* implies the scales and dandruff of a mental leprosy or disease, which obscures the natural purity and transparency of awareness-being, just as clouds temporarily occupy the sky, which in itself is perfectly limpid, luminous, and transparent (*sereno e splendido*). Thus Beatrice's "clear answering," on the threshold of the Empyrean, sweeps away the hypnosis of space and time as self-subsistent realities to reveal the elemental simplicity of Truth-Intellect-Being, the all-encompassing expanse that—focused on itself in a dimensionless point—reveals and knows itself as both what sees and what is seen. *Come stella in cielo il ver si vide* ("Like a star in the sky truth was seen / saw itself"): an intelligence reaches the Empyrean when it understands that what alone exists in an absolute sense is a dimensionless power of sight, apart from which nothing is.

5

Sunrises and Sunsets

We should now be in a better position to understand the first twelve verses of *Paradiso* 29. Those verses, with their enigmatic astronomical simile of "Latona's children," are set off from the textual narrative and mark the center of the pilgrim's sojourn in the *Primo Mobile*. Indeed, at least by one way of counting, they mark its exact center: they are preceded by 187 lines (from Dante's arrival in the *Primo Mobile* at *Paradiso* 27.100), and followed by 187 lines (to the narrative end of Dante's ascent to the Empyrean, at *Paradiso* 30.54). If Dante structured this intentionally, it may not be a coincidence that the digits of 187 numerologically add up to seven, a number Dante conjures by evoking two and five just after the pilgrim's entry into the *Primo Mobile*; moreover, 2 times 187 (or seven) numerologically gives 5, the number of the world. As we saw in the "Time" section of the preceding chapter, seven for Macrobius represents the Neoplatonic world soul, the nexus between the One and the Many, as for the patristic tradition it represents the Holy Spirit; seven also denotes the completion of the work of creation. Cicero (whom Macrobius is glossing) says that seven is "the knot of almost everything" (*rerum omnium fere nodus est*). In particular, we saw that seven is the number of man, the bridge or knot (like the *Primo Mobile* itself) between Creator and creation, between the self-subsistent and the contingent, between intellect (a three) and matter (a four). We shall argue that those opening four tercets, which make a seven bracketed by sevens, mark a turning point or bridge, perhaps parallel to the "pivot" of conversion between earthly cupidity and selfless love that Singleton traced—as another pivotal seven framed by sevens—at the center of the entire *Comedy*. There may also be a link to proud Niobe (*Pg* 12.37–39), standing between seven and seven children killed by Apollo (in an acrostic spelling *uom* ["man"]), after having scorned Apollo's mother Latona for having only two children (Apollo and Diana). We shall see that pride, the downfall of man, is not to know both Latona's children (*ambedue li figli di Latona* [*Pd* 29.1]) as oneself, not to know oneself as both Apollo and Diana.[1]

Latona's Children

Before examining the simile of Latona's children, let us briefly look at the passage it introduces. In lines 13–36, Beatrice gives an account of the creation of the angels, which is in fact a full-fledged account, and the final account in the *Comedy*, of the creation of the world:

> Non per aver a sé di bene acquisto,
> ch'esser non può, ma perché suo splendore
> potesse, risplendendo, dir "*Subsisto*"
> in sua etternità di tempo fore,
> fuor d'ogne altro comprender, come i piacque,
> s'aperse in nuovi amor l'etterno amore.
> Né prima quasi torpente si giacque;
> ché né prima né poscia procedette
> lo discorrer di Dio sovra quest' acque.
> Forma e materia, congiunte e purette,
> usciro ad esser che non avia fallo,
> come d'arco tricordo tre saette.
> E come in vetro, in ambra o in cristallo
> raggio resplende sì, che dal venire
> a l'esser tutto non è intervallo,
> così 'l triforme effetto del suo sire
> ne l'esser suo raggiò insieme tutto
> sanza distinzïone in essordire.
> Concreato fu ordine e costrutto
> a le sustanze; e quelle furon cima
> nel mondo in che puro atto fu produtto;
> pura potenza tenne la parte ima;
> nel mezzo strinse potenza con atto
> tal vime, che già mai non si divima.[2]   (*Pd* 29.13–36)

We have already discussed lines 22–36 in the third section of chapter 2; I shall not repeat those remarks here, but only add some observations. Intellect-Being can gain nothing by giving itself to, or qualifying itself as, finite attribute and identity ("not for gain of good unto Himself, which cannot be" [13–14]); creation is thus a free act of love. Consciousness or Intellect is intrinsically reflexive (a *splendore*, which means "reflection"): pure awareness is awareness of itself.[3] This reflexivity (consciousness perfectly turned on itself) is the act of existence or being, the ultimate ontological principle: it is Aristotle's "thought that thinks itself." In itself Intellect-Being is "outside" the world: it has no extension in either time ("in His eternity outside of time" [16]) or space ("beyond every other encompassing" [16]). In other words, Intellect-Being is not a thing, but an unlimited power of self-determination or self-giving ("eternal love" [18]), a power to identify itself as or with finite attribute. This power of self-identification can freely ("as it pleased it" [17]) and instantly multiply itself to infinity ("open itself into new loves," that is, into finite intelligences) by "re-reflecting" itself to itself (risplendendo). It does this so that its own self-awareness (splendore) may re-reflect itself to itself as a new and apparently autonomous entity ("so that it could, re-reflecting, say 'I subsist'" [15]). Intellect-Being can only re-reflect itself to itself by distinguishing a new "I am" within the "I AM" of pure conscious being, which means to limit or qualify its experience of self as something: this is to take on, or give itself to, finite attribute and identity. One might say the world exists because conscious being has a penchant for giving content to its "I"; that penchant is love. Notice that it is ultimately the divine self-awareness (splendore) that says "I subsist," through or as each finite (created) intelligence. Indeed salvation, or angelic self-knowledge, is to know, through the surrender of self, that there is ultimately only one reality that says "I" in all conscious beings: it is God, the ground of all being. Salvation or understanding is to experience one's own "I" as not other than God's, as everything and nothing; this is to assimilate one's "I" to Christ's, which alone is to know Christ, or give birth to Christ. What separates man from God and the angels is that God and the angels know who they are, what their "I" ultimately designates, while humans have forgotten. This "forgetting" is original sin, the bewitching or obscuring of divine self-awareness—the ultimate ontological principle—by the attachment to the body and the senses.

Spatial and temporal extension, and thus all acts, events, or change (all prima and poscia, "before" and "after") arise with determinate form, which means that creation ex nihilo is not an act or event ("neither before nor after did the moving of God upon these waters proceed" [20–21]). "These waters" are the ocean of formless being of Genesis, and in particular the aquae super firmamentum, the "waters" crystallized as the Primo Mobile, where the pilgrim is, above the sphere of constellations.⁴ The discorrer di Dio is the informing power of the Word (Genesis 1.2), which in fact "arises" in the Primo Mobile, the nexus between self-subsistent Intellect and the sensible world. "Nor before, as if inert, did He lie" (19): there is no time when (or place where) conscious being does or does not experience itself as, or give itself to, spatiotemporal extension. The notion is incoherent: the spatiotemporal world does not itself exist in space and time; space-time is not a "something" to make the world out of, or in. In this sense, the world is parvenza, appearance.

Creation is thus not an act; much less is it a process in time. Dante compares the instantaneous re-reflection of Intellect-Being as determinate form to the instantaneous self-manifestation (reflection) of an invisible ray of light when it enters a translucent or transparent substance (amber, crystal, or glass), causing the entire object to glow without any lapse of time (intervallo [25–27]).

As we have seen, by medieval optics the reflection of light is simultaneous with its emanation, as, analogously, the infinite sequence of integers arises simultaneously with the concept of number, or as the moon reflects the light of the sun instantaneously, in no time. As a ray of light becomes visible by being reflected within a substance, so the reflexivity (*splendore*) of conscious being (*suo sire*) manifests itself by re-reflecting itself as attribute, again, in no time. The parallel goes deeper, because the reflection in amber too is, strictly speaking, a re-reflection (*risplende*): for Dante the ultimate source of visible light, the sun, is already a mirror (*specchio*), reflecting the intelligible light/power of sight of the divine mind within the world as sensible light, which reveals the world to the senses and sustains it. The perfect reflexivity (*splendore*) of consciousness corresponds to light (being, truth, the power to see); its re-reflection corresponds to contingent attribute and identity, what is seen. The first reflection is invariable and self-subsistent; the re-reflection is variable and contingent.[5]

That Beatrice calls the angels "pure act" (*puro atto* [33]) has generated some confusion. In Christian thought, strictly speaking, only God is pure actuality. Insofar as angelic intelligences have identities and are thus distinguished one from another, they are not the act of existence (or perfect reflexive act of intellection or understanding) itself, and they therefore have a degree of potentiality (dependence or contingency); only in God is understanding, or the "power of sight" (*intelligere*), identical with the act of existence itself (*esse*). Dante does refer to angels as both "pure form" and "pure act" (22, 32–33), and he observes in the *Monarchia* (1.3.7) that "their being is nothing other than their act of understanding" (*earum esse nichil est aliud quam intelligere*), statements some have claimed show Averroistic influence (identifying the angels with God as first causes). This interpretation is unnecessary and unlikely: in medieval philosophy "act" is often used interchangeably with "form," a "pure form" is simply an immaterial substance, and therefore what Beatrice means by *puro atto* is simply angels. Moreover, Dante's phrase in the *Monarchia* simply repeats the Aristotelian maxim (often quoted by Aquinas) that "being in rational creatures is intellection or understanding" (*esse in intelligentibus est intelligere*), as in non-rational living creatures it is life (*esse in viventibus est vivere*). This maxim simply summarizes what we learned in the first section of chapter 3: the soul or form through which a living or rational creature exists is one, and is defined by its highest faculty. Dante is not confusing or identifying the angels with God; in fact, in the *Convivio* (3.12.12) Dante says that "the supreme act (actuality)" is in God alone, and "cannot be anywhere else, except insofar as it derives from Him" (*in lui è ... sommo atto, che non può essere altrove, se non in quanto da esso procede*). In *Paradiso* 29, Beatrice is simply saying, again, that the angels "reside" in the Empyrean, as "subsistences" not subject to the power of any thing, "uninfected" by the potentiality or contingency that is matter, and not "blinded to" or alienated from the ultimate ontological principle by their existence through finite (determinate) form. In all these senses, they may be said to be pure form or actuality.[6]

As we have seen, finite form is nothing but a qualification or limitation of the act of existence; matter is the potentiality of some forms (strictly spatiotemporal ones) to give way to others. This is why Beatrice goes on (37–45) to reject the notion that the angels were created "before the rest of the world was made" (*anzi che l'altro mondo fosse fatto*). Apart from the testimony of Scripture ("the writers of the Holy Spirit"), even reason "sees it somewhat, which would not admit that the movers could be so long without their perfection." The perfection or entelechy of angelic intelligences is to determine and govern, through the motion of the spheres, the succession of ephemeral material forms that constitute sublunar experience. This observation further confirms what Beatrice has already said: immaterial and material substances arose instantaneously and simultaneously from Intellect-Being. "Con-created with the substances were their order and structure or organization" (31–32): to create the substances that constitute the world is to create the varied essences and dependencies, the varied balances of form and matter, actuality and potency, that constitute the ontological hierarchy. A substance (*sustanza*) is either an immaterial or material form; matter (which is not a substance) comes into being with the latter.

Beatrice concludes her lesson by saying of the angels, "Now you know where and when these loves were created, and how; so that three flames of your desire are already quenched" (*Or sai tu dove e quando questi amori / furon creati e come: sì che spenti / nel tuo disïo già son tre ardori* [46–48]). The statement is virtually tongue-in-cheek: if some of Dante's ardor for understanding is satiated, it is because he has understood that there is no where, no when, and no how in the creation of the world. Understanding comes when one *sees* how Heaven and all nature depend on one extensionless principle. It is yet again for Intellect to see and know itself in us, which is to see truth or being (the *vero*). It is not a question of information, concepts, sensory experience, or natural science.

By referring to the "where" and "when" of creation at the end of her account, Beatrice is also directing the reader back to the opening twelve lines of the canto, which introduced her talk, and which end with the words *ubi* and *quando*. To realize how pervasive, and how debilitating, the imagined distinction between "Dante-theologus" and "Dante-poeta" has been in Dante criticism, we need only observe that in so many discussions of Beatrice's creation discourse, almost no one (with the exception of Alison Cornish) has asked why it is preceded by the simile of Latona's children. For most, the simile is a "misplaced ostentation of erudition," a gratuitous interruption in a continuing lesson on angelology that began in *Paradiso* 28, an artifice to make the poem's style rarer and more precious.[7] In reading the *Comedy*, such instinctive responses should only make us inquire more insistently what Dante is up to. This investigation of what Dante may be up to in the simile will constitute the third of my three expositions of the *Comedy*'s poetics "in action."

I have argued that Dante's *Primo Mobile* represents the nexus or turning point between God and creation, eternity and time, self-subsistence and contingency, the One and the Many. We should first note that the twelve-line exordium of *Paradiso* 29, which marks the precise center of the pilgrim's sojourn in the *Primo Mobile,* dividing it in equal halves, itself divides in half with perfect symmetry:

> Quando ambedue li figli di Latona,
> coperti del Montone e de la Libra,
> fanno de l'orizzonte insieme zona,
>   quant' è dal punto che 'l cenìt inlibra
> infin che l'uno e l'altro da quel cinto,
> cambiando l'emisperio, si dilibra,
>   tanto, col volto di riso dipinto,
> si tacque Bëatrice, riguardando
> fiso nel punto che m'avëa vinto.
>   Poi cominciò: "Io dico, e non dimando,
> quel che tu vuoli udir, perch' io l'ho visto
> là 've s'appunta ogne *ubi* e ogne *quando.*"[8]   (*Pd* 29.1–12)

As Durling and Martinez have observed, these lines begin and end with the word *quando* ("when"); the center of the twelve lines, or threshold to the second half of the simile, is marked by the words *emisperio* ("hemisphere") and *dilibra* ("unbalances"); the word *punto* ("point") is balanced around this midpoint in the fourth and ninth lines, occupying the same metrical position in both; the tercets bracketing the midpoint are symmetrically balanced by *quanto* ("as long") and *tanto* ("so long"), both in initial position; multiplicity (*ambedue,* "both") in the first line is balanced by unity (*s'appunta,* "comes to a point") in the last.[9]

Both in its structure and in its meaning, the simile enacts and describes a balance, what Durling and Martinez call "an instant of cosmic equilibrium" (209). "Both Latona's children" are Apollo and Diana, the sun and the moon. When the plane of the horizon bisects ("makes a *zona* [girdle] or *cinto* [belt] for") both at once, they are on opposite sides of the earth, under the opposing constellations of Aries and Libra: the moon is setting at the instant the sun is rising, or vice versa. Dante pictures the sun and moon as hanging like the pans of a balance from a point directly above wherever the observer happens to be: the zenith. At the mathematical instant (*punto*) that the "pans" of the scale are both bisected by the horizon, they are in balance (*'l cenìt inlibra*); by the "next" mathematical instant (i.e., in no time at all, since time is infinitely divisible and continuous), they are out of balance (*si dilibra*): they have switched hemispheres. Whether it is the sun that is rising and the moon that is setting, or vice versa, depends upon whether the sun "is covered by" Aries and the moon by Libra, or vice versa. As Alison Cornish has pointed out—and it is a fundamental observation—this is precisely what the text does not tell us. We know we are in an equinox, in a perfect balance between day and night, light and darkness, summer and winter, but we do not know which way the balance is tipping. If the sun is in Aries, then we are in the vernal equinox, and the sun is rising: we are on the threshold of day, summer, light, and life; if the sun is in Libra, then we are in the autumnal equinox, and it is evening: we are going into night, winter, darkness, and death.[10]

So how long is Beatrice silent? As long as the sun and moon, in their revolution, are perfectly bisected by the plane of the horizon. In other words, an extensionless instant in time, or *punto*; as Dante explains in the *Convivio* (2.13.26–27), a *punto* is unmeasurable, infinitely small. Beatrice is silent no time at all. Dante emphasizes the importance of the simile and sets it off as the fulcrum of the *Primo Mobile*, itself the fulcrum of all reality, by its apparent gratuitousness: it seems simply to interrupt a discourse on angels that began in *Paradiso* 28, and the pause it designates is no pause at all. Yet that no-pause, that nothingness in time of the present instant, is made to seem a cosmic expanse by the simile itself. What is Beatrice looking at in an extensionless point of time? *Il punto che m'avëa vinto* ("the point that conquered me"): the infinitesimal burning point Dante saw in *Paradiso* 28. That point, as we saw, is the all-encompassing Empyrean, infinite Being-Light-Love-Bliss, the dimensionless, all-projecting focal point of pure self-awareness. In gazing "where all *where* and *when* come to a point," Beatrice is seeing nothing, that is, no thing, but the source of all things. More precisely, she is seeing the nexus between God and creation, "where, when, and how" space and time arise from, or within, Intellect-Being itself.

In Aristotelian physics, the present instant (the now or *nunc*), like a point on a line, has no extension; it is simply the limit that divides and unites two successive intervals. Those intervals are the arbitrary units or "numbering" by which the movement or change of bodies is measured, which is why time and space have no existence apart from each other. Since both space and time are infinitely divisible, they are in one sense nothing in themselves: time is not "made of" present moments, just as space is not "made of" mathematical points. The present instant or *nunc* is not itself in time and does not constitute time, even though the continuum of time may be conceived as the constantly changing now. Motion or change, the "root" of time, has no being in itself either: it is nothing but the becoming of what does have being. Captured at any instant, motion or becoming is the unfulfilled potentiality of finite (material) being. The now is the actuality or existence or subsistence of what has being; any potentiality (capacity for change) in that being implies duration, an unfolding actualization, and thus a before and after: such a thing exists in time. One could say that a changing present instant (duration) is a finite or transitory participation in being, in the eternal now. The dimensionless instant or present moment thus mediates being and time: it is the nexus, the point of identity and distinction, between self-subsistent and contingent (ephemeral) being; it is the point through which all finite (spatiotemporal) being participates in Being. The present instant is thus the extensionless now of the act of creation, the Christic knot or point between creator and created. We shall see that that dimensionless now of the act of creation is what the simile of Latona's children represents; we have already seen that it is the subject of the discourse the simile introduces.[11]

The simile balances a dimensionless spatiotemporal *punto* against the cosmic expanse of time and space: the latter is seen to have no being apart from the former. But an extensionless spatiotemporal point does not exist in space-time, which shows, yet again, that neither does space-time. So where is it that all *where* and *when* come to a point? As we saw in the second section of chapter 3, especially in discussing Richard of St. Victor and Bonaventure, space-time comes to a point when or where or as the finite human intellect, existing within and as the world, enters itself, focusing itself in a dimensionless point of self-awareness or self-knowledge, through which it passes over into pure Intellect-Being-Truth, thus experiencing itself as the ground of all being, the ground of all being as itself. This is the point from which depend "heaven and all nature," as Beatrice said of the *punto* in *Paradiso* 28, quoting Aristotle's phrase for the ultimate ontological principle, which he too—at the foundation of the whole medieval tradition—defined as the reflexivity of conscious being, *noesis noeseos noesis*. We saw in fact that the nexus between creator and spatiotemporal creation is the innermost or highest peak, point, or spark of the human mind, through which divine self-subsistent Intellect awakens to itself as or through man, thus revealing itself within and as the spatiotemporal world. Fusing the divine and the animal, the eternal and the temporal, the three intellective faculties with the four material elements, man—like the *Primo Mobile* itself, and like this simile composed of four tercets—is a seven, the nexus or bridge or frontier (*confinium*) between the One and the Many.

The balance the simile describes is between the sun and the moon in opposition. As the invariant and unfailing source and sustainer of cosmic light and life, the sun, Dante says in the *Convivio* (3.12.7), is the most worthy exemplar of God; indeed the sun god, Apollo, is the god of light, understanding, pure intellect, revelation, prophecy, divine inspiration, and salvation, attributes that make him an image of Christ, as well as the presiding deity of the *Paradiso*, which opens by invoking him. The realm of the inconstant moon, of the contingent re-reflection of the light of the sun, is Diana's or Persephone's kingdom: finite being, memory, mind, nature, change, ephemerality, temporality, shadow, mortality. As we saw in the second section of chapter 4, the moon is thus marked (at least to sublunar vision) with the dark signs of difference and otherness, the obscuring of light that leads to the sin of Cain and to death. The balance between the moon and the sun, belted together (*cinto*) by the horizon, is the balance or nexus between the contingent world and the ground of its being; it is the yoking together of the mortal and the divine in the human being, a "yoking" perfectly revealed in Christ. This balance or nexus thus has a moral dimension: it is also, in every finite (created) intellect, the ambiguous or undecided balance between day and night, between the eternal and the temporal, between the self-subsistent and the contingent, between self-knowledge and the hypnosis of finite being. That moral dimension or tension, in both angels and humans, will occupy the rest of Beatrice's discourse in *Paradiso* 29, from line 49 to the end of the canto.[12]

Beatrice treats the angels first. At the instant the angels were created, Augustine explains—and Alison Cornish reminds us—they turned to contemplate themselves. At that moment they were morally neutral, poised between night and day in a *cognitio vespertina* ("twilight knowledge"), but by the "next" instant (i.e., in no time, since again an instant is extensionless, and time is infinitely divisible), they "chose sides": they either recognized themselves as dependent upon (reflections of) one self-subsistent reality, as "one with" the ground of all finite being, or they did not. As Beatrice expresses the alternative, either they remained (*rimase*) where they were (the Empyrean) and began their contemplation and praise of the divine (52–54), recognizing, in their modesty, that their being and understanding depended entirely on divine goodness, and receiving, because of their humility and love, an illuminating grace that stably exalted their vision above themselves (58–66); or else they precipitated from the Empyrean into Hell, disturbing the earth (the substratum or lowest-lying of the elements [*il suggetto d'i vostri alimenti*]; 49–51), as the result of the accursed pride of Lucifer (55–56), who is now constrained in the center of the earth by the weight of the world, or more precisely, by every thing that has weight (*da tutti i pesi del mondo costretto* [57]). An angel thus falls or alienates itself from the Empyrean by experiencing itself as only an autonomous and self-subsistent identity, which is to eclipse or block the light of Intellect-Being in oneself through ego and pride; this is to bear upon oneself the entire burden of "otherness," the alienation from Being that is matter. As Augustine puts it, it is to pass into night (*facti sunt nox*). The angels not blinded to Being by their being this-or-that awakened instead to the morning of divine knowledge (*cognitio matutina*), what Beatrice has just described in *Paradiso* 28 (116–117) as "this sempiternal spring which nocturnal Aries does not despoil" (*questa primavera sempiterna / che notturno Ariëte non dispoglia*): Aries appears at night in the autumn when the sun is in Libra, an autumn that for these angels never comes. For Augustine, as Cornish points out, these two states of angelic knowledge constitute the literal sense of the assertion in Genesis (1.4–5) that "God separated the light from the darkness, calling the light Day and the darkness Night"; they also account for morning and evening in the first days, given that the sun was created only on the fourth day. Self-contemplation is simultaneous with, but logically prior to, the seeing or failure to see the divine light, just as (Aquinas observes) the shining of the sun is simultaneous with, but logically prior to, its reflection from the moon. In sum, for each angel, as for every finite intellect, the instant of first creation—which, we might add, is not essentially different from every other instant any thing exists—is either morning or evening, the vernal or autumnal equinox, the threshold to light and life or to darkness and death.[13]

The angels who followed Lucifer in disturbing the substratum or lowest of the elements did so "before one could reach twenty counting" (*né giugneriesi, numerando, al venti / si tosto* [49–50]). Most have thought that Dante is describing some passage of time between the creation and (the end of) the fall of Lucifer, but as Cornish points out, for Augustine and Aquinas the creation and the sin of Lucifer are simultaneous, though logically distinct; Cornish convincingly makes the same case for Dante by linking the states of angelic knowledge to the instant of balance in the opening simile. Indeed, Dante says in the

Convivio (2.5.12) that a tenth of the angels were lost *tosto che furono creati* ("as soon as they were created"), nor is there any delay in the choice of the good angels in *Paradiso* 29. We saw in chapter 4 that Dante compared the emanation of both space and time to the generation of number, and that there is no process in that generation: to have the concept of number (any number) is to have all numbers. The emphasis on *numerando*, isolated in the verse, should remind us of the relentless "numbering" of rings, or generation of space, in *Paradiso* 28: Dante is playing not on the process of counting, but on "how" one number gives rise to another: instantaneously, intrinsically. Cornish realizes the number twenty must here have symbolic force, and she finds it readily in the *Convivio*'s explanation (2.14.3–4) that "twenty signifies the movement of alteration," because it alters ten with the first of the other nine digits. To this observation we may add that two is the number of local movement; ten, we know, is the number of perfection, of the Empyrean. Twenty, we might conclude, represents alteration or change within—which can only be alienation from—the Empyrean, the "home" of all unobstructed vision.

That the fall was simultaneous with creation accords with the sign on the gate of Hell (*If* 3.7–8): "Before me no thing was created if not eternal, and eternal I endure" (*Dinanzi a me non fuor cose create / se non eterne, e io etterno duro*). The possibility of self-alienation is one with, logically but not temporally successive to, the self-qualification or self-giving of Intellect-Being as attribute and identity, in particular as finite intelligence, which is indeed eternal. Evil is not created, and nothing is created evil. The confusions implicit in the temporal picture of creation, almost universal among Dantists (even, as we saw in chapter 4, among the Thomists), have spawned a host of illusory problems around Hell's gate and Lucifer's fall. The earth had to exist for the gate of Hell to exist within it, and Lucifer, falling, "disturbed the substratum or lowest-lying of your elements" (*Pd* 29.51), creating the mountain of Purgatory (*If* 34.121–126): if the ephemeral elements were created "later," then where was Hell, and what did Lucifer upset? Because creation is not a process in time, Beatrice's *suggetto* (*subiectum* or substratum) may be understood either as earth (the lowest-lying element) or as sublunar matter in a generic sense (proximate matter or *complession potenziata*, composed of the four elements), but not as prime matter, which is nothing and thus cannot be upset, nor as Augustinian *materia informis*, because for Dante (as for Augustine) there was no moment when the world was only partially formed.[14]

To know that the opening simile of *Paradiso* 29 applies not only to angelic intelligence, but equally, or perhaps principally, to human intellect, we need only remember the age-old metaphor that has accompanied us through the preceding chapters: the human being is the horizon between eternity and time, between God and creation, between the self-subsistent and the contingent. To use Dante's exact words in the *Monarchia* (3.15.3–4): "man alone among beings is the link [*medium*] between the corruptible and the incorruptible; hence philosophers rightly compare ['assimilate'] him to the horizon, which is the link [*medium*] between two hemispheres" (*homo solus in entibus tenet medium corruptibilium et incorruptibilium; propter quod recte a phylosophis assimilatur ori-*

zonti, qui est medium duorum emisperiorum). As the belt or girdle balancing and yoking the sun and moon, the horizon of the simile, and indeed the *Primo Mobile* as a whole, is the human soul or intelligence itself, the dimensionless point or nexus or bridge between Intellect-Being and space-time. The horizon linking sun and moon is the boundary between the inward and outward orientation of the mind, between, on the one hand, feeding on the ground of being within oneself through self-knowledge and Christic awakening (the sun rises, and the moon sets), and on the other, the insatiable desire or *cupidigia* of the mind that—petrified through its self-identification as this-or-that and thus tinted with death—seeks to feed on ephemeral finite being through the senses, like Pyramus, or Ulysses, or Francesca (the moon rises, and the sun sets). The boundary is one between life and death, light and darkness, day and night, self-knowledge and self-alienation, salvation and damnation.

As a point of conversion or turning or awakening, the *punto che m'avëa vinto,* the point that conquered Dante in *Paradiso* 28, and that Beatrice is gazing upon in *Paradiso* 29, explicitly conjures, symmetrically balances (the phrase occurs five cantos from either end of the poem), and ironically contrasts with Francesca's *solo un punto fu quel che ci vinse* ("one point alone it was that conquered us" [*If* 5.132]); to make sure we don't miss the point, so to speak, Dante repeats the phrase in *Paradiso* 30.11–12: the "point that seems encompassed by what it encompasses" is the "point that conquered me" (*al punto che mi vinse, / parendo inchiuso da quel ch'elli 'nchiude).* The point that conquered Francesca, interrupting her reading so that she and Paolo "that day read no further" (*If* 5.138), was an eclipse of the light of Intellect-Being in her by the body, a failure of self-knowledge and love, a failure to recognize Paolo as herself. That point of eclipse and sensuality is in ironic contrast to the moment of Augustine's conversion in the *Confessions* (8.12): weeping in agony and doubt, Augustine hears a voice chanting "Pick up and read" (*tolle lege).* Seizing the book of the apostle Paul, he reads, "Not in riots and drunken parties, not in eroticism and indecencies, not in strife and rivalry, but put on the Lord Jesus Christ and make no provision for the flesh in its lusts" (Romans 13.13–14). Augustine too stops reading, but because of a sunrise, not a sunset: "I neither wished nor needed to read further" (*nec ultra volui legere, nec opus erat).* Light dawned instantly, Augustine says, all shadows of doubt were expelled, and he found peace (contrast Francesca's *dubbiosi disiri* and thirst for peace [*If* 5.120, 92, 99]). The day-night contrast is explicit in the lines that immediately precede the ones Augustine quotes: "it is the hour now for you to awake from sleep. For our salvation is nearer now than when we first believed; the night is advanced, the day is at hand. Let us then throw off the works of darkness and put on the armor of light; let us conduct ourselves properly as in the day" (Rom. 13.11–12). As Augustine, reading, made the apostle Paul and Paul's text the go-between or Gallehaut between himself and God, so Francesca makes a text, and he who wrote it, the Galleotto (137) between herself and Paolo. That Francesca was probably (mis)reading a prose Lancelot meant to warn her against adultery, a fact she might have discovered had she read further, only compounds the irony.[15]

Statius, on the other hand, (mis)reading the Fourth Eclogue (5–7) of the pagan poet Vergil, was brought out of the shadows into the light of the sun (*Pg* 22.61–62): he recognized Christ in what for Vergil was not Christ, which is to make day out of night, another sunrise of reading. To awaken to Christ (through reading) is ultimately to become (one with) Christ, or to give birth to Christ, as the Incarnation and Resurrection imagery that surrounds Statius's introduction into the poem, announcing his final liberation from the ephemeral, underscores (*Pg* 20.133–141, 21.7–13). The act of reading, Dante is telling us, is itself a point of balance between day and night, life and death, salvation and damnation: we, the readers of Dante's poem, in the very now, instant, or act of reading the poem, are placed on the horizon between the eternal and the ephemeral, between self-knowledge and self-alienation. This now or moment of reading is for each of us either a sunrise (and moonset) into eternal life and freedom, or a sunset (and moonrise) into mortality and unquenchable desire.[16]

The eclipse or blocking of light is built into Dante's simile: although the sun and moon are in opposition at every full moon, if they are in perfect opposition, as specified here, the moon will be in the shadow cast by the earth, and the light of the sun will be blocked. Dante has described a lunar eclipse. In the *Paradiso*—as John Kleiner has shown—eclipse unfailingly evokes Crucifixion. He also points out that the planetary alignment in *Paradiso* 29 corresponds to the eclipse-Crucifixion of the mirror experiment in *Paradiso* 2: the sun corresponds to the lamp, the earth to the observer's body, and the moon to the central mirror. One might think of the simile of Latona's children as a cosmic re-enactment of the mirror experiment of *Paradiso* 2: the body or earth (matter) is in danger of blocking the light of Intellect-Being (the lamp or sun) in the finite mind (the mirror or moon), so that the mind sees (reflects) only body, and not the light that lies behind (sustains) body. It is how the body becomes a *parete / al sol*, a wall to the sun (*Pg* 26.22–23), leading to the fate of Pyramus and Thisbe, the death and suicide that are frustrated desire.[17]

Paradiso 29 is in fact all about eclipse-Crucifixion: it contains a trinity of eclipses. Besides this one in the opening simile, we are told that the angels *non hanno vedere interciso / da novo obietto* (79–80): their sight is not obstructed or cut off by anything new, that now is but once was not. What is and once was not is all of creation, paradigmatically the world of space and time, most paradigmatically matter, the earth—that great blocker of light—from which the human body is made. For the angelic vision (and for the human intellect assimilated to it), nothing is "other" or "new": to "see" the ground of being (the "face of God" [77]) is to know all things as oneself: it is to "see through" earth-matter-body, to see that nothing is added to the ground of being by its self-qualification as this-or-that. As we shall see, the third eclipse is explicitly the eclipse that accompanied the Crucifixion (97–102); it is evoked also at *Paradiso* 27.35–36, when Saint Peter speaks of the corruption and greed of modern popes, which is emblematically an eclipse or Crucifixion of Christ in the world, a failure to see, be, and reveal Christ. Crucifixion is eclipse itself: that Intellect-Being, reflected as the human intelligence, cannot recognize itself, even when it confronts or reveals itself to itself (incarnates) in human form, is the paradigm of eclipse, the blocking of light and intellect by body. Indeed it is a self-eclipse, as Beatrice underlines: at the Crucifixion of Christ the moon did not "interpose" itself between the sun and the earth; rather "the light hid itself" (*la luce si nascose / da sé* [100–101]). But that very eclipse, the willing self-sacrifice or self-crucifixion of *what is*, is a self-revelation: it was the Crucifixion (and accompanying eclipse) that first awakened the centurion and his men to Christ. Incarnation and Crucifixion, revelation and eclipse, are inseparable from each other. *What is* eclipses itself by revealing itself as or through finite form; it reveals itself by eclipsing itself as (sacrificing) finite form. A pervasive medieval tradition in fact links Incarnation and Crucifixion by thinking of Christ as both the rising sun (*sol oriens*) and the setting sun (*sol occidens*). This idea has never been more profoundly and perfectly expressed than in the dimensionless instant or point of *Paradiso* 29's exordium, a nexus-balance-knot-yoking of creator and creation that is simultaneously and undecidably a sunrise and a sunset.[18]

The trinity of eclipses-Crucifixions in *Paradiso* 29 is the culmination of a trinity of eclipses-Crucifixions in the *Paradiso*, evoked and linked, as Kleiner has suggested, by the opening simile of Latona's children. The first of the three occurs upon entering the heaven of the moon in *Paradiso* 2: it is the mirror experiment. The second is evoked upon entering the heaven of the sun, in *Paradiso* 10. There Dante entreats the reader (7–24) to gaze at that (dimensionless and invisible) point in the sky where the oblique motion of the sun along the ecliptic crosses or "strikes" (*percuote*) the contrary motion of the sphere of fixed stars along the celestial equator. That point of intersection is either one of the two equinoctial junctions: as Dante explains in the *Convivio* (3.5.8,13), the sun crosses the celestial equator when it is in Aries and when it is in Libra, at the threshold of summer or of winter. Kleiner notes that both Aries and Libra are associated with Christ: Aries as the paschal lamb, and Libra as the scales of justice or judgment. Freccero has observed that the intersection of the two contrary motions makes a Greek cross, the Platonic celestial *chi* (X) that, in a tradition derived from the *Timaeus* (34c–36e), represents the nexus between the Same (the One) and the Other (duality–multiplicity–finite being); the phrase *l'uno e l'altro*, "the one and the other," occurs twice in the passage. In the *Timaeus*, that nexus or cross is the creative act of the Demiurge, by which the world arises from soul, from conscious being. The exegetical tradition of course identified that cross with the cross of Christ, the Word through which all things were made. In *Paradiso* 10, Dante has instructed us to look at a cross that is not there: there is nothing there to see, unless we have eyes to see it. To see it is to see the nexus between creator and creation; it is yet again to have seen oneself, through the sacrifice of self. The failure to see that nexus or cross is evoked in *Paradiso* 10 by the word *eclisso* (eclipse), which—as Kleiner points out—occurs here (60) as also in *Paradiso* 2 and 29. Through the opening phrase of *Paradiso* 29, "both Latona's children" (*ambedue li figli di Latona*), Dante is directing us back to *Paradiso* 2 and 10, the cantos of the moon and the sun, linking their eclipses-Crucifixions to the culminating eclipse-

Crucifixion of the exordium of *Paradiso* 29. As Kleiner puts it, Dante is balancing the cantos of the sun and moon from the zenith, the *Primo Mobile*, precisely as the simile describes. Kleiner also points out that all three cantos mark thresholds or transitions: between earth and Heaven (*Pd* 2), from the earth's shadow to beyond it (*Pd* 10), between space-time and the Empyrean (*Pd* 29). We might add that all three cantos stress the reader's (or pilgrim's) responsibility to see or look on his own, and to understand without further guidance (*Pd* 2.94–97, 124–126; 10.7–13, 22–27; 29.46–48, 67–69).[19]

Indeed salvation is at hand, if we would only awake and see: indeed the sun is in Aries, and it is the vernal, not autumnal, equinox. The instantaneous now, our moment of reading, is a sunrise, an eternal springtime, if we would only see it. It must be the vernal equinox, because we are in the *Primo Mobile*, the nexus, point, or instant (the eternal now) through which creation arises from Intellect-Being, and at the instant of first creation, both the Christian tradition and Dante tell us, the cosmos was ordered in a vernal equinox. That nexus, point, or instant of creation is also the dimensionless point through which created intelligence, focused upon itself, sacrifices all finite form and returns to its source. This is the crucifixion of self, and at the moment of Crucifixion too, the Christian tradition tells us, and the evocations of eclipse and crucifixion in *Paradiso* 29 remind us, the cosmos was ordered in a vernal equinox. Indeed, in *Paradiso* 10 Dante "transfixes" the sun (Apollo-Christ), as well as himself, on the cross of Same and Other, One and Many, that he has described (28–32): the sun is in Aries ("conjoined with the part noted above" [*con quella parte che su si rammenta congiunto*]), and the pilgrim is with the sun (*e io era con lui*). This means that Dante's own journey from the earth to the Empyrean, from space-time to its source—a journey or self-crucifixion that reverses, so to speak, the act of creation, and which is the now or present moment of the poem's narrative—occurs on the vernal equinox, as we know also from the opening of the poem (1.38–40), as well as the opening of the *Purgatorio* (2.1–6) and the *Paradiso* (1.37–45). In the balance of day and night that is the vernal equinox, the pilgrim enters Hell at sunset and emerges to Purgatory and salvation at dawn. The "act" of creation, the Crucifixion, the pilgrim's journey, and (in the terms Dante has set) our present act of reading the poem are all a timeless instant of revelation-salvation, in which the ground of being manifests or awakens to itself within and as the finite, that is, in and as us. Assimilated to an angelic intelligence through this awakening, the human intellect recognizes all that it sees as itself. It knows itself as both Apollo and Diana: sun and moon, eternity and time, self-subsistent and created, the source and the reflection. Knowing itself, it knows Christ, the nexus of love-being-understanding that bridges or yokes all duality within itself. Through this perfection of selfless love, self-sacrifice, and self-knowledge, the human being lives in time and space unbound by time and space, a mortal creature untouched by mortality and ephemerality: it is completely free. To be completely free, not in the power of space-time or anything it contains, is to live in the Empyrean. It is where the pilgrim will find himself in the next canto, and we too, if we are going with him.[20]

Ciance

Angelic intelligence constitutes the theme of *Paradiso* 28 and 29 not because it is interesting in itself, but precisely because there is almost nothing to know about it. Angels are almost perfectly simple: they are a power of sight or self-knowledge, which assimilates them, in different degrees, to the *punto*, to the perfect reflexivity of conscious being (*Pd* 28.101–102). The sweetness or bliss an angel experiences depends upon the intensity of its love, which in turn depends on its power to see into (to know itself as one with) the unqualified truth-being-awareness, or power of sight, in which every intelligence finds rest (28.106–111, 29.139–141); this unqualified power of sight is the reality in which all things ultimately consist, and which gives being to all things (29.144–145).

Angels are of interest because of *how* they can be known: not by concepts, images, ideas, reasoning, philosophy, or preaching, but only by assimilating one's own intelligence or power of sight to theirs. This is to know from direct experience what an angel is, and how it sees; it is to become its neighbor in the Empyrean, by knowing the ground of all being as not other than oneself. In short, it is to achieve salvation. To know the angels is to see their seeing, so to speak, which is to see seeing itself. For Dante such sight—the truth-being-awareness, or reflexivity of conscious being, that is revealed through the surrender of self—is the source and ground of all authority and revelation, of all true philosophy and preaching. It alone leads to human unity, understanding, conversion, salvation, and love; all else is *ciance*, the idle chatter, imaginings, wanderings, ratiocinations, and hypocrisy of minds bewitched by the ephemeral, of intelligence eclipsed by ego and finite identity. The distinction between seeing and thinking, and the designation of the former as the ground of authority, understanding, and salvation, are the real subject of *Paradiso* 28 and 29. As Contini showed, the obsessive thematic words of *Paradiso* 28 are *vedere* and *vero*, seeing and truth/being; these are key terms also in *Paradiso* 29, in which the awakening of intellect to itself in the now of creation, an awakening encoded in the exordium and creation discourse, gives way to a sustained attack on bad philosophy and preaching.[21]

In the last section of chapter 4, we discussed *Paradiso* 28 up to the point in which Dante's intelligence, like a limpid sky that laughs at the refuse and fog that had obscured it (82–84), has been cleared of the illusion that space is a self-subsistent "something," so that "as a star in the sky truth was seen/saw itself" (*come stella in ciel il ver si vide* [87]). After this "clearing," Beatrice proceeds to distinguish and order the hierarchy of angelic intelligences by name (98–129), a classification that reflects "how sublime they are in their seeing" (*quanto a veder son soblimi* [102]), or "how far their sight sinks into the truth/reality in which every intellect finds rest" (*quanto la sua veduta si profonda / nel vero in che si queta ogne intelletto* [107–108]). How can a human know this classification? Only by having "been there," by having visited the Empyrean, by seeing the angels' seeing. Since to establish a hierarchy of angels is not really to convey information, but to put a list of names in order, Beatrice's point in establishing the definitive order is to underline *that* and *how* she knows, which is to establish the authority and revelatory power, and the ground of the authority and revelatory power, of the text that records her voice: the *Comedy*. Dionysius the Areopagite, says Beatrice, contemplated these orders with such love or desire that he named and distinguished them as she does (*Dionisio con tanto disio / a contemplar questi ordini si mise, / che li nomò e distinse com' io* [130–132]); note that Dionysius agrees with Beatrice, and not vice versa, as in *Purgatorio* 29.100–105 John the Evangelist agrees with Dante (in correcting or "departing from" Ezekiel), and not Dante with John. To gaze with loving desire on angelic intelligence, as Dionysius does, is to identify with or see an unobstructed power of sight, which is for *what is* to see itself; it is not to reason or philosophize. Gregory the Great, on the other hand—like the philosophizing Dante of the *Convivio* (2.5.6), which Beatrice is here correcting—got it wrong, and "divided himself" (*si divise*) from Dionysius. A loving seeing leads to unity and truth; mere philosophizing, imagining, or speculation leads to division and error. In fact as soon as Gregory "opened his eyes in this heaven," he laughed at his previous ignorance (*sì tosto come li occhi aperse / in questo ciel, di sé medesmo rise* [134–135]), not unlike the sky laughing at the fog that had obscured it before truth was seen/saw itself. Dionysius was able to "reveal such a hidden truth on earth" while still alive (*se tanto secreto ver proferse / mortale in terra* [136–137]) because he was merely reporting the testimony of one— Saint Paul—who had directly seen Heaven and the truth of these spheres (*chi 'l vide qua sù gliel discoperse / con altro assai del ver di questi giri* [138–139]). In fact Paul, like the pilgrim Dante, had been rapt to Heaven by special grace (*If* 2.28–30). Dante presents himself as both Dionysius and Paul: he reports Beatrice's testimony as Dionysius reported Paul's; but Dante had to open his eyes in Heaven himself—like Paul, and like the beatified Dionysius—to "receive" that testimony. The *Comedy* is telling us that its authority and its status as revelation are grounded not in imagination, learning, or reasoning, but in seeing. To see the *vero*, truth/being, is for seeing to see itself, to awaken to itself as the ground of all being. For Dante, the words of one in whom this has happened have authority: they alone reveal truth, *what is*; they alone lead to conversion, unity, understanding, and salvation.[22]

After her creation discourse in *Paradiso* 29, Beatrice tells Dante that if he has "taken in her words" he can now contemplate angelic nature on his own, without further guidance (*Omai dintorno a questo consistorio / puoi contemplare assai, se le parole / mie son ricolte, sanz' altro aiutorio* [67–69]). But she does give further guidance, another seventy-five lines of it, all the way to the end of the canto. She does this because on earth, thinking in our schools and preaching in our pulpits, we get it all backward: instead of assimilating our intelligence to that of angels through love and contemplation, we assimilate theirs to ours by projecting our blindness, mental chatter, and ignorance onto them. This is to miss the entire point of angels, what they reveal to us about us: it is to invert the good news of salvation, to eclipse Christ, to alienate ourselves from ourselves, to make even angelic intelligence the occasion for endless sophistry and empty imaginings. Beatrice says:

Ma perché 'n terra per le vostre scole
si legge che l'angelica natura
è tal, che 'ntende e si ricorda e vole,
   ancor dirò, perché tu veggi pura
la verità che là giù si confonde,
equivocando in sì fatta lettura.[23]   (*Pd* 29.70–75)

Beatrice is again distinguishing seeing from thinking: angels see, humans (normally) think. To think that angels think is equivocally to apply terms derived from finite human experience to angels, which is a failure to see truth instead of merely thinking about it, which in turn is a failure to know as the angels do, or as the pilgrim does after his intelligence has been "cleared" in *Paradiso* 28. To suppose that all knowing is conceptual, and thus sequential in time (discursive), and thus dependent upon memory, is not to have seen the ground of being in or through oneself: it is not to know Christ, not to have seen God. It is an eclipse of the light of being in us.

Angels, on the other hand, never turn their sight from the face of God, in which they see all things (76–78). Angels gaze always on Intellect-Being itself, of which all things are merely a partial participation or qualification, and to which no thing can be an addition; hence no new thing ever intercepts their sight, which is why they do not need to remember things from concepts abstracted ("divided") from those things, or divided from other concepts in time: *però non hanno vedere interciso / da novo obietto, e però non bisogna / rememorar per concetto diviso* (79–81). On earth, we are daydreamers (*là giù, non dormendo, si sogna*), whether we believe we are saying the truth, or intentionally distorting it (*credendo e non credendo dicer vero* [82–84]). If we really loved truth instead of our own egos, instead of our own reputation and fame, we would all be in fundamental agreement in all our philosophizing: *Voi non andate giù per un sentiero / filosofando: tanto vi trasporta / l'amor de l'apparenza e 'l suo pensiero!* ("You mortals do not follow one same path as you philosophize, so much does the love of appearance and the thought of it carry you astray!" [85–87]). True philosophy always leads to unity ("one path"), because it leads the intellect to see itself, and thus leads it toward the self-revelation of the ground of being. When philosophy is bewitched by the lure of the ephemeral, by "the love of appearance and the thought of it," it wanders endlessly and aimlessly in the labyrinth of concepts (thought), having lost the road to understanding. Vanity and ambition lead only to ignorance, as humility and self-sacrifice alone lead to understanding.[24]

Even worse than philosophical sophistry and pride, says Beatrice, is the distortion or manipulation of Scripture to worldly or selfish ends (88–90). The purpose of Scripture, of the Good News (*'l Vangelio*), is to trigger an awakening to the eternal through the surrender of the ephemeral: it is a message sown in the world through the blood of self-sacrifice (91–92). Instead preachers use it to *apparer*, to make a show of themselves through their ingenious fantasies, inventions, fables, jokes, and put-downs (94–96, 103–105, 115–117), while the Gospel itself is suppressed: *Per apparer ciascun s'ingegna e face / sue invenzioni;*

e quelle son trascorse / da' predicanti e 'l Vangelio si tace. It is to feed the sheep with wind (106–108). As an example of these fatuous inventions, Beatrice cites the speculation surrounding the eclipse at the Crucifixion:

> Un dice che la luna si ritorse
> ne la passion di Cristo e s'interpuose,
> per che 'l lume del sol giù non si porse;
>   e mente, ché la luce si nascose
> da sé: però a li Spani e a l'Indi
> come a' Giudei tale eclissi rispuose.[25]   (*Pd* 29.97–102)

In itself it does not seem so egregious to say that the moon turned back in its path to cause the eclipse at the Crucifixion: it was the opinion of many good souls, such as Pseudo-Dionysius, Albert the Great, and Aquinas. Beatrice's point is much deeper: she is again blocking the impulse to think instead of to see, the impulse to conceptualize, to posit "scientific explanations," which leads the intellect away from understanding into the labyrinth of finite names and forms. The purpose of a miracle is to shock and stop the mind, not to give it more grist to process. To feel the impulse to "explain" a miracle is to be blind to its revelation, its function, which is to trigger an awakening to oneself, an awakening to the transcendent, the awakening of the divine to itself in us. To theorize about the eclipse at the Crucifixion is itself an eclipse or Crucifixion: to think about revelation, instead of seeing what is revealed, is a failure to recognize or know Christ. The self-revelation/self-eclipse of the divine, like the self-eclipse of the light of the sun at the Crucifixion, is a principle or event that transcends all names, forms, thoughts, concepts, philosophies, languages, and cultures: it is universal, no less present and immediate to the Spaniards and to the Indians than to the Jews (101–102).[26]

We may conclude that without their egos and wandering minds, all seekers of truth would come to the same revelation: either they would not argue, or they would fall into silence. The ground of being reveals itself only to those who sacrifice their attachment to themselves in its pursuit; the others damn themselves and their followers by chattering *about* salvation, feeding their flocks with wind (106–108). "Christ did not say to his apostles, 'Go, and preach idle chatter to the world' " (*Non disse Cristo al suo primo convento: / "Andate, e predicate al mondo ciance"* [109–110]). Instead he gave them a "true foundation" (*verace fondamento*), so that nothing more or less came from their mouths than served to ignite faith: they relied only on the Good News, on the Gospel message itself, for the defense of truth and the defeat of ignorance (*e quel tanto sonò ne le sue guance, / sì ch'a pugnar per accender la fede / de l'Evangelio fero scudo e lance* [112–114]). The Gospel message is eternal life won through self-sacrifice and divine grace; the "true foundation" of that message is Christ Himself: Incarnation, Crucifixion, and Resurrection. That message has been trivialized into *ciance*: the people have been misled into thinking that salvation can be won through words, or purchased as empty indulgences with counterfeit money (*moneta sanza conio* [115–126]). No one teaches, as the martyred apostles and early popes taught, through the true foundation of their own example, that the cost of salvation is the attachment to mortal life itself (*Pd* 27.40–45, 29.91–92).

After this "digression," on the threshold of the Empyrean, Beatrice tells Dante to "turn his eyes back to the true road" (*Ma perché siam digressi assai, ritorci / li occhi oramai verso la dritta strada* [127–128]; she is evoking the "one path" philosophers fail to follow (85–86), as well as the *diritta via* lost in the *selva* of matter and multiplicity in the first lines of the *Comedy*. Beatrice is redirecting Dante's sight back to the angels, and once more she opposes concepts and speech to seeing. She says of the angels:

> Questa natura sì oltre s'ingrada
> in numero, che mai non fu loquela
> né concetto mortal che tanto vada;
>   e se tu guardi quel che si revela
> per Danïel, vedrai che 'n sue migliaia
> determinato numero si cela.[27]   (*Pd* 29.130–135)

The power of self-multiplication or self-giving of *what is* cannot be grasped by thought or language: to argue or think about the number of angels is another manifestation of ignorance and blindness. To read Daniel's words as intending to refer to one number instead of another is to misread the message of Scripture, to miss what that passage reveals. What the passage reveals can however be *seen* ("if you look at what is revealed by Daniel, you will see . . ." [133–134]). Those who have eyes to see, those who (with the pilgrim) have followed the one path toward self-knowledge and now stand on the threshold of the Empyrean, will see in Daniel's indeterminate number of angels the height and breadth, the sublime majesty and generosity, the self-multiplication and self-reflection—of which the reader's intelligence is itself a ray—of the dimensionless and indivisible eternal power:

> Vedi l'eccelso omai e la larghezza
> de l'etterno valor, poscia che tanti
> speculi fatti s'ha in che si spezza,
>   uno manendo in sé come davanti.[28]   (*Pd* 29.142–145)

Argo

In *Paradiso* 33 Dante repeatedly tries to make the subject of all experience (what sees) into an object of experience (what is seen): he seeks to bring Intellect-Being itself into the realm of attribute, the realm of things that can be remembered. What he is really doing, of course, is underlining the chasm between the two, the utter ineffability of the transcendent. What can be remembered is what can be seen; the power to see cannot be remembered, nor can it be forgotten, though it may be blinded to itself. Dante sums up his defeat in one of the richest similes of the *Comedy*:

> Un punto solo m'è maggior letargo
> che venticinque secoli a la 'mpresa
> che fé Nettuno ammirar l'ombra d'Argo.[29]   (*Pd* 33.94–96)

The *punto* is again the focal point of self-awareness that first appeared in the *Primo Mobile*, "conquering" Dante. Gazing into the divine light, Dante has just conjoined his power of sight with the divine (*i' giunsi / l'aspetto mio col valore infinito* [80–81]), penetrating with his sight so far into the divine light that he has consummated/consumed his individual sight or point of view in it (*Oh abbondante grazia ond' io presunsi / ficcar lo viso per la luce etterna, / tanto che la veduta vi consunsi!* [82–84]), so that he sees all substances and accidents, "what is unfolded as the universe," as one in that light (85–90). Just after the simile, Dante says that his "mind, all rapt [*sospesa*], was gazing fixed, motionless and intent, ever more enkindled in its gazing" (*Così la mente mia, tutta sospesa, / mirava fissa, immobile e attenta, / e sempre di mirar faceasi accesa* [97–99]). Through this *punto* of ever-intensifying absorption, intellect turned fully upon itself passes over into the ground of all being: the mind is perfectly withdrawn or suspended (*sospesa*) from the re-reflection of Intellect-Being that is space and time. Hence it is an "experience" that has no extension in time, either long or short, and no location or spatial dimension (attributes). It is the self-experience of the source of space and time, unmeasurable in space or time.

Like the exordium of *Paradiso* 29, the *Argo* simile balances the dimensionless source or ground of all experience against the vast dimensions of its self-manifestation or self-expression as space and time. Dante balances the *punto* of divine self-awareness against the gigantic scope of its quest, when it has reflected as a finite human intelligence and identified itself with spatiotemporal attributes, to seek itself and reawaken to itself. As so often in Dante, the human intelligence's quest for understanding is represented by a small vessel navigating the ocean of being, which is also the space-time continuum in all its modifications. In medieval chronicles, the *Argo* was emblematically the first ship, and the *Argo*'s voyage emblematically the first human quest or enterprise. The twenty-five centuries since the *impresa* of Jason and the Argonauts represent the entire historical span of the human quest for understanding up to Dante's time: the sum of human aspiration in history. Dante balances all of human aspiration in time and space against the dimensionless, extensionless *punto* of self-knowledge, which is both the goal of that aspiration and its source. It is the equilibrium of the *Comedy* itself, which—on the pivot of the *Primo Mobile*—balances the Empyrean (the *punto* of self-knowledge of the concluding cantos of the *Paradiso*) against the entirety of human experience in space and time: the rest of the *Comedy*. As Robert Hollander has observed, Dante's voyage, which the *Paradiso* insistently links to Jason's (most overtly in the first cantos and here in the last), is the other terminus of the history of quest that began with Jason; at the center of that history, bracketed by thirteen centuries on either side, is the Incarnation.[30]

The shadow or trace (*ombra*) cast on the ocean of being by the human quest for understanding, by intellect's quest to return to itself, are the forms of myth (*Argo*): the images of religion, mythology, art, and poetry. Those images endure through history (*venticinque secoli*) because, like the *Comedy*'s Beatrice, they bewitch the mind: through them intellect glimpses and focuses on itself and begins to pursue and feed on itself, ultimately to awaken to its own transcendence. Thus Jason and his deeds are remembered in vivid detail after twenty-five centuries, while the experience of the goal itself, the reflexive self-seeing of the *punto*, occurs out of space and time, leaving no trace, no form, nothing to remember. The experience of the *punto* is an ecstatic suspension from or oblivion of all thought, image, and attribute, hence its "lethargy" or "unwillingness" (*letargo*) to be brought into memory, into the realm of the finite.

Neptune "marvels" (*ammirar*) at the *Argo*'s shadow. Indeed it is singular that a finite embodied intelligence in space-time should navigate the ocean of being in the quest for understanding: it is the mystery of creation. The mystery is that Intellect-Being should voluntarily reflect or alienate itself from itself as attribute and identity, through which it casts a shadow on itself, the restlessness of thirst or desire or "otherness," while yet it lovingly sustains and guides itself back to itself, as Neptune protects and supports the *Argo*. When Intellect reflected in space-time as human intelligence finally reaches itself (its source), following its own guideposts—the enduring forms of revelation, religion, myth, and poetry—it becomes absorbed in itself, love feeding on love, until in its perfect self-knowledge it awakens to the collapse of all reality into a dimensionless burning point of love, being, awareness, and bliss. Of that point, nothing can be said; one can only see it, which is to be it.

Conclusion

Is Dante Telling the Truth?

Dante's *Comedy* is built on the principle that when the individual subject of experience, having shed the *scoglio* or slough (*Pg* 2.122–123) of the exclusive self-identification with the finite, fully awakens to itself, it finds itself in the Empyrean, knowing itself as (one with) the awareness-actuality-being-love that—since it is nothing in itself—is not *in* the world, but rather *contains* the world. One could argue—in Dante's time it would have taken little argument—that this principle, variously expressed and conceived, is the foundation and life of all philosophy, spirituality, art, and meaning; experienced as a transformation of understanding and behavior, it is revelation. The essential insight that underlies the principle is that the individual subject of experience, though it may be "in" the world, is ultimately not part of the world: it is not simply a thing. The mind, as a collection of thoughts and ideas, and the finite self and individuality (the human being or body or soul), are all part of the world and can be described; the metaphysical subject, the source and ground of mind or soul, of all thought and perception, is not a thing, not part of the world: of that ground, nothing can be said. The "metaphysical subject" corresponds to what we have called the extensionless point of awareness: the point through which Bonaventure said one is "totally transferred and transformed into God," through which the ultimate attributeless subject of experience reveals itself as oneself and as the ground of all reality. In the *Comedy* the limit of the world, and thus of all attribute, is the *Primo Mobile*, the horizon between creation and creator, between the world and its ground: it is the "boundary" that "only one who encompasses it can understand" (*quel precinto / colui che 'l cinge solamente intende*) [*Pd* 27.113–114]). One may describe everything that is seen, but not what is ultimately doing the seeing.

The metaphysical "I" (the "I AM" revealed to Moses) is the attributeless, "transparent" foundation of the world, one with the world but radically distinct from it, as (to use a Wittgensteinian, and perhaps also Dantean, image) the seeing eye is one with its visual field, and yet is not contained in that field but lies outside it.[1]

The Limit of the World

Everything except the subject is unnecessary and contingent, the key notions that underlie the Christian understanding of the world as "created." Thus value or meaning (aesthetic, ethical, moral, or spiritual) cannot be grounded in the attributes of the world, or it would be contingent and arbitrary: it would not be value or meaning. It must be grounded in non-contingency and thus must lie outside the world, in the ultimate subject of experience, of which nothing can be said. That meaning or value cannot derive from the world itself, but can only manifest itself by "taking on" and "sacrificing" finite form, is the very foundation of medieval thought, and it is the foundation of Dante's poetics, which have thus variously been called "incarnational" or "equinoctial," a poetics of "conversion," "martyrdom," "crucifixion," or "transfiguration," which we (using Dante's own image in the *Primo Mobile*) have analyzed as a poetics of sunrises and sunsets, of self-eclipse and self-revelation.[2]

In a medieval context, meaning or value must thus be grounded in the transcendent, not the contingent. Any meaning recognized in the contingent and ephemeral—in the world—must be grounded in the non-contingent and transcendent, in Dante's Empyrean, so to speak. Christianity calls such self-revelation of meaning (of truth or being) in the finite the "Word," or "Christ." It is another way of saying, as we did in chapter 3, that for the medieval understanding, the world is a long string of zeros, of no meaning in itself, unless one puts a "1" in front of it, endowing it with incalculable value and significance. That "1" is the "metaphysical subject" or ground of experience, which the Western tradition has variously called Being, Intellect, the One, the act of existence, pure Form, God, the Creator, or "the thought that thinks itself." The transcendent subject manifests or experiences itself in the world as value: beauty, truth, love, bliss, and goodness, or, to use Dante's key term, *dolcezza*, sweetness, the experience of the loving subsumption (not cancellation!) of all limitation and identity into infinity and unity. In poetry, this sweetness or beauty is the dissolution of finite reference as words become revelatory, become music.[3]

Pace Dante's Ulysses, who in fact ends up in Hell, understanding cannot come from yet a little more worldly experience or scientific exploration. The mystery of life is the mystery of the world's (and one's own) *being*, the mystery probed by Christianity through the concept of creation. The world itself cannot resolve the mystery of its own being, which is precisely why the pilgrim Dante travels from within to beyond space-time and looks back, on the threshold of the *Primo Mobile*, to see the world as a limited whole, from the outside, so to speak. In Christian terms, it is to see the world as created (ontologically not self-sufficient), and from the perspective of a creator (non-contingency, an "outside" the world): in a medieval context, such a perspective alone can lead to understanding, alone preserves meaning, alone addresses the mystery or the "mystical" that drives the human quest for understanding. Language, thought, and propositions can all express the structure and articulation of reality, but they can say nothing about the subject of experience itself, because it is not part of that structure; there is nothing to say about it. The non-contingent subject—the limit of the world, the foundation of experience, the transcendent or "higher," the metaphysical "I" reflected in each "I"—without which the world has no meaning, indeed no existence, cannot be put into words; it can only reveal itself; else it would be simply another thing in the world.[4]

Understood within its own context, the purpose of the *Comedy* is to trace the path toward, and to trigger, understanding/revelation, the awakening of the subject of all experience to itself in us. Since both the path and the goal are practical—they consist in a change of life, experience, and vision, in the dissolution of the ego—the *Letter to Cangrande* acutely insists that the aim of the *Comedy* is practical (moral), not speculative, and that if the *Comedy* occasionally treats questions "in the form proper to speculative philosophy . . . it is not for the sake of speculation, but for a practical purpose" (*si in aliquo loco . . . pertractatur ad modum speculativi negotii, hoc non est gratia speculativi negotii, sed gratia operis* [40–41]). The point of the *Comedy* is that understanding *is* practical. It must not be confused with anything that can be thought or taught, with any "doctrine" or "belief." Understanding-happiness-salvation, for Dante, is not a set of ideas; it is to have experienced the true nature and foundation of reality, to know it as oneself, and thus to live it. This is the foundation of ethics, and of all political and social reform: such experience alone is capable of changing, rather than just temporarily suppressing, human behavior. The *Comedy* tells us that there is no path to understanding, happiness, or immortality that does not go through self-sacrifice, through the death to blind self-interest that is an awakening to love, to freedom, to the infinite in and as the finite: to Christ.[5]

The preceding chapters have suggested that although—from a medieval point of view—no metaphysical picture or "philosophy" can itself constitute or deliver understanding (enlightenment, revelation, salvation), a metaphysics that equates Intellect and Being and is thus implicitly non-materialistic and non-dualistic may not hinder, and may even (as in the case of Augustine) constitute fertile ground for, the germination of understanding (conversion). This is the case of Platonic, Aristotelian, and medieval philosophy, whose underlying principle may be expressed in four words: no mind, no matter. *Forma dat esse materiae*, form gives being to matter, and pure Form is pure Intellect or Being. Matter is ontologically dependent upon Intellect (consciousness or awareness), but Intellect is self-subsistent, because it is nothing in itself, it is the act of being. In more or less rigorous and consistent guises, this principle grounds the thought of virtually every Western philosopher between the pre-Socratics and the trio of Gassendi, Hobbes, and Descartes, a span of two thousand years. To realize the distance that separates us from the *Comedy*'s own metaphysical framework, we need only observe that the principle *No mind, no matter* has essentially been reversed in the modern worldview, whose implicit metaphysical picture could perhaps be described as a materialistic psychophysical dualism or late existentialism descended from the Enlightenment. Like every materialist movement of thought, the materialism and empiricism inaugurated by the Enlightenment was a necessary reaction to the degeneration of philosophical and spiritual inquiry into religious dogma (a disguise for political tyranny) and into unquestioned, and thus uncomprehended, philosophical "doctrines." Historically, such reactions have not dominated long once they have cleared the ground: one thinks of the Epicureans in the West, or the Cārvāka in Indian philosophy. Even in our own time, materialist and empiricist assumptions are being strained by advances in physics, and by a renewed thirst for meaning and transcendence. The ground-clearing has however also been beneficial to readers of Dante, who are now less likely than their predecessors to assume that they can understand the *Comedy* simply because they are familiar with Christian, or Scholastic, "doctrine."[6]

In both Western and Eastern thought, the (non-materialistic) non-duality implicit in the underlying principle *No mind, no matter* is usually more or less qualified, or rather disguised, by dualistic elements. Within Christian thought, this is principally the dualism Creator/creation, God/soul, or form/matter. Those who regard Christianity as irreducibly dualistic forget that the second term of each of these pairs has no being apart from the first. The mystical import of the Incarnation and the Trinity is that each of these dualities, so real to human conceptual understanding, is ultimately not two, though they are not the same (non-duality must not be confused with "monism," which is usually, although not always, non-duality misunderstood). Indeed, like Christianity, Vedic non-duality too embraces dualism as one of its guises. Even the strictest of all non-dualistic philosophical traditions, Śaṅkarācārya's Advaita ("not-dual") Vedanta, allows the concept of Īśvara, the Absolute determined as a personal god or object of adoration. This concept springs from the realization that *in fact* understanding comes with the gradual surrender of the individual ego and will to a self-subsistent reality that must be conceived as "other" as long as the exclusive identification with the finite endures. Śaṅkara's system is but one of the Vedantic traditions; Madhva and Rāmānuja, the other principal commentators on the great synopsis of Vedic revelation, the *Brahmasūtra* of Bādarāyana, explain it with a dualistic or qualifiedly dualistic terminology almost identical to that of the main currents of Christian thought. The truth is that what has been said of Indian philosophy applies equally to medieval Christian thought: it "believes that reality is *ultimately* one and *ultimately* spiritual." If the *Comedy* has a philosophical or theological foundation and "message," that is it.[7]

It is only natural that non-duality should be expressed in dualistic terminology and imagery. It can be expressed in no other terms. Terms such as *matter, time, intellect, I,* and *God* denote *things,* to the common understanding. As long as human consciousness has a particular *veduta,* or point of view, it experiences itself as other than the ultimate ontological principle and thus cannot recognize its identity with its own experience. This dualism, like that between the pilgrim Dante and Beatrice, or between the aspirant and the divine, is an inescapable stage, and a usually insurmountable obstacle, in the progress toward understanding (the "vision of God"). Indeed Aquinas thought, at least for a time, that in this life one could not experience Intellect-Being in itself.

The result is that the understanding/revelation that underlies and motivates the formulas of non-dualistic philosophical-spiritual traditions is easily obscured and in danger of being lost. Instead of revealing truth, those formulas end up entombing it. This has already happened whenever revelation has turned into a set of (dualistic) doctrines that are familiar to all, but whose radical import is understood, experienced, and lived by almost none. Dante felt this was the case in his time: it is the world he portrays. The wisdom-seeking Ulysses of the *Comedy* is asleep to himself, as is the passionate and ingenuous Francesca. So are all the churchmen and philosophers who think that truth is something that can be taught, one set of ideas and doctrines (*dottrina*) to be acquired instead of another. So are all the "believers" who imagine that "eternal life" is compatible with their possessive instinct (*cupidigia*) and unreflecting physicalism (the implicit assumption that the physical world is now self-subsistent, even if it was once "created," whatever that could mean). Dante celebrates Saint Francis and Saint Dominic as defenders of the truth not because they taught again truths already known to all, but because—from his point of view—they *saw* the truth, the irreducible reality in which all things and thoughts consist, and they lived and spoke grounded in their direct experience of it. For Dante *that* is what it means to "defend" truth.

Since the Enlightenment, Western Christianity has come to call "mysticism" the texts in which the non-duality implicit in the tradition of Christian thought is more apparent. (That such a term came to seem necessary is a mark of the new unintelligibility and marginalization of these texts: they were no longer seen as the experiential core of the tradition.) Yet that non-duality is foundational: Augustine, for example, is the Christian philosopher who perhaps most emphasizes the essential difference between created and uncreated being, between man and God. He is also one of the greatest of Christian mystics, who taught his heirs that God, as the being of all finite being, can be known, that is, experienced directly, only by seeking within oneself; God cannot be known as "other." Being cannot be an object of knowledge, because it is the ultimate subject of all experience. This is simply, again, non-duality: if in the end there are not two self-subsistent principles in the world, to know the final ontological reality is to experience oneself as that reality. To see God is to see the power to see that is God: it is to see *as* God. In Christian terms it is to become deiform, assimilated to an angelic intelligence. To know God is, as the inscription on the great temple of Apollo at Delphi commanded, to know oneself.[8]

Revelation is thus not only a historical event, although for Christianity it is anchored and embodied in a single historical event, of which every awakening to God is an image, a parallel historical event. To awaken to the transcendent (in oneself) is to receive Christ's message, to know Christ; it could happen either before or after the life of Christ, whether or not one had ever heard that name. For Dante, no one reaches the Empyrean who does not believe in Christ, either before or after His life and Crucifixion (*Pd* 19.103–105, 32.22–27). What is at first sight startling is that Dante's blessed are divided *equally* between those who lived before Christ and those who lived after: *Or mira l'alto proveder divino: / ché l'uno e l'altro aspetto de la fede / igualmente empierà questo giardino* ("Now gaze in wonder on the depth of divine providing: that one and the other perspective of faith shall fill this garden equally" [32.37–39]). In other words, salvation is not more available or readily won if one knows of the historical Jesus, His life and His teachings, than if one does not. To know *about* Christ is not to *know* Christ; many who call on Christ are farther from Him than others who have never heard the name (19.106–114). For Dante the advent of Christ is the fulcrum of history and of the cosmos, but not in the sense that those who lived before Christ are damned and only those who lived after can be saved: that would reduce Christ's revelation to triviality. It is the fulcrum because for Dante the touchstone of salvation, and the resolution of the mystery of life, consists in the capacity to *recognize* Christ, which means either to be awake to (to expect), or to awaken to, the revelation of the infinite in the finite, the divine in the human, that is Christ. It is to know that one's being and freedom depend upon the loving self-sacrifice of the self-subsistent to and as the contingent, which triggers the loving self-sacrifice of the contingent to and as the self-subsistent: it is to know Christ in and as oneself. Hence the line of demarcation that divides Dante's Empyrean rose between "the one and the other perspective of faith" also unites them. That line culminates at one end in Mary, who, as the last to recognize and accept Christ before His birth, brought Him into the world, and at the other in John the Baptist, who, by recognizing and accepting Christ after His birth, was the first to reveal Him to others (*Pd* 32.28–33). Yet again, Dante is telling us that to know Christ is not to profess a set of beliefs and doctrines. Almost everyone in Dante's time did that.

Giorgio Padoan points out that the *Letter to Cangrande* defends the reality of the poet's transcendent experience by comparing it to biblical examples (Paul's *raptus*, the disciples' presence at the Transfiguration, Ezekiel's vision), and by referring the reader to experiences described by Richard of St. Victor, Augustine, and Saint Bernard. He also notes that the *Letter* cites Richard's "book on contemplation" (probably the *Beniamin maior*), whose conspicuous aim is to theorize such transcendent experience as a "possibility always and continuously open to humanity." Étienne Gilson links the pilgrim's final vision to those described by Bonaventure, whose point again is that such experience is available to all. Padoan makes another important observation: the *Letter* does not say that the aim of the *Comedy* is to persuade those who live in sin to repent, as Dante's son Pietro would have it, but rather to bring back *all* humanity (*viventes in hac vita*) to the road lost by its leaders, delivering humanity from slavery into freedom, from Egypt to Jerusalem. In other words, the *Letter* conceives the *Comedy*'s aim as the redemption of all humanity, by leading it to the direct experience of the divine. (Who but the author of the *Comedy* would make such a claim for it?) Dante's prophetic urgency should be understood in this light: he is not interested in indoctrination, in restating religious or philosophical beliefs his contemporaries could already recite only too well by rote. His contemporaries, and especially the leaders of the church, were simply using those doctrines to make their slumber more comfortable. Dante aimed to awaken them, at any cost to himself and to their illusions.[9]

Nardi suggested that Dante is the harbinger, and cisalpine counterpart, of the great flowering of fourteenth- and fifteenth-century German mysticism. Philosophically, and perhaps temperamentally too, Dante's nearest kinsman may be Meister Eckhart, his exact contemporary (1260–1327). Both had the unconventional audacity and fearless self-assurance of those who seem to speak from some direct experience of truth, some self-identification with the nothingness that disguises/reveals itself as all things. What has been said of Eckhart might be said of Dante too: he "was a breaker of shells, not as an iconoclast breaks them, but as life breaks its shells by its own resurgent power"; as Eckhart himself says, "If you want the kernel, you must break the shell." As breakers of shells, both Dante and Eckhart were perceived by ecclesiastical authority as threatening or subversive. The testimony of those who see does not sit comfortably with the apparatus of ideas, conventions, and power structures that in time, in any religious tradition, come to entomb revelation, if it is not constantly renewed, re-revealed, reexperienced. In the fourteenth century Eckhart was condemned; the *Comedy* was banned by the Dominicans and escaped the *Monarchia*'s inquisitorial condemnation only because it was written in the vernacular and could disguise itself as a poetic fiction. This is perhaps why the *Letter to Cangrande* (and Dante's son Pietro, in the prologue to his commentary) says that the literal sense of the *Comedy*, which claims to reveal "the state of souls after death" (a phrase repeated verbatim in thirteenth- and fourteenth-century inquisitorial manuals), is "poetic and fictive" (8–9); if taken as some kind of true or revealing vision—which the poem itself insists it is— the *Comedy* could not have escaped condemnation. That in our time the *Comedy* (at least in Italy) is the glory of Catholic literature does not mean that it is better understood, but probably that it is *less* understood: its revelatory challenge has been defused and accommodated within convention and accepted ideas.[10]

Theologus *and* Poeta

Augustine's spiritual-intellectual trajectory, as he himself traces it (principally in the *Confessions*), moves from an infatuation with language in itself, represented by rhetoric and the hypnotic and sensual lure of poets' fables, through a conversion (in an act of reading) that is a renunciation of that infatuation, now seen as a perversion of intelligence and language through sensory desire and self-centeredness, arriving ultimately to feed on the "circumcised" Word of Scripture, on language that is not fable or fiction or an end in itself, but is rather, like Christ, an Incarnation of the Word, a soul of divinity or spirit given body by the letter of the text. That Scripture is the body or veil of spirit does not mean that some passages of Scripture are not figurative or allegorical even in their literal sense; it does mean that the letter of Scripture is not empty, worldly motivated imagining, not language contaminated by ego and desire, by a finite point of view. Indeed the attempt to read figurative passages of Scripture literally, blind to what they signify, is the death of the soul itself; it is to turn oneself from a human into an animal, not unlike Francesca reading the prose Lancelot. Since in Scripture letter and spirit are related as body to soul, to read only literally is to read carnally, not to see the divine in or through the finite, to see only externally into law and ritual, and not inwardly into revelation and life, to be nourished only by an external rain, without being directed by it to the internal fountain. It is a failure of self-knowledge, a failure to receive or awaken to Christ. As Paul reiterated, in a theme that determined a thousand years of meditation on reading, "the letter brings death, but the spirit brings life."[11]

Poets (and many of the "writers of the Holy Spirit" were poets or used poetic techniques) can write figuratively or metaphorically, weaving fictions that allegorically denote other meanings, but in such allegories (as in the "allegory of poets") a finite ego or intelligence is veiling an intended meaning in a poetic invention; the invention gives way to what it denotes, which can be autonomously designated, as in a personification (like Lady Philosophy in the *Convivio*, or Lady Poverty in *Paradiso* 11). Here mere poetic (imaginative) allegorizing stops, and signifying ends; if, however, the poet is divinely inspired, a writer of Scripture, we have only just reached the true literal sense (what the author intends). Such an inspired text will typically, by the canons of medieval exegesis (laid out by Dante in *Convivio* 2.1.2–8 as the "allegory of the theologians"), have three further dimensions of meaning beyond this literal sense: an allegorical, spiritual, or typological sense; a moral or tropological sense; an anagogical, mystical, or revelatory sense. A pervasive medieval ditty explains these senses: *Littera gesta docet, quid credas allegoria, / Moralis quid agas, quo tendas anagogia* ("The letter teaches events [deeds], allegory what you should believe, the moral sense what you should do, anagogy what you should aim for"). In other words, the literal sense of an inspired text is, broadly conceived, *historia*, the actual events of sacred history, the unfolding of divine revelation in the world, and clearly distinguished from *fabula*, the inventions of secular poets. In those sacred events, which normally constitute the literal sense of an inspired text, one may discover a spiritual meaning, or lesson of faith, which is often more fully revealed through an analogous subsequent (or prior) event of sacred history, paradigmatically the life of Christ; thus, for example, many events of the Old Testament "typologically" foreshadow or "figure" events to come in the New Testament. This is the allegorical, spiritual, figural, or typological meaning. From the events of sacred history one may also draw precise moral lessons, practical guidelines for action; this is the moral or tropological sense. Finally, the events point to an ultimate revelation or unveiling to come, in which the fullness of their meaning will be disclosed: this is the anagogical meaning (*anagogein* means "to lead upward" or "to launch a ship"). Unlike the other three senses of Scripture, this meaning or revelation cannot be put into words: it is the *sovrasenso* ("oversense," or meaning "beyond the senses" [*Cv* 2.1.7]), which transcends all thought, history, and language. It is usually indicated as the union of the soul with God, the happiness of heaven, the hope of future blessedness, the life of eternal glory, the salvation of the soul, the second coming, God's providential plan, or, to use Dante's own phrase in the *Convivio* (2.1.7), *le superne cose de l'etternal gloria* ("the supernal things of eternal glory"). It is the ultimate self-disclosure of the Spirit embodied in the letter of Scripture, in the events of sacred history.[12]

Dante's son Pietro, like other early commentators, sought to "deny the undeniable": to convince readers that a poem whose world they could not help treating as real, as *historia*, was really all a fiction. This was intended to save Dante from charges of heresy (which by law would have ruined Pietro too), for it was only too evident that the claim that he had penetrated the secrets of God, that he was another writer of the Holy Spirit, was implicit (when not explicit) in Dante's enterprise. The task of the commentators was more arduous in face of what Teodolinda Barolini has called the *Comedy*'s "ubiquitous truth claims," which aim at placing the *Comedy* on the same ontological footing as physical reality and as Scripture. Padoan underlines the audacity of these claims in a medieval context and concludes that to "minimize or deny all this means giving up the attempt to understand why Dante could call his poem 'holy' [*sacro*]; it means running the risk of a total misunderstanding of the *Comedy*."[13]

We have seen that the traditional ecclesiastical view of poetry was clear enough: to quote Robert Hollander, "secular literary activity was at the very best both suspect and limited in its possibilities." In no case did it have access to the truths of theology; any truth it did contain was restricted and approximate. As Hollander summarizes the point, "poets were and are liars." Dante's inversion of this attack, while part of a medieval tradition oᶠ poetic self-defense and of a late-medieval *translatio auctoritatis*, a transference of authority to the vernacular and secular, is breathtaking in its audacity: "I, poet, am the voice of truth, my fantastic narrative (Geryon and lizard-thieves included) reveals truth, is true, and will live forever in the world; you, corrupt clergy, false custodians of the Word which *I* reveal, are liars: you conceal, distort, disguise, eclipse truth, and you will be swept away by the *fortuna* to come, in the wake of truth's self-defense (of which my *Comedy* is the first thunderbolt)."[14]

Dante's challenge was designed to offend everybody. In fact, from his day to ours, everyone has had an interest in ignoring it or defusing it: those who wanted to defend the *Comedy* from the church's attack; those who wanted to defend the church from the *Comedy*'s attack; the defenders of the church's privileged position as sole dispenser of revealed truth; those who wanted to appropriate the *Comedy* as a voice of the church; the lovers of secular literature, who, as the new humanism took hold, gloried more and more in the fantastic nature of poetry; those whose traits and actions were attacked by the *Comedy* (almost everyone); and those who were made uncomfortable by the idea that the *Comedy* has any "message" or revelation at all, any implicit or explicit challenge to their own understanding or life. It took only a few years, and the arrival of the Renaissance, to defuse the "prophetic" urgency of the *Comedy* and reduce it to poetic fancy. In Padoan's words, "Between Dante the prophet and Dante the poet, it was the second who belonged to the future; but thus re-dimensioned, he was already no longer the true Dante."[15]

As Barolini has observed, the sleeping dog of Dante's truth-claims lay largely undisturbed for six centuries until Bruno Nardi kicked it rudely in 1941 in an essay called "Dante profeta." Nardi's fundamental point is that Dante considered the *Comedy* not "poetic fiction" or "literary artifice," but the account of a "true prophetic vision" (285), and that to refuse or fail to accept this is to misunderstand Dante's *poema sacro* (295). Nardi concludes that Dante "treats the objects of his vision as reality," not as a *bella menzogna* (311), not as a beautiful lie to "represent a moral idea" (316): Dante believed he saw Hell, Purgatory, and Paradise "as they truly are in reality" (308).[16]

Nardi's formulations raise a problem that persists in much discussion about how the "allegory of theologians" requires us to treat the literal level of Dante's poem as "true," as *historia*: he gives no coherent account of what that claim comes to, what it is asserting. We must remember that in medieval metaphysics, the human intellect, when dissociated from the body (as in prophetic dreams or visions), is assimilated to angelic intelligence, which means that finite form can arise within it without a *mezzo* (duality), without the interposition of the bodily senses; such form is not less real than the physical world.[17] What makes such a vision "real" or "true"? How is it related to physical reality? In what sense is the spatiotemporal world, that great modern guarantor of truth-claims, itself true or real? What the *Comedy* is claiming by claiming to be true or real is by no means obvious. Indeed, that is the point of the poem.

One thing is clear: one cannot reduce such claims to some notion of objectively reporting prior spatiotemporal events. As the *Comedy*'s cosmology demonstrates, such events or things, taken in themselves, are at the opposite extreme from truth or being: they are *brevi contingenze*, brief contingencies. Matter in the medieval world is potentiality, an extreme qualification of being into ephemerality, limitation, and contingency: insofar as a thing is material, it does *not* exist, is not true, and is not actual or real. To say that the modern Western world tends to see things differently is an understatement. As long as modern readers unproblematically identify reality or truth with *brevi contingenze*, the sublunar events or things that Dante calls *ultime potenze* (*Pd* 13.61–66), they will not fully penetrate the *Comedy*, its poetics, or its truth-claims. In medieval metaphysics, all determinate form, including the sensible world, is in some sense fiction: it is non-self-subsistent, a "new thing," and only partially, relatively, and contingently participates in, or manifests, truth, reality, or being.

The crucial principle is supplied to the Middle Ages by Aristotle and quoted in the *Letter to Cangrande* (14): *sicut res se habet ad esse, sic habet se ad veritatem* ("as a thing is related to being, so is it related to truth"). As the *Letter* explains (14–16), to be is not the same as to be this-or-that: a thing is true insofar as *what* it is (its essence) is not other than *that* it is (its being). The two are identical, of course, only in God, Intellect-Being itself. We could say, then, that in Dante's context a poetic narrative is true to the extent that it is "transparent to," not other than, *what is*. A narrative is true or real that embodies, mediates, or unveils the ultimate subject or ground of experience: this can only mean that through such a narrative, the divine, reflected in or as the intelligence of the reader, recognizes itself and awakens to itself. Thus the *Comedy* presents itself as the presenter (not representer) of God's own self-revelation through word and image, from transcribing God's own writing on the gate of Hell into *terza rima* (*If* 3.1–9), to transcribing God's purgatorial sculpture or "visible speaking" (whose first subject is His self-revelation or Incarnation in the world) into poetry (*Pg* 10.28–45, 94–96), to transcribing God's "sky-writing" in the Heaven of Jupiter—words written with things (individual souls), which become a visual image, which in turn speaks, revealing its message—into and as the *Comedy* itself (*Pd* 18.70–111, 19.7–148). The world, and every embodied intelligence, is simultaneously a sunrise and a sunset: creation simultaneously reveals and disguises, manifests and eclipses, pure Form or Being. Read with eyes that see, Scripture and the *Comedy* are meant to be, like Mary who gives birth to Christ, unambiguous sunrises, overpowering the sunset on the same horizon (*Pd* 31.118–120) to reveal the ground of reality. Such texts turn evening knowledge into morning knowledge; they free human intelligence bewitched by complete self-identification with the body, by the experience of the world as "other." As Dante will come to see it, this is the awakening to new life invoked in, but not delivered by, the *Vita Nova*; it is the awakening traced in the arduous journey of the *Comedy*.[18]

It is not surprising, then, that Dante's great definition of poetry in the *De vulgari eloquentia* makes no mention of content: *si . . . recte consideremus [poesis] nichil aliud est quam fictio rhetorica musicaque poita* ("if we consider correctly poetry is nothing but an invention or fiction composed through rhetoric and music"). Although poetry for Dante will normally have a subject matter and various possible interpretations, including allegorical meanings, it has no content, because its content is no thing. If a poem cannot bear anagogical interpretation (as presumably the poems of the *Vita Nova* and *Convivio*, whose "sense" Dante at least partially "opens" in prose, cannot), its "content" could be termed *dolcezza* or *armonia*; if it can (as in the *Comedy*), that content could be indicated as the ground and source of all things, of oneself. When Dante calls the forms that poetry gives to reality *fictio* (invention or fiction), he is not opposing them to, but aligning them with, the *brevi contingenze* that constitute human experience. Both are relatively unreal, contingent, ephemeral, and illusory, yet in a lyric poem both can communicate at least *dolcezza* or *armonia*, the intuition of infinity and unity in the multiple and particular (even if the result may be, as in Casella's song of *Purgatorio* 2, to mesmerize us and suspend our journey toward understanding); in a divinely inspired narrative that signifies with things and events as Scripture does, both *fictio* and *brevi contingenze* can be seen—by those who can see—to embody truth, to reveal truth. Forms that endure in time, like the myth/history of the Argonauts (to use Dante's own example), or Icarus, or Dante's own Geryon or Empyrean rose, share in—and in the hands of the inspired poet can reveal—being, at least as much as any ephemeral physical detail or event of our own lives or of our collective life, which is why Dante makes no distinction between history and myth. At least in principle, Dante's early and open-ended definition of poetry is not superseded by the "prophetic claims" of the *Comedy*; it is their foundation, the key to the poem's transcendent enterprise and truth-claims. There is no distinction between *theologus* and *poeta* in the *Comedy* because the *Comedy* has no content, no teaching or message that can be put into words, except as the *Comedy* itself. Understanding or revelation is not a set of ideas: it is to awaken to oneself, which is to encompass the world.[19]

Anagogy

The patristic exegetical tradition bequeathed to the Middle Ages a sense, variously interpreted, that Scripture is the Word Incarnate, spirit embodied in the letter, a soul of spiritual sense veiled or given form by a body of literal meaning. For Augustine as for Dante, language, as used by the center of desire (*cupidigia*) that is the individual ego, tends to become simply body, eclipsing soul: such language is the emblem of temporality, mortality, ephemerality, changeability; it is the instrument of narcissism, finite self-absorption, sensual untruth, sterile and fruitless virtuosity. To echo R. A. Shoaf's meditation on language as currency in Dante, instead of being exchanged for meaning, opening itself to the Other, language and image tainted by desire become fraudulent, falsified, a coin that usurps the place of reality and is greedily appropriated for its own sake as desire reified. It is the falsification of intellect, of the divine in the human (or perhaps, as Wittgenstein would say of most philosophy, it is the bewitching of intelligence by means of language). Such are the fables of poets, sensuous and hypnotic images of human desire obsessed with itself, a "dying *in* wanting," like Narcissus, instead of a "dying *to* wanting," like Paul (240). This is the realm of hypnotic and alluring untruth. But in the hands of the writers of the Holy Spirit (selfless love), of those who mirror reality as themselves without projecting self and desire into it, who are dead to self-interest and awakened to Christ, who open their mouths to praise and not to consume, language remains currency, figures and images that, though they necessarily obscure the light or soul (as the letter must always veil the spirit), yet "disfigure" and cancel themselves: they may be exchanged, cashed in, for what they promise. Such language is one with faith, with openness or expectation, a currency stamped with the image of Christ: in Shoaf's version of an ancient phrase, it "purchases invisibles with visibles" (88). Such language is true, reveals truth, mediates truth, gives form to truth, and embodies truth. In Augustinian terms, to communicate the Word in words is to mediate the eternal point or *now* of divine self-knowledge into the temporality of human language and experience, as soul or spirit uneclipsed by body or the letter. It is again Augustine's own experience of conversion through reading, and the precise inversion of Francesca's reading.[20]

To put it yet another way, in terms drawn from A. C. Charity: the letter of

Scripture is the story of the progressive self-disclosure of the divine in history, in human experience, in the world. The literal sense of Scripture is the account of the self-manifestation of the divine in things, in concrete experience; it is not simply words that seek to designate or describe the divine, allegorically or otherwise: Scripture signifies *in rebus*, not *in verbis*. (Wittgenstein would say that what is higher makes itself manifest in life and action and our use of language; it cannot itself be put into words.) The life of Christ, seen typologically as the fulfillment or transfiguration of history, an event that reveals the significance of every other event, also makes a claim on every other event: it reveals the role and ultimate aim of each particular, what it tends toward, its anagoge. This is to say that history, read scripturally or typologically as the self-disclosure of the divine, makes a transformative demand on us as part of history: we ourselves are called to be part of that self-disclosure. As Charity puts it, typology is not merely descriptive of parallels between sacred events; such events have an "afterlife," an application both in history as a whole, and specifically in each individual, in the present moment. That application or "sub-fulfillment" is not speculation or philosophy or beliefs; it is facts, things, events, as real and concrete as those of the literal sense of Scripture, as the world. In other words, the claim of history, or of a narrative that typologically discloses the meaning of history or human experience, can only be conversion, awakening, becoming what one is revealed to be, which is to conform one's life to Christ's. To use another Wittgensteinian phrase, Scripture seeks to prevent understanding unaccompanied by inner change. The phrase applies perfectly also to the *Comedy*.[21]

In the wake of Auerbach, Singleton, Charity, Hollander, Padoan, Mineo, and Sarolli, among others, it seems evident (though not all would agree) that the *Comedy* means to signify as the *Letter to Cangrande* says it does: by the "allegory of theologians," scripturally, typologically, and figurally.[22] This claim has much less to do with the application of fourfold allegory (which in fact the *Letter* does not attempt) than with the text's character, motivation, and authority. Based on my analysis of Dante's text and his philosophical context, one can conclude that in Dante's own understanding, the *Comedy* is not simply a poetic fable, although it is indeed in some sense a *fictio* or invention; the poem's literal sense is not ontologically deracinated and discardable, not simply a poetic cipher for doctrines, beliefs, or teachings that could be autonomously expressed (hence the *Letter to Cangrande* makes little attempt to express the spiritual and anagogical meaning in its own exegesis, or does it in banal clichés); the poem is instead grounded in history, the history of one, many, and all human beings, in the totality and individuality of human experience, which of course includes myth, art, literature, and all psychic life; the narrative discloses the sense of that history or experience typologically and Christically; its literal sense is thus presented as no less real than what it figurally signifies, both in the paradigmatic life of Christ and in the reader's; that literal sense, whether "the state of souls after death" or Dante's own emblematically transfigured biography, is a narrative that discloses the meaning of the events and things it recounts through projection into past and future history, both individual and

universal; this projection, through which history and the individual are unveiled to themselves as a disclosure of the transcendent in the contingent, is
meant to make a transformative claim on each reader and each age; this is to
say that by signifying with things, with the concreteness of experience, and not
simply with words, images, or ideas, the poem is meant to bear an anagogical
sense or thrust, which no philosophy, theology, or mere poetic invention could
bear, and which is one with the the practical, ethical claim the poem makes on
the reader; the author of the poem, therefore, is situating himself not as a finite
ego or intelligence, a voracious and distorting center of desire, but rather as
the prophetic voice of the seer, a selfless mirror of reality, awakened to Truth,
to the ground of all things, capable of being all and shedding all, a mouth that
praises and does not consume; in other words, the author is presenting himself as a scribe of the Holy Spirit, of selfless love, which is in fact what he says
he is.

As Charity observes, the typology of Scripture makes a claim on the reader
that must be answered, or rather is answered, in the reader's response, and
that response is either *yes* or *no*. Christ is a mirror to oneself; to ask Christ who
He is is meaningless, for the answer can only be, "Who do *you* say that I am?"
In the same way, the *Comedy*'s outrageous challenge—like that of Scripture—
enacts a response: whether the *Comedy* is what it would have us accept it to be
is in practice answered by each reader with *yes* or *no*; undecidedness, intellectual detachment, scholarly skepticism, "scientific objectivity," or an aesthetic
response that is not simultaneously ethical is of course *no*. The *Comedy*'s incarnational poetics reenact in the reader the moment of cosmic equilibrium
evoked in the *Primo Mobile* through the opening simile of *Paradiso* 29: within
the terms the *Comedy* has established, our acceptance or rejection of its authority, of its claim on us, is an acceptance or rejection of Christ, of ourselves;
it is to recognize or fail to recognize the ground of our own being. To accept
is itself conversion, sunrise, a self-recognition of the divine in us; it is a typological conformation of our life journey, through self-surrender and redemption, to that of the pilgrim, which in turn is typologically conformed to Christ's.
In other words, the *Comedy* mirrors us to ourselves and places us where we
place ourselves. It balances us on the pivot of the *Primo Mobile*: *yes* means we
have—or rather something in us (that is not a thing) has—recognized the
Empyrean as its home; *no* means we live with Francesca and Ulysses in the
flux of the ephemeral, that their world is our world, that we have lost the "1"
in front of the world's string of zeroes. In the same way, Augustine says, he
would know that Moses spoke the truth in Genesis not from Moses, but from
himself: "within me, in the innermost dwelling of my thought, Truth, neither
Hebrew nor Greek nor Latin nor barbarian in speech, without mouth or tongue
as instrument, without audible syllables, would say: 'He speaks the truth.' "[23]

We have said that in medieval interpretation only a text rooted in life,
history, and experience, a text that does not signify only with words, images,
and ideas, but with the fabric of life itself, can bear an anagogical sense, a
revelation that transcends thought and experience, a meaning that cannot be
put into words, a transformative claim on the future, that is, on each reader.

This study has shown that the anagogical meaning of such a text, the future and final self-disclosure of what has simultaneously veiled and unveiled itself in an "inspired" narrative of history and human experience, can be understood as the awakening of Intellect-Being-Love to itself, in the reader, as the ground and totality of all finite being, apart from which nothing is. It is to awaken to oneself as everything and nothing, as in time and out of time, as in the world and beyond it. It is the revelation the Christian tradition calls "Christ."

The anagogical import of the *Comedy* is thus the restoration and fulfillment of the original and "intended" condition of man, before he lost himself in the bewitching flux of multiplicity and change. This is why Adam says, in *Paradiso* 26 (133–138), that in Adam's original language, in the garden of Eden on Mount Purgatory, God named Himself/was named *I*, which is the root of *io* ("I," as well as "one"); as we saw in *Paradiso* 29, eternal love re-reflected itself to itself in finite intelligences so that it could say *Subsisto*, "I am." It is in fact how God was to name Himself to Moses too, on another mountain, Mount Sinai. Only later, says Adam, after the Fall, after the loss of Eden, and in the flux of ephemerality that submerges all things, including language and signs (124–132), did God's name become *El*, the "Other," "He," "That." Indeed, says Adam, human language is like *fronda / in ramo*, leaves on a tree, which come and go (137–138). Adam lost Eden by seeking himself—he himself was the "the apple created fully ripe" (91–92)—as "other" than himself, in the fronds of the tree of creation (64–66), thus trespassing the mark (117) or horizon that divides inside from outside, praise from *cupidigia*, selflessness from selfishness, morning from evening, self-knowledge from insatiable desire, eternal Awareness-Love from its reflection as finite form. The prophetic stance of the *Comedy* is one with its anagogical import; the poem's prophecies (*veltro, DXV, fortuna*) coincide to say that the divine cannot and will not permanently eclipse itself in the world and in human experience, but by its own nature must reawaken to itself, by whatever mechanism and in whatever time that awakening occurs. To deliver that message is itself to effect the awakening, to make others see what, or rather as, the prophet sees.[24]

From what has been said here, we can imagine that Dante would smile appreciatively at Singleton's famous phrase, "the fiction of the *Divine Comedy* is that it is not fiction," but he would answer: "you have not seen the point, the *punto*." The poem's poetics, its typological and anagogical thrust, the basis of its claim to prophetic truth and its claim on the reader, is grounded in its metaphysical ontology: in the self-experience of the subject of all experience, the awakening to what is not in the world, but lies outside it. The thrust of the *Comedy* is that its letter is ontologically continuous with Scripture, physical reality and history, while at the same time it *also* points to itself as artifice, representation, *fictio*, myth, a body or veiling of soul or spirit. Perhaps the most vivid example of this self-unmasking of the letter as fraudulent, as an eclipse or theft of what it reveals, in this most self-conscious of literary texts, is Dante's introduction of Geryon (*If* 16.124–132). Geryon is a *ver c'ha faccia di menzogna* ("a truth that has the face of a lie"), but Dante guarantees that he actually saw Geryon by swearing *per le note / di questa comedìa* ("by the notes of this comedy"). As Hollander has observed, Dante lays the veracity of the entire *Comedy* on the line to back up the veracity of this "poetic object that has every appearance of being a lie, a poet's fiction." This is appropriate, for, as Hollander points out, "if [Dante] did not actually see Geryon he did not actually see anyone or anything else." However this is not a trivial irony, an "authorial wink," as Hollander suggests, but a profound revelation of the nature of the poem and its import.[25]

Barolini's revision of Singleton's formula is exact: "the *Commedia* is a nonfalse error, a *non falso errore*, not a fiction that pretends to be true but a fiction that IS true." This is Dante's understanding of his own poem. It is also—and this is the fundamental point—his understanding of all finite reality, of all human experience: contingent form in time disguising and yet revealing (in the proper narrative) the timeless and dimensionless act of being in which it alone and entirely consists. This is also the nature of Scripture, which must "communicate" or "reveal" non-contingent self-awareness (Truth) through spatiotemporal contingencies (*Pd* 4.40–48). It is also—as embodied in an "inspired" narrative—the nature of myth, art, poetic invention, the imaginative and psychic life of humanity. An "accurate report of how things are in space-time," like the pseudo-concept "scientifically observable facts," would be simple fiction, body without soul, letter without spirit, zeros without a "1," contingent ephemera without meaning or being. It would be to exchange a picture of reality for reality. The *Comedy* is telling us that although all language, thought, image, and finite experience is (in relation to the ground of being) fraudulent, in the proper narrative—as in Scripture or the *Comedy* itself—it can also come to reveal what it eclipses, present what it steals away.[26]

Barolini has analyzed the narrative strategies through which "the *Commedia* makes narrative believers of us all" and how it is that the text forces us to "accept the possible world . . . that Dante has invented." She shows how Dante draws us into the *Comedy*'s frame of reference so deeply that we are unable to question the premises or assumptions of that world except on its own terms, which really amounts to a failure to recognize that there are any such assumptions at all. In light of our study, we can imagine that Barolini's "de-theologizing" exegesis would again make Dante smile, and this time he would answer, "Yes, but go further." The hypnosis or loss of perspective that makes us accept the *Comedy*'s world as real, that draws us into its hall of mirrors, is precisely what draws us into the hall of mirrors that is the sensible world, and makes us accept *it* as non-contingent and non-ephemeral, that is, as unqualifiedly "real." It is what makes us think of physical reality as a self-subsistent "thing" autonomous from our own being, and makes us consider ourselves ephemeral things within that world. The analysis Barolini has applied to the *Comedy* is the analysis the *Comedy* asks us to apply to *all* of our experience. The narrative techniques that force our assent to the *Comedy*'s "possible world" are not just tricks: they are what make illusion possible, what make finite experience coextensive with the field of our vision, so that we cannot see through it, around it, or beyond it to see our own seeing. They are what make the world "real" and God a concept or abstraction in that world. Like the world, the *Comedy* makes us accomplices in its fiction, so that we cannot "suspend our suspension of disbelief." The *Comedy* reveals the roots of our bewitchment by reenacting that bewitchment.[27]

How does one begin to see beyond the limit of the world, to awaken to oneself? The *Comedy*'s answer is: by assimilating as oneself, through poetic re-creation, the entire breadth of possible experience in space and time, as concrete, particular, inescapable reality. To reveal truth such poetry must be written and read by selfless love, as Augustine required, by an "I" willing to shed all in order to become all; only then will the narrative typologically point to and embody the self-disclosure of the ground of being in the world and become the account (cosmological, political, moral, artistic, psychological, spiritual) of an awakening—the narrator's and the reader's both—from the confining limits of that world. The narrative of the *Comedy* places all finite form on the same ontological level: ancient history, mythology, art, literary inventions, current events, Scripture, and personal experience. It is a relentless assault on the conventional boundary between reality and fiction; it annihilates the careful medieval distinction among *historia, argumentum,* and *fabula,* among what happened, what could have happened but did not, and what could not have happened. It fictionalizes historical characters and historicizes fictional characters until we can no longer say which is which. Having been led to experience the sense in which fiction is reality, the reader is thus simultaneously led, like the pilgrim, to experience the sense in which finite reality is fiction. The identification with the totality of possible experience, ontologically equalized, becomes an exercise of love, a de-petrification of the finite intelligence, which begins to dissolve its exclusive self-identification with a particular finite identity and its attachments. This expansion of love and understanding is the journey of moral transformation traced in the narrative, a journey of self-examination, of transfigurative suffering or self-sacrifice, of progressive surrender, and of contemplation. Philosophical-theological inquiry, fused as one with the moral journey and with poetic experience, dissolves conceptual illusion, the distortions in understanding that impede awakening; beauty, the substance of poetry itself (sweetness, harmony, music), suspends the mind from concepts, judgment, and fear to mediate an intimation of the infinite in the particular, to deliver the awakening shock of the transcendent, to focus the human thirst for freedom and being. Gradually gaining perspective, the subject of all experience, reflected as a finite power of awareness and love, begins to awaken to itself, ultimately to discover itself, on the threshold of the Empyrean, as an extensionless point, immune to and yet containing as itself all space and time, the horizon and nexus between contingency and self-subsistence. This is the sunrise of revelation on the horizon of the human soul through which one enters the Empyrean, fully free, and sees the entire cosmos as a limited whole, wholly contained within one's own being. It is to experience oneself as one thing, all things, and no thing, through the love that moves the sun and other stars.[28]

Epilogue

No Mind, No Matter

Medieval thought suggests that the idea that matter ontologically depends on intellect (consciousness) may be less incoherent than the idea that intellect depends on matter. There are a number of difficulties with materialism.

1. Materialism involves a naive notion of matter that cannot sustain analysis: as Aristotle saw clearly, any attempt to characterize matter is simply the description of a form that "matter" has assumed, not of matter itself.
2. No materialist, neither Empedocles, Epicurus, Gassendi, nor Descartes, has been able to account for such phenomena as consciousness, self-awareness, thought, volition, will, sensation, and emotion without introducing non-material principles into his system, such as God, intellect, or love.
3. It is difficult for materialism to provide a non-arbitrary answer to the question, "Why is there something rather than nothing?" In (non-materialistic) non-duality the distinction between something and nothing dissolves: they are not two.
4. The direct awareness of being conscious is the one non-contingent certainty of human experience, grounding both Aristotle's ontology and (in disguised form) Descartes's epistemology. But to pose a duality between subject and object of knowledge, as Descartes or any materialist is forced to do, is already skepticism: skepticism consists not in failing to find an ingenious way to bridge the duality, but in positing the gap at all.
5. The experience of things as self-subsistent can be readily subsumed under Intellect-Being as one facet of its self-experience

(as, analogously, a dream-world is inescapably "real" to one situated within it), while the reverse is unintelligible.

I have observed that scientific advances may undercut both materialism and dualism. A simple sketch might suggest some avenues of reflection.[1] The first point is that the notion of the "ultimate building block" of matter, the irreducible particle that could give meaning to the word "matter," does not exist, at least not in an unequivocal sense. Throughout history, materialism has rested on atomism, the notion of an indivisible particle as the ultimate ontological reality. If in recent years physicists have settled on six types of quarks and their brethren (muons, taus, electrons, and neutrinos, among others), along with the anti-particles to each of these, as the ultimate particles of our universe, this is not because other particles are excluded by theory (indeed dozens have been discovered), but because the energy required to produce them is so great that they would not seem to be part of the current physical system as we understand it. This is not very stable ground: besides the fact that each particle and its anti-particle annihilate each other instantly to produce pure energy, the picture has to be completed with force particles (gluons, photons, weak gauge bosons, and presumably gravitrons), at least one of which (the weak gauge boson) has mass, and all of which further blur any constitutive notion of "matter." Moreover, many physicists have begun to think of all these particles as different manifestations of a "more ultimate" stringlike particle that, like a loop of resonating string, is capable of carrying different frequencies and thus producing different phenomena. Strings are quite enchanting: their size (they stand to protons as protons do to the solar system) makes them "inaccessible to any conceivable experiment": they are far more subtle than any of the phenomena (such as the wavelength of any form of radiation) by which we can know anything about them. They also entail a universe that exists in at least ten dimensions. In any event, according to quantum theory, as well as any of the "supersymmetrical" theories that have grown from it, all particles (or strings) are waves, and all waves and forces are also particles; all particles can be transmuted into other particles, and all mass is interchangeable with energy, in particular with electromagnetic radiation. This "unity of matter" dissolves the notion that matter consists in something "material," as Aristotle explained to us about 2,300 years ago. The great physicist Werner Heisenberg observes, "The smallest units of matter are, in fact, not physical objects in the ordinary sense of the word; they are forms, structures, or—in Plato's sense—Ideas, which can be unambiguously spoken of only in the language of mathematics." Heisenberg makes the connection with Aristotelian hylomorphism explicit:

> All the elementary particles are made of the same substance, which
> we may call energy or universal matter; they are just different forms
> in which matter can appear. If we compare this situation with the
> Aristotelian concepts of matter and form, we can say that the matter

of Aristotle, which is mere "potentia," should be compared to our concept of energy, which gets into "actuality" by means of the form, when the elementary particle is created.[2]

The interdependence of space and time, fused in the concept of four-dimensional space-time, is a fundamental axiom of the theory of relativity. We have seen that Dante conceives the *Primo Mobile*, the source of all being in space-time, as pure motion, *ubi* plotted against *quando*, conceptually insepa-rable from each other. General relativity dissolves the notion of space-time as a matrix autonomous from its articulation as form (from the "things" it "con-tains"): indeed mass is simply a "condensation" of space-time, that is, of an energy field. In accordance with this idea, we have seen that in hylomorphism space-time is not a thing: it is the character common to all finite attribute, the "common form" of all material form. Contemporary physics goes even farther: it requires that "everything that ever existed or can exist is already potentially there in the nothingness of space." Every point in a vacuum is "filled with the vibrations of every possible quantum"; any of these vibrations, if given energy, can "increase to the level of becoming real particles." This means that matter and the vacuum can be transmuted into each other, a fact that, as the physicist Heinz Pagels observes, *creatio ex nihilo* has addressed for centuries. "Theoret-ical and experimental physicists are now studying nothing at all—the vacuum. But that nothingness contains all of being."[3]

Relativity tells us that all spatiotemporal attributes (dimension, mass, and rate of change) are a function of velocity. The speed of light constitutes the limit of motion, and thus the boundary of space-time; it is the constant of conversion between matter and energy or electromagnetic radiation. The sub-stance and limits of the physical universe seem in some sense to consist in the nature of light, broadly conceived, and its mysterious convertibility into spatiotemporal form, and thus into gravity. Bonaventure and other proponents of the "metaphysics of light" would not be surprised; Dante, whose *Comedy* describes physical reality as the contingent "re-reflection" of the self-subsistent light that is the Empyrean, might wonder at our long recalcitrance.

What science has not yet probed is the convertibility between light-energy-vacuum (or strings) and consciousness, what Dante calls *luce intellettual*. This is to be expected: to use Wittgenstein's image, the visual field does not include the eye itself; what alone is absent from any description of experience is the subject of experience, because nothing can be said about it, it is nothing.[4] One of the most revolutionary developments of modern physics, however, is the realization that every description of reality is simply a picture that is in part determined by the act of observation itself. The observing subject's point of view as an entity within the world, its frame of reference, and the questions it asks are all factors that determine its picture of the reality it seeks to describe: they are part of that picture. The "world in itself" may be approximated and imaged—but never grasped or communicated—by descriptions, concepts, or equations: reality lies beyond, beyond all concept, all description, all thought, all image. That beyond, the architects of quantum physics unanimously concluded, lies in consciousness itself. There is no such thing as the world "in itself" autonomous of consciousness.[5]

Virtually all the physicists who developed quantum physics thus sought to reverse our implicit assumption that "matter" is self-subsistent. As early as 1927 Sir Arthur Eddington remarked, "Recognizing that the physical world is entirely abstract and without 'actuality' apart from its linkage to consciousness, we restore consciousness to the fundamental position instead of representing it as an inessential complication occasionally found in the midst of inorganic nature at a late stage of evolutionary history."[6] The same conclusion was reached by Heisenberg, who often expressed this conviction by saying that Platonic idealism was essentially correct, and far more accurate as a picture of the world than the atomism of Democritus or Leucippus. Heisenberg's opinion has some weight, because he was, with Erwin Schrödinger, the principal architect of quantum physics.[7]

More philosophically acute than virtually any other modern physicist, Schrödinger objected to the notion of the interference between subject and object in scientific observation because he realized that the duality between them is itself an illusion. Mind and world are numerically one:

> It is the same elements that go to compose my mind and the world.
> ... The world is given to me only once, not one existing and one
> perceived. Subject and object are only one. The barrier between
> them cannot be said to have broken down as a result of recent experience in the physical sciences, for this barrier does not exist.
>   The reason why our sentient, percipient, and thinking ego is
> met nowhere within our scientific world picture can easily be indicated in seven words: because it is itself that world picture. It is
> identical with the whole and therefore cannot be contained in it as
> part of it.[8]

The "individual mind" that would interact with its own observations is not the real subject, but itself an object within its self-experience as subject: that finite point of view is continuous with the world, a part of experience. The true subject cannot interact with its experience: it is nothing in itself, it *is* its experience. The region in which all minds "overlap is the construct of the 'real world around us' "; but the multiplicity of minds itself "is only apparent, [for] in truth, there is only one mind." Consciousness is ultimately one: the subject of all experience is singular and attributeless. We discussed this point in analyzing the Aristotelian conception of intellect: all attribute or description (one, many, inside, outside) is metaphorical in relation to consciousness. Schrödinger concludes that the true "I" is the conscious ground upon which the experiences and memories that constitute each sense of personal identity are collected; since that "I" has itself no attributes except existence, it identifies itself with these collections, and the sense of "being this-or-that" is born. There is in this sense only one "I": no "intelligible *scientific* meaning" can be given to the notion of "someone else."[9] Schrödinger's statements on metaphysical questions point directly to what we have learned from Dante: "So, in brief, we do not belong to this material world that science constructs for us. We are not in it; we are outside. We are only spectators. The reason why we believe that we are in it, that we belong to the picture, is that our bodies are in the picture."[10]

Schrödinger's assertions of the ontological primacy of consciousness resemble Eddington's and Heisenberg's: "It would seem queer, not to say ridiculous, to think that the contemplating, conscious mind that alone reflects the becoming of the world should have made its appearance only at some time in the course of this 'becoming,' should have appeared contingently, associated with a very special biological contraption [the brain]."[11] A millennium of philosophical and spiritual inquiry, in both West and East, would agree.

By postulating the quantum in 1900 Max Planck became the father of modern physics; he was awarded the Nobel Prize in 1918. He too asserted the absolute independence of the "I-awareness" from the entire chain of causality and said that this "is a truth that comes from the immediate dictate of the human consciousness." It is remarkable that he too, in harmony with a central image of this study, calls I-awareness (the subject of experience) "a point, one single point in the immeasurable world of mind and matter."[12]

In more recent times, there has been a small epidemic of books assessing the relations between the new physics and "Eastern philosophy," Western "mysticism," idealism, and theories of consciousness.[13] The discussion gains urgency from experiments that have confirmed what physicists call non-locality, a phenomenon intrinsic to quantum probability and mathematically predicted by John Bell in 1964. Non-locality amounts to saying that apparently isolated phenomena can influence each other *simultaneously*, faster than any particle or wave could reach one from the other. In other words, causality seems to be capable of ignoring that absolute which is the speed of light; this undermines any commonsense notion of causality at all. The fact that "information gets around" superluminally, ignoring any constraints of spatiotemporal extension, would suggest that all experience is in some sense one and indivisible (it is not made of "locally connecting separate parts"): it is coherent only if conceived as a whole. It also implies that "what the world consists in," the ground of its being, is not subject to the constraints that operate within the world. In some sense, the very notion of locality—of position, distance, and separation in space-time—is an illusion. Reality is ultimately one, and ultimately dimensionless. Dante might say that he tried to awaken us to this experience of reality in the *Comedy*: consciousness, *luce intellettual*, is the omnipresent and indivisible reality in which all finite attribute consists, and it is itself unbound by time, space, or motion, because it is extensionless, a point. Many of the apparent physical paradoxes of Paradise, such as the interpenetration of bodies, or perception "at a distance" with no intervening *mezzo*, or the identity of one and many, equality and inequality, are based on this principle.[14]

What we say we know "theoretically" about the nature of the world is at variance with how we experience it, with what our behavior shows we believe about it. Even without grappling with contemporary physics, we all know that a billiard ball is as spacious as a galaxy: atoms themselves are almost nothing but space, and their electron shells are nothing but a distant haze of sheet lightning. But we play billiards, and the balls do not pass through each other. It is perhaps a question of scale, of perspective, of frame of reference (and, of course, of electromagnetic forces, whatever they are). If we were to see the entire system from the outside in, or from the inside out, as the pilgrim Dante sees the inverted images of creation in *Paradiso* 28, perhaps our familiar, solid, stolid reality would begin to look ethereal, ephemeral, transparent, no more than a luminous, vibrating veil or reflection of our own being, our own seeing, our own infinite love, our freedom, oneness, nothingness. Perhaps some have glimpsed or experienced the world and themselves this way, and perhaps the texts and signs they leave behind them are like fireflies, moving, beckoning, momentary traces of light in the suspended twilight of our half-understanding. Perhaps the *Comedy* is such a text. Perhaps that is why, after six centuries, we still circle around it, like moths drawn to a flame, craving the light, but afraid of the form-devouring fire.[15]

Notes

INTRODUCTION: NON-DUALITY AND SELF-KNOWLEDGE

1. "The one fundamental question . . .": Barolini, *Undivine Comedy* 4; "the central problem . . .": Hollander, "Dante *Theologus-Poeta*" 61; "exceptional and exceptionally insistent . . .": Franke, *Dante's Interpretive Journey* 154; "like perhaps no other . . .": 152. It has been argued that . . . : see Franke, esp. 152–171, 177–185; Singleton: "Irreducible Dove" 129, *Elements of Structure* 62. Drawing on the philosophical hermeneutics of Heidegger and Gadamer, Franke sees every event of reading the *Comedy* as an act of (revelatory) interpretation, of experiencing and appropriating truth: "the truth or disclosure of reality" becomes "an event that intrinsically involves the one to whom the disclosure is made, that is, the interpreter or reader" (233; the crucial passages of Franke's argument are reprinted in "Reader's Application"). Franke's move is elegant, but if it is fruitful and true to Dante, it is because of the assonance between Heideggerian and medieval metaphysics.

2. See "Friendship and Discourse" and "Simpleness."

3. Noakes, "Double Misreading."

4. As I have sought to show . . . : "The Metaphysical Basis of Dante's Politics." Nardi: *Saggi di filosofia dantesca* viii; see also Barbi, "Nuovi problemi" 53–54, for a similar warning. For the fragmentary and secondhand nature of Dante's own reading, see Barański, "Iter ideologico" 9–22.

CHAPTER 1: THE EMPYREAN

1. The quoted remark is Taylor's (*Aristotle* 69); Aristotle, however, was seeking an explanatory cosmological system, while Eudoxus (and later Ptolemy) were aiming only at predictive astronomical computing techniques (see, e.g., Hanson, *Constellations and Conjectures* 64–66, 145–165). For the circular motion of the *aether*, see Aristotle, *De Caelo* 1.2–3, *Physics* 8.7–8; for the concentric physical spheres, *Metaphysics* 12.8, *De Caelo* 2.7–8; for the Platonic elements of Aristotle's cosmology, see especially *De Caelo* 2.12,

1.3.270b.1–10, *Metaphysics* 12.7. Particularly lucid accounts of Aristotelian cosmology and its background are Toulmin and Goodfield, *Fabric of the Heavens* 79–114; Dicks, *Early Greek Astronomy* 194–219; Hanson, *Constellations and Conjectures* 35–88; Pederson, *Early Physics and Astronomy* 24–76; and the introduction to Elders, *Aristotle's Cosmology*. Dicks (216), Elders (27–33), Randall (*Aristotle* 161), Moraux ("Méthode d'Aristote" 184–185), Solmsen ("Platonic Influences" and *Aristotle's System*), and Düring ("Aristotle and the Heritage") are among those who underline the Platonism of Aristotle's cosmology.

2. Beyond the convex outer surface: *De Caelo* 1.9.278b.22–279b.1; quotation: 279a.17–19. The principal texts for the Unmoved Mover or First Being are *Metaphysics* 12.6–8 and *Physics* 7.1, 8.4–7,10; for the terminus of the chain of causality, see *Metaphysics* 2.2, cited in the *Letter to Cangrande* (20.55). The description of the Prime Mover in this paragraph is culled from *Metaphysics* 12.7. Parts of the *De Caelo* (especially books 1 and 2) seem still to allow for Platonic self-moved movers, ruled out in the *Physics* and *Metaphysics*, which are presumably later. Hence in the context of the *De Caelo* (e.g., 2.3.286a.9–11), the eighth sphere, as itself divine, could be both *primum mobile* and *primum movens*; other passages (e.g., 2.6.288a.27–b7) already suggest an Unmoved First Mover. See Elders, *Aristotle's Cosmology* 29–33, and Dicks, *Early Greek Astronomy* 211–214. Complex combinations of regular motions: *Metaphysics* 12.8.1073b.1–1074a.15. For the number of Aristotle's spheres, ranging between forty-seven and sixty-one, and a precise explanation of how the system worked, see Hanson, "On Counting Aristotle's Spheres" and *Constellations and Conjectures* 66–80; and Dicks, *Early Greek Astronomy* 200–203.

3. Some (e.g., Roger Bacon) who thought the sphere of fixed stars had a third motion (trepidation) posited two mobile spheres beyond the eighth. For Aristotle's "movers," see *Metaphysics* 12.8; for their identification with angelic intelligences (rejected by Albert and others), see Weisheipl, "Celestial Movers," and Bemrose, *Dante's Angelic Intelligences* 37–55; in Dante, see, e.g., *Cv* 2.5.14–18; *If* 7.74; *Pd* 12.97–98, 28.78. The tension between Aristotelian cosmology and Ptolemaic geometry is traced by Grant, *Planets, Stars, and Orbs* 275–308; Hanson, *Constellations and Conjectures* 145–165; and Toulmin and Goodfield, *Fabric of the Heavens* 128–149, who remark the religious aspect assumed by Aristotelian cosmology (128). For a more detailed discussion of the Aristotelian-Ptolemaic basis of Dante's cosmology, see Boyde, *Philomythes and Philosopher* 132–171; Tonquédec, *Questions* 7–29, 56–63; Duhem, *Système du monde*, vol. 3; Grant, *Planets, Stars, and Orbs*; useful short accounts may be found in Andriani, *Forma del paradiso* 8–22; Ghisalberti, "Cosmologia nel Duecento," who stresses the variety of Dante's cosmological sources; Faes de Mottoni, "Universo" 830–831; Hartner, "Astronomy from Antiquity to Copernicus"; and Crombie, *Augustine to Galileo* 52–62. Dante's certain or possible astronomical sources include Alfraganus, *Libro dell'aggregazione*; Sacrobosco, *De spera*; Restoro [Ristoro] d'Arezzo, *Composizione del mondo*; Brunetto Latini, *Livres dou Tresor* 1.103–120; Campanus of Novara, *Theorica planetarum*; Albertus Magnus, *De caelo et mundo*; Aquinas, commentary on Aristotle's *De caelo et mundo*; and al-Bitrūjī [Alpetragius], *De motibus celorum*; see also Orr, *Dante and the Early Astronomers*.

4. *Veramente, fuori di tutti questi [cieli mobili], li catolici pongono lo cielo Empireo, che è a dire cielo di fiamma o vero luminoso* (*Cv* 2.3.8).

5. Aristotle's theory of place: *Physics* 4.4–5; motion referred to place: 4.4.212a.14–20; impossibility of void: 4.6–9; nothing beyond eighth sphere: *De caelo* 1.9.278b.35–279a.18 (quoted above); motion of eighth sphere and place: *Physics* 4.5.212a.31–212b.24; the thought that thinks itself: *Metaphysics* 12.7.1072b.14. For the history of

solutions to the problem of the motion of the eighth sphere, see Duhem, *Système du monde* 7:158–302, translated in *Medieval Cosmology* 139–268; Grant, *Planets, Stars, and Orbs* 122–135; Nardi, "Dottrina dell'Empireo" 167–174.

6. Catholics needed a place . . . : see, e.g., Hugh of St. Victor, *De sacramentis* 1.5.1, 2.18.16,20; Peter Lombard, *Sententiae* 4.49.1; Bonaventure, *Commentaria in Sententiarum* 2.d2.p2.a2.q1–2, 4.d45.a1.q2; Albertus Magnus, *Scripta in Sententiarum* 4.44.45; and Thomas Aquinas, *ST Supplement* 69.3, *Scriptum super Sententiarum* 3.d22.q3.m3.1. The history of the Empyrean is traced by Grant, *Planets, Stars, and Orbs* 371–389; Nardi, "Dottrina dell'Empireo" (discussed in this paragraph); Duhem, *Système du monde* 7:197–202, translated in *Medieval Cosmology* 173–178 and partially in Čapek, *Concepts of Space and Time* 43–45; Mellone, "Empireo" and *Dottrina sulla prima creazione* 22–57; Bernard, "Ciel"; Litt, *Corps célestes* 255–261; Maurach, *Coelum Empyreum*; and McDannell and Lang, *Heaven: A History* 80–88. Martinelli ("Dottrina dell'Empireo") provides a wealth of references. For popular representations of paradise, see Morgan, *Dante and the Medieval Other World* 166–195. Nardi: "Dottrina dell'Empireo" 175–204; the Empyrean as world-soul or link: 179–181. Besides Pre-Socratic, Gnostic, and Chaldean sources, the key stages in this Neoplatonic legacy of the Empyrean as Nardi traces it are Plato, *Republic* 10.616b, *Timaeus* 8–9; Plotinus, *Enneads* 4.3.17, 4.8.8, 5.1.6–7, 5.3.12 (stressing the analogy of the sun), 5.5.9; Proclus (source of the play on *topos* and *tupos*), as referred by Simplicius, *In Aristotelis Physicorum* 4.5. World contained in soul: "Soul is not in the universe, on the contrary the universe is in the Soul; bodily substance is not a place to the Soul; soul is contained in Intellectual-Principle [*nous*] and is the container of body" (Plotinus, *Enneads* 5.5.9 [MacKenna]). See also *Timaeus* 36d: "Now when the creator had framed the soul according to his will, he formed within her the corporeal universe." One is reminded also of Dante's blessed souls, whose features are hidden within their own luminosity.

7. Basil, *Exegetic Homilies [Hexaemeron]* 1.5; Martianus Capella, *Marriage of Philology* 2.200–203; Isidore of Seville, *De natura rerum* 12; Bede, *De natura rerum* 7, *Commentarium in Pentateuch* 2. For the early history of the Empyrean and its patristic sources, see Maurach, *Coelum Empyreum*. *Glossa ordinaria* quotation: *Caelum, non visibile firmamentum, sed empyreum, idest igneum, vel intellectuale, quod non ab ardore sed a splendore dicitur, quod statim repletum est angelis.* The gloss is probably by Anselm of Laon. According to Genesis, God created *caelum* (1.1), then *firmamentum* to divide the waters above the firmament from those below it (1.6–7). *Caelum* was identified with the Empyrean; *firmamentum* usually with the eighth sphere of fixed stars; the suprafirmamental waters, in "crystalline" form, were identified with the ninth and/or sometimes with a tenth (or eleventh) moving sphere. In the latter case the Empyrean became the eleventh (or twelfth) sphere; see, e.g., Campanus of Novara, *Theorica planetarum* 4.325–340.

8. Ibn ʿArabī: *al-Futūḥāt*. For Islamic conceptions of Paradise and their relation to Dante's Empyrean, see, e.g., Asín Palacios, *Dante e l'Islam* 209–259, *Abenmasarra y su escuela* 212ff., and Corti, " 'Commedia' di Dante e l'oltretomba islamico"; for parallels between the *Comedy* and Jewish mysticism, see Stow, *Dante e la mistica ebraica*. Strohmaier (*Von Demokrit bis Dante*) studies parallels with the *Comedy* in both Islamic and Jewish mysticism, qualifying the former; Baffioni ("Aspetti delle cosmologie") provides a recent and balanced overview of the question; Cantarino, "Dante and Islam," presents an extensive earlier survey. Other references: Michael Scot, *Commentary* 283 (see Nardi, "Dante e Alpetragio" 153–156, and Vasoli's commentary to *Cv* 2.3.5); Pseudo-Grosseteste, *Summa philosophiae* 15.3, 16.4; Albertus Magnus, *Summa theologiae* 1.t18.q73.m2.a1, *Scripta in Sententiarum* 2.2.3–5; Aquinas, *Scriptum super*

Sententiarum 2.d2.p2.a1.q2, *ST* 1a.66.3, 1a.61.4. Nardi traces the Neoplatonic lineage in "Dottrina dell'Empireo" 187–204.

9. Bonaventure quotation: *Commentaria in Sententiarum* 2.d2.p2.a1.q1; Albert [Hugh of Strassburg] quotation: *caelum est corpus purum, natura simplicissimum, essentia subtilissimum, incorruptibilitate solidissimum, quantitate maximum, materia purissimum* (*Compendium theologicae* 2.4). The decree of 1244 states: *firmiter . . . credimus, quod idem locus corporalis, scilicet celum empireum, angelorum et animarum sanctarum erit et corporum glorificatorum* (Denifle, *Chartularium* 128 [1:171]); the error condemned is that glorified souls should end up in the crystalline heaven instead of in the Empyrean with the angels. On the corporality of the Empyrean: Alexander of Hales, *Summa theologica* 2.47.2; Richard of Middleton, *Super Sententiarum* 2.d2.a3.q1; Bonaventure, *Commentaria in Sententiarum* 2.d2.p2.a1.q1–2; and Aquinas, *ST* 1a.61.3. Aquinas on the Empyrean made of quintessence: *Scriptum super Sententiarum* 2.d14.q1.a2; *Questiones Quodlibetales* 6.11.19.

10. Bede: *Hexaemeron* 1; *Glossa ordinaria*: *Liber genesis* 1.1; Peter Lombard: *Sententiae* 2.2.4–5; and Aquinas: *ST* 1a.66.4 (*Communiter dicitur, quatuor esse primo creata; scilicet naturam angelicam, caelum empyreum, materiam corporalem informem et tempus*). Pseudo-Grosseteste, *Summa philosophiae* 9.4, 15.2–3, 16.4; Richard of Middleton, *Super Sententiarum* 2.d2.a3.q3; Albertus Magnus, *Scripta in Sententiarum* 2.2.4–5; and Bonaventure, *Commentaria in Sententiarum* 2.d2.p2.a1.q1–2. Aquinas: against influence, *Scriptum super Sententiarum* 2.d2.q2.a2–3; probable influence, *ST* 1a.q66.a3.ad2 (c. 1268); final position, *Questiones Quodlibetales* 6.11.19 (c. 1272). On this retraction (extremely rare in Aquinas), see Litt, *Corps célestes* 255–261. For an overview of the question of the Empyrean's influence, see Grant, *Planets, Stars, and Orbs* 378–382.

11. That to be in the Empyrean was itself to see God was definitively fixed in 1336 by the constitution *Benedictus Deus* of Benedict XII; see Bernard, "Ciel" 2510. Bonaventure: *Commentaria in Sententiarum* 2.d2.p2.a1.q2, 2.d13.p2.a2; *Breviloquium* 2.3.4; see also Nardi, "Dottrina dell'Empireo" 202; Mellone, "Empireo" 670–671. For the "metaphysics of light," see Hedwig, *Sphaera Lucis*; Baeumker, *Witelo*, esp. 357–459; Mazzeo, *Medieval Cultural Tradition* 56–90; McEvoy, "Metaphysics of Light"; Lindberg, "The Genesis"; and McKeon, *Study of the* Summa philosophiae 156–174.

12. The *Liber de intelligentiis* is printed in Baeumker, *Witelo* 1–71; Grosseteste's *De luce* is also available in English (*On Light*). On Grosseteste's philosophy of light, see Speer, "Physics or Metaphysics?"; Crombie, *Robert Grosseteste*, esp. 104–116, 128–134; Lindberg, *Theories of Vision* 94–102; and McEvoy, "Ein Paradigma." Bonaventure on light as common form: *Commentaria in Sententiarum* 2.d13, and 2.d12.a2.q1 (*Lux est natura communis, reperta in omnibus corporibus, tam caelestibus quam terrestribus*); light manifest in things: 2.d13.a2.q2, and 2.d13.a1.q1 (*Proprissime* ["in a strict sense"] . . . *Deus lux est, et quae ad ipsum magis accedunt, plus habent de natura lucis*); Empyrean as light: *Breviloquium* 2.3.5, *Commentaria in Sententiarum* 2.d13.a2.q2, 2.d2.p2.a1.q1 (*Lux est forma totius orbis primi*).

13. Aquinas on light not a substance: *ST* 1a.67.1–2, *Scriptum super Sententiarum* 2.q13.a1.ad3; light as metaphor, quality of Empyrean: *Quodlibetales* 6.12.19, *Scriptum super Sententiarum* 2.q13.a1.ad2, *ST* 1a.67.3. Bonaventure on light as form: *Commentaria in Sententiarum* 2.d12.a2.q1, 2.d13; on ambiguity, e.g., 2.d13.a1.q1 (of the Augustinian proposition that God is light in a strict sense, he says, *Dicendum quod verum est quantum ad proprietatem vocabuli, non est tamen verum quantum ad usum communem*). The orthodoxy of Christian "light metaphysicians" and Aquinas's debt to them is noted by McEvoy, "Metaphysics of Light" 140–141.

14. Quotation: Mellone, *Dottrina* 23. For this evolution, see Nardi, "Dottrina

dell'Empireo" 204–211 (which stresses the continuities); Mellone, "Empireo" 669–670, *Dottrina* 22–57; Étienne Gilson, "Recherche de l'Empyrée"; and Foster, "Tommaso d'Aquino" 641; on the Empyrean in the *Convivio*, see also Nardi, "Note al *Convivio*" 65–75. Martinelli ("Dottrina dell'Empireo") alone denies an evolution.

15. "This is the crowning edifice of the world, in which the entire world is contained, and outside of which nothing exists; and it does not exist in place but was formed only in the first Mind, which the Greeks call Protonoe."

16. *Cv* 2.3.10, 12. "Restfulness and peace are the marks of this dwelling-place of that most high Godhead who alone fully sees Himself. According to the teaching of Holy Church, which cannot lie, this is the dwelling-place of blessed spirits; and it will be clear to anyone who properly grasps his meaning that Aristotle implies the same view in the first part of *On the Heavens and the Earth.* . . . This is the splendor to which the Psalmist referred where he says to God: 'Your splendor rises up above the heavens' " [Ryan].

17. Étienne Gilson: "Recherche de l'Empyrée" 150 (*Comment Dieu et des esprits incorporels peuvent-ils se trouver quelque part?*); Gilson also notes (151) that Aristotle had not placed a heaven beyond the Primum Mobile (*Aristote n'avait rien fait de tel*). For the problem of "locating" Aristotle's immaterial mover, see Lang, "Aristotle's Immaterial Mover."

18. *On the Heavens [De Caelo]* 1.9.279a.15–22. Étienne Gilson instead cites 1.9.279a.11; Nardi ("Dottrina dell'Empireo" 205) cites instead 1.3.270b.1–10 and 1.2.269b.16; the latter passage, which is really about the *ether*, is quoted in the *Letter to Cangrande* (27.75).

19. *Cv* 2.3.8–9. "However, Catholics hold that beyond all these [moving heavens] there lies the Empyrean Heaven, meaning the heaven of flame or of light. They hold that this is motionless because it possesses in its every part the perfection required by its matter. It is this quality that causes the First Moving Heaven to move with the utmost speed, for since in every part of that ninth heaven bordering the Empyrean there burns an ardent longing to be united to every part of that most divine heaven which is at rest, it revolves inside that heaven with a desire so intense that its speed is almost beyond comprehension" [Ryan].

20. Aristotle: *Metaphysics* 11.9, 12.7, *Physics* 8.6–10; see also *De Caelo* 1.3–8. Lloyd (*Aristotle* 137–144) gives a particularly insightful account of Aristotle's Unmoved Mover. Compare the *Letter to Cangrande* (25.71): *Omne quod movetur, movetur propter aliquid quod non habet, quod est terminus sui motus* ("Everything that moves moves for something it does not have, which is the goal of its motion.") For references to the *ens primum quietum et sempiternum* (a phrase echoed in the *Letter's* description of the Empyrean [24.67]), see Martinelli, "Dottrina dell'Empireo" 74–82.

21. "Recherche de l'Empyrée" 149; previous quotation, 155. Ghisalberti ("Cosmologia" 40) points out that Albert and Aquinas do not mention the Empyrean in their commentaries on Aristotle's *Physics* and *De caelo* but accept it in their theological treatises. For all of Paradise as "no place," see Brandeis, *Ladder of Vision* esp. 157.

22. "We have issued forth from the greatest body to the heaven that is pure light: light of the intellect, full of love, love of the true good, full of joy, joy that transcends every sweetness."

23. Spatiotemporal allusions to the Empyrean in the *Comedy* include *If* 2.84 (*ampio loco*); *Pg* 26.63 (*'l ciel . . . ch'è pien d'amore e più ampio si spazia*); and of course all of the visual spectacles of *Pd* 30–33.

24. "Your high desire shall be fulfilled up in the last sphere, where are fulfilled all others, and my own. There every desire is perfect, mature, and whole; in that

[sphere] alone is every part where it always was, for it is not in a place, and it does not im-pole itself."

25. "There is a Light above that makes the Creator visible to every creature that has its peace only in seeing Him. That light spreads in a circular form, so much that its circumference would be too wide a girdle for the sun. Its whole expanse is made by a ray reflected from the summit of the First Moved Sphere, which from it draws life and power."

26. See Nardi, "Dottrina dell'Empireo" 208; Mellone, *Dottrina* 39–41; Foster, "Tommaso d'Aquino" 641; and Stormon, "Problems of the Empyrean." For the *lumen gloriae*, see, e.g., Aquinas *ST* 1a.12.5–6, *SCG* 3.53; in Dante, see Simon Gilson, *Medieval Optics* 233–239, and Fallani, "Visio beatifica" 1071.

27. See Mellone, "Empireo" 669, *Dottrina* 47–48.

28. Martinelli, "Dottrina dell'Empireo"; see also Simon Gilson, *Medieval Optics* 234–235. Before Nardi's and Mellone's clarifications, Busnelli assumed, but did not argue, that Dante's Empyrean was Thomistic, that is, both corporeal and spiritual (see, e.g., *Concetto e ordine* 1.53). Aristotle's phrase for the Unmoved Mover: *Metaphysics* 12.7.1072b14; no size or parts: *Physics* 8.10.266a10–267b26. Difficulties with Martinelli's interpretations include: he reads *contenta* in the *Letter to Cangrande* (24.67) to mean the angels and blessed, instead of the moving spheres (in response see Cecchini's introduction to his edition of the *Letter* [p. xlviii]); he maintains that angels and the blessed need a physical place (for counterevidence see Mellone, *Dottrina* 48); he himself demonstrates that the locution *in sempiterna quiete permanente* used for the Empyrean in the *Letter* (24.67) refers, in its proper sense, to First Being or divine nature, not a created thing; he maintains, implausibly, that the Empyrean is "intellectual" only in the sense that it is invisible (the *Primo Mobile* is also invisible); he maintains that Dante *implies* the creation of the Empyrean in the creation of the angels; as he acknowledges, *Pd* 29.35–36 excludes the Empyrean as a created heaven; he is reduced to saying that Dante equates the Empyrean with the divine mind *formaliter* but not *essentialiter*; he is reduced to saying that both the Empyrean and *Primo Mobile* are the "greatest body."

29. "The nature of the universe that holds the center still and moves all the rest around it begins here as from its starting point; and this Heaven has no other *where* than the divine mind, in which are kindled the love that turns it and the formative influence it rains down. Light and love enclose it in a circle, as it does the others, and this enclosing, he alone who girds it understands."

30. *Il est absolument certain que Dante parle ici du cristallin comme inclus sous la pensée divine, seul lieu qu'on puisse lui attribuer, bien qu'elle même n'ait pas de lieu* ("Recherche de l'Empyrée" 160). Russell's remarks on Dante's Empyrean in "History of Heaven" (178–180) are quite accurate.

31. *Dottrina* 33–34. Mellone's reading is followed by the commentators Porena and Chimenz (with variations), and by Bosco-Reggio (at *Pd* 27.109–111); it is implicitly followed by Martinelli, "Dottrina dell'Empireo" 80–81. That on the contrary Dante essentially identifies the Empyrean with the divine mind and the *lumen gloriae* is the central point of Nardi's essay on the Empyrean (see 207–209).

32. *Intende* can have a double sense as "understand" or "will consciously to an end, i.e., create"; see, e.g., Albertus, *Scripta in Sententiarum* 2.d38.a2.q2; Aquinas, *SCG* 2.42; Nardi, "Se la prima materia"; and Martinelli, "Dottrina dell'Empireo" 81n61.

33. "That One and Two and Three which ever lives and reigns ever in Three and Two and One, uncircumscribed, and circumscribing all."

34. For the *coelum Trinitatis*, see, e.g., Albertus, *Scripta in Sententiarum* 2.d2.a7–8; Alexander of Hales, *Quaestiones* 47.2.1–2; and Vincent of Beauvais, *Speculum naturale* 3.84–85; as metaphor, see, e.g., Albertus, *Summa de creaturis* 1.10.2 (*Est enim caelum Trinitatis nihil aliud quam excellentia virtutis eius* [of God], *quae continet et ambit omnia creata* ["The caelum Trinitatis is thus nothing but the eminence of the power of God, which contains and encompasses all created things"]); see also Mellone, *Dottrina* 23–24, and Martinelli, "Dottrina dell'Empireo" 113n131; in Dante, see Mellone, "Empireo" 669, *Dottrina* 23–24, 29–30, 33–36, 48–49; Martinelli, "Dottrina dell'Empireo" 113n131, 132; and Nardi, "Dottrina dell'Empireo" 190. The Trinity revealed to Dante in the Empyrean: *Pd* 23.71–108; 31.25–29; 33.106–141. *Pd* 33.49–54 and 31.1–12 visualize the communion of souls in a reality that transcends individuality; the Trinitarian image of *Pd* 33.109–114 is a *travagliare* of the *semplice sembiante* of the Empyrean's light itself, due to changes within the pilgrim.

35. For example, Augustine's remark (*Genesi ad litteram* 4.28) that Christ is said to be light in a proper, not figurative sense, a statement often echoed (e.g., Aquinas *ST* 1a.67.1, Bonaventure (*Commentaria in Sententiarum* 2.d13.a1.q1); see also Augustine, *Soliloquies* 1.1.3, *Contra Faustum* 20.7, *De Trinitate* 7.4.

36. In addition to passages already cited, see also *Pd* 3.32; *Pd* 14.46–60; *Pd* 29.14–18, 25–30; and the light imagery of *Pd* 30–33, especially *Pd* 33.52–57, 76–90, 100–114, 124–132, 140–141.

37. For the "metaphysics of light" in Dante, see esp. Nardi, *Sigieri di Brabante* 33–37, 66 (amplified in "Intorno al Tomismo" 187–188), "Dottrina dell'Empireo" 202–203, 207–214; Simon Gilson, *Medieval Optics* 146–239; Mazzeo, "Light Metaphysics," *Structure and Thought* 7–19, 141–145, *Medieval Cultural Tradition* 91–132; Guidubaldi, *Dante Europeo*, esp. 2.173–452, 3.225–351; Negri, "Luce nella filosofia"; Boyde, *Dante Philomythes* 208–214; Corti, *Percorsi dell'invenzione* 147–163; and Cantarino, "Dante and Islam." Thomistic objectors, stressing light as poetic metaphor: e.g., Calò, Review of *Sigieri di Brabante* 270–271; Mandonnet, *Dante le théologien* 251–252; Busnelli, *Cosmogonia* 14–19; Mellone and Bufano, "Luce" 712–713; and Mellone, *Dottrina* 36–41. Negri and Simon Gilson correct the overidentification of the "metaphysics of light" with Neoplatonism, most evident in Mazzeo. That light in the *Paradiso* represents substantiality: Mazzeo, *Structure and Thought* 16, and Chiarenza, "Imageless Vision" 83–84.

38. E.g., Aquinas, *ST* 1a.2.3, 1a.46.1–2; *De aeternitate mundi*, *SCG* 2.31–38; see, e.g., Copleston, *Aquinas* 117–119; Étienne Gilson, *Christian Philosophy of Aquinas* 178–179.

39. Aristotle, *Posterior Analytics* 1.2, 2.11, *Physics* 1.1. Translating *aition*: Evans, *Aristotle* 83; the "question" comes from Taylor, *Aristotle* 50; see also Randall, *Aristotle* 34, and William Ross, *Aristotle* 73. The empiricist notion that temporal cause and effect is "something" intrinsic to reality persists despite Hume's attacks. It particularly annoyed Wittgenstein: "Superstition is nothing but belief in the causal nexus" (*Tractatus* 5.1361; see also 6.37, and *Culture and Value* 62).

40. Michael Scot, *Commentary* 283, and Nardi, "Note al Convivio" 67–74. What seems philosophically naive or imprecise in the *Convivio* ("Note al Convivio" 75) may be a deliberate effort to cut through excessive subtleties and find a new and accessible language for philosophy (see Vasoli's introduction to the *Convivio*, lxxvii).

41. Avicenna: *Metaphysica* 9.2; Algazel: *Philosophia* 1.4.2; Nardi: "Note al Convivio" 67–74; see also *Cv* 2.3.5: philosophy requires *un primo mobile semplicissimo* ("a Primo Mobile free of all multiplicity").

42. The expression for the Empyrean "containing all bodies and contained by

none" is a commonplace in the tradition: see, e.g., Bonaventure, *Commentaria in Sententiarum* 2.d14.p2.a1.q3, 2.d2.p2.a1.q1; Campanus of Novara, *Theorica planetarum* 4.335; Duhem, *Medieval Cosmology* 174–175. Mazzeo: *Medieval Cultural Tradition* 101; Martinelli: "Dottrina dell'Empireo" 117–124, " 'Esse' ed 'essentia' " 649–657. I shall not engage the question of the authenticity of the *Letter to Cangrande*, although my own inclination accords with Étienne Gilson's: "to me it seems to express admirably the spirit and, as it were, the essence of the *Divine Comedy*" (*Dante and Philosophy* 278n2). Poets make little attempt to say in prose what for them can be said only in poetry; if it were otherwise, they would not be poets, or their poetry would not be very good. Hence their peculiar reticence, apparent naiveté, or peripheral concerns ("missing the point") when they explicate their own texts.

43. The principal text for essence and existence in Aquinas is *On Being and Essence* [*De ente et essentia*], esp. 1.4, 4.2–8, 5.2–4. Gilson quotations: *God and Philosophy* 67–72; see also, e.g., *Being and Some Philosophers*, esp. 154–189. Kahn ("Why Existence Does Not Emerge" 323–324) links the new concept of existence in the Islamic world to the notion of creation, which involves radical contingency.

44. Ex. 3.14. On the "sublime truth" (*sublimis veritas*) that God's essence is His act of being, see, e.g., Aquinas, *SCG* 1.22, and Étienne Gilson, *Christian Philosophy of Thomas Aquinas* 84–95.

45. I draw the phrase "Neoplatonizing Aristotelianism" from Bazán's foreword to the *Book of Causes* (2). The *Letter to Cangrande*'s argument summarizes apothegms 1–18 (Proposition 1) of the *Liber de causis*, quoting the opening apothegm and 9.92.

46. God not a carpenter: Aquinas, *SCG* 3.65.9, and Augustine, *Genesi ad litteram* 4.12. God doing: from C.F.J. Martin, *Thomas Aquinas* 104; see Étienne Gilson, *Christian Philosophy of Aquinas* 101–102. Giving and sustaining being: e.g., Aquinas, *ST* 1a.q104.1; God everywhere: *ST* 1a.q8. Augustine quotations: *Confessions* 1.2.2. Boyde: *Dante Philomythes* 209. For the "Christian distinction" beween creator and creation, see Sokolowski, *God of Faith* esp. 21–52.

47. *Letter to Cangrande* quotation: *divinus radius sive divina gloria "per universum penetrat et resplendet"*: *penetrat quantum ad essentiam; resplendet quantum ad esse*. On the "reality" of the essence-existence distinction in Aquinas (not explicit in the *De ente et essentia*), see, e.g., *Scriptum super Sententiarum* 1.d13.q1.a3, *De veritate* 27.1.ad8; also Wippel, *Metaphysical Themes* 107–161 and "Essence and Existence"; Owens, "Quiddity and Real Distinction" 19–22; Fabro, *La nozione metafisica* 212–244; Sweeney, "Existence/Essence"; and Te Velde, *Participation and Substantiality*. The *Letter's* distinction against contemporary background: Martinelli, " 'Esse' ed 'essentia.' " Nardi argued ("Punto sull'Epistola" 222–223) that the *Letter's* distinction between essence and existence is not true to Dante's "strictly Neoplatonic" derivation of the Many from the One; but Dante was not a strict Neoplatonist, and the *Letter* does not deny, as he implies it does, that essence is a limitation or determination of being.

48. See Mellone, *Dottrina* 32–35, "Empireo" 669.

49. "Within the heaven of divine peace revolves a body in whose causal power lies the being of all that it contains. The following heaven, which has so many eyes [things to show] distributes this being through diverse essences, distinct from it and contained by it."

50. Pseudo-Dionysius: *Divine Names* 5.10; Nardi: "Dottrina dell'Empireo" 179–181, 212–214.

51. Soul and body: e.g., Plotinus, *Enneads* 4.3.4, 4.3.8–9; Plato, *Timaeus* 34b–37c; and Aristotle, *De anima* 2.2.414a20. No distinction between Empyrean and divine mind: see, e.g., Nardi, "Caduta di Lucifero" 229.

52. The *Primo Mobile* as final cause: Mellone, *Dottrina* 32–33; and Nardi, "Dante e Alpetragio" 165. *Meta* as turning-post: see, e.g., Bosco-Reggio's commentary at *Pd* 27.108.

CHAPTER 2: MATTER

1. *Vita Nova*: con ciò sia cosa che . . . *localmente mobile per sé, secondo lo Phylosofo, sia solamente corpo* . . . ("since . . . according to the Philosopher, only a body is by its nature subject to local motion . . ." [25.2]); see Mugnai, "Mobile." Aristotle: no place or void without body, *Physics* 4.1–9; no time wihout movement: 4.10–14; for the contrast with Descartes, see Mensch, "Aristotle and the Overcoming"; for the relation to modern physics, see Maudlin, "Substances and Space-Time."

2. "Dottrina dell'Empireo" 209; see also, e.g., "Dottrina delle macchie" 19–20.

3. *Metaphysics* 7.3.1029a20. In the Middle Ages this became the formula *nec quid, nec quale, nec quantum, nec aliquid eorum quibus ens determi:iatur.* The principal Aristotelian texts for the form-matter distinction are *Physics* 1.4–9, *Metaphysics* 7.3,7–8, *Generation and Corruption* 2. On the general conception of matter in Aristotle, see, e.g., Gill, *Aristotle on Substance*; Sokolowski, "Matter, Elements and Substance"; Fred Miller, "Aristotle's Use of Matter"; and Skemp, "*Hule* and *Upodoxe*."

4. For the identity *hyle-silva*, see, e.g., Chalcidius, *Timaeus a Calcidio* (esp. 295–297); Bernardus Sylvestris, *De mundi universitate* 1.1.18–22, 1.2.23–25; and Isidore of Seville, *Etymologiarum* 13.3.1. The connection with Dante's *selva oscura* has been noted since Landino's commentary; see also Ragni, "Selva" 141, and Hallock, "Dante's *Selva Oscura*."

5. Copper as form of water: *Metaphysics* 5.4.1015a10. Prime matter only in form: see esp. *Generation and Corruption* 2.1.329a24–35, 2.5.332a35; unknowable in itself: *Metaphysics* 7.10.1036a8, *Physics* 3.6.207a25. The other principal texts for prime matter are *Metaphysics* 5.4.1015a7–10, 7.3.1028b33–1029a33.

6. Form immanent, not transcendent: *Metaphysics* 5.4.1015a7–11, 5.24.1023a31–32, 7.8.1033a24–1034a5. The point that Plato stands at the head of a dualist view of what is now called the mind-body problem, and Aristotle at the head of a non-dualist view, is made by G.E.R. Lloyd, *Aristotle* 186; see, e.g., Aquinas, *ST* 1a.76.4. For the Augustine-Plotinus-Plato link, see Étienne Gilson, *History of Christian Philosophy* 74, 593, and Augustin Mansion, "L'immortalité de l'âme" 456–465; see also Olshewsky, "On the Relations." The Platonic authorship of the *Alcibiades* was unquestioned in antiquity.

7. Prime matter not anything: "Aristotle has ruled out the following kinds of universal substratum: incorporeal, corporeal, void, plenum, extension, triangles, objects of mathematics, Timaean space, some one of the elements, something over and above the elements" (Charlton, "Did Aristotle Believe" 135). Key entries in the forty-year debate on whether Aristotle "believed in prime matter" include King, "Aristotle Without"; Solmsen, "Aristotle and Prime Matter"; Charlton, "Did Aristotle" (which includes the history of the notion, 141–145, suggested also by King) and "Prime Matter"; C.J.F. Williams, "Prime Matter"; Robinson, "Prime Matter"; Stahl, "Stripped Away"; Sheldon Cohen, "Aristotle's Doctrine"; Graham, "The Paradox"; and Polis, "A New Reading"; see also McMullin, *The Concept of Matter*. Augustine: *De Genesi ad litteram* 1.14–15, *De Genesi contra Manichaeos* 1.5–7, *Contra Faustum* 20.14; see also *Confessions* 12.5–6 and 12.15.22.

8. Aquinas: *ST* 1a.66.1; see also 1a.69.1, 1a.74.3, *De potentia* 4.1. Augustine on "instantaneous" creation: e.g., *De Genesi ad litteram* 1.15; 4.26,28,33; 5.3,23; *Confessions*

12.12–13. On the patristic notion of prime matter, see Sorabji, *Time, Creation and the Continuum* 292–294.

9. The distinction between *materia informis* and *materia prima* is stressed in O'Keeffe, "Dante's Theory of Creation" 51–52. Bonaventure: *Commentaria in Sententiarum* 1.d19.p2.q3, 2.d12.a1.q1–3; Duns Scotus: e.g., *Reportata Parisiensia* 2.d12.q1–2, *Quaestiones super Metaphysicorum* 7.5. *Rationes seminales* as exegetical: see Copleston, *History of Philosophy* 2:75–77. David Knowles: *Evolution of Medieval Thought* 44, 34. Matter as most distant from God: e.g., Aquinas, *ST* 1a.q115.a1.ad4; *SCG* 3.69.

10. Plotinus's principal treatment of matter is *Enneads* 2.4, especially sections 14–16.

11. Matter concreated with form: *SCG* 4.63, *ST* 1a.q7.a2.ad3; 1a.q84.a3.ad2; incorruptible: *ST* 1a.104.4.

12. For the congruence between Aristotelian and contemporary concepts of matter, see Suppes, "Aristotle's Concept"; the epilogue outlines other parallels.

13. *Monarchia* 1.3.8–9: *Necesse est multitudinem rerum generabilium ut potentia tota materie prime semper sub actu sit: aliter esset dare potentiam separatam, quod est inpossibile*; 2.2.2–3: *Restat quod quicquid in rebus inferioribus est peccatum, ex parte materie subiacentis peccatum sit . . . et quod quicquid est in rebus inferioribus bonum, cum ab ipsa materia esse non possit, sola potentia existente, per prius ab artifice Deo sit. . . .* On the three principles of natural things, see *Cv* 2.13.17, and *If* 25.100–102.

14. See also *Cv* 2.14.10: *le cose naturali corruttibili . . . cotidianamente compiono loro via, e la loro materia si muta di forma in forma* ("corruptible natural things . . . complete their course day by day, and their matter changes from form to form"). Dante often refers to this capacity to "receive" changing form as *cera*, "wax": e.g., *Pd* 1.40–42, 8.127–129, 13.67–69.

15. "Those in whom pure act was produced were the summit of the universe. Pure potentiality held the lowest place; in the middle such a bond tied up potentiality with act that it is never unbound."

16. Nardi argued for the first position in *Sigieri di Brabante* 23–32, "Intorno al tomismo" 182–184, "Noterelle polemiche" 132–133, "Dante e Pietro d'Abano" 43–45, "Rassegna bibliografica" 309–312, and "Meditantur sua stercora" 57–59; he argued for the second position in " 'Tutto il frutto ricolto' " 260–262; in "Il tomismo secondo Emilio Brodero" 369 he says that Dante's position is "agostinian[a] e scotistic[a]" (curious, since the two views are incompatible). The first position was attacked by the Thomists Calò (Review of *Sigieri di Brabante* 264–270); Moretti, "La filosofia di Dante: Le creature" 52–54; Busnelli, *Cosmogonia* 20–49; and Mandonnet, *Dante le théologien* 247–248, 275–276. Nardi's second position was adopted by Mellone (*Dottrina* 60–68) and (with some reservations) Bemrose (*Dante's Angelic Intelligences* 194). For lucid surveys of the controversy, see Bruce-Jones, "L'importanza primaria"; Mellone, *Dottrina* 58–60; Mazzoni's introduction to his edition of the *Questio* (712–724); and the appendix ("The Angels and Prime Matter") in Bemrose, *Dante's Angelic Intelligences*. The commentary tradition is uniformly confused.

17. "And as in glass, in amber or in crystal, a ray shines so that there is no interval between its coming and its being fully there, so did the triform effect ray forth from its Lord in all its being, all at once, without distinction of beginning. Order and structure was concreated with the substances; and those were at the top in whom . . ."

18. Aristotle, *De sensu* 6.446b27; *De anima* 2.7.418b20–28; see, e.g., Aquinas, *ST* 1a.67.2, 1a.q45.a3.ad3; Bonaventure, *Commentaria in Sententiarum* 2.d13.a3.q1.

19. Nardi said that the concept of matter in the *Monarchia* and *Convivio* is "completely different" from that of the *Comedy* ("Rassegna bibliografica" 309–310; see also

"Dante e Pietro d'Abano" 45, and "Meditantur sua stercora" 57–58). Mellone concurs: the *Monarchia* and *Comedy* present "opposite conceptions," the former Aristotelian-Thomistic, the latter Augustinian-Scotistic (*Dottrina* 67–70); Bemrose calls the *Comedy*'s views a "striking departure" from the *Monarchia* and Aristotelianism (*Dante's Angelic Intelligences* 201). Nardi ended up dating the *Monarchia* before the *Comedy* ("Tre pretese fasi" 294–301) and denying that Dante wrote the *Questio* at all ("Caduta di Lucifero" 241–265).

20. *Forma sustanziäl*: e.g., *Pg* 18.49; *formas particulares*: *Mn* 1.3.9; *suggetto*: e.g., *VN* 20.7 (*Pd* 2.107 and 29.51 are ambiguous); *subietto*: e.g., *Cv* 4.14.10, 3.11.13; *subiectum*: e.g., *Mn* 1.11.4, 3.4.13; *complession potenziäta*: *Pd* 7.140; *subiectum mixtum et complexionatum*: *Questio* 47. Also referring to mixtures of elements: *Cv* 4.21.4; 4.23.7; *Pg* 25.51; *Mn* 1.3.6 (in minerals); to the totality of such mixtures: *Pd* 17.38 (*la vostra matera*).

21. *Mondana cera*: *Pd* 1.41; *cera mortal*: *Pd* 8.128; *cera dedutta*: *Pd* 13.67, 73; *sorda*: *Pd* 1.129; *inobedientiam materie*: *Questio* 44. See also *Cv* 3.4.7, 3.6.6, 3.2.4, 4.5.4; *Questio* 74. "Wax perfectly readied or disposed" (*a punto la cera dedutta*) at creation of Adam and birth of Christ: *Pd* 13.67–87. Matter, not form, cause of imperfection: see also *Cv* 3.2.4; *Mn* 2.2.3.

22. *Sustanze separate da materia, cioè intelligenze, le quali la volgare gente chiamano Angeli* (*Cv* 2.4.2); see also, e.g., *Cv* 3.4.9 (*sustanze partite da materia*).

23. Nardi: "Se la prima materia"; see also "Intorno al tomismo" 185–186, "Dante e Pietro d'Abano" 45, "Tutto il frutto ricolto" 256–258, and "Meditantur sua stercora" 57–58. Nardi's understanding of *intendere* is supported by Corti (*Felicità mentale* 116, 125) and accepted by Foster ("Tommaso d'Aquino" 636); it was anticipated, in a less subtle form, by Moore ("Dante's Theory of Creation" 141–142). (Nardi points out ["Intorno al tomismo" 186, "Rassegna bibliografica" 310, and "Se la prima materia" 202] that Dante is not asking "how" but "if the first matter . . .": "how" would restrict the question to the old Augustinian-Aristotelian debate about whether matter has any actuality [form] in itself, i.e., whether it can be known in itself or only through the analysis of substantial material forms.) *Intendere* as *intelligere*: Busnelli, *Cosmogonia* 37–42, "Un famoso dubbio"; see also Calò, Review of *Sigieri di Brabante* 268–270; O'Keeffe, "Dante's Theory of Creation" 53–54. For a balanced summary of the controversy, see Vasoli's notes to his edition of the *Convivio* (at 4.1.8), and now see Sasso, "*Se la materia*"; for other bibliography, see Mellone, "Esemplarismo divino" 222. Bemrose gives useful clarifications in *Dante's Angelic Intelligences* 186–190; see also De Bonfils Templer, "La prima materia."

24. Nardi: see references in previous note. Others: e.g., Foster, "Tommaso d'Aquino" 636–637, and Corti, *Felicità mentale* 125–126.

25. *In alcuno modo queste cose nostro intelletto abbagliano . . . che lo 'ntelletto nostro guardar non può, cioè Dio e la etternitate e la prima materia: . . . quello che sono intender noi non potemo, se non cose negando si può apressare alla sua conoscenza, e non altrimenti* (*Cv* 3.15.6).

CHAPTER 3: FORM

1. Compare Wittgenstein *Tractatus* 6.44; see 6.372.

2. Geach: in Anscombe and Geach, *Three Philosophers* 75, where he also refers Aristotle's remark (probably from *Metaphysics* 7.3.1029a33). Aristotle against Platonic forms: e.g., *Metaphysics* 1.6–7, 1.9, 7.6, 7.14; form immanent: *Metaphysics* 5.4.1015a7–11, 5.24.1023a31–32, 7.8; form makes substance: *Metaphysics* 7.3.1029a29–30,

7.6.1031b20, 7.7.1032b1–2, 7.11.1037a29–30; 8.1.1042a17; form as actuality, perfection, cause: *Metaphysics* 5.2.1013b22–23, 5.24.1023a34, 8.2–3.1043a28–31; substance known through form: *De anima* 3.8.431b29; matter unknowable: *Metaphysics* 7.10.1036a8, *Physics* 3.6.207a25; form as universal: e.g., *Categories* 5 and 17, *De interpretatione* 7.17a38–b15, *Metaphysics* 7.8.1034a5–8, 7.11.1036a28, 7.13, 13.10, *Parts of Animals* 1.4.644a24–25; immaterial forms: *Metaphysics* 1071b4–23, *De anima* 1.4.408b18–19, 3.5; forms in mind: *De anima* 3.4–5. Some useful discussions of form in Aristotle are: A. C. Lloyd, *Form and Universal*; Joseph Owens, *The Doctrine of Being*, esp. 176–188, 386–395, 457–473; Furth, "Specific and Individual Form" and "Aristotle on the Unity"; Sykes, "Form in Aristotle"; Regis, "Aristotle on Universals"; Lacey, "*Ousia* and Form"; Jeannot, "Plato and Aristotle"; Suzanne Mansion, "Ontological Composition"; Gail Fine, "Forms as Causes"; Leszl, "Knowledge of the Universal"; Lesher, "Aristotle on Form"; Shields, "Generation of Form"; Hamlyn, "Aristotle on Form"; G. E. R. Lloyd, *Aristotle*; William Ross, *Aristotle*, esp. 173–183; Evans, *Aristotle*, esp. 61–101; Witt, *Substance and Essence*; Aubenque, *Problème de l'être*; Matthen, "Individual Substances"; Georgiadis, "Two Conceptions of Substance"; Novak, "A Key to Aristotle's 'Substance' "; Michael Woods, "Universals and Particular Forms" and "Particular Forms Revisited"; Yu, "Two Conceptions of Hylomorphism"; Burger, "Is Each Thing the Same"; Terrell Bynum, "A New Look"; Bernard Williams, "Hylomorphism"; Sellars, "Substance and Form"; Albritton, "Forms of Particular Substances"; Annas, "Aristotle on Substance" and "Forms and First Principles"; and Maierù, "Forma."

3. Aquinas: e.g., *ST* 1a.65.4, 1a.110.2. Hierarchy of being in Aristotle: see esp. *De caelo* 1.9.279a22–30, 2.12.292a22–b25; *Metaphysics* 9.8.1050b5–6; "what it is to be" quotations: A. C. Lloyd, *Form and Universal* 47; "infected with potentiality": William Ross, *Aristotle* 183; "where there is a better" quotation: Aristotle, Fragment 16 (from *On Philosophy*); see Jaeger, *Aristotle* 158. The fundamental study of the "great chain of being" in Western thought is Lovejoy's book of that name (for Aristotle, see esp. 55–59); see also Solmsen, "Antecedents of Aristotle's Psychology"; Kahn, "Place of the Prime Mover"; William Ross, *Aristotle* 178; G. E. R. Lloyd, *Aristotle* 293–297; Jaeger, *Aristotle* 158, 340, 382; and Donald Morrison, "Evidence for Degrees."

4. A transcendent Form: see Jaeger, *Aristotle* 382. Helpful in thinking about Aristotle's thoughts on thinking are Kosman, "What Does the Maker Mind Make?" (particularly insightful) and "Perceiving That We Perceive"; Skousgaard, "Wisdom and Being" (excellent); Horne, "Randall's Interpretation"; Augustin Mansion, "L'immortalité de l'âme"; Anscombe, "On the Notion"; Anscombe and Geach, *Three Philosophers*; Mensch, "Aristotle and the Overcoming"; James Martin, "Aquinas as a Commentator"; Benardete, "Aristotle, *De anima*"; Owens, "A Note on Aristotle"; Robinson, "Form and the Immateriality"; Rodier, *Traité de l'âme*; Sorabji, *Time, Creation and the Continuum* 137–156 and "Body and Soul in Aristotle"; William Ross, *Aristotle* 135–160, 184–191; Allan, *Philosophy of Aristotle* 45–92, 117–122; Everson, "Psychology"; Irwin, "Aristotle's Philosophy of Mind"; De Corte, *Doctrine de l'intelligence*, esp. 32–63; Nardi, "Introduzione"; Modrak, *Aristotle: Power of Perception*, esp. 113–154, "An Aristotelian Theory," and "The *Nous*-Body Problem"; Barnes, "Aristotle's Concept of Mind"; Hartman, *Substance, Body, and Soul*, esp. 220–269; Heinaman, "Aristotle and the Mind-Body Problem"; Shields, "Soul as Subject," "Soul and Body," and "Some Recent Approaches"; Terrell Bynum, "A New Look"; Robinson, "Mind and Body" and "Aristotelian Dualism"; Nussbaum, "Aristotelian Dualism"; Olshewsky, "On the Relations"; Peccorini, "Aristotle's Agent Intellect" and "Divinity and Immortality"; Schiller, "Aristotle and the Concept"; Kahn, "Sensation and Consciousness," "Aristotle on Thinking," and "Aristotle and Altruism"; Williams and Hirst, "Form and Sensation"; Block, "Aristotle

and the Physical Object"; Hamlyn's notes to his translation of the *De anima*; Frede, "On Aristotle's Conception" and "Théorie aristotélicienne"; Wilkes, "*Psuche* versus the Mind"; Cohen, "Credibility"; Hardie, "Concepts of Consciousness"; Lear, "Active Episteme"; Lowe, "Aristotle on Kinds of Thinking"; A. C. Lloyd, "Non-Discursive Thought"; Manning, "Materialism, Dualism and Functionalism"; Rist, "Notes"; Franks, "*Nous* as Human Form"; Sprague, "A Parallel"; and Granger, *Aristotle's Idea*.

5. Nutritive and sensitive soul: *De anima* 2.2–4, 3.12, *Generation of Animals* 2.3.736b21–28; sensation: 2.5–3.2; *nous*: 3.3–8.

6. *Protrepticus*: in Aristotle, *Complete Works* 2403–2416; see also Hutchinson, "Ethics" 196–197.

7. On the Unmoved Mover and *nous*, see, e.g.: Owens, "Relation of God to World"; Kosman, "Divine Being and Divine Thinking" (particularly insightful); Lang, "God or Soul"; Stewart, "Aristotle's Doctrine"; Gerson, *God and Greek Philosophy* 82–141; Norman, "Aristotle's Philosopher-God"; Kahn, "The Place of the Prime Mover"; Ross's commentary to *Metaphysics* 12.7 (2.372–382); Patzig, "Theology and Ontology"; Berti, "Concetto di atto"; and Franks, "Relation of the Sublunary."

8. Compare Kahn ("Aristotle on Thinking" 375): "The self-awareness of *nous* just is the formal structure of the universe *become aware of itself.* This is partially realized in us to the extent that we live the life of *theoria*, fully realized in the divine intellect." Non-Aristotelian possibility: however, Kahn ("Aristotle and Altruism") understands *nous* as the true self, a divine interpersonal or superpersonal principle in which all are one, grounding Aristotle's theory of friendship. Highest ideal: see, e.g., Aristotle, *Nicomachean Ethics* 10.7.1177a12–17, and the *Protrepticus*; see also Atherton, "Aristotle."

9. Nardi: "Conoscenza umana" 143, and see *Soggetto e oggetto* 15–17, 68; Hicks: in his edition of the *De anima* ("We find nothing in Aristotle but the development in systematic form of the Platonic heritage" [xxxvi]); Taylor: *Aristotle* 30–31. For Aristotelian Platonism, see, e.g., G. E. R. Lloyd, *Aristotle* 19–67; Jaeger, *Aristotle* 11–38, 105–123; Owen, "Platonism of Aristotle," and De Vogel, "Legend of the Platonizing Aristotle" (both qualifying Jaeger); and Driscoll, "Platonic Ancestry." Gentile: "Filosofia di Dante" 179–181. Knowles points out that unlike Aristotle Plato never analyzed the soul by a rigorous metaphysics: "he remained in this respect primarily a moralist, an educationalist and a practical psychologist" (*Evolution of Medieval Thought* 188). Aristotle grants transcendence to Intellect alone: the point is made by Marenbon, *Early Medieval Philosophy* 7. Dante: '*l maestro di color che sanno* (*If* 4.131), *maestro e duca della ragione umana* (*Cv* 4.6.8), '*ngegno [singulare] e quasi divino* (4.6.15), *dove aperse la bocca la divina sentenza d'Aristotile, da lasciare mi pare ogni altrui sentenza* (4.17.3); *filosofo sommo* (4.6.16), *glorioso filosofo* (3.5.7), *maestro delli filosofi* (4.8.15), '*l maestro vostro* (*Pd* 8.120), *il mio maestro* (*Cv* 1.9.9), *lo maestro della nostra vita* (4.23.8). Dante discusses Aristotle's authority in *Convivio* 4.6.6–17; for Dante's teeming references to "the Philosopher," see De Matteis, "Aristotele."

10. "The errors of Descartes": Grene, *Knower and the Known* chap. 3. For idealism as a post-Cartesian development ("Greek philosophy does not know the problem of proving in a general way the existence of an external world. That problem is a modern invention." [33]), see the fundamental article by Burnyeat, "Idealism and Greek Philosophy"; see also Sorabji, *Time, Creation and the Continuum* 287–296. On consciousness and Cartesianism, see, e.g., Wilkes ("*Psuche* versus the Mind" 111–116), who also points out the etymology of the word "consciousness"; and Dennehy, "Ontological Basis"; on Cartesian versus Aristotelian mind, see also Kahn, "Sensation and Consciousness"; Hardie, "Concepts of Consciousness"; Rorty, *Philosophy and the Mirror* 45–51; and Anscombe, "On the Notion." "Innocent and cheerful": applied to

Democritus by Lacey ("Materialism" 530). Nardi: *Soggetto e oggetto* 69; see also Kahn ("Aristotle on Thinking"), who comes to the same conclusion. Saint Francis: *Fioretti* chap. 29 (95–98). The exorcism—Nardi delicately does not report it—was to tell Satan, the next time he appeared, *Apri la bocca, e mo' vi ti caco* ("Open your mouth, and I'll just shit in it"). When Brother Ruffino followed the saint's advice, the devil was so insulted he caused a landslide on his way out.

11. Theophrastus: fragments collected in appendix to the Hicks edition of Aristotle's *De anima*, and in Barbotin, *Théorie aristotélicienne* 245–273; Alexander of Aphrodisias: *De anima* 3.5 (on divine union in Alexander, see Merlan, *Monopsychism* 16–41); Themistius: *In De anima* 3.4–5; Augustine: e.g., *De Genesi ad litteram* 12.31, *De Trinitate* 9.7.12; Bonaventure: e.g., *Commentaria in Sententiarum* 3.d23.a2.q2, 1.d15–16, 2.d24.p1.a2.q4, *Collationes in Hexaemeron* 1.13; Avicenna: *Liber de anima*; Averroës: *Commentarium magnum in De anima*; Albertus Magnus: *De anima, Scripta in Sententiarum* 1.B.5; Aquinas: *Sentencia libri De anima* 3.4, *De unitate* (in *Aquinas against the Averroists*). See also: Huby, "Stages in the Development" 134–135; Blumenthal, "*Nous Pathetikos*"; Robinson, "Form and the Immateriality"; Hamelin, *Théorie de l'intellect*; Hoenen, "Metaphysik und Intellektlehre"; Knowles, *Evolution of Medieval Thought* 191–198; Kretzman, Kenny, and Pinborg, *Cambridge History* 595–628; Owens, "Faith, Ideas"; Étienne Gilson, *Philosophy of Bonaventure* 309–364; Leaman, *Averroes* 82–116; Lee, "St. Thomas and Avicenna"; Herrera, "An Episode"; Reyna, "On the Soul"; and Dewan, "St. Albert, St. Thomas." The surveys in Nardi's "Introduzione" and "Conoscenza umana" and in Vasoli's "Intelletto" are still useful.

12. For the pervasiveness of Platonism in medieval thought and the complexity of its sources, see, e.g., Gersh, *Middle Platonism and Neoplatonism* and "Platonism—Neoplatonism—Aristotelianism," and Klibansky, *Continuity of the Platonic Tradition*. For the principle of self-knowledge across many traditions, see Perry, *Treasury of Traditional Wisdom* 859–868, 887–890.

13. Plato: e.g., *Symposium* 201d–212a, *Theaetetus* 176b, *Phaedrus* 243e–257b, *Republic* 7.514a–518b; divine origin of soul: *Timaeus* 90b–d; soul as middle being: *Timaeus* 35a; understanding born suddenly: *Letter VII* 341c–d (quote: 341d); *Alcibiades I:* esp. 132c–d (the paternity of the *Alcibiades* was not doubted in antiquity). On Plato's "mysticism," see, e.g., Festugière, *Contemplation et vie contemplative*, and McGinn, *Foundations of Mysticism* 24–35. Cicero: e.g., *Tusculan Disputations* 1.22.52, *De legibus* 1.22.58, 1.23.60–61, and *Somnium Scipionis* 8.26 (in *Laelius* volume). For an exhaustive history (in three volumes) of the *Gnothi seauton*, see Courcelle, *Connais-toi toi-même*.

14. Porphyry: *On the Life of Plotinus* 23. Philosophy as experience: e.g., *Enneads* 4.8.1, 6.9.9; the One transcends thought and duality: e.g., 3.8.11, 3.9.7, 5.3.12–13, 5.6.1–3, 5.6.6, 6.9.3–4, 6.9.6 (see also Gerson, *God and Greek Philosophy* 185–226); One-Many: 5.1.8 (see also Bussanich, "Plotinus's Metaphysics"); soul and intellect: e.g., 3.6.3, 4.8.2–4, 5.2.1 (and see Blumenthal, "On Soul and Intellect," and Gerson, *Plotinus* 42–64); part of soul remains with Intellect: 4.8.7–8, 6.7.13; emanation like light: e.g., 5.1.6 (and see Armstrong, " 'Emanation' in Plotinus"); emanation timeless: 3.5.9, 6.4.11; turning back on itself: 5.1.6–7, 5.2.1; Dante: see, e.g., Freccero's "Pilgrim in a Gyre."

15. Soul as frontier: *Enneads* 4.4.2–3, 4.8.4 (see Clarke, "Living on the Edge" 185); self as *nous*: 4.4.3, 4.7.10, 5.8.3 (and see Armstrong, "Aristotle in Plotinus"); "shock of beauty," soul becomes love: 1.6.1–4, 6.7.22 (see McGinn, *Foundations of Mysticism* 48); self-surrender: 5.5.8, 6.5.12, 6.9.7, 6.9.11; "all and one": 6.5.7; divine within us: 5.1.5–7, 10–13 (see McGinn, *Foundations of Mysticism* 51); self-knowledge and God: esp.

6.7.35–36, 6.9.9–11; "the man is changed . . .": *Enneads* 6.9.10 (MacKenna translation). See also Hadot, *Plotinus* 23–47 and "Neoplatonist Spirituality" (the best short account of self-knowledge and divine union in Plotinus); O'Daly, *Plotinus' Philosophy of the Self*; Kenney, "Mysticism and Contemplation"; Rist, "Plotinus and Christian Philosophy" 213–230; Arnou, *Désir de Dieu*; Rappe, "Self-Perception in Plotinus"; and Armstrong, *Architecture of the Intelligible* esp. 29–47 and "Apprehension of Divinity."

16. Plotinus and Christianity: see, e.g., Madec, " 'Platonisme' des pères," with extensive bibliography; McGinn, *Foundations of Mysticism* 54–55; Armstrong, "Salvation, Plotinian and Christian" and "Man in the Cosmos"; Rist, "Plotinus and Christian Philosophy"; and Finan and Twomey, *Relationship between Neoplatonism and Christianity*; for an emphatic statement, see Inge, *Philosophy of Plotinus* 7–15. Kingdom within: Luke 17.21; finding treasure, etc . . . : Matt. 13.44–52 (see also 10.39, 16.25, 19.29); Moses: e.g., Ex. 34; Paul: 2 Cor. 12.1–6; Peter, James and John: Matt. 17.1–9, Mark 9.2–10, Luke 9.28–36; pure in heart: Matt. 5.8; be perfect: Matt. 5.48; seeking life: Matt. 10.39; image we reflect: 2 Cor. 3.17–18; Christ within: Gal. 2.19–20 (see also 2.20, 3.27); God is love: 1 John 4.8; dwell in God: 14.23, 17.21–23. For many of these passages and others, see McGinn, *Foundations of Mysticism* 62–83; see also Margaret Smith, *Introduction to Mysticism* 25–33. Botterill provides a lucid account of the history of deification in *Dante and the Mystical Tradition* 196–221.

17. "Flight of the alone": *Enneads* 6.9.11 (line 50); "God became man . . .": Clement of Alexandria, *Protrepticus* (*Exhortation to the Greeks*) 1.8; become gods . . . : e.g., *Stromateis* 2.22.131, 5.10.63, 7.16.101 (see McGinn, *Foundations of Mysticism* 107); Clement quotation: *Paedagogus* 3.1; Origen on reading spiritually: e.g., *Commentary on John* 10.10; "letter that kills": 2 Cor. 3.6 (see McGinn, *Foundations of Mysticism* 111–112); virgin soul gives birth: *Commentary on Matthew*, fragment 281 (see McGinn, *Foundations* 378n192 for other references); intellect deified: *Commentary on John* 32.27; human nature becomes divine: *Against Celsus* 3.28 (see McGinn, *Foundations* 128–129). Athanasius: *Contra gentes* 2.30. Gregory of Nyssa: passage from *Commentary on the Canticle*, Sermon 2 (804a–808b), quoted from *Glory to Glory* 159–163.

18. Augustine and (Neo)Platonism: see, e.g., *City of God* 8.4–13, and McEvoy, "Neoplatonism and Christianity"; Madec, "Le néoplatonisme dans la conversion d'Augustin"; O'Meara, "Augustine and Neo-Platonism"; Nash, "Some Philosophic Sources"; Rist, *Augustine* 3–4; McGinn, *Foundations of Mysticism* 242–243; Armstrong, "St. Augustine and Christian Platonism"; and Sorabji, *Time, Creation and the Continuum* 157–173; for context, see Armstrong, *Cambridge History*. Books of the Platonists: *Confessions* 7.9.13–7.10.16; reverence for Plotinus, e.g., *City of God* 10.2, *Trinity* 4.20, *Against the Academics* 3.18.41, and see McEvoy, "Neoplatonism and Christianity" 155, 169; "by the Platonic books . . .": *Confessions* 7.10.16; "You were within . . .": 10.27.38; perfect prayer: *Soliloquies* 2.1; *noli foras ire*: *Of True Religion* 72 (see also *Against the Academics* 1.1, 1.23, 2.2, 2.4–5, 2.8; *Trinity* 9.4, 10.1–16); sharpen mind . . . : *On Psalms* 41.10; sweetness: 41.9; touches God: *Sermons* 117.5; withdrawing what was added: *Trinity* 10.11; attachment: *Soliloquies* 1.12; inner light: e.g., *Confessions* 9.10, *Literal Meaning* 5.16, 12.31; participation in Christ: *Trinity* 4.4; Trinity within: 9–15, esp., e.g., 9.12.18, 14.12.15; share in Christ: e.g., *Saint Augustine on the Psalms* 69.1, 85.1, *Homilies on John* 21.8 (and see McGinn, *Foundations of Mysticism* 248–251); "the Light itself is one . . .": *Confessions* 10.24.52; "seen by a power of sight . . .": *Trinity* 1.11. See also the famous accounts of "inward travel" in *Confessions* 7.17 and 9.10, and the analysis of Paul's rapture in *Literal Meaning* 54–56. For Augustinian introspection and self-knowledge, see, e.g., O'Daly, *Augustine's Philosophy of Mind* 207–216; Cousins, "Intravi in intima mea"; and A. C. Lloyd, "Nosce Teipsum."

19. Inset passage: *Mystical Theology* 1.1–3. Soul divinized . . . : see, e.g., *Divine Names* 1.5.593C, 1.7.596C, 2.11.649B, 5.10.825B, 13.2.977C. Soul in circle . . . : 4.9.705A, and see Ritacco-Gayoso, "Intelligible Light and Love"; godlike oneness: 1.4.589D; Light beyond deity . . . : 1.5.593C. For a subtle and rich treatment of Dionysian mysticism and its sources, see De Andia, *Henosis*. Eriugena: e.g., *Periphyseon* 3.19. For Eriugena's great "mystical" metaphysics, one of the most probing philosophical syntheses of the Middle Ages, but largely unknown after 1225, see Moran, *Philosophy of John Scotus Eriugena* (although I remain unconvinced that Eriugena's metaphysics, any more than that of any other medieval philosopher, is well characterized by the term "idealism"). For brief surveys of Pseudo-Dionysius's influence in the Middle Ages, see the introductions (by Pelikan and Leclercq) to *Complete Works*, and Rorem, *Pseudo-Dionysius* 214–225.

20. Sweetness of God . . . : e.g., *On Loving God* [*De diligendo Deo*] 9.26, 15.39, 8.25; "drunk with love . . .": 10.27 (Bernard is citing 1 Cor. 6.17); surrender self-will . . . : 10.27–29; understanding through experience: e.g., *On Song of Songs* [*Sermo super Cantica Canticorum*] 74.5–7, 4.1, 22.2; self-knowledge: e.g, *De gradibus* 1.2, 3.6, 4.13,15, 5.18, 10.28, 11.39, *On Loving God* 2.2, 2.4, *De conversione ad clericos* 2.3, *De diversis* 40.3–4 (precept from Heaven, citing Juvenal, *Satires* 11.27, through Macrobius, *Commentary on Dream of Scipio* 1.9.1: see Courcelle, *Connais-toi toi-même* 1.59, 262), *On Song of Songs* 35–37, 50.6 (for other references see Courcelle 258–272); drinks at own well . . . : *De consideratione* 2.3.6; "middle place": *On Song of Songs* 5.5; whose image . . . : 36.6, 2.2; Christ gives us back to ourselves: *On Loving God* 5.15; through Christ . . . : e.g., *On Song of Songs* 6.3, 20.6, 32.2, 71. For Bernard, see McGinn, *Growth of Mysticism* 158–224, and "Love, Knowledge, and *Unio Mystica*" 62–64; and Botterill, *Dante and the Mystical Tradition*.

21. *Gnothi seauton*: *Twelve Patriarchs* [*Benjamin Minor*] 78; inner sweetness . . . : 37, 84, *Mystical Ark* [*Benjamin Major*] 5.5; "ravished into the abyss . . .": *Four Degrees* (from *Selected Writings* 228); knows nothing: *Mystical Ark* 3.6; "everything celestial . . .": 3.7; reasoning useless: *Patriarchs* 74; return to yourself: *Mystical Ark* 3.6, 4.16; mountain of self-knowledge: *Patriarchs* 78; know God: 83; Plato and Aristotle: 75; soul is mirror: 71–72, *Mystical Ark* 5.14; wiped clean . . . : *Patriarchs* 83; forgetting everything . . . : 84, *Mystical Ark* 4.23; fly in contemplation: 5.4; love God alone: 4.16; mind forgets itself . . . : 4.22, 5.5, 5.7; peak of mountain, point: 4.23, 5.2; divine favor: 5.16; mind enlarged . . . : 5.12, 5.14; dawning: 5.2, 5.9.

22. Inset passage: *Soul's Journey* [*Itinerarium mentis in Deum*] 4.1. *Apex mentis* . . . : e.g., 1.6, 7.4, *Commentaria in Sententiarum* 2.d8.p2.a1.q2, *Sermo V de Epiphania* (9.162); mind enters itself . . . : *Soul's Journey* 1.2, 1.4; "everything sensible . . .": *Triple Way* [*De triplici via*] 1.15–17; focuses itself . . . : *Soul's Journey* 5–7; pass over into Truth . . . : 7.4; direct experience of God . . . : e.g., *Triple Way* 1.18, *Knowledge of Christ* [*De scientia Christi*] epilogue, *Breviloquium* 5.6.6–7; path to this experience . . . : as in *Triple Way*, and see McGinn, *Flowering of Mysticism* 102; Christ as medium: e.g., *Commentaria in Sententiarum* 1.Proem, 1.d27.p2.q2, 3.d19.a2.q2, *Collationes in Hexaemeron* 1.11–39, 3.2, *De reductione artium* 23 (see McGinn, *Flowering of Mysticism* 88–93, 100, 107–110); contemplating Christ . . . : e.g., *Soul's Journey* 6.4–6, 7.1–2; Francis: e.g., *Life of St. Francis* [*Legenda major*] 13.3, 15.1, *Soul's Journey* 7.3, *Collationes in Hexaemeron* 22.23 (see McGinn, *Flowering of Mysticism* 93–101, and Cousins, "Francis of Assisi"). See also McGinn, "Ascension and Introversion." For the *apex mentis* and *scintilla animae*, see the appendix to chap. 11 of De Andia's *Henosis*.

23. For Aquinas's reception, see Hillgarth, "Who Read Thomas Aquinas?"; C. F. J. Martin (*Introduction to Medieval Philosophy* 121–136) gives a lively account of Aquinas's

"synthesis" and its rejection. Participates in being . . . : e.g., *Truth [De veritate]* 1.1.ad5, 8.6, 8.10–11, *Metaphysics* 6.3.1205, 11.7.2263, *ST* 1a.5.2, 1a.14.4, 1a.16.3, 1a.45.7, 1a.81, 1a2ae.62.4, 2a2ae.84.2; see also Bogliolo, *Essere e conoscere* 9–15, and Gilson, *Christian Philosophy of St. Thomas* 110–112, for lucid summaries; for the unity of the "transcendentals" and their centrality in Aquinas's thought, see Aertsen, e.g., "What Is First" and "Philosophical Importance." Everything participates in divine . . . : *ST* 1a.44.1, 1a.44.3 (see A. N. Williams, "Deification in the *Summa Theologiae*" 241); "God is the beginning . . .": 1a.2.Proem; God as Intellect: 1a.14.1, 1a.14.4; humans as frontier: *Scriptum super Sententiarum* 3.Prologus, see also *ST* 1a.77.2, *De ente et essentia* 4.29, and the treatment of the "border" in Quinn, *Aquinas, Platonism*; as horizon: *Commentary on Book of Causes* 9 [61] (see Clarke, "Living on the Edge" 192–193); culmination of physical world: *ST* 1a.96.2; 1a.91.1, *Questiones de anima* 1, *Scriptum super Sententiarum* 2.d1.q2.a3; *Quodlibetal Questions* 4.q3 (and see, e.g., Clarke, "Living on the Edge" 192; Étienne Gilson, *Spirit of Medieval Philosophy* 219; and Bogliolo, *Essere e conoscere* 125). Clarke: "Living on the Edge" 193; and Bogliolo: *Essere e conoscere* 125 (but the idea goes back to Maximus the Confessor and Saint Iraeneus: see Armstrong, "St. Augustine and Christian Platonism" 19–23). Purpose of life is deification: e.g., *ST* 1a2ae.q3.a7.ad2, q.112.a1, *SCG* 3.25, and see A. N. Williams, "Deification in the *Summa Theologiae*" (esp. 243); deiformity: e.g., *ST* 1a.12.5–6 (and see Williams 223–226); "essence of God . . .": *ST* 1a.12.5 (see also 1a2ae.28.3, and Kwasniewski, "St. Thomas, *Extasis*, and Union"); "both what is seen . . .": *SCG* 3.51.2; "ontological divide": A. N. Williams, "Deification in the *Summa Theologiae*" 221, 225. For an analytic arrangement of Aquinian texts related to intellect, see Labeaga, *Vita Intellettiva*.

24. "Knows itself . . .": *ST* 1a.87.1; human knowing: e.g., 1a.84–88; cannot know in this life: 1a.12.11, 1a.88.1, *SCG* 3.42–46; see also Kenny, *Aquinas on Mind* esp. 119–127, and Hackett, *Aquinas on Mind and Intellect*. "I cannot do any more . . .": quoted from Torrell, *Saint Thomas Aquinas* 289; for a "physicalist" interpretation, see Weisheipl, *Friar Thomas d'Aquino* 320–323. Underhill: *Mysticism* 83.

25. Eckhart dates: 1260–1327 (Dante: 1265–1321); counterpart: the parallel is suggested by, e.g., Giorgi, *Dante e Meister Eckhart* (see also Fels, *Dante und Meister Eckhart*; Underhill, *Mysticism* 463; and Nardi, *Sigieri di Brabante* 70). Ground of the soul . . . : e.g., German Sermons 2, 5b, 15, 22, 48 (in *Essential Sermons*), Latin Sermon 4.1.28 (in *Teacher and Preacher*), and see McGinn, "Love, Knowledge, and *Unio Mystica*" 75 and "Theological Summary" 42–44; "my eye and God's eye . . .": German Sermon 12; "some people think . . .": 6; "nothing but one": 40; God's being is soul's being: 6; give birth to Christ . . . : 6; "the Father gives birth . . .": 6; uncreated spark . . . : 48, 52; soul virgin and wife: 48; seeking nothing outside: 6; wanting nothing . . . : 52; "God is free of all things . . .": 52; equal to God: 6. (German Sermons 12 and 40 in *Teacher and Preacher*; the others in *Essential Sermons*.) For a balanced assessment of Eckhart's antinomies, see Copleston, *History of Philosophy* 3.183–195; for how his "dialectical" method led to his condemnation, see McGinn, "Eckhart's Condemnation Reconsidered"; for his relation to the Neoplatonic tradition, see Woods, "Meister Eckhart and the Neoplatonic Heritage"; for Eckhart's understanding of the "I," see Mojsisch, "Dieses Ich." In the Vedantic tradition, Eckhart's fundamental insight is captured in the maxim *Brahmavid Brahmaiva Bhavathi* (the knower of Brahman becomes Brahman himself).

26. On self-knowledge and divine union, see Dupré, "Mystical Experience of the Self" and "*Unio Mystica*"; on man as horizon and microcosm, see Clarke, "Living on the Edge" (with many references and examples); see also Étienne Gilson, *Spirit of Medieval Philosophy* 209–228. Nasr (e.g., "God is Reality," *Knowledge and the Sacred*) has

long argued that we must rediscover ourselves (and proper metaphysics) in order to recover the "reality" of God. For particularly good samplings of Christian "mystical" texts, see Dupré and Wiseman, *Light from Light*; Egan, *Anthology of Christian Mysticism*; and Petry, *Late Medieval Mysticism*; the best "interfaith" collection is Perry, *Treasury of Traditional Wisdom*. The best "universal" account of mysticism is Spencer, *Mysticism in World Religion* (less successful are, e.g., Otto, *Mysticism East and West*; Zaehner, *Mysticism Sacred and Profane*; and Carmody and Carmody, *Mysticism*).

27. Gandhi called this effect *satyāgraha*, the force of truth or being.

28. For cogent reflections on how inadequate metaphysics lead to "extrinsic" ethics, see Burrell, "Creation, Metaphysics, and Ethics."

29. On "negative theology," see, e.g., Armstrong, "Negative Theology" and "The Escape of the One," and Carabine, *Unknown God*. For the One and Many across many spiritual traditions, see Perry, *Treasury of Traditional Wisdom* 775–790. An ancient Vedic tradition also defines *Brahman* or *atman* only through negation (*neti neti*, "not this, not this"); see *Brihadāranyaka Upaniṣad* 4.2.4 (in *Upaniṣads*). In its purest form, as in some forms of Buddhism, the practice of negation rejects all talk of God, which (in an ironic reversal) leads some who think God is something to call Buddhists atheists. For a perceptive account of nothingness in modern Buddhist thought, see Yusa, "Contemporary Buddhist Philosophy." Plotinus: *Enneads* 5.2.1 and 6.9.4 (see also Perl, "Power of All Things"); Augustine: *Soliloquies* 1.29; Pseudo-Dionysius: *Divine Names* 2.11.649B, 5.10.825B, 13.2.977C; Richard of St. Victor: *Mystical Ark* 4.17; Aquinas: *ST* 1a.8.1, 1a.8.2, 1a.8.4, 1a.q11.a1.ad2; Eckhart: German Sermon 4 (in *Teacher and Preacher* 250).

30. Eckhart: German Sermon 4 (*Teacher and Preacher* 250); Richard of St. Victor: *Mystical Ark* 4.20.

31. "Behold now the height and breadth of the Eternal Goodness, since it has made itself so many mirrors wherein it is reflected, remaining in itself One as before."

32. *Così la bontà di Dio è ricevuta altrimenti dalle sustanze separate, cioè dalli Angeli, che sono sanza grossezza di materia, quasi diafani per la purità della loro forma; e altrimenti dall'anima umana, che, avegna che da una parte sia da materia libera, da un'altra è impedita, sì com'è l'uomo ch'è tutto nell'acqua fuor del capo, del quale non si può dire che tutto sia nell'acqua né tutto fuor da quella; e altrimenti dalli animali, la cui anima tutta in materia è compresa, ma, tanto dico, alquanto è nobilitata; e altrimenti dalle piante, e altrimenti dalle minere, e altrimenti dalla terra che dalli altri, però che è materialissima, e però remotissima e improporzionalissima alla prima simplicissima e nobilissima vertute che sola è intellettuale, cioè Dio.*

33. *E avegna che posti siano qui gradi generali, nondimeno si possono porre gradi singulari: cioè che quella riceve, dell'anime umane, altrimenti una che un'altra. E però che [nel]l'ordine intellettuale dell'universo si sale e discende per gradi quasi continui dalla infima forma a l'altissima [e dall'altissima] alla infima, sì come vedemo nell'ordine sensibile; e tra l'angelica natura, che è cosa intellettuale, e l'anima umana non sia grado alcuno, ma sia quasi l'uno all'altro continuo per li ordini delli gradi, e tra l'anima umana e l'anima più perfetta delli bruti animali ancor mezzo alcuno non sia; e noi veggiamo molti uomini tanto vili e di sì bassa condizione, che quasi non pare [loro] essere altro che bestia: e così è da porre e da credere fermamente, che sia alcuno tanto nobile e di sì alta condizione che quasi non sia altro che angelo. Altrimenti non si continuerebbe l'umana spezie da ogni parte, che essere non può. E questi cotali chiama Aristotile, nel settimo dell'Etica, divini.* For Dante's "obsession" with the ladder of being, see Boyde, *Philomythes* 128–131.

34. *Homo solus in entibus tenet medium corruptibilium et incorruptibilium; propter*

quod recte a phylosophis assimilatur orizonti, qui est medium duorum emisperiorum (3.15[16].3–4). Comparison to the horizon: *Liber de causis* 2.22; see also Albertus, *De anima* 2.1.8.

35. *Onde, con ciò sia cosa che ciascuno effetto ritegna della natura della sua cagione ... ciascuna forma ha essere della divina natura in alcuno modo: non che la divina natura sia divisa e comunicata in quelle, ma da quelle [è] participata, per lo modo quasi che la natura del sole è participata nell'altre stelle. E quanto la forma è più nobile, tanto più di questa natura tiene: onde l'anima umana, che è forma nobilissima di queste che sotto lo cielo sono generate, più riceve della natura divina che alcun'altra.*

36. Albert: *De caelo* 2.3.6; Averroës: in Duhem, *Medieval Cosmology* 481–482, from *De Caelo* 2.49 (see Grant, *Planets, Stars, and Orbs* 393–395); Dante: *Pd* 2.112–148. Some (e.g., Albert of Saxony) thought that the stars were also faintly self-luminous in addition to the light they received from the sun; some (e.g., Macrobius and Avicenna) thought all the stars except the moon were entirely self-luminous. For a full discussion, see Grant, *Planets, Stars, and Orbs* 393–402. Dante sometimes speaks as if the sun is the sole source of all sensible light (e.g., *Cv* 2.13.15, 3.12.7 [again compared to the relation of divine to created intellect], *Pd* 20.4–6, 23.29–30); other times, as in *Pd* 2.142–148 and *Monarchia* 3.4.18, he implies the stars have some self-luminosity.

37. *E però che naturalissimo è in Dio volere essere—però che, sì come nello allegato libro si legge, "prima cosa è l'essere, e anzi a quello nulla è"—, l'anima umana essere vuole naturalmente con tutto desiderio; e però che 'l suo essere dipende da Dio e per quello si conserva, naturalmente disia e vuole a Dio essere unita per lo suo essere fortificare.* The "book mentioned" is again the *Liber de causis*: *Prima rerum creatarum est esse, et non est ante ipsum creatum aliud* (4.37). By saying that "the first of created things is being," the *Liber* reflects the Neoplatonic idea that Being is the first hypostasis of the One, which is beyond (determinate) existence; but Dante (perhaps through Albert) understands *esse* in an Aristotelian sense, as the actuality that constitutes all that is, which is why he drops the word *creatarum*. See Nardi, "Citazioni" 95–98.

38. *Omnis essentia, preter primam, est causata. ... Quidquid causatum [est, est causatum] vel a natura vel ab intellectu, et quod a natura, per consequens causatum est ab intellectu, cum natura sit opus intelligentie; omne ergo quod est causatum, est causatum ab aliquo intellectu vel mediate vel inmediate. ... Et sic, quemadmodum prius devenire erat ad primam causam ipsius esse, sic nunc essentie et virtutis. Propter quod patet quod omnis essentia et virtus procedit a prima, et intelligentie inferiores recipiunt quasi a radiante et reddunt radios superioris ad suum inferius ad modum speculorum. Quod satis aperte tangere videtur Dionysisus de Celesti Hierarchia loquens. Et propter hoc dicitur in libro De Causis quod "omnis intelligentia est plena formis." Patet ergo quomodo ratio manifestat divinum lumen, idest divinam bonitatem, sapientiam et virtutem, resplendere ubique.*

39. "The glory of Him who moves all things penetrates through the universe, and reglows in one part more, and in another less. I have been in the heaven that most receives of His light, and I saw things which whoever descends from up there has neither the knowledge nor the power to relate, because, as it draws near to its desire, our intellect enters so deep that memory cannot follow it."

40. *Letter to Cangrande* 28. See also Vasoli, "Intelletto" 465, and Nardi's fundamental essay, "Perché 'dietro la memoria non può ire' "; also Migliorini Fissi, "Nozione di *deificatio*." On the word "intelletto" in Dante, see Heiney, "*Intelletto* and the Theory of Love," with the corrections of Scott, "Dante's Use of the Word *Intelletto*." Thirst of intellect: see also *Cv* 2.14.20, *Pd* 24.1–3.

41. "O fantasy, who sometimes snatch us so from outward things that we give

no heed, though a thousand trumpets sound around us, who moves you if the senses offer you nothing? A light moves you that takes on form in heaven, whether by itself, or by a will that downward guides it."

42. Knowledge begins from sensation: *Cv* 2.4.17, *Pd* 4.10–12, 2.52–57; for a detailed account, see *Cv* 3.9.6–16. Estimative faculty: *Pd* 26.73–75, *Pg* 29.43–51, 18.22–23, *Cv* 3.9.9, 4.8.6–8. Imaginative faculty: *Pg* 17.13–18, 9.13–18, *Cv* 2.9.4. Human assimilated to angelic intelligence: see Nardi, "Conoscenza umana" 140–141, "Dante e Pietro d'Abano" 55–58.

43. Angelic intelligences one: see also *DVE* 1.2.3. A point on which Dante never wavers: see, e.g., *Mn* 1.15.8–10, *Cv* 4.21, *Pg* 25.61–78; also Nardi, "Concetto dell'impero" 238–239, and a sensitive treatment in Imbach, *Dante, la philosophie* 180–189. For a contrasting view, and a lucid survey of the issues and positions, see Marenbon, "Dante's Averroism."

44. No thought without phantasms . . . : *Cv* 3.4.9,11; see Aristotle, *De anima* 3.7–8. Reason limited: e.g., *Pg* 3.34–36, *Pd* 19.52–57. Angelic (and beatified) intellect versus human reason: e.g., *DVE* 1.2.3, *Pd* 29.76–81, 8.85–90, 9.73–81, 17.36–45, 21.83–90, *Cv* 3.6.5–6, *Mn* 1.3.7; see also Aquinas, *ST* 1a.58.4, 1a.59.1.

45. "It is necessary to speak so to your faculty, since only through sense perception does it apprehend that which it afterwards makes fit for the intellect. For this reason Scripture condescends to your capacity, and attributes feet and hands to God, while meaning something else; and Holy Church portrays to you with human aspect Gabriel and Michael and the other who made Tobit whole again."

46. "All have delight to the degree that their sight penetrates into the depths of the Truth in which every intellect finds rest. From this you can see how the state of blessedness is founded on the act of vision, not in the act of love, which follows after; and what measures their seeing is their merit, which is born from grace and well-directed will: so from step to step the progression goes."

47. See also *Pd* 10.124–126, 29.139–141.

48. "I remember that because of this I was bolder in sustaining it, until I united my gaze with the Infinite Power. Oh abounding grace whereby I presumed to fix my seeing through the Eternal Light so far that all my sight was spent within it!

49. "In its depth I saw ingathered, bound by love in one single volume, that which is dispersed in leaves throughout the universe: substances and accidents and their behavior, as though fused together in such a way that what I say is but a simple light. I believe I saw the universal form of this knot, because saying this, I feel my joy increase."

50. The numerological evocation of *interna* and *squaderna* was noted by Singleton, gloss to *Pd* 33.87. On the "nodo," see Dronke, "Conclusion of Dante's *Commedia*" 31–32, and "Boethius, Alanus and Dante"; also the perceptive comments by Carugati, *Dalla menzogna al silenzio* 135, and Shapiro, *Dante and the Knot of Body and Soul* 1–44; for the precise literal meaning of Bonagiunta's "nodo," see Pertile, "Il nodo di Bonagiunta." For the "book of creation," see the classic essay by Curtius in *European Literature* 302–347, esp. 326–332.

51. Dante explains the distinction between substance and accident in *Mn* 3.11.5; for the theoretical complications involved in the idea of accidental forms—in abstraction, some of them share qualities of substantial forms—see also 1.11.3–4.

52. Aquinas: *ST* 1a.12.5–6; 2a2a.175; see also Foster, "Dante's Vision of God," and Palgen, "Scoto Eriugena, Bonaventura e Dante."

53. "That circling which, thus begotten, appeared in you as reflected light, when my eyes had dwelt on it for some time, seemed to me painted with our image within

itself and in its own color, so that my sight was entirely set upon it. As is the geometer who wholly applies himself to measure the circle, and does not find, thinking, the principle he needs, such was I at that new sight: I wished to see how the image conformed to the circle and how it has its place within it; but my own wings were not sufficient for that: but then my mind was struck by a flash of light that met its desire. Here power failed my high fantasy; but already my desire and will were revolved, like a wheel that is evenly moved, by the love that moves the sun and the other stars."

54. Saint Bernard: *On Loving God* 10.27; see Hollander, "Invocations of the *Commedia*" 35. For particularly sensitive readings of these concluding lines, see Pertile, "Poesia e scienza," and Chiavacci-Leonardi's commentary (3:904–905, 925–929); see also Battaglia, "L'umano e il divino," and Pertile, "*Paradiso*, XXXIII." Measuring the circle: compare *Cv* 2.13.27, *Mn* 3.3.2, and see Thomas Hart's complex analysis in " 'Per misurar lo cerchio' "; "imago": see Boitani, "The Sybil's Leaves" 111; square as animal nature: *Cv* 4.7.14–15, from Aristotle, *De anima* 2.3.414b28–32. For the image of the circle, see Poulet, *Metamorphoses*, esp. xi–xxvii.

55. "Within that breadth and height my sight did not go astray, but took in all the quantity and quality of that joy. Near and far, there, neither add nor take away: for where God governs with no intermediary, the laws of nature in no way prevail."

56. Form synonymous with existence . . . : see, e.g., *Cv* 2.3.15 and Maierù, "Forma" 971; Nardi, "Averroismo del 'primo amico' " 99. Soul is the act or form of the body: *Cv* 3.6.11–12 (citing Aristotle, *De anima* 2.1); intellect defines human soul: e.g., *Cv* 4.7.15, *Mn* 1.3; our essence depends on intellect: *Cv* 3.15.4.

57. *E quella anima . . . perfettissima di tutte l'altre, è l'anima umana, la quale colla nobilitade della potenza ultima, cioè ragione, participa della divina natura a guisa di sempiterna Intelligenza: però che l'anima è tanto in quella sovrana potenza nobilitata e dinudata da materia, che la divina luce, come in angelo, raggia in quella: e però è l'uomo divino animale dalli filosofi chiamato.*

58. *Solamente dell'uomo e delle divine sustanze questa mente si predica, sì come per Boezio si puote apertamente vedere, che prima la predica delli uomini, ove dice a la Filosofia: "Tu e Dio, che nella mente [te] delli uomini mise"; poi la predica di Dio, quando dice a Dio: "Tutte le cose produci dallo superno essemplo, tu, bellissimo, bello mondo nella mente portante." . . . Onde si puote omai vedere che è mente: che è quella fine e preziosissima parte dell'anima che è deitate.* Boethius: *Consolation of Philosophy* 1.Prose 4.8, 3.Poem 9.6–8. For the affinities of these passages with Albert the Great (linking human and angelic or divine intellect), see Fioravanti, "Dante e Alberto Magno" 99–101.

59. Form not defective: *Cv* 3.6.6; 3.4.7; *Mn* 2.2.3; *Pd* 13.67–72. Perfect knowledge of Christ and Adam: *Pd* 13.70–90. *Cv* 4.21.10: *E sono alcuni di tale oppinione che dicono [che], se tutte le precedenti vertudi [seme, seminante, Cielo] s'accordassero sovra la produzione d'un'anima nella loro ottima disposizione, che tanto discenderebbe in quella della deitade, che quasi sarebbe un altro Dio incarnato;* see also *Cv* 4.5.4.

60. "Dante stresses the natural affinity . . .": remarked by Cesare Vasoli ("Intelletto" 465). *Cv* 3.12.6–7: *lo sole spirituale e intelligibile, che è Iddio . . . lo quale di sensibile luce sé prima e poi tutte le corpora celestiali e [le] elementali allumina: così Dio prima sé con luce intellettuale allumina, e poi le [creature] celestiali e l'altre intelligibili. Cv 2.4.14: con ciò sia cosa che lo divino intelletto sia cagione di tutto, massimamente dello intelletto umano. . . . Inset: Ultimamente, in massima laude di sapienza, dico lei essere di tutto madre [e prima di] qualunque principio, dicendo che con lei Dio cominciò lo mondo e spezialmente lo movimento del cielo, lo quale tutte le cose genera e dal quale ogni movimento è principiato e mosso. . . . nel divino pensiero, ch'è esso intelletto, essa era quando lo mondo fece; onde séguita che ella lo facesse. . . . O peggio che morti che l'amistà di costei fuggite,*

aprite li occhi vostri e mirate: ché, innanzi che voi foste, ella fu amatrice di voi, aconciando e ordinando lo vostro processo; e, poi che fatti foste, per voi dirizzare in vostra similitudine venne a voi.

61. *Filosofia è uno amoroso uso di sapienza, lo quale massimamente è in Dio, però che in lui è somma sapienza e sommo amore e sommo atto: che non può essere altrove se non in quanto da esso procede. È adunque la divina filosofia della divina essenza, però che in esso non può essere cosa alla sua essenza aggiunta; ed è nobilissima, però che nobilissima è la essenza divina; [ed] è in lui per modo perfetto e vero, quasi per etterno matrimonio. Nell'altre intelligenze è per modo minore, quasi come druda della quale nullo amadore prende compiuta gioia, ma nel suo aspetto [mirando], contenta[se]ne la loro vaghezza. . . . Oh nobilissimo ed eccellentissimo cuore, che nella sposa dello Imperadore del cielo s'intende, e non solamente sposa, ma suora e figlia dilettissima!*

62. Aristotle, *Metaphysics* 1.2.982b28–983a10; Prov. 8.22–31, 9.2–5. See also *Cv* 1.1.7, 2.12.9, 2.15.12, 3.14.7, 3.15.16–17, 4.22; Nardi, "Note al 'Convivio' " 47–53, "Dante e la filosofia" 215–220, "Filosofia e teologia" 39–44; Corti, *Felicità mentale* 72–94. *Cv* 4.2.18: *l'anima filosofante . . . contempla lo suo contemplare medesimo . . . rivolgendosi sovra se stessa di se stessa innamorando; Cv* 3.14.13–15: *per le quali tre virtudi si sale a filosofare a quelle Atene celestiali dove li Stoici e Peripatetici e Epicurî, per la luce della veritade etterna, in uno volere concordevolemente concorrono* (3.14.15). See also Foster, "Religion and Philosophy" 65–66; De Bonfils Templer, "Dantesco 'Amoroso uso di sapienza,' " "Ragione e intelletto," and "Genesi di un'allegoria" 86–87; and Dronke, *Dante's Second Love* 60–62 (for *Cv* 4.22.14–18).

63. *La filosofia, fuori d'anima, in sé considerata, ha per subietto lo 'ntendere, e per forma uno quasi divino amore allo 'ntelletto . . . della filosofia è cagione efficiente la veritade . . . fine della Filosofia è quella eccellentissima dile[tta]zione che non pate alcuna intermissione o vero difetto, cioè vera felicitade che per contemplazione de la veritade s'acquista.*

64. Philosophy eclipses attachments: *Cv* 3.14.1,6–8. Devils cannot philosophize: *Cv* 3.13.1–2; the *Convivio* ends (4.30.6) by observing that nobility of character is inseparable from philosophy (see also 4.1.11). Understanding is highest perfection: *Cv* 1.1.1, 3.15.2–5.

65. The most sensitive discussion of the *Convivio*'s Lady Philosophy and her Solomonic and Christic resonance is in Dronke, *Dante's Second Love*, esp. 26–50; in the *Convivio*, see, e.g., 3.14.7, 15.5.16, 3.15.17, 1.1.7. For Lady Philosophy's biblical intertexts, see Vasoli, "La Bibbia nel *Convivio*." Albert: *De anima* 3.3.11–12; Aquinas: *SCG* 3.41–45, 3.48, *Questiones de anima* 16, *ST* 1a.88.1, 1a2ae.q3.a4.ad4, 2a2ae.45. This paragraph is much indebted to the lucid discussion of the "Averroistic" ideal of happiness (in relation to Albert and Aquinas) in Steel, "Medieval Philosophy: An Impossible Project?"

66. For Dante's affinities to lay philosophical culture and to "radical Aristotelian" tendencies see, e.g., Meersseman, "Dante come teologo"; Imbach, *Dante, la philosophie*, esp. 129–148; Dronke, *Dante's Second Love* 41, 51–52; Marenbon, "Dante's Averroism." Those who trace intellectual crises or changes of direction in Dante's career include Nardi, whose many essays are perhaps best summarized in his "Filosofia e teologia" (and see in particular "Dante e la filosofia," and the essays collected in *Dal Convivio alla Commedia*), Corti, *Dante a un nuovo crocevia*, and *Felicità mentale*, esp. 72–155, Barański, "Dante commentatore" and "Iter ideologico," and Gagliardi, *La tragedia intellettuale*; Lanza (*Dante e la gnosi*) considers the *Convivio* an "esoteric" alternative to established Christian orthodoxy. Those who stress the fundamental continuity and coherence of Dante's thought include Imbach (above); Garin, "Il pensiero di

Dante," in *Storia della filosofia* 1.179–206; Scott, "Unfinished *Convivio*" and "Dante and Philosophy"; Carugati, "Retorica amorosa"; and Dronke, *Dante's Second Love*. Étienne Gilson (*Dante and Philosophy* esp. 83–161), Simonelli ("Convivio"), and Vasoli ("Immagine 'enciclopedica' " and his edition of the *Convivio*, lxxx–lxv) stress, as indeed do all the references above, the complexity and autonomy of Dante's positions. For a lucid and balanced account of Dante's intellectual history, see Hollander, *Dante Alighieri* (who makes the point about Beatrice rescuing Dante [135]); Vasoli ("Filosofia e teologia") gives a survey of related critical writings to 1965.

67. Poet of rectitude: e.g., *DVE* 2.2.7–8; *Cv* 1.1, 1.8–9, and esp. book 4; *Letter to Cangrande* 13.40; *Pg* 32.103, 33.52, *Pd* 17.124–142. Primacy of *scienza morale*: *Cv* 2.13.8, 2.14.14–15, 2.14.18; see Étienne Gilson, *Dante and Philosophy* 99–142, and Nardi, "Dante e la filosofia." Aim of *Comedy* is action: *Letter to Cangrande* 16; Imbach (*Dante, la philosophie* 138) links Dante's stress on moral philosophy to his lay audience, whom he aims to guide and instruct.

68. *"Riso de l'universo"*: *Pd* 27.4; see 20.13, 23.59, 30.26, *Pg* 32.5. Reading Vergil: see Leo, "Unfinished *Convivio*." The conviction that literature constitutes a privileged access to understanding, and a means of moral conversion, grounds much of Giuseppe Mazzotta's illuminating work: on Dante, see *Dante, Poet of the Desert* (esp. 192–226), and *Dante's Vision*. On poetry and understanding in Dante, see Foster, "Dante, Poet of the Intellect."

69. *Cv* 3.12.13: *Nell'altre intelligenze [la divina filosofia] è per modo minore; Cv* 2.8.15: *La quale noi non potemo perfettamente vedere mentre che 'l nostro immortale col mortale è mischiato.*

70. *In alcuno modo queste cose nostro intelletto abbagliano, in quanto certe cose [si] affermano essere, che lo 'ntelletto nostro guardare non può, cioè Dio e la etternitate e la prima materia.*

71. *Manifestamente adunque può vedere chi bene considera, che pochi rimangono quelli che all'abito da tutti desiderato possano pervenire, e innumerabili quasi sono li 'mpediti che di questo cibo sempre vivono affamati. Oh beati quelli pochi che seggiono a quella mensa dove lo pane delli angeli si manuca! e miseri quelli che colle pecore hanno comune cibo!*

72. *VN* 17–19 correspond to *VN* 10 in the Gorni edition. For Ps. 50 and "Donne ch'avete," see Scott, "Dante's Sweet New Style"; for Dante's other uses of Ps. 50 (the *Miserere*), see Hollander, "Dante's Use of the Fiftieth Psalm." For gluttony as the background for Dante's poetics of praise, see Barolini, *Dante's Poets* 51–52; Abrams, "Inspiration and Gluttony"; and Musa, " 'Sweet New Style.' " On the complex question of the *dolce stil novo*, see the overview in Pasquini, " 'Dolce stil novo,' " and "Mito dell'amore"; Pertile's penetrating "Dante's *Comedy* beyond the *Stilnovo*" and Barański's " 'New Life' of 'Comedy' " both point to the watershed that must separate the *Vita Nova*'s (unredeemed or unredeeming) *stil novo* from the *Comedy*; see also Leonardi, "Cavalcanti, Dante." The identification of Amor with transcendent inspiration (i.e., the Holy Spirit) is supported by (among others) Jacomuzzi, *L'imago al cerchio* 51; Hollander, "Dante's 'dolce stil novo' "; Mazzotta, *Dante, Poet of the Desert* 204–210 (with qualifications); Mazzeo, "Medieval Hermeneutics" 6; Martinez, "Pilgrim's Answer to Bonagiunta" (linking that answer to the divine "I AM" and the pilgrim's self-knowledge); and Aversano, "Sulla poetica dantesca"; for related contexts, see Sarolli, "Dante 'scriba Dei.' " For a possible medieval intertext for *Pg* 24.52–54, in which Amor is explicitly *caritas* (selfless love), see Casella "Rassegna critica" 108, and Corti, *Percorsi dell'invenzione* 93; compare *Mn* 3.4.11 (cited by Hollander, 269n15). The obser-

vation about *cominciando* is in De Robertis, " 'Incipit Vita Nova' " 18. For the phrase *dolce stil novo* itself, in light of Sanguineti's critical edition of the *Comedy*, see the overview in Fenzi, "Dopo l'edizione Sanguineti."

73. "In order that you may know . . . that school which you have followed, and may see if its teaching can follow my word; and that you may see that your way is so far distant from the divine way, as the highest and swiftest of the heavens is remote from earth."

74. It may be, as Hollander argues ("*Vita Nuova*: Dante's Perceptions"), that Dante's *mirabile visione* at the close of the *Vita Nova* does intuit what the *Comedy* will develop as Beatrice's true significance (assuming the last chapter is not a later addition); nevertheless Dante's love story within and after the *Vita Nova* is not one of perfect fidelity. Aquinas: *Scriptum super Sententiarum* 3.35.1.2 (contemplation); *Super evangelium S. Matthaei* 19.2 (asceticism); see Jordan, "Alleged Aristotelianism" 32.

75. Botterill: "Purgatorio XXVII" 400.

76. Sexual concupiscence was the result of the serpent's deception in Eden and marks all fallen humanity, which is generated through carnal desire. See, e.g., Augustine, *De trinitate* 12.5, 12.13–17, *De civitate Dei* 14.16–26, *De Genesi ad litteram* 9.10, 10.12, 11.3; Bonaventure, *Breviloquium* 3.5–7; and Aquinas, *De veritate* 4.50.7–9. See also Freccero, "Firm Foot" 52–53. Most agree that all the penitent must brave the fire: Statius and Virgil too cross it; the angel calls all *anime sante* to enter it (*Pg* 27.10–12); indeed there is no way to avoid it crossing the seventh ledge (see Bosco and Reggio's commentary [2:453]; a dissenting view in Consoli, "Il canto XXVII"). For the medieval concept of Purgatory, and its relation to fire, see Le Goff, *Birth of Purgatory*. For acute analysis (and sources) of Dante's wall of fire, see Pazzaglia "Il canto XXVII" and Dell'Aquila, "Il canto XXVII." All sin a distortion of love: *Pg* 17.70–139. For the universality of sexual *concupiscentia* as emblematic of *cupiditas, radix . . . omnium malorum* (I Tim. 6.10), see, e.g., Augustine, *De Trinitate*, 12.14–15, and Bonaventure, *Breviloquium*, 3.2–6. For *concupiscentia* as a failure of understanding, see Augustine, *Diversis questionibus ad Simplicianum* 1.1.9. Freccero links the barrier of fire to the wolf of the *Comedy*'s prologue scene: "The further one progresses toward virtue, the less serious are the faults remaining to be purged, but the more difficult are they to overcome. . . . The universality of the wolf's reign diminishes the culpability involved in becoming subject to her, and that universality makes it most difficult, if not impossible, to elude her" ("Firm Foot" 51–52). For helpful comments on this section of the chapter I am especially indebted to Robert Hollander, Giuseppe Mazzotta, Zygmunt Barański, Francesco Sberlati, John Scott, Henry Weinfield, Ted Cachey, and Jan Emerson.

77. *If* 12.49, *Pd* 5.79, 27.121, 30.139; for the wolf as universal evil, see *Pg* 20.8–15, *If* 1.49–54.

78. The river/water analogy holds if one remembers that water, *relatively* attributeless compared to a river, here represents the *entirely* attributeless, God, which is thus, strictly speaking, not something things can be "made of." Dante extends the water-God analogy in *Purgatorio* 5, where he spells out the entire cycle river-sea-vapor-cloud-rain-streams-river-ice, each the changing name and form of an underlying unchanging substance.

79. For the "extreme moral danger" of the pilgrim's situation, see Barański, "Structural Retrospection" 20.

80. "As at the name of Thisbe, Pyramus, at the point of death, opened his eyelids and looked at her, when the mulberry turned bloodred, so, my stubbornness being softened, I turned to the wise leader, when I heard the name that is always

springing up in my mind. At which he shook his head and said, 'How now? Do we wish to stay on this side?' then smiled as one does to a child that is won over by an apple."

81. " 'Jealous wall,' they used to say, 'why do you obstruct lovers? / What would it be for you to let us embrace with all our body, / or, if that is too much, for you at least to open up and let us kiss? / We are not ungrateful, we admit that it is to you we owe it / that our words have been given a passage to loving ears.' " I quote the Latin text from Anderson's edition; in English translation from Hill.

82. " 'Pyramus,' she cried, 'what misfortune has taken you from me? / Pyramus, answer! It is your Thisbe, dearest, who / is calling you: listen to me, lift up your drooping head.' / At Thisbe's name, Pyramus raised his eyes that were by now / heavy with death, he saw her and closed them again."

83. Blasucci ("Canto XXVII" 520) notes that the names of Pyramus and Thisbe occupy the same metrical position in both Dante and Ovid, underlining Dante's direct reference to Ovid's text.

84. " 'Your hand,' she said, 'and love / have destroyed you, unhappy one. But I too have a hand strong / for this one thing, and I have love too: it will give the strength to wound. / I shall follow you into extinction and I shall be called the most wretched cause / and companion of your death; and you, who could have been torn from me / by death, alas, alone, cannot now be torn from me even by death.' "

85. Momigliano: note to *Pg* 27.35–36, echoing Tommaseo. The centrality of the tree is underlined by Porcelli, "La vicenda di Dante" 89–90. In private correspondence, Giuseppe Mazzotta points out the profundity of Ovid's analysis of desire: "words that never reach their targets, a time that is never the appointed time, signs that become universal, etc." Although I cannot pursue them here, these themes are particularly significant (as Mazzotta observes) in the narrative context of *Purgatorio* 27. coming on the heels of *Purgatorio* 26, the canto of sensual love, in which Dante's meditation on love poetry culminates with Arnaut Daniel's "spiritualized" rewriting of the Provençal love lyric (*Pg* 26.140–147).

86. Ovid and Dante's *contrapasso*: see Lorch and Lorch, "Metaphor and Metamorphosis" 117. For the vast medieval diffusion of the tale of Pyramus and Thisbe, see, e.g., Schmitt-von Mühlenfels, *Pyramus und Thisbe*; Georg Hart, *Ursprung und Verbreitung* and *Die Pyramus- und Thisbe-Sage*; Glendinning, "Pyramus and Thisbe"; and Van Emden, "Shakespeare and the French Pyramus" For a general account of Ovid's reception, see Wilkinson, *Ovid Recalled*. For references to Pyramus and Thisbe in Italian Duecento poetry, see Contini, "Alcuni appunti su *Purgatorio* XXVII," and especially Ortiz, "La materia epica." Battaglia ("Piramo e Tisbe") argues that the tale of Pyramus and Thisbe had a continuous life from late antiquity throughout the Middle Ages.

87. The infertility of the sexual imagery is stressed by Lorch and Lorch, "Metaphor and Metamorphosis" 119.

88. For tragedy and comedy in relation to the *Comedy*, see, e.g., Barański, "Dante, the Roman Comedians," " 'Significar per verba,' " and "*Comedía*: Notes on Dante"; Hollander, "Virgilio dantesco" (esp. 117–154) and "Tragedy in Dante's Comedy"; Barolini, *Dante's Poets* 188–286 and *Undivine Comedy* (esp. 59, 76, 79); Auerbach, "Sermo Humilis," in *Literary Language* 25–81; and Ferrucci, *Poetics of Disguise* 66–102. Barberi Squarotti ("Premessa allo studio" 395–398) also reads the Pyramus simile as a contrast between a worldly mythological context and the *Comedy*'s eschatological goal. The link *pullos-rampolla* is noted by Lorch and Lorch "Metaphor and Metamorphosis" 120–121; they observe that this is an argument for taking *rampolla* in the

sense of "to sprout" or "flower" or "send forth shoots" rather than "to flow forth like a spring." The commentary tradition supports both readings.

89. For the link between *nome* and *pome* see Lorch and Lorch, "Metaphor and Metamorphosis" 108, 114–116.

90. Luke 17.6: *Dixit autem Dominus / si haberetis fidem sicut granum sinapis / diceretis huic arbori moro / eradicare et transplantare in mare et oboediret vobis*; Ps. 77.47: *et occidit in grandine vineam eorum / et moros eorum in pruina* (the *Psalmi iuxta Hebraicum* reads: *qui occidit in grandine vineas eorum / et sycomoros eorum in frigore*); cited in English from Douay Rheims version (*Holy Bible*). Ambrose: *Expositio evangelii secundum Lucam, ad locum*. *Glossa ordinaria*: *Fructus mori in flore albet, formatus irrutilat, maturitate nigrescit. Sic diabolus, flore angelicae naturae & potestate rutilantis praevaricando terror inhorruit odore, qui per fidem excluditur* (*Biblia sacra, cum Glossa Ordinaria* 5:927a). Hugh of St. Cher: *Opera omnia* 6:235; Hugh's gloss on *moro* is *id est, diabolo*; he goes on to explain that literally and spiritually the text means that saints were chosen for their faith to eject this mulberry from afflicted bodies. Bonaventure: *Commentarius in Evangelium S. Lucae* 17.15–17 (430b–431a). Aquinas, *Catena aurea* 17.3 (2:257–258). Many of these sources are also referred by Cornelius à Lapide, *Commentaria in Sacram Scripturam* 8:633 (available in many editions); for a succinct synthesis of medieval exegesis of the Luke passage, see Freccero, "Sign of Satan" 170–171. For fuller Latin citations, see the earlier version of this essay, "Pyramus at the Mulberry Tree."

91. Augustine: *Hoc est ipsi euangelio crucis dominicae, per poma sanguinea tamquam uulnera in ligno pendentia victum populis praebiturae* (*Quaestiones Evangeliorum . . . in Matthaeum* 2.39.3 [p. 96]). Freccero: "Sign of Satan" 171. Bede: *In Lucae evangelium expositio* 5.17.6 (p. 310). The idea that mulberry leaves kill serpents may derive from Ambrose: *Rubi folia superiacta serpenti interimunt eum* (*Exameron* 3.8 [37; p. 84]); picked up by Isidore of Seville (*Étymologies: Livre XVII* 17.7.19–20), it was repeated by rote in medieval encyclopedias (e.g., Bartholomaeus Anglicus, *De rerum proprietatibus* 17.100; Thomas Cantimpratensis [Thomas de Cantimpré], *Liber de natura rerum* 10.28; Vincent of Beauvais, *Speculum naturale* 13.24). *Glossa ordinaria*: *Dicetis huic arbori moro. Cuius fructus liquorem sanguini similem emittit. . . . Et ideo arbor morus crucem significat, cuius fructus dicitur ipse Christus in ea suo sanguine rubricatus. Hanc autem arborem transtulerunt apostoli de terra Iudeae, & plantauerunt in mari, id est, in latitudine gentium, quae potest dici mare.* (5:927a). Bonaventure: *Huius sanguis accendit nos ad conflictum contra monstra vitiorum* (*Commentarius in Evangelium S. Lucae* 7:430–431).

92. *Quod parvum quantitate, potestate est magnum, ait Chrysost. insinuat ergo minimum fidei magna posse; et Beda: Fides perfecta, ait, est granum sinapis: in facie est humilis, in pectore fervens* (Lapide, *Commentaria* 8:633).

93. *Glossa ordinaria*: *Morus calidae est naturae, per quod charitas intelligitur, quae in pruina occiditur* (3:1029). Manegold de Lautenbach: *Recte ergo per morum, cujus fructus rubicundus est, dilectio proximi designatur, quae in tantum valere debet in nobis ut animam pro fratribus ponamus, et sanguinem effundamus* (*Exegesis de Psalmorum* 903–904); for the attribution to Manegold, see Glorieux, *Pour revaloriser Migne* 52.

94. Freccero: "Sign of Satan" 177–178. Isidore: *Sicomorus, sicut et morus, graeca nomina sunt. Dictus autem sicomorus eo quod sit folia similis moro. Hanc Latini celsam appellant ab altitudine, quia non est breuis ut morus* (*Étymologies* 98–99); the editor observes that Isidore has made *une complète confusion*. Saint Paul: *Nos autem praedicamus Christum crucifixum / Iudaeis quidem scandalum / gentibus autem stultitiam* (1 Cor. 1.23; see Freccero, "Sign of Satan" 177). Albert: *Non enim erat minoris potentiae, vel misericordiae, Lazarum de inferno ad superos revocare ad vitam, quam Zachaeum de bar-*

athro vitiorum revocare ad compunctionis et justificationis gratiam (Enarrationes in secundam partem evang. Lucae 19.4 [p. 548]). For the symbolism of the cross as a tree leading to Heaven, see Greenhill, "Child in the Tree."

95. *"Ovide moralisé"* 2:17–39 (allegory 37–39). The twelfth-century poem is separately published as *Piramus et Tisbé: poème du XIIe siècle*, and more recently as *Piramus et Tisbé; introduzione, testo critico, traduzione e note*. For other medieval Pyramus and Thisbe poems, see n. 115, and Faral, *Les arts poétiques* 331–335. For Dante's familiarity with medieval allegorized Ovids, see Robson, "Dante's Use" 1–38 (in reference to Pyramus, 2–3, 12–13); for qualifications, see Hollander, *Allegory in Dante's* Commedia 202–214.

96. It is book 15 (chaps. 2–15) of his *Reductorium Morale*, often detached and attributed to Thomas Walleys, and recently reprinted as *Metamorphosis Ovidiana moraliter . . . explanata*; the Pyramus tale is on fol. 36r–37v.

97. Pazzaglia, "Canto XXVII" 107; Calì, "Purgatorio XXVII" 94.

98. Beatrice tells Dante to refer her words to the living: *queste parole segna a' vivi / del viver ch'è un correre a la morte* (*Pg* 33.53–54). She is making an implicit contrast with a life that is immune to temporality: those awake to that life are not in need of the message she is ordering Dante to relay. For a full treatment of the metaphor of the race in relation to *cupiditas* and *caritas*, damnation and salvation, see Werge, "The Race to Death."

99. "As soon as I was on the threshold of my second age and had changed life, this one took himself from me and gave himself to another. When from flesh to spirit I had ascended, and beauty and virtue were increased in me, I was less dear and less pleasing to him, and he turned his steps along a way not true, following false images of good, which pay no promise in full."

100. "Never did nature or art present to you beauty so great as the fair members in which I was enclosed, and which are now scattered on the earth; and if the highest beauty thus failed you by my death, what mortal thing should then have drawn you into desire for it? Truly, at the first arrow of deceitful things you should have risen up after me, who was no longer such a thing."

101. For the "morality of language" in Dante, see Barański, "Dante's Biblical Linguistics."

102. The point is forcefully made in Fergusson, *Dante's Drama of the Mind* 161–171; Fergusson emphasizes the sacrificial aspect of Dante's capitulation. See also Swing, *The Fragile Leaves of the Sibyl* 297–298. Picone sees the *transitus per ignem* as a celebratory, not expiatory, rite; the fire is "theophanic" ("Purgatorio XXVII" 394–395).

103. "That sweet fruit which the care of mortals goes seeking on so many branches, this day shall give your hungerings peace." Dante is evoking Boethius, *Philosophiae consolatio* Book 3, Prose 2.

104. Song of Songs: *Sicut malum inter ligna silvarum sic dilectus meus inter filios / sub umbra illius quam desideraveram sedi et fructus eius dulcis gutturi meo*; see also Deut. 33.13–15, Apoc. 18.14. Ambrose: *Expositio Psalmi CXVIII*; this fruit tree's fragrance . . . : 5.9 (*Christus ergo adfixus ad lignum, sicut malum pendens in arbore. . . . Cibus suauis in malo est; ergo cibus suauis est Christus*); Church preaches Fruit of Passion . . . : 5.12; that Christ hung for us: 5.16 (*Pomum est quod [Christus] pependit. Hoc pomum gustauit ecclesia et ait: et fructus eius dulcis in faucibus meis. Et ut scias, qui pomum est dominus*).

105. Ambrose: *Expositio . . . secundum Lucam* 8.90 (*Zacchaeus in sycomoro, nouum videlicet novi temporis pomum. . . . Ad hoc enim Christus aduenit, ut ex lignis non poma,*

sed homines nascerentur); see also 8.81, and Pertile, *Puttana e gigante* 193–194. Albertus Magnus: *Enarrationes* 19.4.

106. Compare Wittgenstein, *Tractatus* 6.371, 6.372, 6.41, 6.4312, 6.4321, 6.44; *Culture and Value* 49e.

107. Double metonymy: e.g., Genesis 2.17, 3.6. Dante uses only *legno*: e.g., *Pg* 24.116, 32.44, 33.56–63; *Pd* 26.115. Child's first desire: *Cv* 4.12.16. References to creation as leaves and branches surround the designation of Adam as *pomo*: Dante says he loves in just measure the leaves (*fronde*) with which the Eternal Gardener's garden is enleaved (*Pd* 26.64–66); he bows to Adam like a frond (*fronda*) bent by the wind but straightened by its own virtue (85–87); mortal usage is ephemeral like leaves on a branch (*fronde in ramo* [137–138]); see also *Pd* 24.115–117, 27.119. As a particular finite being, Dante is the *fronda* of Cacciaguida's root (*Pd* 15.88–89); as an embodiment of conscious being, he is the *pomo* itself. Salvation, the fruition of self-knowledge, is to find the *pomo* in or on the *fronda*. In *Paradiso* 18 (28–33), Cacciaguida compares the heavens of Paradise to the branches of a tree, on which the souls themselves are the fruit.

108. Medieval and modern commentators are virtually unanimous in saying that the gryphon represents Christ; for dissenting views, see Armour, *Dante's Griffin*, Scott, "Beatrice's Reproaches in Eden," and Pertile's response in *Puttana e gigante* 143–162. Dante specifies that the gryphon is a single person in two natures (*Pg* 31.80–81).

109. "Blessed are you, gryphon, who do not pluck with your beak this tree, sweet to the taste, which then afterwards racks the belly."

110. For the precise sense of *Pg* 32.48, see Pertile, *Puttana e gigante* 158–162; thus Christ, the second Adam . . . : see Pertile 148–153, 159–162. Pyramus lost Thisbe: this reading is implicit in another thirteenth-century allegorized Ovid (John of Garland, *Integumenta Ovidii* 51 [lines 181–182]): *Alba prius morus nigredine mora colorans / Signat quod dulci mors in amore latet* ("the mulberry tree, first white, whose mulberries are stained with black, signifies that death lies hidden in sweet love"). Several manuscripts gloss further: *Secundum integumentum, arbor que ferebat prius alba poma signat quod in amore prius est quedam albedo i. quedam dulcedo. Morus autem que postea habuit nigra mora signat quod in fine ex amore sequitur nigredo i. amaritudo s. mors anime* ("The hidden meaning is that the tree which first bore white fruits signifies that in love at first there is some whiteness, that is some sweetness. The mulberry tree which then had black mulberries signifies that in the end out of love blackness follows, that is bitterness, in other words the death of the soul"). The lines and their gloss are picked up by Giovanni del Vergilio; see Ghisalberti, "Giovanni del Virgilio espositore" 55; a similar interpretation is in Benvenuto da Imola's commentary (4:146). *Vermiglio*: Benvenuto says the gryphon's white indicates *carnem humanam puram*; it is mixed with *vermiglio . . . quia sanguine rubricata in . . . passione* (*Comentum* 4:197). White and red also evoke *Song of Songs* 5.10 (*dilectus meus, candidus et rubicundus*), and conventional female beauty in the medieval lyric tradition; on the other hand, *vermiglio* is often Dante's word for blood shed in violence (*If* 12.101; *Pd* 16.154), and for Lucifer's central face (*If* 34.39). For the valences of *vermiglio* in Dante, see Niccoli, "Vermiglio" 5:966, and Armour, *Dante's Griffin* 167.

111. "Your intellect's asleep if it does not deem that for a special reason [the tree] is so lofty and so inverted at the top. And if your vain thoughts had not been as Elsa's water round about your mind, and your delight in them were not like Pyramus at the mulberry tree, you'd recognize in those circumstances [the tree's height and form], in a moral sense, God's justice in forbidding trespass of that tree. But since I see you

turned to stone in your mind, and as a stone, so stained that the light of my speech dazzles you."

112. For the tree, see Pertile, *Puttana e gigante* 163–202. For a concise summary of eucharistic themes in the Ugolino episode, see Durling's note (1:578–580) to his edition of the *Comedy*; Hollander, "Inferno XXXIII, 37–74." "Io son venuto": *Rime* 100.12. For a slightly idiosyncratic interpretation of *impetrato*, see André Pézard, "Dante pétrifié." The link between Medusan petrification and failure of interpretation or understanding is elegantly traced by Freccero, "Medusa: The Letter and the Spirit," esp. 121. For Medusa in the *Rime petrose*, see Durling and Martinez, *Time and the Crystal* 105 and passim. Dante may be evoking the "high" or "tragic" style in *Pg* 33.64–75: in his commentary (2:372), Sapegno notes that Beatrice's words are cryptographic, a *parlar chiuso*. The difficult rhyme on *-elsa* is unique in the *Comedy*.

113. Quotation from Jacoff, "The Rape/Rapture of Europa" 241. For Dante's "Christian" rereading or rewriting of Ovid, see Hawkins, "Transfiguring the Text" and "Dante's Ovid," and Brownlee, "Dante's Poetics of Transfiguration." Picone: "L'Ovidio di Dante" and "Purgatorio XXVII."

114. *Inritor, inquam, abs te uersus istos tuos omni metrorum genere cantando et ululando insectari, qui inter te atque ueritatem inmaniorem murum quam inter amantes tuos conantur erigere; nam in se illi uel inolita rimula respirabant* (De ordine 1.3 [8]; quoted in English from Augustine, "Divine Providence and the Problem of Evil" 247).

115. The parallel to Augustine is proposed by Battaglia, "Piramo e Tisbe" 115n2; Battaglia suggests that in both texts the wall indicates a barrier between the individual and transcendent values. Pyramus and Thisbe symbol of faithful lovers . . . : Ortiz, "Materia Epica" 8–14. In at least one French romance . . . : Alfred Morrison, "Old French Parallels."

116. *De Ordine,* 1.8 [21] (p. 99); "Divine Providence," 259.

117. *Ubi se, inquam, pyramus et illa eius super inuicem, ut cantaturus es, interemerint, in dolore ipso, quo tuum carmen uehementius inflammari decet, habes commodissimam oportunitatem. Arripe illius foedae libidinis et incendiorum uenenatorum execrationem, quibus miseranda illa contingunt, deinde totus adtollere in laudem puri et sinceri amoris, quo animae dotatae disciplinis et uirtute formosae copulantur intellectui per philosophiam et non solum mortem fugiunt uerum etiam uita beatissima perfruuntur* (De ordine 1.8 [24]; "Divine Providence" 262).

118. Dante's references to Augustine are few and usually generic (he names only the *Confessiones, De civitate Dei, De doctrina christiana,* and *De quantitate animae*), but his relation to him is deep and problematic. This is in part because Augustine "negated pagan Rome, discredited Virgil, and refused the idea of temporal beatitude as a legitimate human end" (Hawkins, "Divide and Conquer" 198), but also, as Simone Marchesi will argue in a forthcoming work, because Augustine discredited poetry as a medium of truth and revelation. Hence Dante's tactics of silencing Augustine in the *Comedy* while drawing on him, rewriting him, or (as Marchesi puts it in a private communication) "setting Augustine against Augustine." For these tactics, see Hawkins, "Divide and Conquer"; Hollander, "Dante's Republican Treasury" 66–67; and Mazzotta, *Dante, Poet of the Desert* (esp. 147–191); for Augustinian "intertexts" in the *Comedy*, see, e.g., Pincherle, "Agostino"; Moore, "Dante and St. Augustine"; Gardner, *Dante and the Mystics* 44–76; Tateo, "Percorsi agostiniani"; Chioccioni, *L'Agostinismo nella Divina Commedia*; Calcaterra, "Sant' Agostino nelle opere"; and Freccero, *Dante: The Poetics of Conversion*. Self-dissolving web . . . : see Hawkins, "Augustine, Dante" applying Stanley Fish's notion of "self-consuming artifact" to the *Comedy*.

CHAPTER 4: CREATION

1. The term "non-reciprocal relation of dependence" is from Sara Grant's Teape lectures, *Towards an Alternative Theology*, in which she distills her penetrating work on non-duality in Śaṅkarācārya and Aquinas; see also her "Contemporary Relevance."

2. Aristotle's Neoplatonic commentators: see, e.g., Sorabji, "The Ancient Commentators" 3–5; Merlan: *From Platonism to Neoplatonism*, e.g., 3–4, 229–231, *Monopsychism* 4–84. Cicero: *Academica* 1.4.17; see Blumenthal, "Neoplatonic Elements" 306n6. Simplicius: *In De Caelo* 378.20, *In De anima* 245.12; see Blumenthal, "Neoplatonic Elements" 306. Porphyry: *On the Life of Plotinus* 14.4–8. On Aristotle in Plotinus, see, e.g., Gerson, *God and Greek Philosophy* 186, 191–201; Armstrong, "Aristotle in Plotinus" and *Architecture of the Intelligible Universe*, esp. 6–13, 39–43; Hadot, "Harmony of Plotinus and Aristotle" and "Conception Plotinienne"; Gandillac, "Plotin et la 'Métaphysique' "; and Salmona, "Atto di Aristotele." Al-Fārābī: in *Deux traités philosophiques*. "One example": from Sorabji, "Infinite Power Impressed" 181–183, and see *Matter, Space and Motion* 249–285 (for full Aquinas references, 270n83, 281n129; for full Bonaventure references, 272n90). For whether Aquinas thought Aristotle's world was "created," see his commentary on the *Physics* (8.lect. 3, lect. 21) and *De substantiis separatis* 9; also Johnson, "Did St. Thomas Attribute?" and Dewan, "Thomas Aquinas, Creation." Van Steenberghen: *Histoire de la philosophie* 1.113–114.

3. Nardi ("legend of Dante's Thomism"): "Noterelle polemiche" 124; *Sigieri di Brabante* vii; "Tutto il frutto" 261n. The papal documents are reproduced, with their history, in the appendix to Maritain, *St. Thomas Aquinas*; for the history of the Thomistic movement, see Lobkowicz, "What Happened to Thomism?" For a recent study of Aquinas's implication in the Condemnation of 1277, see Wippel, "Thomas Aquinas and the Condemnation." Foster: "Tommaso d'Aquino" 634, 645, 648. Jordan: "The Alleged Aristotelianism" (esp. 1–5) and "Theology and Philosophy"; for analogous and equally penetrating observations on Bonaventure, see Speer, "Bonaventure and the Question." For a caution about speaking of Dante's "Aristotelianism," see Barański, "Iter ideologico" 22–27.

4. *Parmenides* 166b; see Étienne Gilson, *God and Philosophy* 45.

5. Augustine: the point is made by Knowles, *Evolution of Medieval Thought* 33–35; see also Marenbon, *Early Medieval Philosophy* 15. Porphyry: see Hadot, *Dieu et l'être* 57–63; Hankey, "Aquinas' First Principle" 157; and Cortest, "Was Thomas Aquinas a Platonist?" 215. Aquinas on diverse participation: e.g., *ST* 1a.44.1 (see also Étienne Gilson, *Christian Philosophy of Aquinas* 153–154, and Fabro, *La nozione metafisica* 165); permeated by God: 1a.8.1–4; "governs the lower things": *SCG* 3.83 (summarizing 3.77–82). On "Neoplatonism" in Aquinas, besides his own commentary to the *Liber de causis*, see, e.g., Te Velde, *Participation and Substantiality*; Fabro, *La nozione metafisica* and " "Platonism, Neo-Platonism"; Geiger, *La participation*; Henle, *Saint Thomas and Platonism*; Little, *Platonic Heritage of Thomism*; Fay, "Participation"; Quinn, *Aquinas, Platonism*; and Reichberg, "Communication of the Divine Nature." For a lucid account of the metaphysical relations between Aquinas and Islamic "Neoplatonism," see Burrell, "Aquinas and Islamic"; for an exhaustive study of the relation of created to uncreated being in Aquinas, see Wippel, *Metaphysical Thought*.

6. Nardi: *come nella sua mente si sia insinuata la dottrina della creazione mediata* ("Tutto il frutto" 253). Aquinas: *Questiones de veritate* 5.9 (that *caelestia corpora sint media inter Deum et ista corpora inferiora etiam in via creationis quodammodo . . . alienum est a fide, quae ponit naturam omnium immediate a Deo esse conditam, secundum primam institutionem*). Nardi too admits: e.g., "Dottrina delle macchie lunari" 18–19,

"Dante e Pietro d'Abano" 42–49, and "Intorno al tomismo" 182–197. *Monarchia:* 3.7.6 (*potestatem creandi et similiter baptizandi nullo modo Deus commictere posset, ut evidenter probatur, licet Magister contrarium dixerit in quarto*); Aquinas: *ST* 1a.45.5; Peter Lombard: *Sententiae* 4.5.3.

7. Nardi: e.g., "Dottrina delle macchie lunari" 22; Mellone: "Concorso delle creature" 280, "Emanatismo neoplatonico" 208–212, *Dottrina di Dante* 21n7.

8. "O you who are in your little barks, eager to listen, following my ship that, singing, crosses the deep, turn back to see your shores again: do not commit yourselves to the open sea, for you may, losing me, be left astray. The water I take was never sailed before; Minerva breathes and Apollo guides me, and the nine Muses point out the Bears to me. You other few who raised your necks in time to the bread of angels, on which man feeds here ever unsatiated, you may indeed put out your vessel on the deep salt sea, keeping within the furrow of my wake ahead of the water that flows back smooth again."

9. For the relation between divine inspiration and Dante's navigation imagery, see Stabile's penetrating "Navigazione celeste"; for the revelatory/liturgical connotations of *pan de li angeli*, see O'Brien, " 'Bread of Angels.' "

10. For the theme of unity/diversity, sameness/difference in the canto, see Barolini, *Undivine Comedy* 177–180; a summary of key terms is in Muresu, "Dante tra ragione e intelletto" 19n45. Light ray and virgin maternity: see, e.g., Cosmo, *Ultima ascesa* 410–411, and Stabile, "Navigazione celeste" 118–121. For the interpenetration of bodies in ancient and medieval thought, see Sorabji, *Matter, Space and Motion* 60–122.

11. Cain: see also *If* 20.126. Ulyssean echoes in *Paradiso* 2: see, e.g., Battaglia Ricci, "Ancora sulla struttura" 161–190. *Monarchia: Unum esse videtur esse radix eius quod est bonum, et multa esse eius quod est esse malum. . . . Hinc videri potest quod peccare nichil est aliud quam progredi ab uno spreto ad multa.* (Compare Nisargadatta Maharaj: "There is nothing else. The very idea of 'else' is a disaster and a calamity" [*I Am That* 205].) Stabile ("Navigazione celeste" 125) links the "signs" to interpretation, going from the effect to the cause.

12. For reason versus intellect in *Paradiso* 2, see Muresu's penetrating "Dante tra ragione e intelletto"; for angelic knowledge, see *Cv* 3.6.5–6, *DVE* 1.3.1–3, *Monarchia* 1.3.7, *Pd* 29.76–81, and Boyde, *Dante Philomythes* 191–193. *Ratio* versus *intellectus* in Aquinas: e.g., *ST* 1a.58.3–4, 59.1, 79.8; *Scriptum super Sententiarum* 2.d9.q1.a8, d3.q1.a6; 3.d14.q1.a3, d35.q2.a2; *SCG* 2.91.8, 3.91.4; *Questiones de veritate* 4.1. Muresu notes (17n38) that the word *corpo* recurs nine times in *Paradiso* 2, more than in any other canto of the *Paradiso*. On "rationality" in *Paradiso* 2, see Sebastio, *Strutture narrative* 55–95.

13. "You will certainly see that your belief is plunged deep in error, if you listen well to the argument I shall make against it. The eighth sphere shows you many lights, which both in quality and in size can be seen to be of diverse countenances. If rarity and density alone produced all this, one single power, more or less or equally distributed, would be in all. But different powers must be fruits of [different] formal principles, and it would follow from your argument that those, all except for one, would be destroyed."

14. For this "radical epistemological shift" from the physical to the metaphysical or intelligible, see Pastore Stocchi, "Dante e la luna" 154–155, 157–159, and Nardi, "Dottrina delle macchie lunari" 3–5, 38–39. Nardi points out (5) that the *Convivio*'s "explanation" was restricted to the moon; Beatrice expands the problem to the entire cosmos. The explanation of moonspots as dependent on varying density was appar-

ently rather uncommon: see Grant, *Planets, Stars, and Orbs* 398–399. For the "Averroism" of that position, rejected in the *Paradiso*, see Nardi, "Dottrina delle macchie lunari," Proto, "Dottrina dantesca," and Vasoli, "Canto II del Paradiso."

15. For detailed analysis and diagrams of the experiment, including "performable" possibilities Dante excludes, see Kleiner, *Mismapping the Underworld* 100–107; see also James Miller, "Three Mirrors"; for a photograph of the experiment, see Boyde, "L'esegesi di Dante" 16. Kleiner mentions the Cross in "Eclipses in the *Paradiso*" 20 (an invaluable essay for tracing the links between the Crucifixion and eclipse in the *Paradiso*) and in *Mismapping the Underworld* 112–114, but does not grasp its significance. For the "breaking" of light by body in the *Purgatorio*, see especially 2.16–21, 3.17, 3.26, 3.88–90, 3.96, 5.4–9, 5.25–26, 6.57, 26.7. Vasoli ("Canto II del Paradiso") stresses the importance of the canto as the key to understanding the *Paradiso* (28), but he too misses the significance of the mirror experiment.

16. "Now, as beneath the blows of the warm rays the substrate of the snow is left stripped of both its former color and its cold, so is your intellect left bare, and I now wish to in-form it with light so living that it shall quiver as you look on it."

17. "Within the heaven of divine peace revolves a body in whose power lies the being of all that it contains. The following heaven, which has so many things to show, distributes this being through diverse essences, distinct from it and contained by it. The other circles, by various differentiations, direct the distinctions they possess within themselves to their own ends and sowings. So do these organs of the universe proceed, as you now see, from grade to grade, for they receive from above and operate downward."

18. Nardi: *Sigieri di Brabante* 30, "Dottrina delle macchie lunari" 20–25, and "Citazioni dantesche" 97; see also Mellone, "Concorso delle creature" 278–280.

19. On *trasumanar* and Glaucus, see Botterill, *Dante and the Mystical Tradition* 221–241; on Glaucus, see also Brownlee, "Pauline Vision," and Palgen, "Il mito di Glauco." Picone's reading of the role of Jason in *Paradiso* 2 in "Il corpo della/nella luna" is particularly illuminating.

20. "The motion and the power of the holy spheres must breathe from the blessed movers as the hammer's art does from the smith; and the heaven that so many lights make beautiful takes its stamp from the profound mind that turns it, and of that image makes itself the seal. And as the soul within your dust is diffused through different members and conformed to different potencies, so the intelligence deploys its goodness multiplied among the stars, while revolving upon its own unity."

21. That the moonspots are "appearance" has been suggested several times; e.g., Muresu, "Dante tra ragione e intelletto" 19–20, 22.

22. The *Paradiso*'s exploitation of the correspondence between physical light as understood in Dante's time and the "light of the universe" is noted by Mazzeo, *Medieval Cultural Tradition* 105. For Dante's mirror experiment and the invariance of apparent surface brightness with distance, see Kleiner, *Mismapping the Underworld* 101–104; Peterson, "Dante's Physics" 170–171; and Nardi, "Dottrina delle macchie lunari" 59–61.

23. "To create, properly speaking, is to make out of nothing; but to make is in fact not only to produce something from nothing, but also out of matter" (*Creare proprie est de nihilo facere, facere vero non modo de nihilo aliquid operari, sed etiam ex materia* [Peter Lombard, *Sententiae* 2.1.2]). The term "generation" is Aristotelian; "propagation" is Augustinian (e.g., *De Genesi ad litteram* 5.11.20, and Aquinas, *ST* 1a.45.8); "the work of distinction" is particularly Thomistic: *ST* 1a.65. Aquinas distinguishes "distinction" from final perfection or "adornment" (1a.65.Proem); he treats the latter

in 1a.66–69. That all things participate "directly" in being (are created by God) is underlined by Aquinas at 1a.44.1–2, 1a.45.2; see also 1a.45.5–6, 1a.65.3, 1a.103.5. Aquinas quotation: 1a.q45.a4.ad1, 1a.103.5. Some of the principal Aquinian texts on creation are collected and translated in Aquinas, *Aquinas on Creation*. For penetrating treatments of the concept of creation, see Sokolowski, *God of Faith and Reason*; the essays in Burrell and McGinn, *God and Creation* (especially Burrell, "Creation or Emanation"; Sokolowski, "Creation and Christian Understanding"; and McGinn, "Do Christian Platonists"); Burrell, *Freedom and Creation*; and Ross, "Creation II."

24. Nothing created "first" in time, things "prior" only by nature (logical dependence): e.g., *ST* 1a.66.4; "God created all things immediately, but in the creation itself He established an order among things, so that some depend on others, by which they are conserved in being; though He remains the principal cause of their conservation" (1a.q104.a2.ad1). "Corporeal forms . . . came immediately from God," etc. . . . : 1a.65.4; see 1a.q71.a1.ad1, 1a.65.3, *Questiones de veritate* 5.9, *SCG* 2.43. "No transmutation from potentiality to act": 1a.65.4; see 1a.q71.a1.ad1, 1a.65.3, *Questiones de veritate* 5.9, *SCG* 2.43. There was no becoming: *ST* 1a.104.1. "Had to do something special": 1a.103.6 (Foster's account in "Tommaso" does not grasp clearly enough the non-temporality of the "act" of creation, or the principle that matter is not a thing: e.g., 636, 638). Moment of first creation only conceptually different: "The conservation of things by God is not by a new action, but by a continuation of that action whereby He gives being, which action is without either motion or time; so also the conservation of light in the air is by the continual influence of the sun" (1a.104.a1.ad4). Aquinas on eternity of the world: *De aeternitate mundi*, *SCG* 2.31–38, *Questiones de Potentia* 3.17, *ST* 1a.46.1–2, *Scriptum super Sententiarum* 2.d1.q1.a5–6; many of these texts are collected and translated (along with others by Bonaventure and Sigier de Brabant) in Aquinas, *On the Eternity of the World*. For a lucid and systematic discussion of Aquinas on creation, see Kretzmann, *Metaphysics of Creation*.

25. Different balance: see Foster, "Tommaso" 640, also 636, 638. Nardi saw in this passage a wholesale Avicennian Neoplatonism, in which the sphere of the moon is the *dator formarum* (*Sigieri di Brabante* 27, "Rassegna bibliografica" 312–313, 317–318, "Dante e Pietro d'Abano" 42–43, and "Dottrina dell'Empireo" 212–213). Nevertheless he recognized that nothing in it is incompatible with Aquinas ("Intorno al tomismo" 187). A "Thomistic" interpretation is of course advanced by Calò (Review of *Sigieri di Brabante* 270) and Busnelli (*Cosmogonia* 46–47, 88–90). Mellone ("Concorso delle creature" 276–278, *Dottrina di Dante* 63–64) stresses the Neoplatonic "exemplarism" in the passage but denies that it is Avicennistic. Foster deems Nardi's idea that Dante was describing mediate creation "quite improbable" ("Tommaso" 638, see also 639).

26. "Both that which does not die and that which dies are nothing but the reflected light of that Idea which in his love our Sire begets; for that Living Light which so streams from its lucent source that it is not disunited from it, nor from the Love which is intrined with them, through its own goodness gathers its rays, as though reflected, in nine subsistences, itself eternally remaining One. From there it descends down, from act to act, to the last potentialities, becoming such that finally it makes nothing but brief contingencies, and by these contingencies I mean the generated things which the moving heavens produce with seed and without seed."

27. For the technical meaning of *splendore* and *raggio* in "the usage of philosophers," see *Cv* 3.14.5: "light" (*luce*) refers to light in its source, "ray" (*raggio*) to light between its source and first reflection, and "reflection" (*splendore*) to light as reflected from an illuminated object; for current examples of this usage, see Vasoli's edition of

the *Convivio*, 456–457. First Person as efficient cause: *Pd* 10.1–6, 29.17; Second Person as formal cause: *Cv* 3.15.15–17, *Pd* 10.1–6, 13.53–54, 79–81; Third Person as final cause: *Pd* 10.1–6, 13.79–81; for an overview, see Mellone, "Creazione" 252; in Aquinas, see *ST* 1a.45.6–7.

28. At the end of the section "Dante's Predecessors" in chapter 3.

29. See the section "Dante" in chapter 2.

30. "The Divine Goodness, which spurns all envy from Itself, burning within Itself so sparkles that It displays the eternal beauties. That which is distilled from It without an intermediary thereafter has no end, because when It seals, Its imprint may never be removed. That which rains down from It without an intermediary is fully free, because it [what so rains down] is not subject to the power of the new things."

31. Nardi: e.g., *Sigieri di Brabante* 25, "Rassegna bibliografica" 313–315, "Noterelle polemiche" 130, "Filosofia di Dante" 1174–1175, "Intorno al tomismo" 183, 187, and "Tutto il frutto" 258. In "Filosofia di Dante" (1174) Nardi's caption for this passage is "Creazione immediata e creazione mediata"; Moore ("Dante's Theory of Creation" 135) glosses it by saying, "Here we have at once the vitally important distinction in Dante's system between Mediate and Immediate Creation clearly set forth." Despite O'Keeffe's sharp corrections and clarifications ("Dante's Theory of Creation" 45–49), Moore's confusion (Nardi was not confused, but polemical) is echoed in the modern commentaries: e.g., Singleton, Sapegno, Bosco-Reggio, and Chiavacci Leonardi.

32. "You say: 'I see water, I see fire and air and earth, and all their mixtures come to corruption and last but a little while, and yet these too were created things; so that, if what has been said is true, they ought to be secure against corruption.' The angels, brother, and the pure country you are in now, may be said to be created even as they are, in their entire being; but the elements which you have named, and all the things that are made of them, are informed by created power. Created was the matter that is in them, created was the informing power in these stars that wheel about them."

33. The arguments were chiefly between Busnelli (e.g., *Cosmogonia e antropogenesi* 50–57) and Nardi (e.g., "Rassegna bibliografica" 313–316). In short, Nardi said that sublunar things were not created "directly" by God ("Intorno al tomismo" 189); Busnelli said they were (*Cosmogonia e antropogenesi* 52); Nardi said that if they were, then they would be incorruptible ("Rassegna bibliografica" 315). This last statement, echoed by Bemrose (*Dante's Angelic Intelligences* 95), is false: all things were "directly" created by God, but not all "in their entire being." The principal points of contention in the debate are concisely summarized by Mellone ("Concorso delle creature" 282–284). The "temporal picture" of creation insinuated itself even into Nardi's sharp mind: e.g., "Intorno al tomismo" 182, 184, "Noterelle polemiche" 132–133, and "Rassegna bibliografica" 309–310 (in which he speaks of the world *in via di formazione*, "in the process of formation"). The same confusion between ontological dependence and temporal causality led Foster to say that, according to Aquinas, in the beginning God "did himself" (through an "initial and direct intervention") what "later" God accomplished through the spheres and univocal agents ("Tommaso" 638); Busnelli (*Comsogonia e antropogenesi* 56–57) too says God "did more" in the act of first creation than God "did later." Besides being (or rather, because they are) philosophically muddled, these notions contradict both Aquinas and Dante, as we have seen. Ironically, the same "temporal picture" led Mellone ("Concorso delle creature" 284–286, *Dottrina della creazione* 67) to conclude that Dante said the precise opposite: in the beginning the *spheres* had a special power to produce all things, including the first specimens of

higher animal species (univocal agents), while "later" they simply influenced the action of those agents. As Boyde notes (*Dante Philomythes* 371), for Aquinas this would make Dante a "modern heretic" (*SCG* 2.43). Acknowledging that Dante never mentions such a "special power" of the spheres (except here, in his view), Mellone concludes ("Concorso delle creature" 285): "It does not interest us to explain how the heavens could have exercised this power of theirs" (nor do we care to hear the explanation!). Boyde's position (264–265, 371–372) on Aquinas is the same as Foster's; on Dante it is the same as Mellone's. The Thomist Moretti (incoherently, as Mellone [*Dottrina di Dante* 67] points out) seems to attribute both to Dante ("Filosofia di Dante: concetti metafisici" 82).

34. For aeviternity, see Aquinas, *ST* 1a.10.5–6.

35. "It is the most conformed to It [the divine goodness] and therefore pleases It the most; for the Holy Ardor, which irradiates each thing, is most living in what is most like Itself. The human creature has the advantage of all these gifts, and if one is lacking, it must fall from its noble state. Sin alone is what disfranchises it and makes it unlike the Supreme Good, so that it is little illumined by Its [the Supreme Good's] light."

36. See especially the section "Pyramus and Thisbe" in chapter 3 and the section "Unity in Diversity" of this chapter.

37. "The soul of every beast and of the plants is drawn from a potentiated compound by the ray and motion of the holy lights; but your life the Supreme Beneficence breathes forth without intermediary, and so enamors it of itself [of the Supreme Beneficence] that it desires it ever after."

38. E.g., *Pd* 8.100–148, 16.73–74, 4.58–63.

39. See the section "Aristotle" of chapter 3; the expression "serial concept" is from Evans, *Aristotle* 123–127. *L'anima in vita: Cv* 4.21.5.

40. See the subsection "Philosophy" in the "Dante" section of chapter 3.

41. "Open your breast to the truth that is coming; and know that, as soon as the articulation of the brain is perfected in the fetus, the First Mover turns to it with joy over such art of nature, and breathes into it a new spirit replete with power, which absorbs that which is active there into its own substance, and makes one single soul that lives and feels and circles on itself."

42. The same process is described in *Convivio* 4.21.4–5, in which however more stress is laid on the role of the spheres (*vertù del cielo, vertù celestiale*) in the production of the human animal organism (*anima in vita*). For a particularly lucid overview of the issues involved in Statius's speech, see Boyde, *Dante Philomythes* 270–279; for the vexed details, see Nardi, "Sull'origine dell'anima"; Busnelli, *Cosmogonia e antropogenesi* and *Origine dell'anima*; Bartoli and Ureni, "Controversie medico-biologiche"; Bemrose, " 'Come d'animal divegna fante' "; and chap. 2 of Gragnolati's *Experiencing the Afterlife*; also Trovato, "Due elementi di filosofia." For a detailed overview of the Aristotelian understanding of soul, see Boyde, *Perception and Passion*; for a lucid introduction to soul in Aquinas, see Kretzmann, "Philosophy of Mind." *Sé in sé rigira*: compare *Cv* 2.4.18; "a power to know all things": *Cv* 4.21.5; *Mn* 1.3.9. For the relation of the human being to nature, see also *Mn* 1.3, 1.11.1; *Cv* 3.6.4–6 (what "the angelic intelligences fabricate with the heavens" is not the rational soul, but the *anima in vita* or human organism: compare 3.6.11–12, 3.2.14,17–19, 4.21.4–10) and 4.23.6; also Nardi, "Arco della vita" and "Immortalità dell'anima."

43. "Yet, if the warm Love disposes and imprints the clear Vision of the primal Power, complete perfection is there acquired. Thus was the earth once made fit for the full perfection of a living being; thus was the Virgin made to be with child."

44. "You lie subject, in your freedom, to a greater power and to a better nature, and that creates the mind in you which the heavens do not have in their charge."

45. "And from this you further can infer your resurrection, if you reflect how human flesh was made then when the first parents were both made."

46. Standard view virtually universal: including Nardi ("Tutto il frutto" 263, "Concetto dell'impero" 225–226 [esp. note 26], and "Noterelle polemiche" 131); Foster ("Tommaso d'Aquino" 644); Mellone ("Concorso delle creature" 285, "Creazione" 252); and Bemrose (*Dante's Angelic Intelligences* 109–112); the commentaries include all the ones in the Dartmouth Dante Project, as well as Chiavacci-Leonardi (who tangles with the incoherence of the view in a "Nota integrativa" [3:208]) and Di Salvo. O'Keeffe: "Dante's Theory of Creation" 61–63.

47. *Cv* 1.1.1, 3.15.9–10, 4.13.6–9; see also Nardi, "Conoscenza umana" 137. For the complexity, subtlety, and variety of medieval musings on body and its relation to soul, identity, and resurrection, see Caroline Bynum, e.g., "Why All the Fuss about the Body?" and *Resurrection of the Body*.

48. Besides the more distant evidence of Western hagiography, one interested in the possibility of this power over the body and nature should probably consider, among other recent texts, Paramahansa Yogananda's great *Autobiography of a Yogi*; Murphet's *Sai Baba: Man of Miracles*; and Sandweiss's *Sai Baba: The Holy Man*.

49. See the section "Dante's Predecessors" in chapter 3.

50. "From the time when I had looked before, I saw that I had moved through the whole arc which the first climate makes from its middle to its end; so that, beyond Cadiz, I saw Ulysses' mad crossing, and on this side the shore where Europa made herself a sweet burden. And more of the space of this little threshing-floor would have been disclosed to me, but the sun was proceeding beneath my feet and was a sign and more away."

51. For Dante's frequent assimilation of Jove to God/Christ (e.g., *O sommo Giove / che fosti in terra per noi crucifisso*, "O supreme Jove, who was crucified on earth for us" [*Pg* 6.118–119]), see Bemrose, *Dante's Angelic Intelligences* 126–131. Europa is usually considered an image of the seduction of earthly appearances (e.g., Bezzola, "*Paradiso* 27" 1909). For an illuminating study of the imagery of *Paradiso* 27, see Scott, "Imagery."

52. Canto of transition: see, e.g., Bezzola, "*Paradiso* 27" 1899; Sansone, "*Paradiso* 27" 967; Limentani, "Lectura Dantis: Paradiso XXVII" 31.

53. "Its motion is not determined by another's, but the others are measured by this, just as ten by a half and by a fifth; and how time has its roots in such a flowerpot, and in the others its leaves, may now be manifest to you."

54. *Ordina col suo movimento la cotidiana revoluzione di tutti li altri, per la quale ogni die tutti quelli ricevono [e piovono] qua giù la vertù di tutte le loro parti. . . . Onde, pognamo che possibile fosse questo nono cielo non muovere. . . . da vero non sarebbe quaggiù generazione né vita d'animale o di pianta; notte non sarebbe né die, né settimana né mese né anno, ma tutto l'universo sarebbe disordinato.*

55. *Con lei [la Sapienza] Dio cominciò lo mondo e spezialmente lo movimento del cielo, lo quale tutte le cose genera e dal quale ogni movimento è principiato e mosso.*

56. *Lo tempo, secondo che dice Aristotile nel quarto de la Fisica, è 'numero di movimento, secondo prima e poi'; e 'numero di movimento celestiale,' lo quale dispone le cose di qua giù diversamente a ricevere alcuna informazione.*

57. *Physics* 4.11 (219b.1, 223b.18–24; see also 220a.25).

58. No fundamental unit: *Physics* 4.11 (220a5–25); for an analogous conception

in Wittgenstein, see *Tractatus* 6.3611. Ordinal, not cardinal, number . . . : see *Physics* 219b5–8; 224a1–14. Change occurs only in what has spatial extension . . . : 4.12 (221a1–222a9). Universal measure of time . . . : 4.14 (223b13–224a1); 8. To measure this motion . . . : 4.12 (220b15); 4.14 (223b15). For the Aristotelian conception of time, see Moreau, *L'espace et le temps* 89–158; Owen, "Aristotle on Time" 9–16; Von Leyden, "Time, Number, and Eternity"; Annas, "Aristotle, Number, and Time"; Sorabji, *Time, Creation and the Continuum*; and Ghisalberti, "Nozione di tempo."

59. Mansion: "La théorie aristotélicienne" 279. Both Albert and Aquinas stress . . . : Albert, *Physica* 4.3.4 (Mansion 293); Aquinas, *In octo libros Physicorum* 4.17 [574] (Mansion 303). As Albert and Aquinas do . . . : Albert, *Physica* 4.3.17 (Mansion 295); Aquinas, *In octo libros Physicorum* 4.23 [636] (Mansion 303; and Ghisalberti, "Nozione di tempo" 349–351).

60. Augustine: e.g., *Confessions* 11.10–15, *City of God* 11.6; see also Vasoli, "Tempo" 547. Conscious being above time: compare Aquinas, "Intellect is above time, which is the number of movement of corporeal things" (*Intellectus est supra tempus quod est numerus motus corporalium rerum* [*ST* 1a.q85.a4.ad1]).

61. Martianus Capella: *Marriage of Philology* 7.751. Macrobius: *Commentary on the Dream of Scipio* 1.6.7–8. For an analogous conception of number, as a formal concept given immediately when any object falling under it is given, see Wittgenstein, *Tractatus* 6.022, 4.126, 4.12721.

62. Succession of integers from one: see also *DVE* 1.16.2, *Pd* 28.92–93, *Cv* 2.13.19, 3.15.9, *Rime* 106.72. Aquinas: *Metaphysics* 10.1 lect. 2 (1939), on Aristotle, *Metaphysics* 1052b.20–25; also 4.2, lect. 2–3 (562, 567); 1.5, lect. 3 (66); see also Boyde, *Dante Philomythes* 217–219. Aristotle says (*Metaphysics* 10.1 [1052b.20–25]), "For measure is that by which quantity is known; and quantity *qua* quantity is known either by a 'one' or by a number, and all number is known by a 'one.' Therefore all quantity *qua* quantity is known by the one, and that by which quantities are primarily known is the one itself; and so the one is the starting-point of number *qua* number."

63. Albert: *Physica* 1.5.4. Isidore: *Liber numerorum* 11.60. Martianus Capella: *Marriage of Philology*.

64. Macrobius: *Commentary on Dream of Scipio* 1.6.1–3,18–21; Hugh of St. Victor: *De numeris mysticis* 22. That Dante may be playing on Macrobian numerology is not unlikely: as Rabuse has shown ("Macrobio" 758b), along with the Cacciaguida cantos *Paradiso* 27 contains perhaps the densest set of explicit echoes of the *Commentary on the Dream of Scipio* in the *Comedy*. These echoes include a reference to Scipio (61), prophetic mission (64–66), aspiration to true glory (1–2, 62), looking to earth from the spheres (77–86), an "ancestral" encounter in the spheres (with Saint Peter), and the glory of Rome (61–62). Martianus Capella: *Marriage of Philology*.

65. *[La] Morale Filosofia, secondo che dice Tommaso sopra lo secondo dell'Etica, ordina noi all'altre scienze. Ché, sì come dice lo Filosofo nel quinto dell'Etica, la giustizia legale ordina le scienze ad apprendere, e comanda, perché non siano abandonate, quelle essere apprese e ammaestrate; [e] così lo detto cielo ordina col suo movimento la cotidiana revoluzione di tutti li altri.*

66. Augustine: *On Christian Doctrine* 2.16.25; see also Isidore of Seville, *Liber numerorum* 6.25, and Rabanus Maurus, *De universo* 18.3 (p. 490). Rabanus Maurus: *De universo* 18.3. Isidore: *Liber numerorum* 6.26.

67. On turning, see Freccero, "Pilgrim in a Gyre," esp. 76–81; related to the Pauline modes of vision, see chap. 4 of Mazzeo, *Structure and Thought*; Scrivano ("Paradiso 28" 273) says that in *Paradiso* 28, philosophy gives way to a higher, or mystical,

mode of understanding. As Contini noted ("*Paradiso* 28"), the obsessive theme of *Paradiso* 28 is *vero* (truth), and its relation to *vedere* (seeing); every simile in the canto concerns the power of sight; see also Spera, "Poesia degli angeli" 546.

68. On the identity between note and meter, see also Vandelli ("*Paradiso* 28" 1921) and Contini ("*Paradiso* 28" 1016).

69. For Aristotle, and for the *punto*, see the first two sections of chapter 3; see also Poulet, *Metamorphoses* xi–xxvii.

70. "Perhaps as near as an encircling halo appears to the light that paints it, when the vapor that bears it [the halo] is most dense, at such a distance around the point a circle of fire was whirling so rapidly that it would have surpassed that motion which most swiftly encircles the universe; and this was engirdled by another, and that by a third, and the third by a fourth, by a fifth the fourth, then by a sixth the fifth. Upon that the seventh followed, now extended so wide in girth that the messenger of Juno entire would be too narrow to contain it. So the eighth and the ninth; and each was moving more slowly according as it was in number more distant from the one; and the one from which the pure spark was least distant had the clearest flame, because, I believe, it most en-trues itself in it. My lady, who saw me perplexed and in great suspense, said: 'From that point depends heaven and all nature.' "

71. For the rich semantic history of *pungere* (long associated with sensual passion, Christian writers transformed it into the prod or stimulus of divine love), see Pertile, "Punta del disio." Contini ("*Paradiso* 28" 1018) underlines the same contrast, and connects the *punto* of *Paradiso* 28 with Francesca's. See also Chiampi, "Dante's *Paradiso*" (esp. 261, 265, 274). Molly Morrison ("Dante and Dionysius" 88) points out that for Pseudo-Dionysius too (*Divine Names* 4.693B) angelic intelligences participate in God as a circle's radii share in its central point.

72. "Untimely" (*intempestivo*): Vandelli, "*Paradiso* 28" 1924; he also calls Dante's numbering an "insistent and monotonous hammering" (*un martellare insistente e monotono*). Iris: Vergil, *Aeneid* 5.606–610, 4.693–705; Ovid, *Metamorphoses* 1.270–271, 11.585–632; in Dante, *Pg* 21.50–51, 29.77–78, 25.91–93, *Pd* 12.10–12, 33.118–119. Freccero notes ("Dance of the Stars" 234, 312n) that in the Middle Ages the halo around the moon was also called *Iris* (compare *Pg* 29.77–78).

73. "If the universe were disposed in the order which I see in those wheels, that which is set before me would have satisfied me; but in the world of sense the revolutions may be seen so much the more divine as they are more remote from the center. Thus if my desire is to attain its end in this wondrous and angelic temple, which has only love and light for its confine, I will need to hear why the model and the copy do not go the same way, for by myself I contemplate this in vain." For a sensitive analysis of this inverted astronomical model, see Cornish, *Reading Dante's Stars* 108–118.

74. "Take that which I shall tell you, if you wish to satiate yourself, and make yourself sharp about it. The material spheres are wide or narrow according to the more or less of causal-formative power that is diffused through all their parts. Greater goodness must needs work greater weal (health, blessedness); and the greater body, if its parts are equally complete, contains the greater weal. Hence this sphere, which sweeps along with it all the rest of the universe, corresponds to the circle which loves most and knows most. Wherefore, if you draw your measure round the power, not the semblance, of the substances which appear to you as circles, you will see a wondrous correspondence of greater to more and of smaller to less, in each heaven with respect to its intelligence."

75. "Just as the hemisphere of the air remains splendid and serene when Boreas blows from his milder cheek, purging and dissolving the refuse that had obscured it,

so that Heaven smiles to us with the beauties of its every region, so I became after my lady had provided me with her clear answer, and like a star in heaven the truth was seen [saw itself]."

CHAPTER 5: SUNRISES AND SUNSETS

1. Twice 187: whether by doubling 7 (= 14; 1 + 4 = 5), or by doubling 187 itself (187 + 187 = 374; 3 + 7 + 4 = 14; 1 = 4 = 5). For the meanings associated with two, five, seven, and ten, see the section "Time" of chapter 4. Cicero: *De re publica* 6.18. Singleton: "Poet's Number" esp. 6–7; see also Logan, "Poet's Central Numbers."

2. "Not to acquire good for Himself, which cannot be, but in order that his reflected light might, by re-reflecting, say 'I subsist,' in His eternity out of time, beyond all other encompassing, as it pleased Him, the Eternal Love opened Itself into new loves. Nor did He lie, as if inert, before, for neither before nor after did the moving of God upon these waters proceed. Form and matter, conjoined and simple, came into being that had no defect, as three arrows from a three-stringed bow; and as in glass, in amber or in crystal, a ray shines so that there is no interval between its coming and its its being fully there, so did the triform effect ray forth from its Lord in all its being, all at once, without distinction of beginning. Order and structure was con-created with the substances; and those in whom pure act was produced were the summit of the universe. Pure potentiality held the lowest place; in the middle such a bond tied up potentiality with act that it is never unbound."

3. For the technical meaning of *splendore*, see *Cv* 3.14.5 and Vasoli's comments in his edition (456–457).

4. Waters above the firmament: e.g., Augustine, *De Genesi ad litteram* 1.18–19, 21; and Aquinas, *ST* 1a.68.2–3; see Grant, *Planets, Stars, and Orbs* 103–104, 320–321, 332–334; and Nardi, "Discorrer di Dio" 311–313.

5. The sun as a mirror: *Pg* 4.62–63; see also *Pd* 10.28–30, 10.53, 22.116, 1.38, 20.1, *Cv* 3.5.21, 3.7.2–3, 3.12.7–8, 3.14.2–3, and Bufano et al., "Sole" 298–299. See also the discussion of the "metaphysics of light" in the second section of chapter 1.

6. *Intelligere* identical with *esse* only in God: e.g., Aquinas, *ST* 1a.54.1. On Dante's "Averroism" in this passage: see Vasoli, "Averroè" 476; O'Keeffe, "Dante's Theory of Creation" 63; Maierù, "Atto" 444; Nardi, "Tomismo di Dante secondo Francesco Orestano" 363, "Tomismo di Dante secondo Emilio Brodero" 369, "Filosofia di Dante" 1173; and Bemrose, *Dante's Angelic Intelligences* 61–70.

7. Nardi, Busnelli, Calò, Bersani, and Mellone never mention lines 1–12 in their analyses of *Pd* 29.13–36. In a *lettura* ("*Paradiso* 29" 296), Nardi calls lines 1–12 a "contrived Dantean simile . . . one of the usual expedients of a regulated style to hold the attention of the listener" (*un'artificiosa similitudine dantesca . . . uno dei soliti espedienti di stile regolato per incatenare l'attenzione dell'ascoltatore*); Bufano ("*Paradiso* 29" 20) attributes them to Dante's tendency to "make his exposition more precious" (*impreziosire la sua esposizione*); Vandelli ("*Paradiso* 28" 1916) calls it a successful expedient to "somehow justify" the sudden end of *Paradiso* 28. "Misplaced ostentation of erudition": Boyde's phrase (*Dante Philomythes* 240) for Porena's reaction in "Noterelle dantesche." Besides Cornish ("Planets and Angels," distilled and revised in *Reading Dante's Stars* 119–141), exceptions to this attitude include Boyde, who recognizes a thematic relevance between the simile and the discourse (239–240), and Durling and Martinez (*Time and the Crystal* 208–209), who also recognize the simile's profundity and importance. Getto ("*Paradiso* 29" 1946) is close to the mark when he compares it to the mid-sentence suspension between *Paradiso* 32 and 33; Petrocchi ("Figure dan-

tesche" 4) observes that the cosmic dimensions of the simile make an instant seem an immense temporal space.

8. "When both the children of Latona, covered by the Ram and by the Scales, make the horizon their belt at one same moment, as long as from the instant when the zenith holds them balanced till the one and the other, changing hemispheres, are unbalanced from that belt, for so long, her face painted with a smile, was Beatrice silent, looking fixedly at the point which had overcome me. Then she began, 'I tell, not ask, what you wish to hear, for I have seen it there where every *ubi* and every *quando* comes to a point.' "

9. Durling and Martinez: *Time and the Crystal* 208–209.

10. Alison Cornish: *Reading Dante's Stars* 119–120. Porena ("Noterelle Dantesche" 203) interpreted *si dilibra* as "frees itself"; in response, see Boyde, *Dante Philomythes* 239–240, and Cornish 124–125.

11. The problems of change, continuum, space, and time are treated throughout Aristotle's *Physics*, but principally in 4.10–14, 5, and 6. See also Aquinas's commentary, especially on book 4 (lect. 15–23). For useful overviews, see Ghisalberti, "Nozione di tempo" and Moreau, *L'espace et le temps* 89–177; in Dante, see Masciandaro, *Problematica del tempo*.

12. Apollo as revelation, etc. . . . : *Pd* 1.13–33, 2.8–9, 13.25, *Cv* 4.25.6; see also Padoan, "Apollo," and Castellani, "Heliocentricity"; for the *Paradiso*'s invocation of a "Christlike" Apollo, see Hollander, *Allegory* 204–216; Christ as sun: e.g., *Pd* 23.29, 23.79–84, 25.54; for the relation between God and sun, see Mazzeo, *Structure and Thought* 141–166. The Proserpinan associations of the moon are thoroughly treated by Kerr in chap. 2 of *Proserpinan Memory*; for the contrast between sun and moon, see *Mn* 3.4, and the relative articles in the *Enciclopedia Dantesca*. Belted together: Cornish observes (*Reading Dante's Stars* 122–123) that Dante's *cinto* renders "syzygy," which means "yoked together" and is the technical term for an "oppositional alignment of sun, moon, and earth." Durling and Martinez (*Time and the Crystal* 209) acutely realize that in the simile "the metaphysical relation of God and nature is mirrored in the astronomical relation of sun and moon," but do not develop the suggestion. Von Richthofen ("Twins of Latona") interprets the perfect balance between sun and moon as the perfect equilibrium between papal and imperial power, which is to balance the scales of justice.

13. Cornish: *Reading Dante's Stars* 119–141. Weight of the world: see also *If* 32.73–74, 34.110–111; Mazzotta (*Dante, Poet of the Desert* 163–164) elegantly evokes the assimilation between the Augustinian *pondus amoris* and physical gravity. "Nocturnal Aries": Cornish 140. Augustine: *Genesi ad litteram* 4.22–32, 11.16–30, *City of God* 11.13–22; see also Aquinas, *ST* 1a.63.5–6. Sun produced on fourth day: see also *Mn* 3.4.13. Shining of sun simultaneous with reflection: the analogy is in both Augustine (*Genesi ad litteram* 4.34) and Aquinas (*ST* 1a.63.5); see Cornish 131–132. For how *amor sui* can lead either to *amor Dei* or *contemptus Dei*, see Nardi, "Angeli che non furon ribelli" 346–348.

14. Host of illusory problems: especially between Nardi (e.g., "Noterelle polemiche" 131, "Meditantur sua stercora" 59, "Rassegna bibliografica" 312, and "Caduta di Lucifero") and Thomists (Moretti, "Filosofia di Dante: le creature eterne"; Busnelli, *Cosmogonia e antropogenesi* 45–46; and Calò, Review of Nardi's *Sigieri di Brabante* 267); see also Mellone, *Dottrina di Dante* 64–66, and Bemrose, *Dante's Angelic Intelligences* 185–201. Creation not in time for Augustine: e.g., *Genesi ad litteram* 4.33–35. In the *Questio* Dante gives a strictly natural explanation of the rise of earth over water: see

Pastore Stocchi, "Quaestio" 764; Freccero, "Satan's Fall"; and Mazzoni's introduction to his edition, esp. 712–732. If there is any temporality in Lucifer's fall, as *If* 34.122 suggests (*la terra, che pria di qua si sporse* ["the earth, which first protruded on this side"]), it may be (as Freccero argued in "Satan's Fall" 109) that Lucifer's journey through space occurred in time (as opposed to the pilgrim's ascent from sphere to sphere), or (as Mellone proposed in "Canto XXIX" 202–203) that his expulsion was delayed after his sin. For this temporality, see Cornish, *Reading Dante's Stars* 136–138.

15. On Francesca, see also the subsection "Pyramus and Thisbe" in chapter 3. Francesca's misreading: see Noakes, "Double Mis-Reading"; Poggioli, "Tragedy or Romance?"; and Hatcher and Musa, "The Kiss." For the relations between Augustine, the *Aeneid*, and Francesca's reading, see Hollander, *Allegory* 108–114, and Mazzotta, *Dante, Poet of the Desert* 165–177; Hollander discusses the opposed *punti* in "*Paradiso* XXX.*" The parallel between Francesca's and Augustine's interrupted reading was noticed by Seung, *Fragile Leaves* 299. Rom. 13.11–12: *Hora est iam nos de somno surgere / nunc enim propior est nostra salus quam cum credidimus / nox praecessit / dies autem adpropiavit / abiciamus ergo opera tenebrarum / et induamur arma lucis / sicut in die honeste ambulemus.*

16. For Vergil's Fourth Eclogue as a prophecy of Christ, see Comparetti, *Vergil in the Middle Ages* 96–103. Dante is of course perfectly aware that the "Virgo" of the Eclogue is Astraea, goddess of justice (*Mn* I.11.1, *Ep* 7.6, 11.15). For Statius's "misreadings" of Vergil, see Kleiner, *Mismapping the Underworld* 71–78; Barolini, *Dante's Poets* 258–263; Shoaf, " 'Auri sacra fames' "; Martinez, "*Sacra fame dell'oro*"; Hollander, "Tragedy of Divination" 169–218; Kleinhenz, "Celebration of Poetry"; Brugnoli, "Stazio in Dante" and "Stazio di Dante in Benvenuto"; Chiamenti, *Dante Alighieri traduttore* 131–137; and Marchesi, "Dante's 'Active' Hermeneutics." The Crucifixion/Resurrection imagery surrounding Statius is lucidly laid out by Hollander, *Allegory* 67–69.

17. For the mirror experiment of *Paradiso* 2, see the second section of chapter 4.

18. The lunar eclipse was noticed by Porena in his commentary (3.283); see also Cornish, "Planets and Angels" 7–8, and Kleiner, *Mismapping the Underworld* 99–100. Kleiner: in "Eclipses in the *Paradiso*"; Cornish also notes the three eclipses ("Planets and Angels" 8). As Imbach observes (*Dante, la philosophie* 146–47), the idea that angels learn nothing new contradicts Aquinas, was supported by Sigier de Brabant, and condemned by Tempier in 1277. Awakened the centurion: Matt. 27.45–54, Mark 15.22–39, and Luke 23.44–47.

19. See Kleiner, "Eclipses in the *Paradiso*" and *Mismapping the Underworld* 87–116. For the inscribing of cross and Crucifixion at the center of the *Paradiso*, see Schnapp, *Transfiguration of History* 70–169. Aries and Libra associated with Christ: Kleiner, "Eclipses in the *Paradiso*" 14n11. Freccero: "Pilgrim in a Gyre" 77 and "Dance of the Stars" 239–240; see also Kleiner, *Mismapping the Underworld* 90–94. Balancing the sun and moon: Kleiner, "Eclipses in the *Paradiso*" 26–32; he notes that Dante refers to the moon as Latona's child only three times, *Pd* 29.1, 10.67, and 22.139, the latter being a reference to *Pd* 2.

20. Dante transfixes the sun: Kleiner, *Mismapping the Underworld* 112. "Excellence" of vernal equinox, linked to creation: *If* 1.38–40, *Pg* 2.1–6, 2.55–57, 8.133–135, 11.115–117, 25.2, 32.53–54, *Pd* 1.37–42, *Cv* 3.5.8, 3.5.18. Beginning from equlibrium, poised on the equinox, and then moving back and forth across the equinox through the seasons, the sun establishes the rhythms of sublunar generation and corruption (see Bufano et al., "Sole" 300). Pasquazi ("*Paradiso* 29" 1037) links the cosmic moment when the pilgrim leaves the dark wood in *Inferno* 1 to the moment described in

the opening verses of *Paradiso* 29: both are an emerging from multiplicity and differ-ence. Compare Kabir: "I have brought my love and my silence / into the land where there is no sun and moon, nor day and night" (*Songs of Kabir* 76).

21. Contini: "Paradiso 28." That in *Paradiso* 28 Dante is underlining the "au-thenticity" of his experience (and poetry) is stressed by Padoan ("Canto XXVIII").

22. For the ordering of angelic intelligences in relation to the Trinity and the spheres, see Mellone, "Gerarchia angelica" (with extensive references and bibliogra-phy), and Mellone et al., "Angelo" 268–271. Spera ("Poesia degli angeli" 541) acutely suggests that *Paradiso* 28 presents the angels as a contemplative model for man. For the contrast between human and angelic knowing as underpinning the formal strate-gies of the *Paradiso*, see Barolini, *Undivine Comedy* 22–23, 237–241. For a full treat-ment of the angelic hierarchies in relation to theological authority (especially Pseudo-Dionysius), see Molly Morrison, "Hierarchies at a Crossroads" and "Dante and Dionysius."

23. "But since it is taught in your schools on earth that the angelic nature is such that it understands and remembers and wills, I will speak further, in order that you may see in its purity the truth that is confused down there by the equivocations in such teaching."

24. On angelic knowledge, see Aquinas *ST* 1a.58.1–5; on angelic memory, see also *SCG* 2.101, *Questiones disputatae De veritate* 8.5; also Nardi, "Canto XXIX," and Bemrose, *Dante's Angelic Intelligences* 74–75.

25. "One says that at Christ's passion the moon turned back and interposed it-self, so that the light of the sun did not reach below—and he lies, for the light itself hid itself, so that this eclipse took place for the Spaniards and the Indians, as well as for the Jews."

26. On the eclipse, see Aquinas *ST* 3a.q44.a2.ad2; also Bufano, "Canto XXIX" 9. Petrocchi ("Figure dantesche di Dio" 17) observes that the preaching Beatrice is at-tacking conjures the *Decameron*'s Frate Cipolla.

27. "This [angelic] nature extends so far beyond in number, that there was never speech nor mortal concept that might go so far; and if you look at what is revealed in Daniel, you will see that in his thousands any determinate number is withheld."

28. "By now you see the height and breadth of the Eternal Goodness, since it has made itself so many mirrors in which it divides itself, remaining one in itself as before."

29. "A single moment brings me more forgetfulness than twenty-five centuries have brought to the enterprise that made Neptune wonder at the *Argo*'s shadow."

30. *Argo* first ship: see Curtius, "Ship of the Argonauts." Hollander: *Allegory* 231–232; Hollander's discussion of Jason and this simile (220–232) is particularly insight-ful. Jason in first cantos of *Paradiso*: subliminally in 1.67–69, explicitly in 2.16–18; see also 25.7–8, and Hollander, 220–224. For the simile, see also Dronke, "Conclusion" and "Boethius, Alanus, and Dante"; Chiarenza, "Pagan Images"; Portier, "Argonautes dantesques"; Rabuse, "Un punto solo"; and Tateo, "Percorsi agostiniani."

CONCLUSION: IS DANTE TELLING THE TRUTH?

1. Wittgensteinian image: see *Tractatus* 5.633, and compare (on the metaphysical subject and the limit of the world) 5.631, 5.632, 5.641. For Dante's Empyrean as the "eye of God," see Kay, "Dante's Empyrean."

2. Value or meaning grounded in the non-contingent: compare Wittgenstein *Tractatus* 5.634, 6.41. Incarnational poetics: e.g., Mazzotta, *Dante, Poet of the Desert*

197, and Brownlee, "Language and Desire" 57; equinoctial: Durling and Martinez, *Time and the Crystal* 207; conversion: Freccero, *Poetics of Conversion*; martyrdom, Crucifixion: Schnapp, *Transfiguration of History*; transfiguration: Brownlee, "Dante's Poetics of Transfiguration."

3. *Dolcezza*: *Pd* 33.63, and, e.g., *Pg* 13.16, 27.115, *Pd* 3.38, 19.2, 32.101; in poetry: e.g., *Cv* 1.7.14–15, 3.7.12, *VN* 3.2, 39.8.3, *Pg* 2.113–114, 24.57, 29.22 32.90, *Pd* 10.147, 20.75, 23.97 27.3.

4. Mystery of the world's being: compare Wittgenstein *Tractatus* 6.4312, 6.44, 6.45, 6.371–372; *Culture and Value* 5e. Limit of thought and language: compare *Tractatus* 6.42, 6.522, 7. Wittgenstein's later work is based on the conviction that philosophy does not provide answers to questions: it is a course of therapy that dissolves illusory questions (expressions of self-alienation and unhappiness) by correcting our vision, our power to see. Philosophy is a practical (moral) enterprise. In rough terms, the thrust of the *Philosophical Investigations* is that thought and language arise together as an implicit determination of experience, a positing of rules for a game. To identify or become aware of those rules (to delineate the structure of experience) is not to *explain* the game, but at most a way to become conscious that it *is* a game, that it has no innate "essence" or "reality" to get at that, when known, could "explain" it. The game *is* its rules, but the rules are simply a description of the game: the articulation or structure that is to explain the world constitutes it. This is the insight that lies behind the Aristotelian and medieval understanding of form; to grasp it is to begin to awaken to the nature of reality, to oneself.

5. Allen (*Ethical Poetic*) makes the *Comedy* the paradigm of a late-medieval understanding of poetry as principally ethical or practical. Wittgenstein too remarked that no one can speak the truth who does not live in it: see *Culture and Value* 35, 16, 33, and Monk, *Ludwig Wittgenstein* 361–384.

6. David Loy (*Nonduality* 336, 13–14) calls twentieth-century catastrophe "the cultural bankruptcy of contemporary Western dualism." For a lucid overview of materialism and its motivations, see Campbell, "Materialism" esp. 182.

7. Madhva's dualistic system (Dvaita-vedānta) stresses the distinction between God and the soul, God and matter, individual souls, souls and matter, and individual material substances; the qualified non-dualism of Rāmānuja (Viśiṣṭādvaita-vedānta) emphasizes the objective reality of the world, the eternal individuality of souls, and the absolute transcendence of a personal God to all creation, which exists by Him and through Him only in order to serve Him. What has been said of Indian philosophy: Radhakrishnan and Moore, *Sourcebook* xxv. For a sensitive meditation on recognizing Christ in other traditions, see Panikkar, *Unknown Christ*, and the assessment by Long, "Unknown Christ."

8. The term "mysticism" in its modern sense arose in seventeenth-century France, along with the Enlightenment: see Certeau, " 'Mystique' au XVIIe siècle," and McGinn, *Foundations of Mysticism* 266, 310–313.

9. Padoan: "Mirabile visione" 295–296, referring to *Epistola a Cangrande* 79–80. *Beniamin maior: The Mystical Ark* e.g., 1.6, 4.23. Étienne Gilson: "Conclusion de la *Divine Comédie*."

10. Nardi: e.g., *Sigieri di Brabante* 70. "Breaker of shells": Blakney, in introduction to Eckhart, *Meister Eckhart: A Modern Translation* xiv; Eckhart himself: Sermon 11 (*Meister Eckhart: A Modern Translation* 148). The *Comedy* could not have escaped condemnation: see Simonelli, "L'Inquisizione e Dante" 140.

11. Augustine's trajectory: traced in Vance, *Mervelous Signals* 1–50. Letter as body, spirit as soul: Smalley, *Study of the Bible*, esp. 1–2. Reading figurative passages literally:

Augustine, *De doctrina Christiana* 3.5.9 (see Vance, *Mervelous Signals* 9). External rain versus internal fountain: Augustine, *Genesi contra Manicheos* (on Gen. 2.4–5), cited by Shoaf, *Dante, Chaucer, and the Currency* 59. Paul: 2 Cor. 3.6; see also Rom. 7.6, 8.1–13, 2.28–29.

12. For the transcendence of the anagogical sense, see, e.g., Richard of St. Victor, *Mystical Ark* 366–367. The distinction between "poetical" and "theological" allegory is sharpest in Albert the Great (e.g., *Summae Theologiae* I, 1.5.2) and Aquinas (e.g., *ST* 1a.1.9–10); in medieval practice, however, *fictio* does not necessarily simply imply falsehood. See, e.g., Minnis and Scott, *Medieval Literary Theory*, esp. 386–387, and Grayson, "Dante's Theory," which defines fiction as "simply what the poet makes within him as opposed to what is created or exists outside him" (155). For the links between sacred and profane poetry in the later Middle Ages, see Minnis, *Medieval Theory of Authorship* 138–145; for examples of the varieties of poetic signifying available to Dante in medieval practice, see Dronke, "The *Commedia* and Medieval Modes" 1–31. Figural or biblical exegesis was also applied to profane texts, as noted for example by Auerbach himself ("Figura" 63–64) and by John Scott ("Dante's Allegory" 573). A number of recent essays, such as those by Priest ("Allegory and Reality"), Chiarenza ("Falsity and Fiction"), Giannantonio (*Endiadi*), Barański ("Lezione esegetica"), and Scaglione ("(Christian) Theologians"), have worked to undermine or complicate the "theologians/poets" distinction as applied to the *Comedy*; see also Hollander, "Typology and Secular Literature." For the distinction as presented in the *Convivio*, see now Scott, " 'Veramente li teologi,' " and Fenzi, "L'esperienza di sé." The classic work on the four senses of Scripture is Lubac, *Four Senses of Scripture* (vol. 1 of *Medieval Exegesis*); for crystalline overviews of the two types of allegory, see Hollander, *Allegory* 15–56 and *Dante Alighieri*; Mazzotta's account in *Dante, Poet of the Desert* (227–274) is particularly nuanced, and argues that truth and fiction are not "mutually exclusive categories" in metaphoric language (233). A detailed analysis that has not been superseded is provided by Pépin, *Dante et la tradition* and "Allegoria"; for Dante and the tradition of biblical exegesis, see Lieberknecht, *Allegorese und Philologie*. For other references, see the section on anagogy in this chapter.

13. "Deny the undeniable": Padoan, "Mirabile visione" 292; see also Hollander, *Allegory* 19. Could have ruined Pietro: Simonelli, "L'Inquisizione e Dante" 140. Barolini: "For the Record" 142. For a survey of passages in which the *Comedy* ascribes to itself divine inspiration, see Nardi, "Dante Profeta." Padoan quotation: "Mirabile visione" 290.

14. Hollander: "Dante *Theologus-poeta*" 44–51; quotations: 49, 50; see also the chapter "Poetry and Theology" in Curtius, *European Literature* (214–227). Tradition of poetic self-defense: see Haug, *Vernacular Literary Theory*; *translatio auctoritatis*: a term coined by Minnis, *Medieval Theory of Authorship*, e.g., viii, xiii. Imbach (*Dante, la philosophie*, esp. 129–138) stresses the importance of Dante in a movement of lay appropriation of clerical learning and authority and of the vernacular as its medium.

15. Padoan: "Mirabile visione" 307.

16. Barolini: *Undivine Comedy* 3–4, stressing the historical importance of the event; in "Mirabile visione," Padoan is taking up the banner raised by Nardi. Nardi's ideas are subtly developed in Gorni, "Spirito profetico"; see also Osculati, "La profezia."

17. For example, *Pg* 17.13–18, 9.13–18; *Cv* 2.8.13; see also Nardi, "Conoscenza umana" 140–141 and "Dante e Pietro d'Abano" 55–58.

18. Aristotle: *Metaphysics* 2.1.993b20–30 (in a context arguing toward the

thought that thinks itself, the ground of all being which makes all knowledge possible); see Aquinas, *ST* 1a.2.3, 1a.44.1. The gate of Hell: see Hollander, *Allegory* 72; purgatorial sculpture: Barolini, "Re-Presenting What God Presented," in *Undivine Comedy* 122–142, which makes the crucial distinction between representation and re-presentation; for thematic connections between the three examples, see appendix II of Hollander's *Allegory*. The connection between Mary and sunrise is traced by Pertile, *Puttana e gigante* 69–74.

19. *DVE* 2.4.2. As Mengaldo notes in his commentary, this purely formal definition is "in antithesis to the content-based definitions of poetry" current in Dante's time (162). For the sense of *fictio*, see Paparelli, "*Fictio*." As Simone Marchesi will argue in a forthcoming manuscript, there may well be an evolution in Dante's understanding of *fictio*, evident from his attempts in the *Vita Nova* and *Convivio* to "open" at least some of the import of his poetic *fictio* in prose.

20. Body and soul in Scripture: Smalley, *Study of the Bible* esp. 1–2. Shoaf: *Dante, Chaucer, and the Currency* 7–100, 233–242; "dying in wanting": 240; "purchases invisibles": 88. Mediate eternal into temporal: Vance, *Mervelous Signals* 34–50.

21. Charity: *Events and Their Afterlife*. Transfiguration of history: from Schnapp's book of that title. For Charity's notion of "applied" typology, see *Events and Their Afterlife* esp. 80, 261; conforming one's life to Christ's: see 168. Pasquazi's brief "Interpretazione figurale anagogica" captures its essence.

22. Auerbach: "Figura"; Singleton: *Dante's Commedia: Elements of Structure* 1–17, 84–98, and "Irreducible Dove"; Charity: *Events and their Afterlife*; Hollander: esp. *Allegory, Dante Alighieri*, "Dante Theologus-poeta"; Padoan: "Mirabile visione"; Mineo: *Profetismo e apocalittica*, and Sarolli, *Prolegomena* and "Dante 'scriba Dei.' " See also Mazzeo, "Medieval Hermeneutics."

23. *Confessions* 11.3.5, see Vance, *Mervelous Signals* 41. Franke too stresses the claim of the poem on the "historicity of the reader" as a revelation of the transcendent; for Franke its fiction is true in an existential sense, as an interpretation of a life and history (*Dante's Interpretive Journey* esp. 152–237).

24. For the name of God and the Italian "I," see Hollander, "Babytalk" 128. Martinez points out ("Pilgrim's Answer" 46–49) that the paradigmatic divine name of Ex. 3.14 (*Ego sum qui sum*) is echoed not only in *Pd* 26.133–138, but also by the pilgrim in his statement of poetics (*Pg* 24.52), as well as in the phrases *sé in sé rigira* (*Pg* 25.75, referring to the rational soul) and *sé con sé misura* (*Pd* 19.51, referring to God). Damon observes ("Adam on the Primal Language") that the movement from *I* to *El* is from the direct contemplation and denotation of God to description. Casagrande (" 'I s'appellava' "), following Penna ("El"), links "I" to the Hebrew divine name "Ja" (the *jod*, or letter "I"), signifying the universal and the invisible; "El" is another Hebrew name for God, signifying power. For the political dimension of the restoration of man through Christ, see Kantorowicz, *King's Two Bodies* 451–495.

25. Singleton: "Irreducible Dove" 129, *Dante's Commedia: Elements of Structure* 62. Many have cast doubt on Singleton's claim: see, e.g., Barolini, *Undivine Comedy* 11; Minnis and Scott, *Medieval Literary Theory* 384–385; and Dronke, "*Commedia* and Medieval Modes" 3–4, 126–127. For Geryon as an image of Dante's poetic project, see Ferrucci, *Poetics of Disguise* 66–102; Barolini, *Dante's Poets* 213–214, *Undivine Comedy* esp. 58–73; Barański, "Il 'meraviglioso' e il 'comico' "; and Cachey, "Dante's Journey." Hollander: "Dante *Theologus-poeta*" 76.

26. Barolini: *Undivine Comedy* 13. In *Dante, Poet of the Desert*, Mazzotta stresses the ambiguity of the sign, and thus acutely sees the *Comedy* as a dramatization of the

act of interpretation itself, between the two poles of Francesca and Statius. That all thought and language is fraudulent (*menzogna*) in relation to "mystical" truth is the point of Carugati's *Dalla menzogna al silenzio*; see also Colombo, *Dai mistici a Dante*.

27. Barolini quotations: *Undivine Comedy* 16.

28. Augustine: *De doctrina Christiana* 1.36. *Historia, argumentum, fabula*: see Isidore of Seville, *Etymologiarum* 1.44.5. For a sustained meditation on poetry as alone capable of encompassing and mediating the sense and totality of human knowledge, see Mazzotta's *Dante's Vision*; Mazzotta underlines the transformative power of poetry in "Why Did Dante Write the *Comedy*?"

EPILOGUE: NO MIND, NO MATTER

1. For accounts of recent scientific developments, see, e.g., Greene, *Elegant Universe*; Hawking, *Brief History of Time*; and Pagels, *Cosmic Code*. Ferris, *Coming of Age*, and Herbert, *Quantum Reality*, are good popular accounts. For relativity in particular, see Geroch, *General Relativity*; Mook and Vargish, *Inside Relativity*; and Einstein, *Relativity*. For some of the philosophical and theological implications of these developments, see, e.g., Fine, *Shaky Game*; Bohr, *Philosophical Writings*; Heisenberg, *Physics and Philosophy*; Schrödinger, *Mind and Matter*; Cushing and McMullin, *Philosophical Consequences*; Russel, Murphy, and Isham, *Quantum Cosmology*; Lester Smith, *Intelligence Came First*; Barr, "Four Developments"; and Brockelman, *Cosmology and Creation*. The Neoscholastic movement spawned various attempts to reconcile modern science with Aristotelian-Thomistic hylomorphism. These are usually textbooks of Thomistic metaphysics that address the physics of the era that spawned them. They thus struggle to reconcile hylomorphic "doctrine" with atomism, a hopeless enterprise in any case, and an effort that more recent developments in physics have rendered superfluous. A prime example is Daujat, *Physique moderne*. Selvaggi, *Filosofia del mondo*; Descoqs, *Essai critique*; and Benignus, *Nature, Knowledge, and God* also address the problem. Recent essays include Wallace, "Thomism and the Quantum Enigma"; William Carroll, "Aquinas on Creation"; and Nichols, "Aquinas's Concept." Emerton's *Scientific Reinterpretation of Form* gives a history of the concept of form and its relation to science from ancient times through the eighteenth century.

2. "Inaccessible to any conceivable experiment": Horgan, "Particle Metaphysics" 102. Heisenberg: inset quote, *Physics and Philosophy* 160; "the smallest units . . ." *Across the Frontiers* 116.

3. General relativity dissolves . . . : see Einstein, *Relativity* 155. For a philosophical analysis of the notion of substantival spacetime, see Sklar, *Space, Time, and Spacetime* 155–237. Egginton ("Dante, Hyperspheres") underlines how Dante's medieval conception of space and its relation to matter has proved to be more accurate than the Cartesian-Newtonian picture. "Everything that ever existed . . .": Pagels, *Cosmic Code* 244; "filled with the vibrations . . .": 246; Heinz Pagels observes . . . : 247; "theoretical and experimental . . .": 247.

4. *Tractatus* 5.633–5.6331 ("nothing *in the visual field* allows you to infer that it is seen by an eye"), and the related remarks 5.631–5.632.

5. See Wilber, *Quantum Questions* 1–29. Wilber's book is a clearheaded treatment of the relation between "mysticism" and science and provides a comprehensive anthology of the quantum physicists' writings on religion and "mysticism."

6. *Nature of the Physical World* 332.

7. Some of Heisenberg's remarks are collected in Wilber, *Quantum Questions* 33–73 (see esp. 45–54). Heisenberg invented matrix quantum mechanics, and with it the

uncertainty principle, which gives quantum physics its essential character; Schrödinger independently formulated the wave equation that allows the theory to actually
function and make predictions. Heisenberg was awarded the Nobel Prize in 1932,
Schrödinger in 1933.

8. Schrödinger, *Mind and Matter* 51–52.

9. The region in which all minds . . . : *Mind and Matter* 52–53. Schrödinger
points out that "consciousness is never experienced in the plural, only in the singular" (55), and that we cannot even conceive how it could be otherwise. The true "I" is
the conscious ground . . . : *What Is Life?* 96; no "intelligible scientific meaning" . . . :
My View of the World 21.

10. *Nature and the Greeks* 95–96.

11. *Mind and Matter* 62–63.

12. Planck, *Where Is Science Going?*, in *New Science* 114–115, 118.

13. The books vary widely in scientific and philosophical rigor. Among the best
for scientific precision are Wolfgang Smith, *Quantum Engima*; Capra, *Tao of Physics*
and *Turning Point*; and Zukav, *Dancing Wu Li Masters*. More popular accounts are Talbot, *Mysticism and the New Physics* and *Beyond the Quantum*; and Drees, *Beyond the
Big Bang*. For a skeptical view, see Powers, *Philosophy and the New Physics*.

14. For an account of recent experiments in non-locality, see Chiao, Kwiat, and
Steinberg, "Faster than Light?"; for their implications, see Cushing and McMullin,
Philosophical Consequences. Wittgenstein had already seen that the common notion of
causality is incoherent: it is not a thing, not *in* the world, but a form that descriptions
of experience can take. See, e.g., *Tractatus* 5.136–5.1362, 6.32, 6.36, 6.37. "Information
gets around": Henry Stapp, quoted in Zukav, *Dancing Wu Li Masters* 311; the expression is of course inexact. That the universe is not an aggregate of parts is the point of
Bohm, *Wholeness and the Implicate Order*; see also Kafatos and Nadeau, *Conscious Universe*.

15. What we say we know . . . : see Barfield's *Saving the Appearances*. Billiard
balls: see Ferris, *Coming of Age* 288–289. Perhaps some have glimpsed . . . : recent
testimony to consider might include Yogananda's *Autobiography of a Yogi* and Murphet's *Sai Baba: Man of Miracles*. Fireflies: the title of a collection of aphorisms by
Rabindranath Tagore. The moth and flame: see Dillard, *Holy the Firm*.

Works Cited

Abrams, Richard. "Inspiration and Gluttony: The Moral Context of Dante's Poetics of the 'Sweet New Style'." *MLN* 91 (1976): 30–59.

Aertsen, Jan A. "The Philosophical Importance of the Doctrine of the Transcendentals in Thomas Aquinas." *Revue internationale de philosophie* 52 (June 1998): 249–268.

———. "What is First and Most Fundamental? The Beginnings of Transcendental Philosophy." In *Was ist Philosophie im Mittelalter?* edited by Jan A. Aertsen and Andreas Speer, Miscellanea Mediaevalia, vol. 26, 177–192. Berlin: De Gruyter, 1998.

Ahearn, John. "Binding the Book: Hermeneutics and Manuscript Production in *Paradiso* 33." *PMLA* 97, no. 5 (October 1982): 800–809.

Albertus Magnus, Saint. *Compendium theologicae veritatis.* Vol. 34 of *Opera omnia* (Borgnet edition). Now attributed to Hugh of Strasbourg.

———. *De anima libri tres.* Edited by Clement Stroick. Münster: Institutum Alberti Magni, 1968.

———. *De caelo et mundo.* Vol. 5, pt. 1 of *Opera omnia* (Geyer edition).

———. *De intellectu et intelligibili.* Vol. 9 of *Opera omnia* (Borgnet edition).

———. *Enarrationes in secundam partem evang. Lucae (X–XXIV).* Vol. 23 of *Opera omnia* (Borgnet edition).

———. *Metaphysica.* Vol. 16 of *Opera omnia* (Geyer edition).

———. *Opera omnia ad fidem codicum manuscriptorum edenda. . . .* Edited by Bernhard Geyer. Cologne: Monasterii Westfalorum, 1951–.

———. *Opera omnia ex editione lugdunensi religiose castigata. . . .* Edited by Auguste Borgnet. Paris: Vivès, 1890–1899.

———. *Physica.* Vol. 4 of *Opera omnia* (Geyer edition).

———. *Scripta in quatuor libros Sententiarum.* Vols. 25–30 of *Opera omnia* (Borgnet edition).

———. *Summa de creaturis.* Vol. 34 of *Opera omnia* (Borgnet edition).

———. *Summae Theologiae.* Vol. 31 of *Opera omnia* (Borgnet edition).

al-Bitrūjī [Alpetragius]. *On the Principles of Astronomy.* Arabic and Hebrew texts with translation, analysis, and Arabic-Hebrew-English glossary.

Edited and translated by Bernard R. Goldstein. New Haven: Yale University Press, 1971.

————. *De motibus celorum*. Critical edition of the Latin translation of Michael Scot. Edited by Francis J. Carmody. Berkeley: University of California Press, 1952.

Albritton, Rogers. "Forms of Particular Substances in Aristotle's *Metaphysics*." *Journal of Philosophy* 54, no. 22 (October 1957): 699–708.

Alexander of Aphrodisias. *De anima liber cum mantissa*. Edited by Ivo Bruns. Commentaria in Aristotelem Graeca: Supplementum Aristotelicum, vol. 2. Berlin: Academiae Litterarum Regiae Borussicae, 1887.

————. *The De Anima of Alexander of Aphrodisias: A Translation and Commentary*. Translated by Athanasias P. Fotinis. Washington, D.C.: University Press of America, 1979.

Alexander of Hales. *Quaestiones disputatae "antequam esset frater."* Quaracchi: Collegium S. Bonaventurae, 1960.

————. *Summa theologica*. Florence: Collegium S. Bonaventurae, 1924–1948. 4 vols. in 5.

al-Fārābī. *Deux traités philosophiques: L'harmonie entre les opinions des deux sages, le divin Platon et Aristote et De la religion*. Translated by Dominique Mallet. Damas: Institut Français de Damas, 1989.

————. *Al-Farabi's Philosophy of Plato and Aristotle*. Translated by Madhi. Ithaca: Cornell University Press, 1969.

Alfraganus [al-Farghānī]. *Il "Libro dell'aggregazione delle stelle" (Dante, Conv., II,v,1–34), secondo il codice Mediceo-Laurenziano Pl. 29–Cod. 9 contemporaneo a Dante*. Vols. 87–90 in Collezione di opuscoli danteschi inediti o rari, ed. G. L. Passerini. Edited by Romeo Campani. Città di Castello: Lapi, 1910.

Algazel [al-Ghazālī]. *Logica et Philosophia*. 1506. Facsimile ed., Frankfurt: Minerva, 1969.

Allan, D. J. *The Philosophy of Aristotle*. 2d ed. Oxford: Oxford University Press, 1970.

Allen, Judson Boyce. *The Ethical Poetic of the Later Middle Ages: A Decorum of Convenient Distinction*. Toronto: University of Toronto Press, 1982.

Ambrose, Saint. *Exameron*. In *Opera, pars prima*. CSEL, vol. 32, 1–261. Vindobonae: F. Tempsky, 1897.

————. *Expositio evangelii secundum Lucam*. In *Sancti Ambrosii Mediolanensis Opera, Pars IV*. CCSL, vol. 14. Turnholti: Brepols, 1957.

————. *Expositio Psalmi CXVIII*. In *Opera, pars quinta*. Edited by M. Petschenig. CSEL, vol. 62. Vindobonae: F. Tempsky, 1913.

Andriani, Beniamino. *La forma del paradiso dantesco: il sistema del mondo secondo gli antichi e secondo Dante*. Padova: Cedam, 1961.

Annas, Julia. "Aristotle, Number and Time." *Philosophical Quarterly* 25, no. 99 (April 1975): 97–113.

————. "Aristotle on Substance, Accident and Plato's Forms." *Phronesis* 22, no. 2 (1977): 146–160.

————. "Forms and First Principles." *Phronesis* 19, no. 3 (1974): 257–283.

Anscombe, G. E. M. "On the Notion of Immaterial Substance." In *Substances and Things: Aristotle's Doctrine of Physical Substance in Recent Essays*, edited by M. L. O'Hara, 252–262. Washington, D.C.: University Press of America, 1982.

Anscombe, G. E. M., and P. T. Geach. *Three Philosophers*. Ithaca: Cornell University Press, 1961.

Anselm, Saint. "Monologium." In *St. Anselm: Basic Writings*, translated by S. N. Deane, 81–190. 2d ed. La Salle, Ill.: Open Court, 1962.

————. "Proslogium." In *St. Anselm: Basic Writings*, translated by S. N. Deane, 47–80. 2d ed. La Salle, Ill.: Open Court, 1962.

Aquinas, Saint Thomas. *Aquinas against the Averroists: On There Being Only One Intellect [De unitate intellectus contra Averroistas]*. Includes Leonine critical edition of the text. Translated by Ralph McInerny. West Lafayette, Ind.: Purdue University Press, 1993.

————. *Aquinas on Creation: Writings on the "Sentences" of Peter Lombard (Book 2, Distinction 1, Question 1)*. Translated by Steven E. Baldner and William E. Carroll. Toronto: Pontifical Institute of Medieval Studies, 1997.

————. *In Aristotelis libros De caelo et mundo; De generatione et Corruptione; Meteorologicorum. Expositio cum textu ex recensione Leonina*. Edited by Raimondo Spiazzi. Turin: Marietti, 1952.

————. *Catena aurea in quatuor evangelia*. 8th rev. ed. Turin: Marietti, 1925. 2 vols.

————. *A Commentary on Aristotle's* De anima. Translated by Robert Pasnau. New Haven: Yale University Press, 1999.

————. *Commentary on Aristotle's* De Anima. Translated by Kenelm Foster and Silvester Humphries. 1951. Notre Dame, Ind.: Dumb Ox Books, 1994.

————. *Commentary on Aristotle's* Metaphysics. Rev. ed. Translated by John P. Rowan. 1961. Notre Dame, Ind.: Dumb Ox Books, 1995.

————. *Commentary on Aristotle's* Physics. Translated by Richard J. Blackwell, Richard J. Spath, and W. Edmund Thirlkel. New Haven: Yale University Press, 1963.

————. *Commentary on the* Book of Causes *[Super librum de causis expositio]*. Translated by Vincent A. Guagliardo, Charles R. Hess, and Richard C. Taylor. Washington, D.C.: Catholic University of America Press, 1996.

————. *De aeternitate mundi*. Vol. 43 of *Opera omnia*, 49–89. Rome: Commissio Leonina, 1976.

————. *De ente et essentia*. Vol. 43 of *Opera omnia*. Rome: Commissio Leonina, 1976.

————. *De substantiis separatis*. Vol. 40 of *Opera omnia*, 1–87. Edited by H. F. Dondaine. Rome: Commissio Leonina, 1969.

————. *In octo libros Physicorum Aristotelis expositio*. Edited by P. M. Maggiolo. Turin: Marietti, 1965.

————. *On the Eternity of the World [De Aeternitate Mundi.]* 2d ed. Translated by Cyril Vollert, S. J., Lottie H. Kendzierski, and Paul M. Byrne. 1964. Milwaukee: Marquette University Press, 1984.

————. *Quaestiones de anima*. Translated by James H. Robb. Milwaukee: Marquette University Press, 1984.

————. *Quaestiones disputatae De potentia*. Vol. 2 of *Quaestiones disputatae*. 10th ed. Edited by Raimondo Spiazzi. Turin: Marietti, 1965.

————. *Quaestiones disputatae De veritate*. Vol. 2 of *Quaestiones disputatae*. 10th ed. Edited by Raimondo Spiazzi. Turin: Marietti, 1965.

————. *Quaestiones Quodlibetales*. Edited by Raimondo Spiazzi. Turin: Marietti, 1949.

————. *Quodlibetal Questions 1 and 2*. Translated by Sandra Edwards. Toronto: Pontifical Institute of Mediaeval Studies, 1983.

————. *Scriptum super libros Sententiarum Magistri Petri Lombardi Episcopi Parisiensis*. New ed. Edited by R. P. Mandonnet and Maria Fabianus Moos. Paris: Lethielleux, 1929–1947. 4 vols.

————. *Sentencia libri "De anima."* Edited by René-Antoine Gauthier. Vol. 45, part 1, of *Opera omnia*. Rome: Commissio Leonina, 1984.

————. *[Summa contra gentiles] Liber de veritate Catholicae fidei contra errores infidelium;*

qui dicitur Summa contra gentiles. Textus Leoninus diligenter recognitus. Edited by P. Marc, C. Pera, and P. Caramello. Turin: Marietti, 1961. 3 vols.

———. *Summa contra gentiles*. Translated by Anton C. Pegis. 1955. Notre Dame, Ind.: University of Notre Dame Press, 1975. 5 vols.

———. *Summa theologiae*. Vols. 4–12 of *Opera omnia*. Rome: Commissio Leonina, 1888–1906.

———. *Summa Theologica*. Translated by the Fathers of the English Dominican Province. 1920. Westminster, Md.: Christian Classics, 1981. 5 vols.

———. *Super evangelium S. Matthaei*. 5th rev. ed. Edited by Raffaele Cai. Turin: Marietti, 1951.

———. *Super librum De causis expositio*. Edited by H. D. Saffrey, O. P. Fribourg: Société Philosophique, 1954.

———. *Treatise on Separate Substances*. Translated by Francis J. Lescoe. West Hartford, Conn.: St. Joseph College, 1959.

———. *Truth [De Veritate]*. Translated by Robert W. Muligan, S.J., James V. McGlynn, S.J., and Robert W. Schmidt. 1954. Indianapolis: Hackett, 1994. 3 vols.

———. *On Being and Essence*. 2d ed. Translated by Armand Maurer. Toronto: Pontifical Institute of Medieval Studies, 1968.

Aristotle. *Aristotle's De Anima, in the Version of William of Moerbeke and the Commentary of St. Thomas Aquinas*. Translated by Kenelm Foster and Silvester Humphries. New Haven: Yale University Press, 1951.

———. *Aristoteles Latinus*. Edited by L. Minio-Paluello. Leiden: Brill, 1975–1990.

———. *Aristotle's* Metaphysics: *A Revised Text with Introduction and Commentary*. Edited by W. D. Ross. 1924. Oxford: Oxford University Press, Clarendon, 1948. 2 vols.

———. *The Complete Works of Aristotle*. Rev. Oxford translation. Edited by Jonathan Barnes. Princeton: Princeton University Press, 1984. 2 vols.

———. *De anima*. Edited with commentary by R. D. Hicks. Cambridge: Cambridge University Press, 1907.

———. *De anima: Books II and III*. With passages from book I. Translated by D. W. Hamlyn. Oxford: Oxford University Press, Clarendon, 1993.

Armour, Peter. *Dante's Griffin and the History of the World: A Study of the Earthly Paradise* (Purgatorio, *Cantos XXIX–XXXIII*). Oxford: Oxford University Press, Clarendon, 1989.

Armstrong, A. Hilary. "The Apprehension of Divinity in the Self and Cosmos in Plotinus." In *Plotinian and Christian Studies*, vol. 18, 187–198. London: Variorum Reprints, 1979.

———. *The Architecture of the Intelligible Universe in the Philosophy of Plotinus*. 1940. Amsterdam: Hakkert, 1967.

———. "Aristotle in Plotinus: The Continuity and Discontinuity of *Psyche* and *Nous*." In *Aristotle and the Later Tradition*. Supplementary vol. of *Oxford Studies in Ancient Philosophy*, edited by Henry Blumenthal and Howard Robinson, 117–127. Oxford: Oxford University Press, Clarendon, 1991.

———. " 'Emanation' in Plotinus." In *Plotinian and Christian Studies*, vol. 3, 61–66. London: Variorum Reprints, 1979.

———. "The Escape of the One: An Investigation of Some Possibilities of Apophatic Theology Imperfectly Realised in the West." In *Plotinian and Christian Studies*, vol. 23, 77–89. London: Variorum Reprints, 1979.

———. "Man in the Cosmos: A Study of Some Differences between Pagan Neoplatonism and Christianity." In *Plotinian and Christian Studies*, vol. 22, 5–14. London: Variorum Reprints, 1979.

———. "Negative Theology." In *Plotinian and Christian Studies*, vol. 24, 176–189. London: Variorum Reprints, 1979.

———. "St. Augustine and Christian Platonism." In *Augustine: A Collection of Critical Essays*, edited by R. A. Markus, 3–37. New York: Doubleday, 1972.

———. "Salvation, Plotinian and Christian." In *Plotinian and Christian Studies*, vol. 6, 126–139. London: Variorum Reprints, 1979.

———, ed. *The Cambridge History of Later Greek and Early Medieval Philosophy*. London: Cambridge University Press, 1967.

Arnou, René. *Le désir de Dieu dans la philosophie de Plotin*. 2d ed. 1921. Rome: Gregorian University, 1967.

Ascoli, Albert Russell. "Palinode and History in the Oeuvre of Dante." In *Dante: Contemporary Perspectives*, edited by Amilcare A. Iannucci, 23–50. Toronto: University of Toronto Press, 1997.

———. "The Vowels of Authority (Dante's *Convivio* IV.vi.3–4)." In *Discourses of Authority in Medieval and Renaissance Literature*, edited by Kevin Brownlee and Walter Stephens, 23–46. Hanover, N.H.: University Press of New England, 1989.

Asín Palacios, Miguel. *Abenmasarra y su escuela: orígenes de la filosofia hispanomusulmana*. Madrid: Maestre, 1914.

———. *Dante e l'Islam*. Vol. 1, *L'escatologia islamica nella* Divina Commedia; vol. 2, *Storia e critica di una polemica*. Translated by Roberto Rossi Testa and Younis Tawfik. Milano: Nuova Pratiche Editrice, 1997.

Astell, Ann W. *The Song of Songs in the Middle Ages*. Ithaca: Cornell University Press, 1990.

Athanasius, Saint. *Contra Gentes*. In *Select Writings and Letters of Athanasius, Bishop of Alexandria*, 4–30. Edited by Archibald Robertson. 1891. Nicene and Post-Nicene Fathers of the Christian Church. Grand Rapids, Mich.: Wm. B. Eerdmans, 1991.

Atherton, Patrick. "Aristotle." In *Classical Mediterranean Spirituality: Egyptian, Greek, Roman*, edited by A. H. Armstrong, vol. 15 of *World Spirituality: An Encyclopedic History of the Religious Quest*, 121–134. New York: Crossroad, 1986.

Aubenque, Pierre. *Le problème de l'être chez Aristote*. 4th ed. Paris: Presses Universitaires de France, 1977.

Auerbach, Erich. "Dante's Addresses to the Reader." *Romance Philology* 7 (1954): 268–275.

———. "Figura." In *Scenes from the Drama of European Literature: Six Essays*, 11–76. 1944. New York: Meridian Books, 1959.

———. *Literary Language and Its Public in Late Latin Antiquity and in the Middle Ages*. Translated by Ralph Manheim. Princeton: Princeton University Press, 1965.

Augustine, Saint. *Against the Academics*. Translated by John J. O'Meara. Westminster, Md.: Newman Press, 1950.

———. *The Catholic and Manichaean Ways of Life: De moribus ecclesiae Catholicae et de moribus Manichaeorum*. Translated by Donald A. Gallagher and Idella J. Gallagher. Washington, D.C.: Catholic University of America Press, 1966.

———. *On Christian Doctrine*. Translated by D. W. Robertson, Jr. New York: Macmillan, Library of Liberal Arts, 1958.

———. *The City of God against the Pagans*. Translated and edited by R. W. Dyson. Cambridge: Cambridge University Press, 1998.

————. *Confessions*. Translated by Henry Chadwick. World's Classics. Oxford: Oxford University Press, 1992.

————. *Confessionum libri XIII*. Edited by Lucas Verheijen. *CCSL*, vol. 27. Turnholti: Brepols, 1981.

————. *Contra Faustum*. See *De utilitate credendi*. . . .

————. *De civitate Dei*. Edited by Bernardus Dombart and Alphonsus Kalb. 1928–1929. *CCSL*, vols. 47–48. Turnholti: Brepols, 1955.

————. *De diversis quaestionibus ad Simplicianum*. Edited by Almut Mutzenbecher. *CCSL*, vol. 44. Turnholti: Brepols, 1970.

————. *De doctrina Christiana*. Edited and translated by R. P. H. Green. Oxford: Clarendon Press, 1995.

————. *De Genesi ad litteram libri duodecim*. Edited by Joseph Zycha. *CSEL*, vol. 28. Vindobonae: F. Tempsky, 1894.

————. *De Genesi contra Manichaeos*. Vol. 34 of *PL*. Edited by J.-P. Migne. Paris, 1841–1864.

————. *De moribus ecclesiae catholicae et de moribus Manichaeorum*. Vol. 32 of *PL*. Edited by J.-P. Migne. Paris, 1841–1864.

————. *De ordine*. In *Opera, pars 2.2*. *CCSL*, vol. 29, 87–137. Turnholti: Brepols, 1970.

————. *[De ordine]* "Divine Providence and the Problem of Evil." Translated by Robert P. Russell. In *Writings of Saint Augustine*, vol. 1, 229–334. Fathers of the Church. New York: CIMA Publishing, 1948.

————. *De Trinitate libri XV*. Edited by W. J. Mountain and Fr. Glorie. *CCSL*, vols. 50–50A. Turnholti: Brepols, 1968. 2 vols.

————. *De utilitate credendi, De duabus animabus, Contra fortunatum, Contra adimantum, Contra epistulam fundamenti, Contra Faustum*. Edited by Joseph Zycha. *CSEL*, vol. 25. Vindobonae: Tempsky, 1891.

————. *Homilies on the Gospel of John*. Edited by Philip Schaff. 1886–1890. Nicene and Post-Nicene Fathers of the Christian Church. Grand Rapids: Eerdmans, 1983.

————. *The Literal Meaning of Genesis*. Translated by John Hammond Taylor. Ancient Christian Writers. New York: Newman Press, 1982. 2 vols.

————. *Of True Religion*. Translated by Burleigh. Chicago: Regnery, 1959.

————. *Quaestiones Evangeliorum cum appendice Quaestionum XVI in Matthaeum*. Edited by Almut Mutzenbecher. *CCSL*, vol. 44B. Turnholti: Brepols, 1980.

————. *Saint Augustine on the Psalms*. Translated by Scholastica Hebgin and Felicitas Corrigan. Westminster, Md.: Newman Press, 1960. 2 vols.

————. *Selected Sermons*. Translated and edited by Quincy Howe, Jr. New York: Holt, Rinehart & Winston, 1966.

————. *Soliloquies and Immortality of the Soul*. Translated by Gerard Watson. Warminster, England: Aris & Phillips, 1990.

————. *The Trinity*. Edited by John Rotelle. Translated by Edmund Hill. Brooklyn: New City Press, 1991.

Aurigemma, Marcello. "Primo Mobile." In *ED*, 4:670–671.

Averroës [Ibn Rushd]. *Aristotelis De coelo, De generatione et corruptione, Meteorologicorum, De plantis cum Averrois Cordubensis in eosdem commentariis*. In *Aristotelis opera cum Averrois commentariis*. Venice: Junctas, 1562–1574. Facsimile ed., Frankfurt: Minerva, 1962.

————. *Commentarium magnum in Aristotelis De anima*. Edited by F. Stuart Crawford. *Corpus Commentariorum Averrrois in Aristotelem*. Cambridge: Medieval Academy of America, 1953.

Aversano, Mario. "Sulla poetica dantesca nel canto XXIV del *Purgatorio*." *L'Alighieri*, n.s., 16 (July–December 2000): 123–138.

Avicenna [Ibn Sīnā]. *Liber de anima*. Edited by Simone Van Riet. Louvain: Brill, 1968–1972. 2 vols.

———. *Metaphysica, sive Prima philosophia*. Venice, 1495. Facsimile ed., Louvain: Bibliothèque S.J., 1961.

Baeumker, Clemens. "Dantes philosophische Weltanschauung." *Deutsche Literaturzeitung* 34 (1913): 2760–2761.

———. *Witelo, ein Philosoph und Naturforscher des XIII. Jahrhunderts. Beiträge zur Geschichte der Philosophie des Mittelalters*, vol. 3.2. Münster: Aschendorffschen Buchhandlung, 1908.

Baffioni, Carmela. "Aspetti delle cosmologie islamiche in Dante." In *Il pensiero filosofico e teologico di Dante Alighieri*, ed. Alessandro Ghisalberti, 103–122. Milano: Vita e Pensiero, 2001.

Barański, Zygmunt G. "*Comedìa*: Notes on Dante, the Epistle to Cangrande, and Medieval Comedy." *Lectura Dantis* 8 (1991): 26–55.

———. "Dante and Medieval Poetics." In *Dante: Contemporary Perspectives*, edited by Amilcare A. Iannucci, 3–22. Toronto: University of Toronto Press, 1997.

———. "Dante commentatore e commentato: riflessioni sullo studio dell'*iter* ideologico di Dante."*Letture classensi* 23 (1994): 135–158.

———. "Dante's (Anti-)Rhetoric: Notes on the Poetics of the *Commedia*." In *Moving in Measure: Essays in Honour of Brian Moloney*, edited by Judith Bryce and Doug Thompson, 1–14. Hull, England: Hull University Press, 1989.

———. "Dante's Biblical Linguistics." *Lectura Dantis* 5 (Fall 1989): 105–143.

———. "Dante, the Roman Comedians, and the Medieval Theory of Comedy." *Italianist* 15, Supplement (1995): 61–99.

———. "L'iter ideologico di Dante." In *Dante e i segni: saggi per una storia intellettuale di Dante Alighieri*, 9–39. Napoli: Liguori Editore, 2000.

———. "La lezione esegetica di *Inferno* I: Allegoria, storia e letteratura nella *Commedia*." In *Dante e le forme dell'allegoresi*, edited by Michelangelo Picone, 79–97. Ravenna: Longo Editore, 1987.

———. "Il 'meraviglioso' e il 'comico' (*Inferno*, XVI)." In *"Sole nuvo, luce nuova": saggi sul rinnovamento culturale in Dante*, 153–182. Torino: Scriptorium, 1996.

———. "The 'New Life' of 'Comedy': The *Commedia* and the *Vita Nuova*." *Dante Studies* 113 (1995): 1–29.

———. " 'Significar per verba': Notes on Dante and Plurilingualism." *Italianist* 6 (1986): 5–18.

———. "Structural Retrospection in Dante's *Comedy*: The Case of *Purgatorio* XXVII." *Italian Studies* 41 (1986): 1–23.

Barberi Squarotti, Giorgio. "Premessa allo studio delle similitudini dantesche." In *Filologia e critica dantesca: studi offerti a Aldo Vallone*, 381–402. Firenze: Leo S. Olschki, 1989.

Barbi, Michele. "Nuovi problemi della critica dantesca, IV–VI." *Studi danteschi* 23 (1938): 5–77.

———. *Problemi di critica dantesca: prima serie*. Firenze: Sansoni, 1934.

———. "Razionalismo e misticismo in Dante." *Studi danteschi* 17 (1933): 5–44; 21 (1937): 5–91.

Barbotin, Edmond. *La théorie aristotélicienne de l'intellect d'après Théophraste*. Louvain: Publications Universitaires de Louvain, 1954.

Barfield, Owen. *Saving the Appearances: A Study in Idolatry*. New York: Harcourt, Brace and World, Harbinger, n.d.

Barnes, Jonathan. "Aristotle's Concept of Mind." In *Articles on Aristotle*, vol. 4, *Psychology and Aesthetics*, edited by Jonathan Barnes, Malcolm Schofield, and Richard Sorabji, 32–41. New York: St. Martin's Press, 1978.

Barolini, Teodolinda. *Dante's Poets: Textuality and Truth in the Comedy*. Princeton: Princeton University Press, 1984.

―――. "Detheologizing Dante: For a 'New Formalism' in Dante Studies." *Quaderni d'italianistica* 10, no. 1–2 (1989): 35–53.

―――. "For the Record: The Epistle to Cangrande and Various 'American Dantisti.'" *Lectura Dantis* 6 (Spring 1990): 140–143.

―――. *The Undivine Comedy: Detheologizing Dante*. Princeton: Princeton University Press, 1992.

Barr, Stephen M. "Four Developments in Modern Physics that Subvert Scientific Materialism." In *The Battle for the Catholic Mind: Catholic Faith and Catholic Intellect in the Work of the Fellowship of Catholic Scholars, 1978–95*, edited by William E. May. South Bend, Ind.: St. Augustine's Press, 2001.

Bartholomaeus Anglicus. *De rerum proprietatibus*. Edited by Pontanus a Braitenberg and Georgius Bartholdus. 1601. Facsimile, Frankfurt a. M.: Minerva G.M.B.H., 1964.

Bartoli, Vittorio, and Paola Ureni. "Controversie medico-biologiche in tema di generazione umana nel XXV del *Purgatorio*." *Studi danteschi* 68 (2003): 83–111.

Basil, Saint. *Exegetic Homilies [Hexaemeron]*. Edited by Agnes Clare Way. *Fathers of the Church, A New Translation*, vol. 46. Washington, D.C.: Catholic University of America Press, 1963.

Baswell, Christopher. "The Medieval Allegorization of the *Aeneid*: MS Cambridge, Peterhouse 158." *Traditio* 41 (1985): 181–237.

Battaglia Ricci, Lucia. "Ancora sulla struttura narrativa della *Commedia*." In *Dante e la tradizione letteraria medievale: una proposta per la* Commedia, 161–196. Pisa: Giardini, 1983.

Battaglia, Salvatore. "Piramo e Tisbe in una pagina di Sant'Agostino." *Filologia e letteratura* 9 (1963): 113–122.

―――. "L'umano e il divino nell'ultimo canto del *Paradiso*." In *Esemplarità e antagonismo nel pensiero di Dante*, 2d ed., 201–221. Napoli: Liguori, 1967.

Battistini, Andrea. "Il mondo che si 'squaderna': cosmo e simbologia del libro." In *Letture classensi*, vol. 15, edited by Ezio Raimondi, 61–78. Ravenna: A. Longo, 1986.

Baumgartner, M. "Dantes Stellung zur Philosophie." In *Görres-Gesellschaft zur Pflege des Wissenschaft im Katholischen Deutschland: Zweite Vereinschrift für 1921*, 61–64. Köln, 1921.

Bede, Venerable. *In Lucae evangelium expositio*. Edited by D. Hurst. *CCSL*, vol. 120. Turnholti: Brepols, 1960.

―――. *Opera*. *CCSL*, vols. 118A–123C. Turnholti: Brepols, 1955–1983.

Bemrose, Stephen. "'Come d'animal divegna fante': The Animation of the Human Embryo in Dante." In *The Human Embryo: Aristotle and the Arabic and European Tradition*, edited by G. R. Dunstan, 123–135. Exeter: University of Exeter Press, 1990.

―――. *Dante's Angelic Intelligences: Their Importance in the Cosmos and in Pre-Christian Religion*. Roma: Edizioni di Storia e Letteratura, 1983.

Benardete, Seth. "Aristotle, *De Anima* III.3–5." *Review of Metaphysics* 28, no. 4 (June 1975): 611–622.

Benignus [Gerrity], Brother, F.S.C. *Nature, Knowledge and God: An Introduction to Thomistic Philosophy.* Milwaukee, Wis.: Bruce Publishing Company, 1947.

Benvenuto da Imola. *Comentum super Dantis Aldigherij Comoediam, nunc primum integre in lucem editum.* 1380. Edited by Jacobo Philippo Lacaita. Florence: G. Barbèra, 1887. 5 vols.

Bernard of Clairvaux, Saint. *Five Books on Consideration: Advice to a Pope.* Edited by John D. Anderson and Elizabeth T. Kennan. Cistercian Fathers, vol. 13. Cistercian Publications, 1976.

———. *On Loving God.* With an analytical commentary by Emero Stiegman. Kalamazoo, Mich.: Cistercian Publications, 1995.

———. *On the Song of Songs.* In *The Works of Bernard of Clairvaux.* Edited by Louis Bouyer, et al. Translated by Kilian Walsh. Kalamazoo, Mich.: Cistercian Publications, 1971.

———. *Opera omnia.* 8 vols. Edited by Jean Leclercq, C. H. Talbot, and Henri M. Rochais. Rome: Editiones Cistercienses, 1957–1980.

———. *Selected Works.* Translated by G. R. Evans. Classics of Western Spirituality. New York: Paulist Press, 1987.

Bernard, P. "Ciel." In *Dictionnaire de théologie catholique*, edited by A. Vacant, E. Mangenot, and E. Amann. Paris: Librairie Letouzey et Ané, 1926–1950.

Bernardino Daniello da Lucca. *L'espositione di Bernardino Daniello da Lucca sopra la Comedia di Dante.* 1568. Edited by Robert Hollander and Jeffrey Schnapp. Hanover, N.H.: University Press of New England, 1989.

Bernardo, Aldo. "Dante's Eighth Heaven: Ultimate Threshold to Reality." *Journal of Medieval and Renaissance Studies* 2 (1972): 131–150.

Bernardus Silvestris. *The Commentary on the First Six Books of the* Aeneid *of Vergil Commonly Attributed to Bernardus Silvestris.* Edited by Julian Ward Jones and Elizabeth Frances Jones. Lincoln: University of Nebraska Press, 1977.

———. *Commentary on the First Six Books of Vergil's* Aeneid *by Bernardus Silvestris.* Translated by G. Schreiber and Thomas E. Maresca. Lincoln: University of Nebraska Press, 1979.

———. *De mundi universitate libri duo sive megacosmus et microcosmus.* Edited by C. S. Barach and J. Wrobel. Frankfurt am Main, 1964.

Bersani, Stefano. *Dottrine, allegorie, simboli della* Divina Commedia: *appunti esegetico-critici.* Piacenza: Collegio Alberoni, 1931.

Bersuire, Pierre [Petrus Berchorius]. *Metamorphosis Ovidiana moraliter . . . explanata.* Paris, 1509. Reprint, New York: Garland, 1979.

Berti, Enrico. "Il concetto di atto nella *Metafisica* di Aristotele." In *L'atto aristotelico e le sue ermeneutiche*, edited by Marcello Sánchez Sorondo, 43–61. Roma: Herder-Università Lateranense, 1990.

Bertoni, Giulio. "L'estetica di Dante e il canto XXIX del *Paradiso*." *Archivium Romanicum* 8 (1924): 239–255. Geneva: Leo S. Olschki.

Bezzola, Reto. "*Paradiso* 27." In *Letture dantesche*, edited by Giovanni Getto, 1897–1914. Firenze: Sansoni, 1964.

Biblia Sacra iuxta vulgatam versionem. 4th rev. ed. Edited by B. Fischer, Robertus Weber, and Roger Gryson. Stuttgart: Deutsche Bibelgesellschaft, 1994.

Biondolillo, Francesco. "La poetica di Dante." In *Ore dantesche*, 11–23. Ravenna: A. Longo, 1969.

Blasucci, Luigi. "Canto XXVII." In *Lectura Dantis Neapolitana: Purgatorio*, edited by Pompeo Giannantonio, 515–531. Napoli: Loffredo, 1989.

Block, Irving. "Aristotle and the Physical Object." *Philosophy and Phenomenological Research* 21, no. 1 (September 1960): 93–101.

Blumenthal, Henry J. "*Nous Pathetikos* in Later Greek Philosophy." In *Aristotle and the Later Tradition*. Oxford Studies in Ancient Philosophy: Supplementary vol., edited by Henry Blumenthal and Howard Robinson, 191–205. Oxford: Oxford University Press, Clarendon, 1991.

———. "Neoplatonic Elements in the *De Anima* Commentaries." In *Aristotle Transformed: The Ancient Commentators and Their Influence*, edited by Richard Sorabji, 305–324. Ithaca: Cornell University Press, 1990.

———. "On Soul and Intellect." In *The Cambridge Companion to Plotinus*, edited by Lloyd P. Gerson, 82–104. Cambridge: Cambridge University Press, 1996.

Bobik, Joseph. *Aquinas on Being and Essence: A Translation and Interpretation*. Notre Dame: University of Notre Dame Press, 1965.

Boethius. *Philosophiae consolatio*. Edited by Ludovicus Bieler. *CCSL*, vol. 94. Turnholti: Brepols, 1984.

———. *The Consolation of Philosophy*. Translated by Richard Green. New York: Macmillan, 1962.

Bogliolo, Luigi. *Essere e conoscere*. Studi Tomistici, vol. 21. Città del Vaticano: Libreria Editrice Vaticana, 1983.

Bohm, David. *Wholeness and the Implicate Order*. 1980. London: Routledge, Ark Paperbacks, 1983.

Bohr, Niels. *The Philosophical Writings of Niels Bohr*. 3 vols. 1934–1963. Woodbridge, Conn.: Ox Bow Press, 1987.

Boitani, Piero. "The Sybil's Leaves: A Study of *Paradiso* XXXIII." *Dante Studies* 96 (1978): 83–126.

Bonaventure, Saint. *Breviloquium*. Vol. 5 of *Opera omnia*, 199–291.

———. *The Breviloquium*. Translated by José de Vinck. *The Works of Bonaventure*, vol. 2. Paterson, N.J.: St. Anthony Guild Press, 1963.

———. *Collationes in Hexaëmeron et Bonaventuriana quaedem selecta*. Edited by Ferdinand Delorme. Quaracchi: Collegium S. Bonaventurae, 1934.

———. *Collations on the Six Days*. In *The Works of Bonaventure*, vol. 5. Translated by José De Vinck. Paterson, N.J.: St. Anthony Guild Press, 1970.

———. *Commentaria in quatuor libros Sententiarum Magistri Petri Lombardi*. Vols. 1–4 of *Opera omnia*.

———. *Commentarius in Evangelium S. Lucae*. Vol. 7 of *Opera omnia*.

———. *De triplici via*. Vol. 8 of *Opera omnia*, 3–18.

———. *Disputed Questions on the Knowledge of Christ*. Translated by Zachary Hayes. *The Works of Saint Bonaventure*, vol. 4. New York: Franciscan Institute [St. Bonaventure University], 1992.

———. *Itinerarium mentis in Deum*. Vol. 5 of *Opera omnia*, 295–313.

———. *Legenda major*. Vol. 8 of *Opera omnia*, 504–564.

———. *Opera omnia*. Ad Claras Aquas [Quaracchi]: Editiones Collegii S. Bonaventure, 1882–1902. 10 vols.

———. *Quaestiones disputatae de scientia Christi*. Vol. 5 of *Opera omnia*, 3–43.

———. *Sermones dominicales*. Edited by Iacobus Guidus Bougerol. Grottaferrata: Collegio S. Bonaventura, 1977.

———. *The Soul's Journey into God; The Tree of Life; The Life of St. Francis*. Translated by Ewert Cousins. Classics of Western Spirituality. New York: Paulist Press, 1978.

————. *The Triple Way, or Love Enkindled.* In *Mystical Opuscula.* Translated by José de Vinck. *The Works of Saint Bonaventure,* vol. 1, 59–94. Paterson, N.J.: St. Anthony Guild Press, 1960.

The Book of Causes [Liber de causis]. Translated by Dennis Brand, with a foreword by Bernardo Carlos Bazán. Milwaukee: Marquette University Press, 1981.

Bosco, Umberto. "La 'follia' di Dante." In *Dante vicino,* 2d ed. 1958, 55–75. Caltanisetta-Roma: Sciascia, 1972.

Bosco, Umberto, and Giovanni Reggio, eds. *La* Divina Commedia, *con pagine critiche.* Firenze: Le Monnier, 1988. 3 vols.

Botterill, Steven. "Dante and the Authority of Poetic Language." In *Dante: Contemporary Perspectives,* edited by Amilcare A. Iannucci, 167–180. Toronto: University of Toronto Press, 1997.

————. *Dante and the Mystical Tradition: Bernard of Clairvaux in the* Commedia. Cambridge: Cambridge University Press, 1994.

————. "Purgatorio XXVII." In *Dante's* Divine Comedy: *Introductory Readings (II: Purgatorio).* Special issue, *Lectura Dantis Virginiana,* vol. 2 (supplement to *Lectura Dantis* 12 [Spring 1993]), edited by Tibor Wlassics, 398–410.

Bousset, W. "Platons Weltseele und das Kreuz Christi." *Zeitschrift für die Neutestamentlich Wissenschaft* 14 (1913): 273–285.

Boyde, Patrick. "L'esegesi di Dante e la scienza." In *Dante e la scienza,* edited by Patrick Boyde and Vittorio Russo, 9–23. Ravenna: Longo, 1995.

————. *Dante Philomythes and Philosopher: Man in the Cosmos.* London: Cambridge University Press, 1981.

————. *Perception and Passion in Dante's Comedy.* Cambridge: Cambridge University Press, 1993.

Brandeis, Irma. *The Ladder of Vision: A Study of Dante's Comedy.* Garden City, N.Y.: Doubleday, 1962.

Brockelman, Paul. *Cosmology and Creation: The Spiritual Significance of Contemporary Cosmology.* New York: Oxford University Press, 1999.

Brownlee, Kevin. "Dante's Poetics of Transfiguration: The Case of Ovid." *Literature and Belief* 5 (1985): 13–29.

————. "Language and Desire in *Paradiso* XXVI." *Lectura Dantis* 6 (Spring 1990): 46–59.

————. "*Paradiso* XXVI." In *Dante's* Divine Comedy: *Introductory Readings (III: Paradiso).* Special issue, *Lectura Dantis Virginiana,* vol. 3 (*Lectura Dantis* 16–17 [Spring–Fall 1995]), 388–401.

————. "Pauline Vision and Ovidian Speech in *Paradiso* I." In *The Poetry of Allusion: Virgil and Ovid in Dante's* Commedia, edited by Rachel Jacoff and Jeffrey T. Schnapp, 202–213. Stanford: Stanford University Press, 1991.

Bruce-Jones, John. "L'importanza primaria della materia prima (Why Does Prime Matter Matter?): aspetti della materia nella poesia e nel pensiero di Dante." In *Dante e la scienza,* edited by Patrick Boyde and Vittorio Russo, 213–221. Ravenna: A. Longo, 1995.

Brugnoli, Giorgio. "Lo Stazio di Dante in Benvenuto." In *Benvenuto da Imola: lettore degli antichi e dei moderni, Atti del Convegno Internazionale, Imola, 26 e 27 maggio 1989,* edited by Pantaleo Palmieri and Carlo Paolazzi, 127–137. Ravenna: Longo, 1991.

————. "Stazio in Dante." *Cultura neolatina* 19 (1969): 117–125.

Bufano, Antonietta. "Il canto XXIX del *Paradiso.*" *L'Alighieri: rassegna bibliografica dantesca* 22, no. 1 (January–June 1981): 3–22.

Bufano, Antonietta, and Gian Roberto Sarolli. "Numero." In *ED*, 4:87–96.

Bufano, Antonietta, Giorgio Stabile, Emmanuel Poulle, and Marcello Aurigemma. "Sole." In *ED*, 5:296–304.

Buonaiuti, Ernesto. "La dottrina della creazione e della salvezza nel Canto XIII del *Paradiso*." *Il giornale dantesco* 26 (1923): 1–7.

_____. "Filosofia e religione nel medio evo: San Tommaso e Sigieri di Brabante." *Nuova antologia* 57 (1 May 1922): 32–41.

Burger, Ronna. "Is Each Thing the Same as Its Essence? On *Metaphysics* Z.6–11." *Review of Metaphysics* 41, no. 1 (1987): 53–76.

Burnyeat, M. F. "Idealism and Greek Philosophy: What Descartes Saw and Berkeley Missed." In *Idealism: Past and Present*, Royal Institute of Philosophy Lecture Series, vol. 13, 19–50. Cambridge: Cambridge University Press, 1982.

Burrell, David B., C.S.C. "Aquinas and Islamic and Jewish Thinkers." In *The Cambridge Companion to Aquinas*, edited by Norman Kretzmann and Eleonore Stump, 60–84. Cambridge: Cambridge University Press, 1993.

_____. "Creation, Metaphysics, and Ethics." *Faith and Philosophy* 18.2 (April 2001): 204–221.

_____. "Creation or Emanation: Two Paradigms of Reason." In *God and Creation: An Ecumenical Symposium*, edited by David B. Burrell, C.S.C., and Bernard McGinn, 27–37. Notre Dame, Ind.: University of Notre Dame Press, 1990.

_____. "Simpleness." In *Philosophy of Religion*, edited by Brian Davies, 70–75. Washington, D.C.: Georgetown University Press, 1998.

_____. *Freedom and Creation in Three Traditions*. Notre Dame, Ind.: University of Notre Dame Press, 1993.

_____. "Friendship and Discourse about Divinity: Lest God be god." Chapter 5 of *Friendship and Ways to Truth*. Notre Dame, Ind.: University of Notre Dame Press, 2000.

Burrell, David B., C.S.C., and Bernard McGinn, eds. *God and Creation: An Ecumenical Symposium*. Notre Dame, Ind.: University of Notre Dame Press, 1990.

Busnelli, Giovanni. *Il concetto e l'ordine del Paradiso dantesco*. Città di Castello: Lapi, 1911–1912. 2 vols.

_____. *Cosmogonia e antropogenesi secondo Dante Alighieri e le sue fonti*. Roma, 1922.

_____. "Un famoso dubbio di Dante intorno alla materia prima." *Studi danteschi* 13 (1928): 47–60.

_____. *L'origine dell'anima razionale secondo Dante e Alberto Magno*. 2d ed., 1929.

Bussanich, John. "Plotinus's Metaphysics of the One." In *The Cambridge Companion to Plotinus*, edited by Lloyd P. Gerson, 38–65. Cambridge: Cambridge University Press, 1996.

Buti, Francesco da. *Commento di Francesco da Buti sopra la* Divina Commedia *di Dante Allighieri*. 1858–1862. Edited by Crescentino Giannini. Pisa: N. Lischi, 1989. 3 vols.

Bynum, Caroline Walker. *The Resurrection of the Body in Western Christianity, 200–1336*. New York: Columbia University Press, 1995.

_____. "Why All the Fuss about the Body? A Medievalist's Perspective." *Critical Inquiry* 22 (Autumn 1995): 1–33.

Bynum, Terrell Ward. "A New Look at Aristotle's Theory of Perception." *History of Philosophy Quarterly* 4, no. 2 (April 1987): 163–178.

Cachey, Theodore J., Jr. "Dante's Journey between Fiction and Truth: Geryon Revisited." In *Dante da Firenze all'aldilà: atti del terzo Seminario dantesco internazionale di Firenze (9–11 giugno 2000)*, edited by Michelangelo Picone, 75–92. Firenze: Franco Cesati Editore, 2001.

Calcaterra, Carlo. "Sant' Agostino nelle opere di Dante e del Petrarca." 1931. In *Nella selva del Petrarca*, 247–360. Bologna: Capelli, 1942.

Calì, Piero. "Purgatorio XXVII." In *Dante Commentaries: Eight Studies of the Divine Comedy*, edited by David Nolan, 93–113. Dublin: Irish Academic Press, 1977.

Calò, Giovanni. "Il Canto XXVI del *Paradiso*." Roma: Bontempelli, 1914.

_____. Review of *Sigieri di Brabante nella* Divina Commedia *e le fonti della filosofia di Dante*, by Bruno Nardi. *Bullettino della Società Dantesca Italiana: rassegna critica degli studi danteschi* 20 (1913): 261–283.

Campanus of Novara. *Campanus of Novara and Medieval Planetary Theory: Theorica planetarum*. Edited and translated by Francis S. Benjamin, Jr., and G. J. Toomer. Madison: University of Wisconsin Press, 1971.

Campbell, Keith. "Materialism." In *The Encyclopedia of Philosophy*, vol. 5, 179–188. Edited by Paul Edwards. New York: Macmillan and the Free Press, 1967.

Cantarino, Vincent. "Dante and Islam: History and Analysis of a Controversy." In *A Dante Symposium in Commemoration of the 700th Anniversary of the Poet's Birth (1265–1965)*, edited by William De Sua and Gino Rizzo. Chapel Hill: University of North Carolina Press, 1965.

_____. "Dante and Islam: Theory of Light in the *Paradiso*." *Kentucky Romance Quarterly* 15, no. 1 (1968): 3–35.

Capasso, Ideale. *L'astronomia nella* Divina Commedia. Pisa: Domus Galilaeana, 1967.

Čapek, Milič, ed. *The Concepts of Space and Time: Their Structure and Their Development*. Dordrecht and Boston: D. Reidel, 1976.

Capra, Fritjof. *The Tao of Physics: An Exploration of the Parallels between Modern Physics and Eastern Mysticism*. 3d ed. Boston: Shambhala, 1991.

_____. *The Turning Point: Science, Society, and the Rising Culture*. New York: Simon and Schuster, 1982.

Carabine, Deirdre. *The Unknown God: Negative Theology in the Platonic Tradition; Plato to Eriugena*. Louvain Theological and Pastoral Monographs, vol. 19. Louvain: Peeters Press, n.d.

Caraccio, Armand. "Dante entre Saint François et Saint Dominique dans les chants XI et XII du *Paradis*." *Bulletin de la Société d'Études Dantesques du Centre Universitaire Méditerranéen* 15 (1966): 11–19.

Carmody, Denise Lardner, and John Tully Carmody. *Mysticism: Holiness East and West*. New York: Oxford University Press, 1996.

Carroll, John S. *Exiles of Eternity* [Inf.]; *Prisoners of Hope* [Purg.]; *In Patria* [Par.]: *Expositions*. In *DDP*.

Carroll, William E. "Aquinas on Creation and the Metaphysical Foundation of Science." *Sapientia* 54 (1999): 69–91.

Carugati, Giuliana. *Dalla menzogna al silenzio: la scrittura mistica della* Commedia *di Dante*. Bologna: Il Mulino, 1991.

_____. "Retorica amorosa e verità in Dante: il *De Causis* e l'idea della donna nel *Convivio*." *Dante Studies* 112 (1994).

Casagrande, Gino. " 'I s'appellava in terra il sommo bene' (*Paradiso*, XXVI, 134)." *Aevum* 50 (May–August 1976): 249–273.

Casella, Mario. "*Paradiso* 33." In *Letture dantesche*, edited by Giovanni Getto, 2021–2038. Firenze: Sansoni, 1964.

_____. "Rassegna critica." *Studi danteschi* 18 (1934): 105–126.

Cassell, Anthony K. "*Ulisseana*: a Bibliography of Dante's Ulysses to 1981." *Italian Culture* 3 (1981): 23–45.

Castellani, Victor. "Heliocentricity in the Structure of Dante's *Paradiso*." *Studies in Philology* 78, no. 3 (Summer 1981): 211–223.

Cecchetti, Giovanni. "The Statius Episode: Observations on Dante's Conception of Poetry." *Lectura Dantis* 7 (Fall 1990): 96–114.

Certau, Michel de. " 'Mystique' au XVIIe siècle: le problème du langage 'mystique'." In *L'homme devant Dieu: mélanges offerts au Père Henri du Lubac*, vol. 2, 267–291. Paris: Aubier, 1964.

Chalcidius. *Timaeus a Calcidio translatus commentarioque instructus*. In *Corpus Platonicum medii aevi*. 2d ed. Edited by J. H. Waszink and Raymond Klibansky. 1962. Plato latinus, vol. 4. London: Warburg Institute, 1975.

Chance, Jane. "The Origins and Development of Medieval Mythography: From Homer to Dante." In *Mapping the Cosmos*, edited by Jane Chance, 35–64. Houston: Rice University Press, 1985.

Charity, A. C. *Events and Their Afterlife: The Dialectics of Christian Typology in the Bible and Dante*. 1966. Cambridge: Cambridge University Press, 1987.

Charlton, William. "Did Aristotle Believe in Prime Matter?" Appendix in *Aristotle's Physics: Books I and II*, translated by W. Charlton, 129–145. Oxford: Clarendon Press, 1970.

———. "Prime Matter: A Rejoinder." *Phronesis* 28, no. 2 (1983): 197–211.

Chavero Blanco, Francisco de Asís. *Imago Dei: aproximación a la antropología teológica de San Buenaventura*. Publicaciones del Instituto Teológico Franciscano, serie major, vol. 12. Murcia, Spain: Espigas, 1993.

Chiamenti, Massimiliano. *Dante Alighieri traduttore*. Firenze: Le Lettere, 1995.

Chiampi, James T. "Dante's *Paradiso* from Number to *Mysterium*." *Dante Studies* 110 (1992).

Chiao, Raymond Y., Paul G. Kwiat, and Aephraim M. Steinberg. "Faster Than Light?" *Scientific American* 269, no. 2 (August 1993): 52–60.

Chiarenza, Marguerite Mills. "Falsity and Fiction in the 'Allegory of Poets'." *Quaderni d'italianistica* 1, no. 1 (Autumn 1980): 80–86.

———. "The Imageless Vision and Dante's *Paradiso*." *Dante Studies* 90 (1972): 77–91.

———. "Pagan Images in the Prologue of the *Paradiso*." *Proceedings of the Pacific Northwest Council on Foreign Languages* 26, no. 1 (1975): 133–136.

Chiavacci Leonardi, Anna Maria, ed. *Commedia*, by Dante Alighieri. With commentary by Anna Maria Chiavacci Leonardi. I Meridiani. Milano: Arnoldo Mondadori, 1991–1997. 3 vols.

Chimenz, Siro A., ed. *La Divina Commedia di Dante Alighieri*. Torino: UTET, 1962.

Chioccioni, Pietro. *L'agostinismo nella Divina Commedia*. Firenze: Olschki, 1952.

Cicero. *De natura deorum; Academica*. Translated by H. Rackham. 1951. Loeb Classical Library, vol. 268. Cambridge: Harvard University Press, 1994.

———. *De re publica; De legibus*. Translated by Clinton Walker Keyes. 1928. Loeb Classical Library, vol. 213. Cambridge: Harvard University Press, 1994.

———. *Laelius, On Friendship (Laelius De amictia) and The Dream of Scipio (Somnium Scipionis)*. Edited and translated by J. G. F. Powell. Warminster: Aris and Phillips, 1990.

———. *Tusculan Disputations*. Translated by J. E. King. 1927. Loeb Classical Library, vol. 141. Cambridge: Harvard University Press, 1989.

Clarke, W. Norris, S.J. "Living on the Edge: The Human Person as 'Frontier Being' and Microcosm." *International Philosophical Quarterly* 36, no. 2 (June 1996): 183–199.

Clement of Alexandria. *Le pédagogue*. Translated by Bernardette Troo and Paul Gau-
riat. Les pères dans la foi, vols. 44–45. Paris: Migne (Brépols), 1991.

———. *Protrepticus*. Edited by M. Marcovich. Leiden: Brill, 1995.

———. *Stromateis: Liber 1–3*. Translated by John Ferguson. Washington, D.C.: Catholic University of America Press, 1991.

———. *Les stromates*. Translated by Marcel Caster. Sources chrétiennes, vols. 30, 38,
278–279, 428, 446. Paris: Editions du Cerf, 1951–.

———. *The Exhortation to the Greeks*. In *Clement of Alexandria*. Translated by G. W.
Butterworth. 1919. Loeb Classical Library, vol. 92, 3–263. Cambridge: Harvard
University Press, 1982.

Cohen, S. Marc. "The Credibility of Aristotle's Philosophy of Mind." In *Aristotle Today:
Essays on Aristotle's Ideal of Science*, edited by Mohan Matthen, 103–125. Edmonton, Alberta: Academic Printing, 1987.

Cohen, Sheldon. "Aristotle's Doctrine of the Material Substrate." *Philosophical Review*
93, no. 2 (April 1984): 171–194.

Colombo, Manuela. *Dai mistici a Dante: il linguaggio dell'ineffabilità*. Firenze: La Nuova
Italia, 1987.

Comparetti, Domenico. *Vergil in the Middle Ages*. Translated by E.F.M. Benecke. 1885.
Princeton: Princeton University Press, 1997.

Consoli, Domenico. "Il canto XXVII del *Purgatorio*." In Purgatorio: *letture degli anni
1976–'79* [Casa di Dante in Roma], 627–655. Roma: Bonacci, 1981.

Contini, Gianfranco. "Alcuni appunti su *Purgatorio* XXVII." In *Un'idea di Dante: saggi
danteschi*, 171–190. 1959. Torino: Giulio Einaudi, 1976.

———. "*Paradiso* 28." In *Lectura Dantis Scaligera*: Paradiso, 999–1030. Firenze: Felice Le Monnier, 1968.

Copleston, Frederick C., S.J. *Aquinas*. Baltimore: Penguin Books, 1955.

———. *A History of Philosophy*. 9 vols. 1946. New York: Doubleday, Image Books,
1985.

———. *Medieval Philosophy*. 1952. New York: Harper and Row, Harper Torchbooks,
1961.

Cornish, Alison. "Planets and Angels in *Paradiso* XXIX: The First Moment." *Dante
Studies* 108 (1990): 1–28.

———. *Reading Dante's Stars*. New Haven: Yale University Press, 2000.

Corrigan, Kevin. "A Philosophical Precursor to the Theory of Essence and Existence
in St. Thomas Aquinas." *Thomist* 48, no. 2 (April 1984): 219–240.

Cortest, Luis. "Was Thomas Aquinas a Platonist?" *Thomist* 52, no. 2 (April 1988): 209–
219.

Corti, Maria. "La *Commedia* di Dante e l'oltretomba islamico." *L'Alighieri* 5 (January–
June 1995): 7–19.

———. *Dante a un nuovo crocevia*. Firenze: Libreria Commissionaria Sansoni, 1981.

———. *La felicità mentale: nuove prospettive per Cavalcanti e Dante*. Torino: Giulio Einaudi, 1983.

———. "La filosofia aristotelica e Dante." In *Letture classensi*, vol. 13, edited by Maria
Corti, 111–123. Ravenna: A. Longo, 1984.

———. *Percorsi dell'invenzione: il linguaggio poetico e Dante*. Torino: Giulio Einaudi,
1993.

Cosmo, Umberto. "L'ultima ascesa: introduzione alla lettura del *Paradiso*." In *Vita di
Dante*, by Umberto Cosmo, edited by Bruno Maier. Firenze: La Nuova Italia, 1965.

Cotter, James Finn. "Dante and Christ: The Pilgrim as *beatus vir*." *Italian Quarterly* 38,
no. 107 (1987): 5–19.

Courcelle, Pierre. *Connais-toi toi-même, de Socrate à Saint Bernard.* Paris: Études Augustiniennes, 1974–1975. 3 vols.

Cousins, Ewert H. "Francis of Assisi: Christian Mysticism at the Crossroads." In *Mysticism and Religious Traditions,* edited by Steven T. Katz, 163–190. Oxford: Oxford University Press, 1983.

———. " 'Intravi in intima mea': Augustine and Neoplatonism." *Archivio di filosofia* 51, no. 1–3 (1983): 281–292.

Cristiani, Marta. "Ragione." In *ED,* 4:831–841.

Croce, Benedetto. *La poesia di Dante.* Bari: Laterza, 1921.

Crombie, A. C. *Augustine to Galileo: The History of Science, A.D. 400–1650.* London: Falcon Press, 1952.

———. *Robert Grosseteste and the Origins of Experimental Science (1100–1700).* Oxford: Oxford, Clarendon Press, 1953.

Curtius, Ernst Robert. *European Literature and the Latin Middle Ages.* Translated by Willard R. Trask. Princeton: Princeton University Press, 1953.

———. "The Ship of the Argonauts." In *Essays on European Literature,* translated by Michael Kowal, 465–496. 1950. Princeton: Princeton University Press, 1973.

Cushing, James T., and Ernan McMullin, eds. *Philosophical Consequences of Quantum Theory: Reflections on Bell's Theorem.* Notre Dame, Ind.: University of Notre Dame Press, 1989.

D'Amore, Benedetto, O.P. "Il problema del fondamento nella metafisica di S. Tommaso." *Sapienza* 26, no. 3–4 (1973): 463–469.

D'Andrea, Antonio. "L' 'allegoria dei poeti': Nota a *Convivio* II.1." In *Dante e le forme dell'allegoresi,* edited by Michelangelo Picone, 71–78. Ravenna: Longo Editore, 1987.

Damon, Philip. "Allegory and Invention: Levels of Meaning in Ancient and Medieval Rhetoric." In *The Classics in the Middle Ages,* edited by Aldo S. Bernardo and Saul Levin. Binghamton, N.Y.: Center for Medieval and Early Renaissance Studies, 1990.

———. "Adam on the Primal Language: *Paradiso* 26.124." *Italica* 38, no. 1 (March 1961): 60–62.

Dante Alighieri. *La Commedia secondo l'antica vulgata.* Rev. ed. Edited by Giorgio Petrocchi. Firenze: Le Lettere, 1994. 4 vols.

———. *Convivio.* Edited by Franca Brambilla Ageno. Firenze: Le Lettere, 1995. 3 vols.

———. *Il Convivio.* Critical edition by Maria Picchio Simonelli. Bologna: Pàtron, 1966.

———. *Il Convivio.* Edited by Giovanni Busnelli and G. Vandelli. In *Opere di Dante.* 2d ed. Firenze: Le Monnier, 1964.

———. *Convivio.* Edited by Cesare Vasoli. In *La letteratura italiana: storia e testi,* vol. 5, tome I, part 2. Milano–Napoli: Ricciardi, 1988.

———. *[Convivio] Dante's Il Convivio.* Translated by Richard H. Lansing. New York: Garland, 1990.

———. *[Convivio] The Banquet.* Translated by Christopher Ryan. Saratoga, Calif.: ANMA Libri, 1989.

———. *[Convivio] Das Gastmahl.* Translated by Thomas Ricklin, with introduction and commentary by Francis Chevenal. 4 vols. Hamburg: F. Meiner, 1996–.

———. *Dantis Alagherii Comedia.* Critical ed. by Federico Sanguineti. Firenze: Edizioni del Galluzzo, 2001.

———. *De vulgari eloquentia.* Edited by Pier Vincenzo Mengaldo. In *La letteratura italiana: storia e testi,* vol 5, tome 2, 3–237. Milano–Napoli: Ricciardi, 1979.

_____. *The Divine Comedy of Dante Alighieri*. Translated by Allen Mandelbaum. New York: Bantam Books, 1986. 3 vols.

_____. *The Divine Comedy*. Translated by Charles S. Singleton. Bollingen Series. Princeton: Princeton University Press, 1973. 6 vols.

_____. *The Divine Comedy*. Translated by John D. Sinclair. 1939–1946. New York: Oxford University Press, 1971. 3 vols.

_____. *The Divine Comedy*. In *The Portable Dante*. Translated by Mark Musa. New York: Penguin Books, 1995.

_____. *Epistola a Cangrande*. Edited by Enzo Cecchini. Firenze: Giunti, 1995.

_____. *Epistole*. Edited by Arsenio Frugoni and Giorgio Brugnoli. In *La letteratura italiana: storia e testi*, vol. 5, tome 2, 505–643. Milano–Napoli: Riccardo Ricciardi, 1979.

_____. *Monarchia*. Edited by Bruno Nardi. *La letteratura italiana: storia e testi*, vol. 5, tome 2, 239–503. Milano–Napoli: Riccardo Ricciardi, 1979.

_____. *Monarchy*. Translated and edited by Prue Shaw. Cambridge: Cambridge University Press, 1996.

_____. Monarchy *and Three Political Letters*. Translated by Donald Nicholl and Colin Hardie. 1947. Westport, Conn.: Hyperion Press, 1979.

_____. *Questio de aqua et terra*. Edited by Francesco Mazzoni. In *La letteratura italiana: storia e testi*, vol. 5, tome 2, 691–880. Milano–Napoli: Riccardo Ricciardi, 1979.

_____. *Rime*. Edited by Gianfranco Contini. In *La letteratura italiana: storia e testi*, vol. 5, tome 1, part 1, 251–552. Milano–Napoli: Riccardo Ricciardi, 1984.

_____. *Vita Nova*. Edited by Guglielmo Gorni. Torino: Giulio Einaudi, 1996.

_____. *Vita Nuova*. Edited by Domenico De Robertis. *La letteratura italiana: storia e testi*, vol. 5, tome 1, part 1, 1–247. Milano–Napoli: Riccardo Ricciardi, 1974.

Dartmouth Dante Project. Edited by Robert Hollander. 1988. Department of Comparative Literature, Princeton University, 1999. telnet:library.dartmouth.edu.

Daujat, Jean. *Physique moderne et philosophie traditionnelle*. Tournai: Desclée, 1958.

Dauphiné, James. *Le cosmos de Dante*. Paris: Société d'édition "Les Belles Lettres," 1984.

Davies, Brian. *The Thought of Thomas Aquinas*. Oxford: Oxford University Press, Clarendon, 1992.

De Andia, Ysabel. *Henosis: L'union à Dieu chez Denys l'Aréopagite*. Leiden: E. J. Brill, 1996.

De Bonfils Templer, Margherita. "Il dantesco 'amoroso uso di Sapienza': sue radici platoniche." *Stanford Italian Review* 7, no. 1–2 (1987): 5–28.

_____. "Genesi di un'allegoria." *Dante Studies* 105 (1987): 79–94.

_____. "La prima materia de li elementi'." *Studi danteschi* 58 (1986): 275–291.

_____. "Ragione e intelletto nel *Convivio*." In *Italiana*, edited by Albert N. Mancini, Paolo Giordano, and Pier Raimondo Baldini, 77–86. River Forest, Ill.: Rosary College, 1988.

De Corte, Marcel. *La doctrine de l'intelligence chez Aristote*. Paris: Librairie Philosophique J. Vrin, 1934.

De Libera, Alain. *Penser au moyen âge*. Paris: Editions de Seuil, 1991.

De Matteis, Maria C. "Aristotele." In *ED*, 1:372–377.

De Robertis, Domenico. " 'Incipit vita nova' (*V.N.*, 1): poetica del (ri)cominciamento." In *La gloriosa donna de la mente*, edited by Vincent Moleta, 11–19. Firenze: Leo S. Olschki, 1994.

De Vogel, C. J. "The Legend of the Platonizing Aristotle." In *Aristotle and Plato in the*

Mid-Fourth Century, edited by I. Düring and G. E. L. Owen, 248–256. Göteborg: Elanders Boktryckeri Aktiebolag, 1960.

Dell'Aquila, Michele. "Il canto XXVII del *Purgatorio*." In *Miscellanea di studi danteschi, in memoria di Silvio Pasquazi*, 313–324. Napoli: Federico & Ardia, 1993. 2 vols.

Demers, G. E. "Les divers sens du mot 'ratio' au moyen âge." *Études d'histoire littéraire et doctrinale du XIIIe siècle* 1 (1932): 105–139.

Denifle, Heinrich, and Emil Chatelain. *Chartularium Universitatis Parisiensis*. Paris: Delalain, 1889–1897.

Dennehy, Raymond. "The Ontological Basis of Certitude." *Thomist* 50, no. 1 (January 1986): 120–150.

Descoqs, Pedro, S.J. *Essai critique sur l'hylémorphisme*. Bibliothèque des archives de philosophie. Paris: Gabriel Beauchesne, 1924.

Deutsch, Eliot. *Advaita Vedanta: A Philosophical Reconstruction*. 1969. East-West Center Books. Honolulu: University Press of Hawaii, 1973.

Dewan, Lawrence, O. P. "St. Albert, St. Thomas, and Knowledge." *American Catholic Philosophical Quarterly* 70, no. 1 (Winter 1996): 121–135.

———. "Thomas Aquinas, Creation, and Two Historians." *Laval théologique et philosophique* 50 (1994): 363–387.

Di Salvo, Tommaso, ed. *La* Divina Commedia *annotata e commentata da Tommaso Di Salvo con illustrazioni*. 3 vols. Bologna: Zanichelli, 1993.

Dicks, D. R. *Early Greek Astronomy to Aristotle*. Ithaca: Cornell University Press, 1970.

Dillard, Annie. *Holy the Firm*. New York: Harper & Row, 1977.

Drees, Willem B. *Beyond the Big Bang: Quantum Cosmologies and God*. La Salle, Ill.: Open Court, 1990.

Driscoll, John. "The Platonic Ancestry of Primary Substance." *Phronesis* 24, no. 3 (1979): 253–269.

Dronke, Peter. "Boethius, Alanus and Dante." In *The Medieval Poet and His World*, 431–438. Rome:, 1984.

———. "The *Commedia* and Medieval Modes of Reading." In *Dante and Medieval Latin Traditions*, 1–31. Cambridge: Cambridge University Press, 1986.

———. "The Conclusion of Dante's *Commedia*." *Italian Studies* 49 (1994): 21–39.

———. *Dante's Second Love: The Originality and the Contexts of the* Convivio. Occasional Papers, no. 2. Leeds: Society for Italian Studies, 1997.

Duhem, Pierre. *Medieval Cosmology: Theories of Infinity, Place, Time, Void, and the Plurality of Worlds*. Edited and translated by Roger Ariew. Chicago: University of Chicago Press, 1985.

———. *Le système du monde: histoire des doctrines cosmologiques de Platon à Copernic*. Paris: Hermann, 1913–1959. 10 vols.

Duns Scotus, John. *Opera omnia*. 26 vols. New ed. 1891–1895. Westmead: Gregg International, 1969.

———. *Quaestiones super libros Metaphysicorum Aristotelis*. Edited by R. Andrews. St. Bonaventure, NY: Franciscan Institute, 1997.

———. *Questions on the* Metaphysics *of Aristotle*. Translated by Girard J. Etzkorn and Allan B. Wolter. St. Bonaventure, N.Y.: Franciscan Institute, 1997.

Dupré, Louis. "The Mystical Experience of the Self and Its Philosophical Significance." *Proceedings of the American Catholic Philosophical Association* 48 (1974): 149–165.

———. "*Unio Mystica*: the State and the Experience." In *Mystical Union and Monotheistic Faith: An Ecumenical Dialogue*, edited by Moshe Idel and Bernard McGinn, 3–23. New York: Macmillan, 1989.

Dupré, Louis, and James A. Wiseman, eds. *Light from Light: An Anthology of Christian Mysticism.* New York: Paulist Press, 1988.

Düring, Ingemar. "Aristotle and the Heritage from Plato." *Eranos* 62 (1964): 84–99.

Durling, Robert M., ed. and trans. *The Divine Comedy of Dante Alighieri.* Introduction and notes by Ronald L. Martinez and Robert M. Durling. 3 vols. New York: Oxford University Press, 1996.

Durling, Robert M., and Ronald L. Martinez. *Time and the Crystal: Studies in Dante's Rime Petrose.* Berkeley: University of California Press, 1990.

Eckhart, Meister. *The Essential Sermons, Commentaries, Treatises, and Defense.* Translated by Edmund Colledge and Bernard McGinn. Classics of Western Spirituality. New York: Paulist Press, 1981.

————. *Meister Eckhart: A Modern Translation.* Translated by Raymond Bernard Blakney. New York: Harper and Row, Harper Torchbooks, 1941.

————. *Meister Eckhart, Teacher and Preacher.* Edited by Bernard McGinn. The Classics of Western Spirituality. New York: Paulist Press, 1986.

Eddington, A. S. *The Nature of the Physical World.* The Gifford Lectures, 1927. New York: Macmillan Company, 1929.

Egan, Harvey, S.J. *An Anthology of Christian Mysticism.* Collegeville, Minn.: Liturgical Press, Pueblo, 1991.

Egginton, William. "On Dante, Hyperspheres, and the Curvature of the Medieval Cosmos." *Journal of the History of Ideas* 60, no. 2 (April 1999): 195–216.

Einstein, Albert. *Relativity: The Special and the General Theory.* Translated by Robert W. Lawson. New York: Crown, 1961.

Elders, Leo. *Aristotle's Cosmology: A Commentary on the* De Caelo. Assen: Van Gorcum, 1965.

Emerton, Norma E. *The Scientific Reinterpretation of Form.* Cornell History of Science Series. Ithaca, N.Y.: Cornell University Press, 1984.

Enciclopedia Dantesca. 5 vols. plus appendix. Edited by Umberto Bosco. 1970–1978. 2d ed. Roma: Istituto dell'Enciclopedia Italiana, 1984.

Eriugena, John Scotus. *Periphyseon (The Division of Nature).* Translated by I. P. Sheldon-Williams, revised by John J. O'Meara. Montréal: Bellarmin, 1987.

L'esperienza mistica di Dante nelle indicazioni dell'esegesi Trecentesca. Primi risultati di una ricerca di gruppo effettuata nell'Istituto di Studi Danteschi dell'Università Cattolica del Sacro Cuore. Firenze: Leo S. Olschki, 1969.

Evans, J. D. G. *Aristotle.* New York: St. Martin's Press, 1987.

Everson, Stephen. "Psychology." In *The Cambridge Companion to Aristotle,* edited by Jonathan Barnes, 168–194. Cambridge: Cambridge University Press, 1995.

Ewert, Alfred. "Art and Artifice in the *Divina Commedia.*" In *Centenary Essays on Dante,* by members of the Oxford Dante Society, 77–90. Oxford: Clarendon Press, 1965.

Fabro, Cornelio. *La nozione metafisica di partecipazione.* 2d ed. 1939. Torino: Società Editrice Internazionale, 1950.

————. "Platonism, Neo-Platonism and Thomism: Convergencies and Divergencies." *New Scholasticism* 44 (1970): 69–100.

Faes de Mottoni, Barbara. "Universo." In *ED,* 5:830–833.

Fallani, Giovanni. *Dante poeta teologo.* Milano: Marzorati Editore, 1965.

————. "Visio beatifica." In *ED,* 5:1070–1071.

Faral, Edmond. *Les arts poétiques du XIIe et du XIIIe siècle: recherches et documents sur la technique littéraire du moyen âge.* Paris: Librairie Ancienne Honoré Champion, 1924.

Fay, Thomas A. "Participation: The Transformation of Platonic and Neoplatonic Thought in the Metaphysics of Thomas Aquinas." *Divus Thomas* 76 (1973): 50–64.

———. "The Problem of Intellectual Intuition in the Metaphysics of Thomas Aquinas." *Sapienza* 27, no. 3–4 (1974): 352–359.

Fels, Heinrich. "Dante und Meister Eckhart." *Deutsches Dante-Jahrbuch* 27 (1948): 171–187.

Fenzi, Enrico. "Dopo l'edizione Sanguineti: dubbi e proposte per *Purg.* XXIV 57." *Studi danteschi* 68 (2003): 67–82.

———. "L'esperienza di sé come esperienza dell'allegoria (a proposito di Dante, *Convivio* II i 2)." *Studi danteschi* 67 (2002): 161–200.

Fergusson, Francis. *Dante's Drama of the Mind: A Modern Reading of the* Purgatorio. Princeton: Princeton University Press, 1953.

Ferrero, Augusto. *Il Canto XXVII del* Purgatorio *letto da Augusto Ferrero nella Sala di Dante in Orsanmichele*. Firenze: G. C. Sansoni, 1910.

Ferris, Timothy. *Coming of Age in the Milky Way*. New York: Doubleday, Anchor Books, 1988.

Ferrucci, Franco. *The Poetics of Disguise: The Autobiography of the Work in Homer, Dante, and Shakespeare*. Translated by Ann Dunnigan. Ithaca, N.Y.: Cornell University Press, 1980.

———. "Tre note dantesche." *Lettere italiane* (1997): 89–92.

Festugière, André Jean. *Contemplation et vie contemplative selon Platon*. Paris: Librairie Philosophique J. Vrin, 1936.

Fido, Franco. "Writing Like God—or Better?: Symmetries in Dante's Twenty-Sixth and Twenty-Seventh Cantos." *Italica* 63, no. 3 (Autumn 1986): 250–264.

Finan, Thomas, and Vincent Twomey, eds. *The Relationship between Neoplatonism and Christianity*. Dublin: Four Courts Press, 1992.

Fine, Arthur. *The Shaky Game: Einstein, Realism, and the Quantum Theory*. Chicago: University of Chicago Press, 1986.

Fine, Gail. "Forms as Causes: Plato and Aristotle." In *Mathematics and Metaphysics in Aristotle*, edited by Andreas Graeser, 69–112. Bern: Paul Haupt, 1987.

Fioravanti, Gianfranco. "Dante e Alberto Magno." In *Il pensiero filosofico e teologico di Dante Alighieri*, ed. Alessandro Ghisalberti, 93–102. Milano: Vita e Pensiero, 2001.

Forti, Fiorenzo. "Le Atene celestiali: i magnanimi del sapere." In *Magnanimitade*, 49–81. Bologna: Pàtron, 1977.

Foster, Kenelm, O.P. "Dante, Poet of the Intellect." *New Blackfriars* 46: 442–446.

———. "Dante's Vision of God." In *The Two Dantes and Other Studies*, 66–85. Berkeley: University of California Press, 1977.

———. "Religion and Philosophy in Dante." In *The Mind of Dante*, edited by Uberto Limentani, 47–78. Cambridge: Cambridge University Press, 1965.

———. "Tommaso d'Aquino." In *ED*, 5:626–649.

Francis, Saint. *I Fioretti di San Francesco*. Edited by Giorgio Petrocchi. Alpignano: Tallone, 1973.

Franke, William. *Dante's Interpretive Journey*. Chicago: University of Chicago Press, 1996.

———. "Reader's Application and the Moment of Truth in Dante's *Divine Comedy.*" In *Dante: Contemporary Perspectives*, edited by Amilcare A. Iannucci, 259–280. Toronto: University of Toronto Press, 1997.

Franks, Joan. "*Nous* as Human Form: Reflections on the *De anima.*" *American Catholic Philosophical Association Proceedings* 49 (1995): 249–255.

———. "The Relation of the Sublunary Substances to God in Aristotle." *American Catholic Philosophical Quarterly* 66 (1992): 175–180.

Frattini, Alberto. "Canto XXVII." In *Lectura Dantis Scaligera*: Purgatorio, 995–1036. Firenze: Felice Le Monnier, 1971.

Freccero, John. "The Dance of the Stars: *Paradiso X.*" In *Dante: The Poetics of Conversion*, 221–244.

———. *Dante: The Poetics of Conversion.* Edited by Rachel Jacoff. Cambridge, Mass.: Harvard University Press, 1986.

———. "The Firm Foot on a Journey without a Guide." In *Dante: The Poetics of Conversion*, 29–54.

———. "Medusa: The Letter and the Spirit." In *Dante: The Poetics of Conversion*, 119–135.

———. "Pilgrim in a Gyre." In *Dante: The Poetics of Conversion*, 70–92.

———. "Satan's Fall and the *Quaestio de Aqua et Terra.*" *Italica* 38 (1961): 99–115.

———. "The Sign of Satan." In *Dante: The Poetics of Conversion*, 167–179.

Frede, Michael. "On Aristotle's Conception of the Soul." In *Essays on Aristotle's De anima*, edited by Martha C. Nussbaum and Amélie Oksenberg Rorty, 93–107. Oxford: Oxford University Press, Clarendon, 1992.

———. "La théorie aristotélicienne de l'intellect agent." In *Corps et âme: sur le De anima d'Aristote*, edited by Gilbert Romeyer Dherbey, 377–390. Paris: Librairie Philosophique J. Vrin, 1996.

Furth, Montgomery. "Aristotle on the Unity of Form." In *Aristotle Today: Essays on Aristotle's Ideal of Science*, edited by Mohan Matthen, 77–102. Edmonton, Alberta: Academic Printing, 1987.

———. "Specific and Individual Form in Aristotle." In *Biologie, logique et métaphysique chez Aristote*, edited by Daniel Devereux and Pierre Pellegrin, 85–111. Paris: Éditions du Centre National de la Recherche Scientifique, 1990.

Gagliardi, Antonio. *La tragedia intellettuale di Dante: Il* Convivio. Catanzaro: Pullano, 1994.

Gandillac, Maurice de. "Plotin et la *Métaphysique* d'Aristote." In *Études sur la Métaphysique d'Aristote: actes du VIe Symposium Aristotelicum*, edited by Pierre Aubenque, 247–259. Paris: Librairie Philosophique J. Vrin, 1979.

Gardner, Edmund G. *Dante and the Mystics: A Study of the Mystical Aspect of the Divina Commedia and Its Relations with Some of Its Mediaeval Sources.* 1913. New York: Haskell House, 1968.

Garin, Eugenio. *Storia della filosofia italiana.* 3 vols. 2nd ed. Torino: Einaudi, 1966.

Geiger, L. B. *La participation dans la philosophie de saint Thomas d'Aquin.* 1942. Montréal: Institut d'Études Médiévales, 1952.

Gellrich, Jesse. *The Idea of the Book in the Middle Ages.* Ithaca: Cornell University Press, 1985.

Gentile, Giovanni. "La filosofia di Dante." In *Studi su Dante*. Vol. 13 of *Opere complete di Giovanni Gentile*, edited by Vito A. Bellezza. 1921. Firenze: Sansoni, 1965.

Georgiadis, Constantine. "Two Conceptions of Substance in Aristotle." In *Substances and Things: Aristotle's Doctrine of Physical Substance in Recent Essays*, M. L. O'Hara, 172–187. Washington, D.C.: University Press of America, 1982.

Geroch, Robert. *General Relativity from A to B.* Chicago: University of Chicago Press, 1978.

Gerrity, Benignus, F.S.C. "The Relations Between the Theory of Matter and Form and the Theory of Knowledge in the Philosophy of Saint Thomas Aquinas." Ph.D. diss., Catholic University of America, 1936.

Gersh, Stephen. *Middle Platonism and Neoplatonism: The Latin Tradition.* 2 vols. Notre Dame, Ind.: University of Notre Dame Press, 1986.

_____. "Platonism—Neoplatonism—Aristotelianism: A Twelfth-Century Meta-physical System and Its Sources." In *Renaissance and Renewal in the Twelfth Century,* edited by Robert L. Benson and Giles Constable, 512–534. Toronto: University of Toronto Press, 1991.

Gerson, Lloyd P. *God and Greek Philosophy: Studies in the Early History of Natural Theology.* London and New York: Routledge, 1994.

_____. *Plotinus.* New York: Routledge, 1994.

Getto, Giovanni. "*Paradiso 29.*" In *Letture dantesche,* edited by Giovanni Getto, 1945–1970. Firenze: Sansoni, 1964.

Ghisalberti, Alessandro. "La cosmologia nel Duecento e Dante." In *Letture classensi,* vol. 13, 33–48. Ravenna: Longo, 1984.

_____. "La nozione di tempo in San Tommaso d'Aquino." *Rivista di filosofia neoscolastica* 59 (January–February 1967): 343–371.

Ghisalberti, Fausto. "Giovanni del Virgilio espositore delle *Metamorfosi.*" *Giornale dantesco* 34 (1933): 1–110. Reprint, Firenze: L. S. Olschki, 1933.

Giacon, Carlo. "Avicenna." In *ED,* 1:481–482.

Giannantonio, Pompeo. "Struttura e allegoria nel *Paradiso.*" In *Letture classensi,* vol. 11, 63–80. Ravenna: A. Longo.

_____. *Endiadi: dottrina e poesia nella* Divina Commedia. Firenze: G. C. Sansoni, 1983.

Gill, Mary Louise. *Aristotle on Substance: The Paradox of Unity.* Princeton: Princeton University Press, 1989.

Gilson, Étienne. *Being and Some Philosophers.* Toronto: Pontifical Institute of Medieval Studies, 1949.

_____. *The Christian Philosophy of St. Thomas Aquinas.* Translated by L. K. Shook. 1948. New York: Random House, 1956.

_____. "La conclusion de la *Divine Comédie* et la mystique franciscaine." *Revue d'histoire franciscaine* 1 (1924): 55–63.

_____. *Dante the Philosopher.* Translated by David Moore. New York: Sheed & Ward, 1949. Reprinted as *Dante and Philosophy.* Gloucester, Mass.: Peter Smith, 1968.

_____. *God and Philosophy.* Powell Lectures on Philosophy at Indiana University. 1941. New Haven: Yale University Press, 1969.

_____. *History of Christian Philosophy in the Middle Ages.* New York: Random House, 1955.

_____. *The Philosophy of St. Bonaventure.* Translated by Dom Illtyd Trethowan and Frank J. Sheed. Paterson, N.J.: St. Anthony Guild Press, 1965.

_____. "Poésie et théologie dans la *Divine Comédie.*" In *Atti del congresso internazionale di studi danteschi (20–27 aprile, 1965).* Firenze: Sansoni, 1965–1996.

_____. "A la recherche de l'Empyrée." *Revue des études italiennes* 11 (1965): 145–161.

_____. *The Spirit of Mediaeval Philosophy.* Gifford Lectures 1931–1932. Translated by A. H. C. Downes. 1936. Notre Dame, Ind.: University of Notre Dame Press, 1991.

Gilson, Simon A. *Medieval Optics and Theories of Light in the Works of Dante.* Lewiston: E. Mellen Press, 2000.

Giorgi, Rubina. *Dante e Meister Eckhart: letture per il tempo della fine*. Salerno: Edizioni Ripostes, 1987.

Glendinning, Robert. "Pyramus and Thisbe in the Medieval Classroom." *Speculum* 61, no. 1 (January 1986): 51–78.

Glorieux, Palémon. *Pour revaloriser Migne: tables rectificatives*. Mélanges de Science Religieuse, 9me année (cahier supplémentaire). Lille: Facultés Catholiques, 1952.

[*Glossa ordinaria.*] *Biblia sacra, cum Glossa Ordinaria, primum quidem a Strabo Fuldensi collecta . . . annotatis etiam iis quae confuse antea citabantur locis*. 7 vols. With the *Postilla* of Nicholas of Lyra. Lugduni, 1589.

Gorni, Guglielmo. *Il nodo della lingua e il verbo d'amore*. Firenze: Olschki, 1981.

———. "Spirito profetico duecentesco e Dante." In *Letture classensi*, vol. 13, edited by Maria Corti, 49–68. Ravenna: A. Longo, 1984.

Grabmann, Martin. "Die wege von Thomas von Aquin zu Dante: Fra Remigio de' Girolami O.Pr." *Deutsches Dante-Jahrbuch* 9 (1925): 1–35. Reprinted in *Dante Alighieri: Aufsätze zur Divina Commedia*, edited by Hugo Friedrich, 201–235. Darmstadt: Wissenschaftliche Buchgesellschaft, 1968.

Gragnolati, Manuele. *Experiencing the Afterlife: Body and Soul in Dante and Medieval Culture*. Notre Dame, Ind.: University of Notre Dame Press, forthcoming.

Graham, Daniel W. "The Paradox of Prime Matter." *Journal of the History of Philosophy* 25, no. 4 (October 1987): 475–490.

Granger, Herbert. *Aristotle's Idea of the Soul*. Dordrecht: Kluwer Academic, 1996.

Grant, Edward. *Planets, Stars, and Orbs: The Medieval Cosmos, 1200–1687*. Cambridge: Cambridge University Press, 1994.

Grant, Sara, R.S.C.J. "The Contemporary Relevance of the Advaita of Śaṅkarācārya." In *New Perspectives on Advaita Vedanta: Essays in Commemoration of Professor Richard de Smet*, edited by Bradley J. Malkovsky, 148–163. Leiden and Boston: Brill, 2000.

———. *Towards an Alternative Theology: Confessions of a Non-Dualist Christian*. The Teape Lectures. Bangalore: Asian Trading, 1991. Reprint, Notre Dame, Ind.: Notre Dame University Press, 2002.

Grayson, Cecil. "Dante's Theory and Practice of Poetry." In *The World of Dante: Essays on Dante and His Times*, 146–165. Oxford: Oxford Dante Society, 1980.

Greene, Brian. *The Elegant Universe: Superstrings, Hidden Dimensions, and the Quest for the Ultimate Theory*. New York: W. W. Norton, 1999.

Greenhill, Eleanor Simmons. "The Child in the Tree: A Study of the Cosmological Tree in the Christian Tradition." *Traditio* 10 (1954): 323–371.

Gregory of Nyssa. *From Glory to Glory: Texts from Gregory of Nyssa's Mystical Writings*. Translated and edited by Herbert Musurillo, S.J., and selected by Jean Daniélou, S.J. 1961. Crestwood, N.Y.: St. Vladimir's Seminary Press, 1995.

Gregory, Tullio. "Filosofia e teologia nella crisi del XIII secolo." *Belfagor* 19 (1964): 1–16.

Grene, Marjorie. *The Knower and the Known*. Berkeley: University of California Press, 1974.

Griffiths, Dom Bede. "Toward an Indian Christian Spirituality." In *Prayer and Contemplation*, edited by C. M. Vadakkekara. Studies in Christian and Hindu Spirituality. Bangalore: Asirivanan Benedictine Monastery, n.d.

Grosseteste, Robert. *De luce seu de inchoatione formarum*. Edited by Ludwig Baur. Beiträge zur Geschichte der Philosophie des Mittelalters, vol. 9. Münster: Aschendorff, 1912.

————. *On Light.* Translated by Clare C. Riedl. Milwaukee: Marquette University Press, 1942.

Guerri, Domenico. "Il nome di Dio nella lingua di Adamo scondo il XXVI del *Paradiso* e il verso di Nembrotte nel XXXI dell'*Inferno.*" *Giornale storico della letteratura italiana* 54 (1909): 65–76.

Guidubaldi, Egidio. *Dante europeo.* 3 vols. Firenze: L. S. Olschki, 1965–1968.

Hackett, Jeremiah, ed. *Aquinas on Mind and Intellect: New Essays.* Oakdale, N.Y.: Dowling College Press, 1996.

Hadot, Pierre. "La conception Plotinienne de l'identité entre l'intellect et son objet: Plotin et le *De anima* d'Aristote." In *Corps et âme: sur le* De anima *d'Aristote*, edited by Gilbert Romeyer Dherbey, 367–376. Paris: Librairie Philosophique J. Vrin, 1996.

————. *Dieu et l'être.* Paris: Centre d'études des réligions du livre, 1978.

————. "The Harmony of Plotinus and Aristotle According to Porphyry." In *Aristotle Transformed: The Ancient Commentators and Their Influence*, edited by Richard Sorabji, 125–140. Ithaca: Cornell University Press, 1990.

————. "Neoplatonist Spirituality: 1. Plotinus and Porphyry." Translated by Jane Curran. In *Classical Mediterranean Spirituality: Egyptian, Greek, Roman*, edited by A. H. Armstrong, 230–249. New York: Crossroad, 1986.

————. *Plotinus, or the Simplicity of Vision.* Translated by Michael Chase. Chicago: University of Chicago Press, 1993.

Hagman, Edward. "Dante's Vision of God: The End of the *Itinerarium Mentis.*" *Dante Studies* 106 (1988): 1–22.

Hallock, Ann H. "Dante's *Selva Oscura* and Other Obscure *Selvas.*" *Forum Italicum* 6, no. 1 (March 1972): 57–78.

Hamelin, Octave. *La théorie de l'intellect d'après Aristote et ses commentateurs.* Edited by Edmond Barbotin. Paris: Librairie Philosophique J. Vrin, 1953.

Hamlyn, D. W. "Aristotle on Form." In *Aristotle on Nature and Living Things*, edited by Allan Gotthelf, 55–65. Pittsburgh: Mathesis; Bristol: Bristol Classical Press, 1985.

Hankey, Wayne. "Aquinas' First Principle: Being or Unity?" *Dionysius* 4 (1980): 133–172.

Hanson, Norwood Russell. *Constellations and Conjectures.* Edited by Willard C. Humphreys. Dordrecht: Reidel, 1973.

————. "On Counting Aristotle's Spheres." *Scientia* 98 (1963): 223–232.

Happold, F. C. *Mysticism: A Study and an Anthology.* Rev. ed. 1963. London: Penguin Books, 1990.

Hardie, Colin. "The Symbol of the Gryphon in *Purgatorio* XXIX.108 and Following Cantos." In *Centenary Essays on Dante.* By members of the Oxford Dante Society, 103–131. Oxford: Clarendon Press, 1965.

Hardie, W. F. R. "Concepts of Consciousness in Aristotle." *Mind* 85 (1976): 388–411.

Hardison, O. B., Jr. "Toward a History of Medieval Literary Criticism." *Medievalia et Humanistica* 7 (1976): 1–12.

Hardt, Manfred. "Dante and Arithmetic." In *The Divine Comedy and the Encyclopedia of Arts and Sciences*, edited by Giuseppe Di Scipio and Aldo Scaglione, 81–94. Amsterdam and Philadelphia: John Benjamins, 1988.

Haren, Michael. *Medieval Thought: The Western Intellectual Tradition from Antiquity to the Thirteenth Century.* 2d ed. Toronto: University of Toronto Press, 1992.

Hart, Georg. *Die Pyramus- und Thisbe-Sage in Holland, England, Italien und Spanien.* Passau: A. Liesecke, 1891.

_____. *Ursprung und Verbreitung der Pyramus- und Thisbe-Sage*. Passau: J. Bucher, 1889.

Hart, Thomas E. " 'Per misurar lo cerchio'; (*Par.* XXXIII 134) anu Archimedes' *De mensura circuli*: Some Thoughts on Approximations to the Value of π." In *Dante e la scienza*, edited by Patrick Boyde and Vittorio Russo, 265–335. Ravenna: A. Longo, 1995.

Hartman, Edwin. *Substance, Body, and Soul: Aristotelian Investigations*. Princeton: Princeton University Press, 1977.

Hartner, Willy. "Astronomy from Antiquity to Copernicus." In *Avant, avec, après Copernic: la représentation de l'univers et ses conséquences épistémologiques*, 11–17. Paris: Albert Blanchard, 1975.

Harwood, Sharon. "Moral Blindness and Freedom of Will: A Study of Light Images in the *Divina Commedia*." *Romance Notes* 16, no. 1 (Autumn 1974): 205–221.

Hatcher, Anna, and Mark Musa. "The Kiss: *Inferno* V and the Old French Prose *Lancelot*." *Comparative Literature* 20 (1968): 97–109.

Haug, Walter. *Vernacular Literary Theory in the Middle Ages: The German Tradition, 800–1300, in Its European Context*. Translated by Joanna M. Catling. Cambridge: Cambridge University Press, 1997.

Hawking, Stephen W. *A Brief History of Time: From the Big Bang to Black Holes*. New York: Bantam Books, 1988.

Hawkins, Peter S. "Augustine, Dante, and the Dialectic of Ineffability." In *Ineffability: Naming the Unnamable from Dante to Beckett*, edited by Peter S. Hawkins and Anne Howland Schotter, 5–22. New York: AMS Press, 1984. Reprinted in *Dante's Testaments: Essays in Scriptural Imagination*. Stanford: Stanford University Press, 1999.

_____. "Dante's Ovid." *Literature and Belief* 5 (1985): 1–11.

_____. "Divide and Conquer: Augustine in the *Divine Comedy*." *PMLA* 106, no. 3 (May 1991): 471–482. Reprinted in *Dante's Testaments: Essays in Scriptural Imagination*. Stanford: Stanford University Press, 1999.

_____. "Transfiguring the Text: Ovid, Scripture and the Dynamics of Allusion." *Stanford Italian Review* 5, no. 2 (Fall 1985): 115–139. Reprinted in *Dante's Testaments: Essays in Scriptural Imagination*. Stanford: Stanford University Press, 1999.

_____. "Virtuosity and Virtue: Poetic Self-Reflection in the *Commedia*." *Dante Studies* 98 (1980): 1–18.

Hedwig, Klaus. *Sphaera Lucis: Studien zur Intelligibilität des Seienden im Kontext der mittelalterlichen Lichtspekulation*. Münster: Aschendorff, 1980.

Heinaman, Robert. "Aristotle and the Mind-Body Problem." *Phronesis* 35, no. 1 (1990): 83–102.

Heiney, Donald. "*Intelletto* and the Theory of Love in the Dolce Stil Nuovo." *Italica* 39, no. 3 (September 1962): 173–181.

Heisenberg, Werner. *Across the Frontiers*. Translated by Peter Heath. New York: Harper & Row, 1974.

_____. *Physics and Beyond: Encounters and Conversations*. Translated by Arnold J. Pomerans. New York: Harper & Row, Harper Torchbooks, 1971.

_____. *Physics and Philosophy: The Revolution in Modern Science*. 1958. New York: Harper & Row, Harper Torchbooks, 1962.

Heiser, John H. "Plotinus and Aquinas on *Esse Commune*." *Modern Schoolman* 70, no. 4 (May 1993): 259–287.

Henle, Robert J., S.J. *Saint Thomas and Platonism: A Study of Plato and the Platonic Texts in the Writings of Saint Thomas*. The Hague: Marinus Nijhoff, 1956.

Herbert, Nick. *Quantum Reality: Beyond the New Physics.* New York: Doubleday, Anchor Books, 1985.

Herrera, Robert A. "An Episode in Medieval Aristotelianism: Maimonides and St. Thomas on the Active Intellect." *Thomist* 47, no. 3 (July 1983): 317–338.

Hillgarth, J. N. *Who Read Thomas Aquinas?* Étienne Gilson Series, vol. 13. Toronto: Pontifical Institute of Mediaeval Studies, 1992.

Hissette, Roland. *Enquête sur les 219 articles condamnés à Paris le 7 mars 1277.* Louvain: Publications Universitaires, 1977.

———. "L'implication de Thomas d'Aquin dans les censures Parisiennes de 1277." *Recherches de théologie et philosophie médiévales* 64, no. 1 (1997): 3–31.

Hixon, Lex. *Great Swan: Meetings with Ramakrishna.* Boston: Shambhala, 1992.

Hoenen, Maarten J.F.M. "Metaphysik und Intellektlehre: Die aristotelische Lehre des 'intellectus agens' im Schnittpunkt der mitterlalterlichen Diskussion um die natürliche Gotteserkenntnis." *Theologie und Philosophie* 70, no. 3 (1995): 405–413.

Hollander, Robert. *Allegory in Dante's* Commedia. Princeton: Princeton University Press, 1969.

———. "Babytalk in Dante's *Commedia.*" *Italica* 8, no. 4 (July 1975). Reprinted in *Studies in Dante,* 115–129.

———. *Dante Alighieri.* Roma: Editalia, 2000.

———. "Dante's *Commedia* and the Classical Tradition: The Case of Virgil." In *The Divine Comedy and the Encyclopedia of Arts and Sciences,* edited by Giuseppe Di Scipio and Aldo Scaglione, 15–25. Amsterdam: Benjamins, 1988.

———. "Dante's 'dolce stil novo' and the *Comedy.*" In *Dante, mito e poesia: atti del secondo seminario dantesco internazionale (Monte Verità, Ascona, 23–27 giugno 1997),* edited by Michelangelo Picone and Tatiana Crivelli, 263–281. Firenze: Franco Cesati Editore, 1999.

———. "Dante's Use of the Fiftieth Psalm (a Note on *Purg.* XXX, 84)." *Dante Studies* 91 (1973). Reprinted in *Studies in Dante,* 107–13.

———. "Dante *Theologus-Poeta.*" *Dante Studies* 94 (1976): 91–136. Reprinted in *Studies in Dante,* 39–89.

———. "The Invocations of the *Commedia.*" *Yearbook of Italian Studies* 3 (1976): 235–240. Reprinted in *Studies in Dante,* 31–38.

———. "A Note on *Inferno* XXXIII, 37–74: Ugolino's Importunity." *Speculum* 59 (1984): 549–555.

———. "*Paradiso* XXX." *Studi danteschi* 60 (1988): 1–33.

———. *Studies in Dante.* Ravenna: Longo, 1980.

———. "Tragedy in Dante's *Comedy.*" In *The Classical Tradition: Vergil,* edited by Craig Kallendorf, 253–269. New York: Garland, 1993.

———. "The Tragedy of Divination in *Inferno* XX." In *Studies in Dante,* 131–218.

———. "Typology and Secular Literature: Some Medieval Problems and Examples." In *Literary Uses of Typology from the Late Middle Ages to the Present,* edited by Earl Miner, 3–19. Princeton: Princeton University Press.

———. *Il Virgilio dantesco: tragedia nella* Commedia. Translated by Anna Maria Castellini and Margherita Frankel. Firenze: Olschki, 1983.

———. "*Vita Nuova:* Dante's Perceptions of Beatrice." *Dante Studies* 92 (1974): 1–18. Reprinted in *Studies in Dante,* 11–30.

Hollander, Robert, and Albert L. Rossi. "Dante's Republican Treasury." *Dante Studies* 104 (1986): 59–82.

The Holy Bible Translated from the Latin Vulgate. Douay Rheims version. Revised by Richard Challoner. 1899. Rockford, Ill.: TAN Books and Publishers, 1989.

Horgan, John. "Particle Metaphysics." *Scientific American* 270, no. 2 (February 1994): 96–99, 102–106.

Horne, James R. "Randall's Interpretation of the Aristotelian 'Active Intellect'." *Dialogue* 10, no. 2 (1971): 305–316.

Huby, Pamela. "Stages in the Development of Language about Aristotle's *Nous*." In *Aristotle and the Later Tradition*. Oxford Studies in Ancient Philosophy: Supplementary vol., edited by Henry Blumenthal and Howard Robinson, 129–143. Oxford: Oxford University Press, Clarendon, 1991.

Hugh of St. Cher. *[Opera omnia in universum Vetus et Novum Testamentum] Opus admirabile, omnibus concionatoribus ac s. theologiae professoribus pernecessarium.* . . .Lugduni: Sumptibus Societatis Bibliopolarum, 1645. 8 vols.

Hugh of St. Victor. "De numeris mysticis sacrae scripturae." Chapter 15 of *De scripturis et scriptoribus sacris*. In *PL*, vol. 175, 22–23.

———. *On the Sacraments of the Christian Faith (De sacramentis)*. Edited and translated by Roy J. Deferrari. Cambridge, Mass.: Medieval Academy of America, 1951.

Hutchinson, D. S. "Ethics." In *The Cambridge Companion to Aristotle*, edited by Jonathan Barnes, 195–232. Cambridge: Cambridge University Press, 1995.

Iannucci, Amilcare A. "Autoesegesi dantesca: la tecnica dell' 'episodio parallelo'." In *Forma ed evento nella* Divina Commedia, 83–114. Roma: Bulzoni, 1984.

———. "Casella's Song and the Turning of the Soul." *Thought* 65 (1990): 27–46.

———. "Forbidden Love: Metaphor and History (*Inferno* 5)." In *Dante: Contemporary Perspectives*, edited by Amilcare A. Iannucci, 94–112. Toronto: University of Toronto Press, 1997.

Ibn al-ʿArabī. *[al-Futūḥāt al-Makkīya] Les illuminations de la Mecque: textes choisis.* Translated into French or English under the direction of Michel Chodkiewicz. Paris: Sindbad, 1988.

Imbach, Ruedi. *Dante, la philosophie et les laïcs*. Fribourg: Editions Universitaires, 1996.

Inge, William Ralph. *The Philosophy of Plotinus*. The Gifford Lectures at St. Andrews, 1917–1918. 3d ed. London: Longmans, 1929. 2 vols.

Irwin, T. H. "Aristotle's Philosophy of Mind." In *Psychology*, edited by Stephen Everson, vol. 2, 56–83. Cambridge: Cambridge University Press, 1991.

Isidore of Seville. *De natura rerum liber*. Edited by Gustavus Becker. Amsterdam: Hakkert, 1967.

———. *Etymologiarum sive Originum libri XX*. Edited by W. M. Lindsay. Oxford: Oxford University Press, 1911. 2 vols.

———. *Étymologies: Livre XVII (De l'agriculture)*. Edited and translated by Jacques André. Paris: Les Belles Lettres, 1981.

———. *Liber numerorum qui in sanctis scripturis occurrunt*. In *PL*, vol. 83.

———. *Traité de la nature [De natura rerum]*. Edited by Jacques Fontaine. Bordeaux: Féret, 1960.

Jacoff, Rachel. "The Rape/Rapture of Europa: *Paradiso* 27." In *The Poetry of Allusion: Virgil and Ovid in Dante's* Commedia, edited by Rachel Jacoff and Jeffrey T. Schnapp, 233–246. Stanford, Calif.: Stanford University Press, 1991.

Jacomuzzi, Angelo. "La *Divina Commedia*: figura, allegoria, visione." *Rivista di storia e letteratura religiosa* 6, no. 1 (1970).

———. *L'imago al cerchio e altri studi sulla* Divina Commedia. 1968. Milano: Franco-Angeli, 1995.

Jacopo della Lana. Commedia *di Dante degli Allaghieri col Commento di Jacopo della*

Lana bolognese. Edited by Luciano Scarabelli. Bologna: Tipografia Regia, 1866–1867. In *DDP*.

Jaeger, Werner. *Aristotle: Fundamentals of the History of His Development*. 2d ed. Translated by Richard Robinson. London: Oxford University Press, 1948.

Jaki, Stanley L. *Genesis 1 through the Ages*. London: Thomas More Press, 1992.

Jallonghi, Ernesto. *Il misticismo bonaventuriano nella* Divina Commedia. Edited by Diomede Scaramuzzi. Città di Castello: Società Anonima Tipografica "Leonardo da Vinci," 1935.

Jeannot, Thomas M. "Plato and Aristotle on Being and Unity." *New Scholasticism* 60, no. 4 (Autumn 1986): 404–426.

Jeauneau, Edouard. *Lectio Philosophorum: recherches sur l'École de Chartres*. Amsterdam: Hakkert, 1973.

John of Garland. *Integumenta Ovidii: poemetto inedito del secolo XIII*. Edited by Fausto Ghisalberti. *Testi e documenti inediti o rari*, vol. 2. Messina: Giuseppe Principato, 1933.

Johnson, Mark F. "Did St. Thomas Attribute a Doctrine of Creation to Aristotle?" *New Scholasticism* 63 (1989): 129–155.

Jordan, Mark D. *The Alleged Aristotelianism of Thomas Aquinas*. Étienne Gilson Series, vol. 15. Toronto: Pontifical Institute of Mediaeval Studies, 1992.

————. "The Competition of Authoritative Languages and Aquinas's Theological Rhetoric." *Medieval Philosophy and Theology* 4 (1994): 71–90.

————. *Ordering Wisdom*. Notre Dame, Ind.: University of Notre Dame Press, 1986.

————. "Theology and Philosophy." In *The Cambridge Companion to Aquinas*, edited by Norman Kretzmann and Eleonore Stump, 232–251. Cambridge: Cambridge University Press, 1993.

Juvenal. *The Satires*. Edited by John Ferguson. London: Bristol Classical Press, 1999.

Kabir. *Songs of Kabir*. Translated by Rabindranath Tagore. 1915. York Beach, Me.: Samuel Weiser, 1988.

Kafatos, Menas, and Robert Nadeau. *The Conscious Universe: Part and Whole in Modern Physical Theory*. New York: Springer, 1990.

Kahn, Charles H. "Aristotle and Altruism." *Mind* 90, no. 357 (January 1981): 20–40.

————. "Aristotle on Thinking." In *Essays on Aristotle's* De anima, edited by Martha C. Nussbaum and Amélie Oksenberg Rorty, 359–379. Oxford: Oxford University Press, Clarendon, 1992.

————. "The Place of the Prime Mover in Aristotle's Teleology." In *Aristotle on Nature and Living Things*, edited by Allan Gotthelf, 183–205. Pittsburgh: Mathesis; Bristol: Bristol Classical Press, 1985.

————. "Sensation and Consciousness in Aristotle's Psychology." *Archiv für Geschichte der Philosophie* 48 (1966): 43–81.

————. "Why Existence Does Not Emerge as a Distinct Concept in Greek Philosophy." *Archiv für Geschichte der Philosophie* 58, no. 4 (1976): 323–334.

Kantorowicz, Ernst H. *The King's Two Bodies: A Study in Mediaeval Political Theology*. Princeton: Princeton University Press, 1997.

Kay, Richard. "Dante's Empyrean and the Eye of God." *Speculum* 78, no. 1 (January 2003): 37–65.

Kenney, John Peter. "Mysticism and Contemplation in the *Enneads*." *American Catholic Philosophical Quarterly* 71, no. 3 (Summer 1997): 315–337.

Kenny, Anthony. *Aquinas on Mind*. London: Routledge, 1993.

Kerr, John. "*Proserpinan Memory in Dante and Chaucer*." Ph.D. diss., University of Notre Dame, 2000.

King, Hugh R. "Aristotle without *Prima Materia*." *Jounal of the History of Ideas* 17, no. 3 (June 1956): 370–389.

Kleiner, John. "The Eclipses in the *Paradiso*." *Stanford Italian Review* 9, no. 1–2 (1990): 5–32.

———. *Mismapping the Underworld: Daring and Error in Dante's* Comedy. Stanford: Stanford University Press, 1994.

Kleinhenz, Christopher. "The Celebration of Poetry: A Reading of *Purgatorio* XXII." *Dante Studies* 106 (1988): 21–41.

———. "Dante and the Bible: Biblical Citation in the *Divine Comedy*." In *Dante: Contemporary Perspectives*, edited by Amilcare A. Iannucci, 74–93. Toronto: University of Toronto Press, 1997.

———. "The Poetics of Citation: Dante's *Divina Commedia* and the Bible." In *Italiana 1988*, edited by Albert N. Mancini, Paolo A. Giordano, and Anthony J. Tamburri, 1–21. River Forest, Ill.: Rosary College, 1990.

Klibansky, Raymond. *The Continuity of the Platonic Tradition in the Middle Ages*. 1939. Milwood, N.Y.: Kraus International, 1982.

Knowles, David. *The Evolution of Medieval Thought*. 2d ed. Edited by D. E. Luscombe and C.N.L. Brooke. London: Longman, 1988.

Kosman, L. Aryeh. "Divine Being and Divine Thinking in *Metaphysics* Lambda." *Proceedings of the Boston Area Colloquium in Ancient Philosophy* 3 (1987): 165–201.

———. "Perceiving That We Perceive: *On the Soul* III, 2." *Philosophical Review* 84 (1975): 499–519.

———. "What Does the Maker Mind Make?" In *Essays on Aristotle's* De anima, edited by Martha C. Nussbaum and Amélie Oksenberg Rorty, 343–358. Oxford: Oxford University Press, Clarendon, 1992.

Kretzmann, Norman. *The Metaphysics of Creation: Aquinas's Natural Theology in* Summa contra gentiles *II*. Oxford: Oxford University Press, Clarendon Press, 1999.

———. "Philosophy of Mind." In *The Cambridge Companion to Aquinas*, edited by Norman Kretzmann and Eleonore Stump, 128–159. Cambridge: Cambridge University Press, 1993.

Kretzmann, Norman, Anthony Kenny, and Jan Pinborg, eds. *The Cambridge History of Later Medieval Philosophy*. Cambridge: Cambridge University Press, 1982.

Kuksewicz, Zdzislaw. "Criticisms of Aristotelian Psychology and the Augustinian-Aristotelian Synthesis." In *The Cambridge History of Later Medieval Philosophy*, edited by Norman Kretzmann, Anthony Kenny, and Jan Pinborg, 623–628. Cambridge: Cambridge University Press, 1982.

———. "The Potential and the Agent Intellect." In *The Cambridge History of Later Medieval Philosophy*, edited by Norman Kretzmann, Anthony Kenny, and Jan Pinborg, 595–601. Cambridge: Cambridge University Press, 1982.

Kwasniewski, Peter A. "St. Thomas, *Extasis*, and Union with the Beloved." *Thomist* 61, no. 4 (October 1997): 587–603.

Labeaga, José Antonio Izquierdo. *La vita intellettiva: lectio sancti Thomae Aquinatis*. Studi tomistici, vol. 55. Città del Vaticano: Libreria Editrice Vaticana, 1994.

Lacey, Alan Robert. "Materialism." In *The Oxford Companion to Philosophy*, edited by Ted Honderich, 530–532. Oxford: Oxford University Press, 1995.

———. "*Ousia* and Form in Aristotle." *Phronesis* 10, no. 1 (1965): 54–69.

Lanapoppi, Aleramo P. "La *Divina Commedia*: allegoria 'dei poeti' o allegoria 'dei teologi?' " *Dante Studies* 86 (1968): 17–39.

Landino, Cristoforo. *Comento sopra la* Comedia. 1481. Edited by Paolo Procaccioli. Roma: Salerno, 2001.

Lang, Helen S. "Aristotle's Immaterial Mover and the Problem of Location in *Physics* VIII." *Review of Metaphysics* 35, no. 2 (December 1981): 321–335.

———. "God or Soul: The Problem of the First Mover in *Physics* VII." *Paideia* 7 (1978): 86–104.

Lanza, Adriano. *Dante e la Gnosi: esoterismo del* Convivio. Roma: Edizioni Mediterranee, 1990.

Lapide, Cornelius à. *Commentaria in Sacram Scripturam.* 10 vols. Edited by Sisto Riario Sforza. Naples: I. Nagar, 1854–1859.

Latini, Brunetto. *The Book of the Treasure (Li livres dou tresor).* Translated by Paul Barrette and Spurgeon Baldwin. New York: Garland, 1993.

———. *Li livres dou tresor de Brunetto Latini.* Edited by Francis J. Carmody. Berkeley: University of California Press, 1947.

———. *Il tesoretto.* In *Poeti del Duecento,* edited by Gianfranco Contini, vol. 2, tome 1, 175–284. 1960. Milano: Ricciardi, 1995.

Le Goff, Jacques. *The Birth of Purgatory.* Translated by Arthur Goldhammer. Chicago: University of Chicago Press, 1984.

Leaman, Oliver. *Averroes and His Philosophy.* Oxford: Oxford University Press, 1988.

Lear, Jonathan. "Active Episteme." In *Mathematics and Metaphysics in Aristotle,* edited by Andreas Graeser, 149–174. Bern: Paul Haupt, 1987.

Lee, Patrick. "St. Thomas and Avicenna on the Agent Intellect." *Thomist* 45, no. 1 (January 1981): 41–61.

Leiva-Merikakis, Erasmo. "Fides quaerens experientiam: The Flesh of Dante's Belief." *Faith and Reason* 6 (1980): 203–219.

Leo, Ulrich. "Il Canto XXVII del *Purgatorio.*" In *Letture dantesche,* edited by Giovanni Getto, 1215–1233. Firenze: Sansoni, 1964.

———. "The Unfinished *Convivio* and Dante's Rereading of the *Aeneid.*" *Medieval Studies* 13 (1951): 41–64.

Leonardi, Lino. "Cavalcanti, Dante e il nuovo stile." In *Dante: da Firenze all'aldilà; atti del terzo seminario dantesco internazionale,* ed. Michelangelo Picone, 331–354. Firenze: Cesati, 2001.

Lesher, James H. "Aristotle on Form, Substance, and Universals: A Dilemma." *Phronesis* 16, no. 2 (1971): 169–178.

Leszl, Walter. "Knowledge of the Universal and Knowledge of the Particular in Aristotle." *Review of Metaphysics* 26, no. 2 (December 1972): 278–313.

"Le *Liber de causis.*" Edited by Adriaan Pattin, O.M.I. *Tijdschrift voor Filosofie* 28 (1966): 90–203.

"*Liber Scalae Machometi*: die lateinische Fassung des Kitab al mi'radj." Edited by Edeltraud Werner. Düsseldorf: Droste, 1986.

Liber Scalae Machometi. In *Il Libro della scala e la questione delle fonti arabo-spagnole della* Divina Commedia. Edited by Enrico Cerulli. Studi e Testi, no. 150. Città del Vaticano: Biblioteca Apostolica Vaticana, 1949.

Il libro della scala di Maometto. Translated by Roberto Rossi Testa. Milano: Studio Editoriale, 1991.

Lieberknecht, Otfried. *Allegorese und Philologie: Überlegungen zum Problem des Mehrfachen Schriftsinns in Dantes* Commedia. Stuttgart: Franz Steiner Verlag, 1999.

Limentani, Uberto. "Lectura Dantis: *Paradiso* XXVII." In *Moving in Measure: Essays in Honour of Brian Moloney,* edited by Judith Bryce and Doug Thompson, 31–48. Hull, England: Hull University Press, 1989.

Lindberg, David C. "The Genesis of Kepler's Theory of Light: Light Metaphysics from Plotinus to Kepler." *Osiris*, n.s., 2 (1986): 5–43.

———. *Theories of Vision from al-Kindi to Kepler.* Chicago: University of Chicago Press, 1976.

Litt, Thomas. *Les corps célestes dans l'univers de Saint Thomas d'Aquin.* Louvain: Publications Universitaires, 1963.

Little, Arthur. *The Platonic Heritage of Thomism.* Dublin: Golden Eagles Books, 1950.

Lloyd, A. C. *Form and Universal in Aristotle.* ARCA Classical and Medieval Texts, Papers and Monographs, vol. 4. Liverpool: Francis Cairns, 1981.

———. "Non-Discursive Thought: An Enigma of Greek Philosophy." *Proceedings of the Aristotelian Society*, n.s., 70 (1969–1970): 261–274.

———. "Nosce Teipsum and Conscientia." *Archiv für Geschichte der Philosophie* 46 (1964): 188–200.

Lloyd, G. E. R. *Aristotle: The Growth and Structure of His Thought.* Cambridge: Cambridge University Press, 1968.

Lobkowicz, Nicholas. "What Happened to Thomism? From *Aeterni Patris* to *Vaticanum Secundum*." *American Catholic Philosophical Quarterly* 69, no. 3 (Summer 1995): 397–423.

Logan, J. L. "The Poet's Central Numbers." *MLN* 86 (1971): 95–98.

Lombardi, Bonaventura. *La Divina Commedia di Dante Alighieri, col Comento del p. Bonaventura Lombardi, M.C. 1791.* Prato: D. Passigli, 1852.

Long, Jeffery D. "The Unknown Christ: An Assessment of Raimundo Panikkar's Model for Inter-Religious Dialogue." *Humanitas: A Journal of the College of Arts and Letters. University of Notre Dame* 6, no. 1 (Spring 1991): 35–46.

Lorch, Maristella, and Lavinia Lorch. "Metaphor and Metamorphosis: *Purgatorio* 27 and *Metamorphoses* 4." In *Dante and Ovid: Essays in Intertextuality*, edited by Madison U. Sowell, 99–121. Binghamton, N.Y.: MRTS, 1991.

Lovejoy, Arthur O. *The Great Chain of Being: A Study of the History of an Idea.* The William James Lectures, Harvard University, 1933, 1936. Cambridge, Mass.: Harvard University Press, 1964.

Lowe, Malcolm F. "Aristotle on Kinds of Thinking." *Phronesis* 28, no. 1 (1983): 17–30.

Loy, David. *Nonduality: A Study in Comparative Philosophy.* New Haven: Yale University Press, 1988.

Lubac, Henri de. *The Four Senses of Scripture.* Vol. 1 of *Medieval Exegesis.* Translated by Marc Sebanc. 1959. Grand Rapids: Eerdmans, 1998.

Lucan. *The Civil War [Pharsalia].* Translated by J. D. Duff. 1928. Loeb Classical Library, vol. 220. Cambridge, Mass.: Harvard University Press, 1988.

Macrobius. *Commentary on the* Dream of Scipio. Translated by William Harris Stahl. 1952. New York: Columbia University Press, 1990.

Madec, Goulven. "Le néoplatonisme dans la conversion d'Augustin: état d'une question centennaire (depuis Harnack et Boissier, 1888)." In *Internationales Symposium über den Stand der Augustinus-Forschung.* Vol. 39.1 of *Res et Signa (Cassiciacum)*, edited by C. Mayer and K. H. Chelius, 9–25. Würzburg: Geissener Augustinus-Studien, 1989.

———. " 'Platonisme' des Pères." In *Catholicisme: hier, aujourd'hui, demain*, edited by G. Jacquemet, vol. 11 (1986), 491–507. 15 vols. Paris: Letouzey et Ané, 1947–2000.

Mahoney, Edward P. "Sense, Intellect, and Imagination in Albert, Thomas, and Siger." In *The Cambridge History of Later Medieval Philosophy*, edited by Norman Kretzmann, Anthony Kenny, and Jan Pinborg, 602–622. Cambridge: Cambridge University Press, 1982.

Maierù, Alfonso. "Atto." In *ED*, 1:442–445.

———. "Forma." In *ED*, 2:969–974.

Mandonnet, Pierre. *Dante le théologien: introduction a l'intelligence de la vie, des oeuvres et de l'art de Dante Alighieri.* Paris: Desclée de Brouwer, 1935.

Manegold de Lautenbach. *Exegesis de Psalmorum Libro.* PL, vol. 93, 903–904.

Manning, Rita. "Materialism, Dualism and Functionalism in Aristotle's Philosophy of Mind." *Apeiron* 19, no. 1 (1985): 11–23.

Mansion, Augustin. "L'immortalité de l'âme et de l'intellect d'après Aristote." *Revue philosophique de Louvain* 51 (1953): 444–72.

———. "La théorie aristotélicienne du temps chez les péripatéticiens médiévaux." *Revue néoscolastique de philosophie,* 2d ser., 36, no. 41 (February 1934): 275–307.

Mansion, Suzanne. "The Ontological Composition of Sensible Substances in Aristotle (*Metaphysics* VII,7–9)." In *Articles on Aristotle,* vol. 3, *Metaphysics,* edited by Jonathan Barnes, Malcolm Schofield, and Richard Sorabji, 80–87. New York: St. Martin's Press, 1979.

Marchesi, Simone. "Dante's 'Active' Hermeneutics in *Purgatorio* XXII: Virgil and Statius as Readers of Poetry." Forthcoming article.

———. "The Reasons of Epic: Virgil's Dido between History and Poetry." Unpublished paper, University of Notre Dame, 1997.

Marenbon, John. "Dante's Averroism." In *Poetry and Philosophy in the Middle Ages: A Festschrift for Peter Dronke,* edited by John Marenobon, 349–374. Leiden: Brill, 2001.

———. *Early Medieval Philosophy (480–1150): An Introduction.* Rev. ed. London: Routledge, 1988.

Maritain, Jacques. *St. Thomas Aquinas.* Translated by Joseph W. Evans and Peter O'Reilly. 1930. Cleveland: World, Meridian, 1958.

Martianus Capella. *The Marriage of Philology and Mercury.* Vol. 2 of *Martianus Capella and the Seven Liberal Arts.* Translated by William Harris Stahl and Richard Johnson. New York: Columbia University Press, 1977.

———. *Martianus Capella.* Edited by James Willis. Leipzig: Teubner, 1983.

Martin, C. F. J. *An Introduction to Medieval Philosophy.* Edinburgh: Edinburgh University Press, 1996.

———. *Thomas Aquinas: God and Explanations.* Edinburgh: Edinburgh University Press, 1997.

Martin, James T. H. "Aquinas as a Commentator on *De anima* 3.5." *Thomist* 57, no. 4 (October 1993): 621–640.

Martinelli, Bortolo. "La dottrina dell'Empireo nell'*Epistola a Cangrande* (capp. 24–27)." *Studi danteschi* 57 (1985): 49–143.

———. " 'Esse' ed 'essentia' nell'*Epistola a Cangrande* (capp. 20–23)." *Critica letteraria* 12, no. 4 (1984): 627–672.

Martinez, Ronald L. "The Pilgrim's Answer to Bonagiunta and the Poetics of the Spirit." *Stanford Italian Review* 3 (1983): 37–63.

———. "La 'sacra fame dell'oro' (*Purgatorio* 22, 41) tra Virgilio e Stazio: dal testo all'interpretazione." *Letture classensi* 18 (1989): 177–193.

Masciandaro, Franco. *La problematica del tempo nella* Commedia. Ravenna: Longo, 1976.

Mastrobuono, Antonio C. *Dante's Journey of Sanctification.* Washington, D.C.: Regnery Gateway, 1990.

Mattalia, Daniele. *La* Divina Commedia *a cura di Daniele Mattalia.* Milano: A. Rizzoli, 1975.

Matthen, Mohan. "Individual Substances as Hylomorphic Complexes." In *Aristotle Today: Essays on Aristotle's Ideal of Science*, edited by Mohan Matthen, 151–176. Edmonton, Alberta: Academic Printing, 1987.

Maudlin, Tim. "Substances and Space-Time: What Aristotle Would Have Said to Einstein." In *Biologie, logique et métaphysique chez Aristote*, edited by Daniel Devereux and Pierre Pellegrin, 429–470. Paris: Éditions du Centre National de la Recherche Scientifique, 1990.

Maurach, Gregor. *Coelum empyreum: Versuch einer Begriffsgeschichte*. Wiesbaden: Franz Steiner Verlag, 1968.

Mazzeo, Joseph Anthony. "The Analogy of Creation in Dante." *Speculum* 32 (1957): 706–721.

———. "Light Metaphysics, Dante's *Convivio*, and the Letter to Can Grande Della Scala." *Traditio* 14 (1958): 191–229.

———. *Medieval Cultural Tradition in Dante's* Comedy. 1960. Westport, Conn.: Greenwood Press, 1968.

———. "Medieval Hermeneutics: Dante's Poetics and Historicity." *Religion and Literature* 17, no. 1 (1985): 1–24.

———. *Structure and Thought in the* Paradiso. Ithaca, N.Y.: Cornell University Press, 1958.

Mazzotta, Giuseppe. *Dante, Poet of the Desert: History and Allegory in the* Divine Comedy. Princeton: Princeton University Press, 1979.

———. "Dante's Literary Typology." *MLN* 87 (1972): 1–19.

———. *Dante's Vision and the Circle of Knowledge*. Princeton: Princeton University Press, 1993.

———. "Why Did Dante Write the *Comedy*? Why and How Do We Read It? The Poet and the Critics." In *Dante Now: Current Trends in Dantes Studies*, edited by Theodore J. Cachey, Jr., 63–79. Notre Dame, Ind.: University of Notre Dame Press, 1995.

McDannell, Colleen, and Bernhard Lang. *Heaven: A History*. New Haven: Yale University Press, 1988.

McEvoy, James J. "The Metaphysics of Light in the Middle Ages." *Philosophical Studies* 26 (1978): 126–145.

———. "Ein Paradigma der Lichtmetaphysik: Robert Grosseteste." In *Robert Grosseteste, Exegete and Philosopher*, 91–110. Brookfield, Vt.: Ashgate, Variorum, 1994.

———. "Neoplatonism and Christianity: Influence, Syncretism or Discernment?" In *The Relationship between Neoplatonism and Christianity*, edited by Thomas Finan and Vincent Twomey, 155–170. Dublin: Four Courts Press, 1992.

———. "The Sun as *Res* and *Signum*: Grosseteste's Commentary on *Ecclesiasticus* Ch. 43, Vv.1–5." *Recherches de théologie ancienne et médiévale* 41 (1974): 38–91.

McGinn, Bernard. "Ascension and Introversion in the *Itinerarium mentis in Deum*." In *San Bonaventura: 1274–1974*, vol. 3, 535–552. 5 vols. Grottaferrata: Collegio San Bonaventura, 1974.

———. "Do Christian Platonists Really Believe in Creation?" In *God and Creation: An Ecumenical Symposium*, edited by David B. Burrell, C.S.C., and Bernard McGinn, 197–219. Notre Dame, Ind.: University of Notre Dame Press, 1990.

———. "Eckhart's Condemnation Reconsidered." *Thomist* 44, no. 3 (July 1980): 390–414.

———. *The Flowering of Mysticism: Men and Women in the New Mysticism, 1200–1350*. In *The Presence of God: A History of Western Christian Mysticism*. New York: Crossroad, 1998.

_____. *The Foundations of Mysticism: Origins to the Fifth Century*. In *The Presence of God: A History of Western Christian Mysticism*. New York: Crossroad, 1991.

_____. *The Growth of Mysticism: Gregory the Great through the Twelfth Century*. In *The Presence of God: A History of Western Christian Mysticism*. New York: Crossroad, 1996.

_____. "Love, Knowledge and *Unio Mystica* in the Western Christian Tradition." In *Mystical Union and Monotheistic Faith: An Ecumenical Dialogue*, edited by Moshe Idel and Bernard McGinn, 59–86. New York: Macmillan, 1989.

_____. "Theological Summary." In *Meister Eckhart: The Essential Sermons, Commentaries, Treatises, and Defense*, translated by Edmund Colledge and Bernard McGinn, 24–61. New York: Paulist Press, 1981.

McKeon, Charles King. *A Study of the* Summa philosophiae *of the Pseudo-Grosseteste*. New York: Columbia University Press, 1948.

McMullin, Ernan, ed. *The Concept of Matter*. Notre Dame, Ind.: University of Notre Dame Press, 1963.

Meersseman, Gilles G. "Dante come teologo." In *Atti del congresso internazionale di studi danteschi, Firenze, 20–27 aprile 1965*, 177–195. Firenze: Sansoni, 1965.

Mellone, Attilio P. "Il canto XXIX del *Paradiso*." *Nuove letture dantesche [Casa di Dante in Roma]*, vol. 7, 193–214. 8 vols. Firenze: Le Monnier, 1968–1976.

_____. "Il concorso delle creature nella produzione delle cose secondo Dante." *Divus Thomas (Piacenza)* 56 (1953): 273–286.

_____. "Creazione." In *ED*, 2:251–253.

_____. "Emanatismo neoplatonico di Dante per le citazioni del *Liber de causis?*" *Divus Thomas (Piacenza)* 54 (1951): 205–212.

_____. "Empireo." In *ED*, 2:668–671.

_____. "L'esemplarismo divino secondo Dante." *Divinitas* 9 (1965): 215–243.

_____. "Gerarchia angelica." In *ED*, 3:122–124.

_____. *La dottrina di Dante Alighieri sulla prima creazione*. Nocera (Salerno): Convento S. Maria degli Angeli, 1950.

_____. "Il primo mobile." In *Lectura Dantis Modenese: Paradiso*, 231–249. Modena: Comitato Provinciale Dante Alighieri, 1986.

Mellone, Attilio, Antonietta Bufano, and Fernando Salsano. "Luce." In *ED*, 3:706–732.

Mellone, Attilio, Fernando Salsano, and Pier Vincenzo Mengaldo. "Angelo." In *ED*, 1:268–272.

Mensch, James R. "Aristotle and the Overcoming of the Subject-Object Dichotomy." *American Catholic Philosophical Quarterly* 65, no. 4 (Autumn 1991): 465–482.

Merlan, Philip. *From Platonism to Neoplatonism*. 2d ed. The Hague: Martinus Nijhoff, 1960.

_____. *Monopsychism Mysticism Metaconsciousness: Problems of the Soul in the Neoaristotelian and Neoplatonic Tradition*. 2d ed. The Hague: Martinus Nijhoff, 1969.

Michael Scot. *The Commentary Attributed to Michael Scot*. In *The Sphere of Sacrobosco and Its Commentators*. Edited and translated by Lynn Thorndike, 248–342. Chicago: University of Chicago Press, 1949.

Migliorini Fissi, Rosetta. "La nozione di *deificatio* nel *Paradiso*." *Letture classensi* 9–10 (1982): 39–72.

Miller, Fred D. "Aristotle's Use of Matter." *Paideia* 7 (1978): 105–119.

Miller, James. "Three Mirrors of Dante's *Paradiso*." *University of Toronto Quarterly* 46, no. 3 (Spring 1977): 261–279.

Mineo, Nicolò. "Per l'interpretazione del canto XXIX del *Paradiso*." In *Saggi danteschi*, vol. 2 of *Bibliologia e critica dantesca: saggi dedicati a Enzo Esposito*, edited by Vincenzo De Gregorio. 2 vols. Ravenna: Longo, 1997.

_____. *Profetismo e apocalittica in Dante*. Catania: Università di Catania, 1968.

Minnis, A. J. *Medieval Theory of Authorship: Scholastic Literary Attitudes in the Later Middle Ages*. 2d ed. Philadelphia: University of Pennsylvania Press, 1988.

Minnis, A. J., and A. B. Scott, eds. *Medieval Literary Theory and Criticism, c.1100–c.1375: The Commentary-Tradition*. Rev. ed. Oxford: Oxford University Press, Clarendon, 1988.

Modrak, Deborah K. W. "An Aristotelian Theory of Consciousness." *Ancient Philosophy* 1, no. 2 (Spring 1981): 160–170.

_____. *Aristotle: The Power of Perception*. Chicago: University of Chicago Press, 1987.

_____. "The *Nous*-Body Problem in Aristotle." *Review of Metaphysics* 44, no. 4 (June 1991): 755–774.

Moevs, Christian. "God's Feet and Hands (*Paradiso* 4.40–48): Non-Duality and Non-False Errors." *MLN* 114 (1999): 1–13.

_____. "Is Dante Telling the Truth?" *Lectura Dantis* 18–19 (Spring–Fall 1996): 3–11.

_____. "The Metaphysical Basis of Dante's Politics." Forthcoming in *Dante's Cultures: Acts of the Fourth International Dante Seminar, September 26–27, 2003*.

_____. "The *Primo Mobile* as a Pot of Time: *Paradiso* 27.115–120." *Romance Notes* 40, no. 3 (2000): 247–257.

_____. "Pyramus at the Mulberry Tree: De-Petrifying Dante's Tinted Mind." In *Imagining Heaven in the Middle Ages: A Book of Essays*, edited by Jan Swango Emerson and Hugh Feiss, O.S.B, 211–244. New York: Garland, 2000.

Mojsisch, Burkhard. " 'Dieses Ich': Meister Eckhart's Ich-Konzeption." In *Sein—Reflexion—Freiheit: Aspekte der Philosophie Johannn Gottlieb Fichtes*, edited by Christoph Asmuth, 239–252. Amsterdam: B. R. Grüner, 1997.

Momigliano, Attilio, ed. *La Divina Commedia commentata da Attilio Momigliano*. 3 vols. 1946–1951. Firenze: Sansoni, 1980.

Monk, Ray. *Ludwig Wittgenstein: The Duty of Genius*. New York: Penguin Books, 1990.

Mook, Delo E., and Thomas Vargish. *Inside Relativity*. Princeton: Princeton University Press, 1987.

Moore, Edward. "Dante and St. Augustine." In *Studies in Dante*, first series, 291–294. 1896. New York: Haskell House, 1968.

_____. "Dante's Theory of Creation." In *Studies in Dante*, fourth series, 134–165. 1917. New York: Haskell House, 1968.

_____. "The Reproaches of Beatrice." In *Studies in Dante*, third series, 221–252. 1903. New York: Haskell House, 1968.

Moran, Dermot. *The Philosophy of John Scottus Eriugena: A Study of Idealism in the Middle Ages*. Cambridge: Cambridge University Press, 1989.

Moraux, Paul. "La méthode d'Aristote dans l'étude du ciel: *De Caelo* I.1–II.12." In *Aristote et les problèmes de méthode*, 173–194. Louvain: Publications Universitaires, 1961.

Moreau, Joseph. *L'espace et le temps selon Aristote*. Padova: Antenore, 1965.

Moretti, P. "La filosofia di Dante: i concetti metafisici di atto e potenza." *Il VI centenario dantesco* 1 (1914): 81–82.

_____. "La filosofia di Dante: le creature eterne e il senso di un emistichio dantesco nel canto III dell'*Inferno*." *Il VI centenario dantesco* 1 (1914): 52a–54b.

_____. "La filosofia di Dante studiata con Dante." *Il VI centenario dantesco* 6 (1919): 111a–120b.

Morgan, Alison. *Dante and the Medieval Otherworld.* Cambridge: Cambridge University Press, 1990.

Morrison, Alfred J. "Old French Parallels to *Inf.* V. 127–138." *Modern Language Notes* 18, no. 3 (March 1903): 94–95.

Morrison, Donald. "The Evidence for Degrees of Being in Aristotle." *Classical Quarterly,* n.s., 37, no. 2 (1987): 382–401.

Morrison, Molly Georgette. "Dante and Dionysius: The Articulation of the Heavenly Vision of Canto 28 of the *Paradiso.*" *Cincinnati Romance Review* 17 (1998): 86–92.

————. "Hierarchies at a Crossroads: Dante's Angels, Popes and the Cosmic Nexus of Divine and Earthly Truth in Canto 28 of the *Paradiso.*" Ph.D. diss., Indiana University, 1996.

Mugnai, Paolo. "Mobile." In *ED,* 3:979–980.

Muresu, Gabriele. "Dante tra ragione e intelletto (*Par.* II)." *La rassegna della letteratura italiana* 91 (1987): 5–23.

Murphet, Howard. *Sai Baba, Man of Miracles.* York Beach, Me.: Samuel Weiser, 1973.

Musa, Mark. "The 'Sweet New Style' That I Hear." In *Advent at the Gates: Dante's Comedy,* 111–128. Bloomington: Indiana University Press, 1974.

Nardi, Bruno. "Gli 'angeli che non furon ribelli né fur fedeli a Dio' (*Inferno,* III)." 1959. In *"Lecturae" e altri studi danteschi,* 57–70.

————. "L'arco della vita (nota illustrativa al *Convivio*)." In *Saggi di filosofia dantesca,* 110–138.

————. "L'averroismo del 'primo amico' di Dante." In *Dante e la cultura medievale,* 81–108.

————. "La caduta di Lucifero e l'autenticità della 'Questio de aqua et terra'." In *"Lecturae" e altri studi danteschi,* 227–265.

————. "Il canto XXIX del 'Paradiso.'" 1956. In *"Lecturae" e altri studi danteschi,* 193–201.

————. "Le citazioni dantesche del 'Liber de causis'." In *Saggi di filosofia dantesca,* 81–109.

————. "Il concetto dell'Impero nello svolgimento del pensiero dantesco." In *Saggi di filosofia dantesca,* 215–275.

————. "La conoscenza umana." In *Dante e la cultura medievale,* 135–172.

————. *Dal* Convivio *alla* Commedia *(sei saggi danteschi).* 1960. Roma: Istituto Storico Italiano per il Medio Evo, 1992.

————. "Dante e Alpetragio." In *Saggi di filosofia dantesca,* 139–166.

————. *Dante e la cultura medievale.* 2d ed. Edited by Paolo Mazzantini. 1942. Roma: Editori Laterza, 1990.

————. "Dante e la filosofia." In *Nel mondo di Dante,* 209–245.

————. "Dante e Pietro d'Abano." In *Saggi di filosofia dantesca,* 40–63.

————. "Dante profeta." In *Dante e la cultura medievale,* 265–326.

————. " 'Lo discorrer di Dio sovra quest'acque.' " In *Nel mondo di Dante,* 305–314.

————. "La dottrina delle macchie lunari nel secondo canto del *Paradiso.*" In *Saggi di filosofia dantesca,* 3–39.

————. "La dottrina dell'Empireo nella sua genesi storica e nel pensiero dantesco." In *Saggi di filosofia dantesca,* 167–215.

————. "La filosofia di Dante." In *Grande antologia filosofica,* edited by Umberto Antonio Padovani, vol. 4, 1149–1253. 35 vols. Milano: Marzorati, 1954–1985.

————. "Filosofia e teologia ai tempi di Dante in rapporto al pensiero del poeta." In *Saggi e note di critica dantesca,* 3–109. Milano: Ricciardi, 1966.

_____. "L'immortalità dell'anima." In *Dante e la cultura medievale*, 225–243.

_____. "Intorno al tomismo di Dante e alla quistione di Sigieri." *Giornale dantesco* 22 (1914): 182–197.

_____. "Introduzione." In *Trattato sull'unità dell'intelletto contro gli averroisti*, by Thomas Aquinas, 7–89. Firenze: G. C. Sansoni, 1947.

_____. "*Lecturae*" e altri studi danteschi. Edited by Rudy Abardo. 1959. Firenze: Le Lettere, 1990.

_____. "Meditantur sua stercora scarabei." *Il nuovo giornale dantesco* 4 (1920): 56–62.

_____. *Nel mondo di Dante*. Roma: Edizioni di "Storia e Letteratura," 1944.

_____. "Note al 'Convivio'." In *Nel mondo di Dante*, 41–90.

_____. "Noterelle polemiche di filosofia dantesca." *Il nuovo giornale dantesco* 1 (1917): 123–136.

_____. "Perché 'dietro la memoria non può ire' (*Paradiso*, I, 9)." In "*Lecturae*" e altri studi danteschi, 267–276.

_____. "Pretese fonti della *Divina Commedia*." In *Dal* Convivio *alla* Commedia, 351–370.

_____. "Il punto sull' *Epistola a Cangrande*." In "*Lecturae*" e altri studi danteschi, 205–225.

_____. "Rassegna bibliografica." Review of Busnelli, *Cosmogonia e antropogenesi*. *Giornale storico della letteratura italiana* 81 (1923): 307–334.

_____. *Saggi di filosofia dantesca*. 2d ed. Firenze: La Nuova Italia, 1967.

_____. " 'Se la prima materia de li elementi era da Dio intesa'." In *Dante e la cultura medievale*, 197–206.

_____. *Sigieri di Brabante nella* Divina Commedia *e le fonti della filosofia di Dante*. Spianate (Pescia): Presso l'autore, 1912.

_____. *Soggetto e oggetto del conoscere nella filosofia antica e medievale*. 2d ed. Roma: Edizioni dell'Ateneo, 1952.

_____. "Sull'origine dell'anima umana." In *Dante e la cultura medievale*, 207–224.

_____. "Il tomismo di Dante e il P. Busnelli S. J." In *Saggi di filosofia dantesca*, 341–380.

_____. "Il tomismo di Dante secondo Emilio Brodero." Appendix in *Nel mondo di Dante*, 368–376.

_____. "Il tomismo di Dante secondo Francesco Orestano." Appendix in *Nel mondo di Dante*, 353–368.

_____. "La tragedia di Ulisse." In *Dante e la cultura medievale*, 153–165.

_____. "Tre pretese fasi del pensiero politico di Dante." In *Saggi di filosofia dantesca*, 276–310.

_____. " 'Tutto il frutto ricolto del girar di queste spere'." In *Dante e la cultura medievale*, 245–264.

Nash, Ronald H. "Some Philosophic Sources of Augustine's Illumination Theory." *Augustinian Studies* 2 (1971): 47–66.

Nasr, Seyyed Hossein. "God Is Reality: Metaphysical Knowledge and Spiritual Realization." In *Ultimate Reality and Spiritual Discipline*, edited by James Duerlinger, 155–166. New York: Paragon House, New Era, 1984.

_____. *Knowledge and the Sacred*. New York: Crossroad, 1981.

Negri, Luigi. "La luce nella filosofia naturale del '300 e nella *Commedia*." *Giornale storico della letteratura italiana* 82 (1923): 325–336.

Niccoli, Alessandro. "Vermiglio." In *ED*, 5:966.

Nicholas of Lyra. *Postilla*. In *Biblia sacra, cum Glossa Ordinaria, primum quidem a*

Strabo Fuldensi collecta . . . annotatis etiam iis quae confuse antea citabantur locis. 7 vols. With the *Postilla* of Nicholas of Lyra. Lugduni, 1589.

Nichols, Terence L. "Aquinas's Concept of Substantial Form and Modern Science." *International Philosophical Quarterly* 36, no. 3 (September 1996): 303–318.

Nisargadatta Maharaj. *I Am That: Talks with Sri Nisargadatta Maharaj.* Edited by Sudhakar S. Dikshit. Translated by Maurice Frydman. 1973. Durham, N.C.: Acorn Press, 1982.

Noakes, Susan. "The Double Misreading of Paolo and Francesca." *Philological Quarterly* 62, no. 2 (1983): 221–239.

Norman, Richard. "Aristotle's Philosopher-God." In *Articles on Aristotle,* vol. 4, *Psychology and Aesthetics,* edited by Jonathan Barnes, Malcolm Schofield, and Richard Sorabji, 93–102. New York: St. Martin's Press, 1978.

Normore, Calvin G. "Who Was Condemned in 1277?" *Modern Schoolman* 72, no. 2–3 (January–March 1995): 273–281.

Novak, Michael. "A Key to Aristotle's 'Substance'." In *Substances and Things: Aristotle's Doctrine of Physical Substance in Recent Essays,* M. L. O'Hara, 190–208. Washington, D.C.: University Press of America, 1982.

Nussbaum, Martha C. "Aristotelian Dualism: Reply to Howard Robinson." *Oxford Studies in Ancient Philosophy* 2 (1984): 197–207.

O'Brien, William J. " 'The Bread of Angels' in *Paradiso* II: A Liturgical Note." *Dante Studies* 97 (1979): 97–106.

O'Daly, Gerard J. P. *Augustine's Philosophy of Mind.* Berkeley: University of California Press, 1987.

————. *Plotinus' Philosophy of the Self.* New York: Harper & Row, 1973.

O'Keeffe, D. "Dante's Theory of Creation." *Revue néoscolastique de philosophie* 26 (1924): 45–64.

O'Meara, John Joseph. "Augustine and Neo-Platonism." *Recherches augustiniennes* 1 (1958): 91–111.

Olshewsky, Thomas M. "On the Relations of Soul to Body in Plato and Aristotle." *Journal of the History of Philosophy* 14, no. 4 (October 1976): 391–404.

Origen. *Against Celsus.* In *The Writings of Origen,* translated by Frederick Crombie. Ante-Nicene Christian Library, vols. 10, 23. Edinburgh: T & T Clark, 1871–1872.

————. *Commentaire sur l'Evangile selon Matthieu.* Translated by Robert Girod. Sources chrétiennes, vol. 162. Paris: Editions du Cerf, 1970.

————. *Commentary on the Gospel According to John.* Translated by Ronald E. Heine. Fathers of the Church, A New Translation, vols. 80, 89. Washington, D.C.: Catholic University of America Press, 1989–93.

Orr, Mary Ackworth. *Dante and the Early Astronomers.* 1956. Port Washington, N.Y.: Kennikat, 1969.

Ortiz, Ramiro. "La materia epica di ciclo classico nella lirica italiana delle origini." *Giornale storico della letteratura italiana* 85 (1924): 1–93.

Osculati, Roberto. "La profezia nel pensiero di Dante." In *Il pensiero filosofico e teologico di Dante Alighieri,* ed. Alessandro Ghisalberti, 39–57. Milano: Vita e Pensiero, 2001.

Ottimo Commento. L'Ottimo Commento della Divina Commedia. Attributed to Andrea Lancia. 1333. Edited by Alessandro Torri. Pisa: N. Capurro, 1827–1829. In *DDP.*

Otto, Rudolf. *Mysticism East and West: A Comparative Analysis of the Nature of Mysticism.* Translated by Bertha L. Bracey and Richenda C. Payne. 1932. New York: Meridian, 1958.

Ovid. *Metamorphoses*. 3d ed. Edited by William S. Anderson. Leipzig: B. G. Teubner Verlagsgesellschaft, 1985.

———. *Metamorphoses I–IV*. Edited and translated by D. E. Hill. Oak Park, Ill.: Bolchazy-Carducci, 1985.

"Ovide moralisé": poème du commencement du quatorzième siècle. 5 vols. Edited by C. De Boer. 1915–1938. Wiesbaden: Martin Sändig, 1966.

Owen, G. E. L. "Aristotle on Time." In *Logic, Science, and Dialectic: Collected Papers in Greek Philosophy*, by G. E. L. Owen, edited by Martha Nussbaum, 295–314. Ithaca: Cornell University Press, 1986.

———. "The Platonism of Aristotle." In *Logic, Science, and Dialectic: Collected Papers in Greek Philosophy*, by G. E. L. Owen, edited by Martha Nussbaum, 200–220. Ithaca: Cornell University Press, 1986.

Owens, Joseph. *The Doctrine of Being in the Aristotelian 'Metaphysics': A Study in the Greek Background of Mediaeval Thought*. 3d ed. Toronto: Pontifical Institute of Mediaeval Studies, 1978.

———. "Faith, Ideas, Illumination, and Experience." In *The Cambridge History of Later Medieval Philosophy*, edited by Norman Kretzmann, Anthony Kenny, and Jan Pinborg, 440–459. Cambridge: Cambridge University Press, 1982.

———. "A Note on Aristotle, *De Anima* 3.4, 429b9." *Phoenix* 30, no. 2 (Summer 1976): 107–118.

———. "Quiddity and Real Distinction in St. Thomas Aquinas." *Medieval Studies* 27 (1965): 1–22.

———. "The Relation of God to World in the *Metaphysics*." In *Études sur la Métaphysique d'Aristote: actes du VIe Symposium Aristotelicum*, edited by Pierre Aubenque, 207–228. Paris: Librairie Philosophique J. Vrin, 1979.

Padoan, Giorgio. "Apollo." In *ED*, 1:318.

———. "Il canto XXVIII del *Paradiso*." In *Nuove letture dantesche*. Firenze: Le Monnier, 1973.

———. "La 'mirabile visione' di Dante e l'*Epistola a Cangrande*." In *Dante e Roma: atti del convegno di studi [Roma, 8–10 aprile 1965]*, 283–314. Firenze: Felice Le Monnier, 1965. Reprinted in *Il pio Enea, l'empio Ulisse* (Ravenna: Longo, 1977), 30–63.

Paganini, C. P. *Chiose a luoghi filosofici della* Divina Commedia; *raccolte e ristampate per cura di Giovanni Franciosi*. Edited by Giovanni Franciosi. Collezione di opuscoli danteschi inediti o rari, vol. 5. Castello: S. Lapi, 1894.

Pagels, Heinz R. *The Cosmic Code: Quantum Physics as the Language of Nature*. 1982. New York: Bantam Books, 1983.

Palgen, Rudolf. "Il mito di Glauco nella *Divina Commedia*." *Convivium* 25 (1957): 400–412.

———. "Scoto Eriugena, Bonaventura e Dante." *Convivium* 25, no. 1 (1957): 1–8.

Panikkar, Raymond. *The Unknown Christ of Hinduism*. London: Darton, Longman & Todd, 1964.

Paparelli, Gioacchino. "*Fictio*: la definizione dantesca della poesia." In *Ideologia e poesia di Dante*, 53–138. Firenze: Olschki, 1975.

Papio, Michael. "Dante's Re-Education of Conscience (*Paradiso* XVII)." *Lectura Dantis* 18–19 (Spring–Fall 1996): 91–110.

Paratore, Ettore. "Ovidio e Dante." In *Nuovi saggi danteschi*, 45–100. Roma: Angelo Signorelli, 1973.

Parma, Giuseppe Benedetto. *Ascesi e mistica cattolica nella* Divina Commedia: *studio filosofico-religioso*. 2 vols. Subiaco: Tipografia dei Monasteri, 1925–1927.

Pasquazi, Silvio. "Dell'interpretazione figurale anagogica." *Rassegna di cultura e vita scolastica* 25, no. 10 (31 October 1971): 1–3.

———. "*Paradiso* 29." In *Lectura Dantis Scaligera*: Paradiso, edited by Mario Marcazzan, 1031–1060. Firenze: Felice Le Monnier, 1968.

Pasquini, Emilio. "Il 'dolce stil novo.' " In *Storia della letteratura italiana*, edited by Enrico Malato, vol. 1, 649–721. 12 vols. Roma: Salerno, 1995–2003.

———. "Le metafore della visione nella *Commedia*." In *Letture classensi*, vol. 16, edited by Aldo Vallone, 129–151. Ravenna: Longo, 1987.

———. "Il mito dell'amore: Dante fra i due Guidi." In *Dante, mito e poesia: atti del secondo seminario dantesco internazionale (Monte Verità, Ascona, 23–27 giugno 1997)*, edited by Michelangelo Picone and Tatiana Crivelli, 283–295. Firenze: Franco Cesati Editore, 1999.

Pastore Stocchi, Manlio. "Dante e la luna." *Lettere italiane* 33, no. 2 (April–June 1981): 153–174.

———. "Quaestio de aqua et terra." In *ED*, 4:761–765.

Patzig, Günther. "Theology and Ontology in Aristotle's *Metaphysics*." In *Articles on Aristotle*, vol. 3, *Metaphysics*, edited by Jonathan Barnes, Malcolm Schofield, and Richard Sorabji, 33–49. New York: St. Martin's Press, 1979.

Pazzaglia, Mario. "Il canto XXVII del *Purgatorio*." In *Nuove letture dantesche*, vol. 5, 103–130. Firenze: Felice Le Monnier, 1972.

Peccorini, Francisco L. "Aristotle's Agent Intellect: Myth or Literal Account?" *Thomist* 40, no. 4 (October 1976): 505–533.

———. "Divinity and Immortality in Aristotle: A 'De-Mythologized Myth?' " *Thomist* 43, no. 2 (April 1979): 217–256.

Pelikan, Jaroslav. "The Odyssey of Dionysian Spirituality." Introduction to *Pseudo-Dionysius: The Complete Works*, translated by Colm Luibheid, 11–24. New York: Paulist Press, 1987.

Penna, Angelo. "El." In *ED*, 2:647.

Pépin, Jean. "Allegoria." In *ED*, 1:151–165.

———. *Dante et la tradition de l'allégorie*. Montréal: Institut d'Études Médiévales, 1970.

Perl, Eric D. " 'The Power of All Things': The One as Pure Giving in Plotinus." *American Catholic Philosophical Quarterly* 71, no. 3 (Summer 1997): 301–313.

Perry, Whitall N. *A Treasury of Traditional Wisdom*. 1971. Cambridge: Quinta Essentia, 1991.

Pertile, Lino. "'Così si fa la pelle bianca nera': l'enigma di *Par.* XXVII, 136–138." *Lettere italiane* 43, no. 1 (January–March 1991): 3–26.

———. "Dante's *Comedy* beyond the *Stilnovo*." *Lectura Dantis* 13 (Fall 1993): 47–77.

———. "A Desire of Paradise and a Paradise of Desire: Dante and Mysticism." In *Dante: Contemporary Perspectives*, edited by Amilcare A. Iannucci, 148–166. Toronto: University of Toronto Press, 1997.

———. "Il nodo di Bonagiunta, le penne di Dante e il Dolce Stil Novo." *Lettere italiane* 46 (1994): 44–75.

———. "*Paradiso*: A Drama of Desire." In *Word and Drama in the* Divine Comedy, edited by John Barnes and Jennifer Petrie, 143–180. Dublin: Irish Academic Press, 1993.

———. "*Paradiso* XXXIII: l'estremo oltraggio." *Filologia e critica* 6 (1981): 1–21.

———. "Poesia e scienza nell'ultima immagine del *Paradiso*." In *Dante e la scienza*, edited by Patrick Boyde and Vittorio Russo, 133–148. Ravenna: A. Longo, 1995.

_____. " 'La punta del disio': storia di una metafora dantesca." *Lectura Dantis* 7 (Fall 1990): 3–28.

_____. *La puttana e il gigante: dal Cantico dei Cantici al Paradiso Terrestre di Dante.* Ravenna: Longo, 1998.

Peter Lombard. *Sententiae in IV libris distinctae.* 3d ed. Grottaferrata: Editiones Collegii S. Bonaventure ad Claras Aquas, 1971.

Peterson, Mark. "Dante's Physics." In *The* Divine Comedy *and the Encyclopedia of Arts and Sciences: Acta of the International Dante Symposium (Hunter College, New York, 1983),* edited by Giuseppe Di Scipio and Aldo Scaglione, 163–180. Amsterdam and Philadelphia: John Benjamins, 1988.

Petrocchi, Giorgio. "Figure dantesche di Dio e degli angeli." *L'approdo letterario* 11 (April–June 1965): 3–18.

_____. *Vita di Dante.* Roma-Bari: Laterza, 1986.

Petry, Ray C. *Late Medieval Mysticism.* Philadelphia: Westminster Press, 1977.

Pézard, André. "Adam joyeux: Dante, *Paradis,* XXVI, 97–102." In *Dans le sillage de Dante,* 135–152. Paris: Société d'Études Italiennes, 1975.

_____. "Dante pétrifié: *Purgatoire,* XXXIII, 74." In *Dans le sillage de Dante,* 185–193. Paris: Société d'Études Italiennes, 1975.

Piché, David. "A Survey of the New Critical Edition of the Condemnation of 1277." Unpublished paper, Notre Dame, Ind., 1997.

Picone, Michelangelo. "Il corpo della/nella luna: sul Canto II del *Paradiso.*" *L'Alighieri,* n.s., 15 (January–June 2000): 7–25.

_____. "Dante and the Classics." In *Dante: Contemporary Perspectives,* edited by Amilcare A. Iannucci, 51–73. Toronto: University of Toronto Press, 1997.

_____. "L'Ovidio di Dante." In *Dante e la "bella scola" della poesia,* edited by Amilcare A. Iannucci, 107–144. Ravenna: Longo, 1993.

_____. "*Purgatorio* XXVII: passaggio rituale e *translatio* poetica." *Medioevo romanzo* 12, no. 2 (August 1987): 389–402.

Pieper, Josef. *Scholasticism: Personalities and Problems of Medieval Philosophy.* Translated by Richard Winston and Clara Winston. 1960. New York: McGraw-Hill, 1964.

Pierotti, Gian Luca. "La 'filia solis' di Bonaventura e i cambiamenti di colore in *Par.* XXVII." *Lettere italiane* 33, no. 2 (April–June 1981): 216–221.

Pietrobono, Luigi. "Filosofia e teologia nel *Convivio* e nella *Commedia.*" *Giornale dantesco* 41 (1938): 13–71.

Pincherle, Alberto. "Agostino." In *ED,* 1:80–82.

Piramus et Tisbé: introduzione, testo critico, traduzione e note. Edited by F. Branciforti. Firenze: L.S. Olschki, 1959.

Piramus et Tisbé: poème du XIIe siècle. Edited by C. De Boer. Les classiques français du moyen âge, vol. 26. Paris: Librairie Ancienne Honoré Champion, 1921.

Placella, Vincenzo. "Filosofia." In *ED,* 2:881–885.

_____. "*Guardando nel suo figlio.*" Napoli: Federico & Ardia, 1990.

Planck, Max. *The New Science: Where Is Science Going?, The Universe in the Light of Modern Physics,* and *The Philosophy of Physics.* N.p.: Meridian Books [Greenwich Editions], 1959.

Plato. *Alcibiades I and II.* In *Plato XII.* Translated by W. R. M. Lamb. 1927. Loeb Classical Library, vol. 201, 93–273. Cambridge, Mass.: Harvard University Press 1986.

_____. *The Collected Dialogues of Plato, Including the Letters.* Edited by Edith Hamilton and Huntington Cairns. Princeton: Princeton University Press, 1961.

————. *Plato: The Republic.* Edited and translated by Paul Shorey. Loeb Classical Library. Cambridge, Mass.: Harvard University Press, 1953–1956. 2 vols.

————. *Timaeus a Calcidio translatus commentarioque instructus.* In *Corpus Platonicum medii aevi.* 2d ed. Edited by J. H. Waszink and Raymond Klibansky. Plato Latinus, vol. 4. London: Warburg Institute, 1975.

Plotinus. *Enneads.* Edited and translated by A. H. Armstrong. 7 vols. Loeb Classical Library. Cambridge, Mass.: Harvard University Press, 1966–88.

————. *The Enneads.* Abridged ed. Translated by Stephen MacKenna. 1917–1930. New York: Penguin Books, 1991.

Poggioli, Renato. "Tragedy or Romance? A Reading of the Paolo and Francesca Episode in Dante's *Inferno.*" *PMLA* 72 (1957): 313–358.

Polis, Dennis F. "A New Reading of Aristotle's *Hyle.*" *Modern Schoolman* 68, no. 3 (March 1991): 225–244.

Porcelli, Bruno. "La vicenda di Dante nel canto XXVII del *Purgatorio.*" In *Studi sulla Divina Commedia,* 85–94. Bologna: Pàtron, 1970.

Porena, Manfredi. "Noterelle dantesche." *Studj romanzi* 20 (1930): 201–215.

Porena, Manfredi, ed. *La Divina Commedia di Dante Alighieri.* 3 vols. 1947. Bologna: Nicola Zanichelli, 1963.

Porphyry. *On the Life of Plotinus and the Order of His Books.* Translated by A. H. Armstrong. 1966. Loeb Classical Library, vol. 440, 1–87. Cambridge, Mass.: Harvard University Press, 1995.

Portier, Lucienne. "Les Argonautes dantesques." *Revue des études italiennes* 11 (1965): 381–392.

Portirelli, Luigi, ed. *La Divina Commedia di Dante Alighieri illustrata di note da Luigi Poritrelli.* Notes to *Paradiso* by G. Ferrario. Milano: Tipografia de' Classici Italiani, 1804–1805. In *DDP.*

Poulet, Georges. *The Metamorphoses of the Circle.* Translated by Carley Dawson and Elliott Coleman. Baltimore: Johns Hopkins University Press, 1966.

Poulle, Emmanuel, and Marcello Aurigemma. "Luna." In *ED,* 3:732–734.

Powell, Robert. *The Wisdom of Sri Nisargadatta Maharaj.* New York: Globe Press Books, 1992.

Powers, Jonathan. *Philosophy and the New Physics.* London: Methuen, 1982.

Priest, Paul. "Allegory and Reality in the *Commedia.*" *Dante Studies* 96 (1978): 127–144.

Proclus. *The Elements of Theology.* 2d ed. Edited and translated by E. R. Dodds. Oxford: Oxford University Press, 1963.

Proto, Enrico. "La dottrina dantesca delle macchie lunari." In *Scritti vari di erudizione e critica in onore di Rodolfo Renier,* 197–213. Torino: Fratelli Bocca, 1912.

Pseudo-Dionysius. *Pseudo-Dionysius: The Complete Works.* Translated by Colm Luibheid. Classics of Western Spirituality. New York: Paulist Press, 1987.

Pseudo-Grosseteste. *Summa philosophiae.* In *Die philosophischen Werke des Robert Grosseteste, Bischofs von Lincoln.* Edited by Ludwig Baur, 275–643. Münster: Aschendorff, 1912.

Quinn, Patrick. *Aquinas, Platonism, and the Knowledge of God.* Aldershot, England: Avebury, 1996.

Rabanus Maurus. *De rerum naturis [De universo].* PL, vol. III, 9–614.

Rabuse, Georg. "Macrobio." In *ED,* 3:757–759.

————. "Un punto solo m'è maggior letargo." *Deutsches Dante-Jahrbuch* 43 (1965): 138–152.

Racci, Manuela. "La metamorfosi dantesca: il percorso di Dante nel testo ovidiano." *Critica letteraria* 22, no. 2 (1994): 211–233.

Radhakrishnan, Sarvepalli, and Charles A. Moore, eds. *A Source Book in Indian Philosophy.* Princeton: Princeton University Press, 1957.

Raffa, Guy P. "Enigmatic 56's: Cicero's Scipio and Dante's Cacciaguida." *Dante Studies* 110 (1992): 121–134.

Ragni, Eugenio. "Selva." In *ED*, 5:137–142.

Raimondi, Ezio. "Ontologia della metafora dantesca." In *Letture classensi*, vol. 15, edited by Ezio Raimondi, 99–109. Ravenna: Longo, 1986.

Ramana Maharshi. *The Spiritual Teaching of Ramana Maharshi.* 1972. Boston: Shambhala, 1988.

Randall, John Herman, Jr. *Aristotle.* New York: Columbia University Press, 1960.

Rappe, Sara. "Self-Perception in Plotinus and the Later Neoplatonic Tradition." *American Catholic Philosophical Quarterly* 71, no. 3 (Summer 1997): 433–451.

Regis, Edward, Jr. "Aristotle on Universals." *Thomist* 40, no. 1 (1976): 135–152.

Reichberg, Gregory Martin. "The Communication of the Divine Nature: Thomas's Response to Neoplatonism." *American Catholic Philosophical Quarterly* 66 (1992): 215–228.

Restoro d'Arezzo. *La composizione del mondo colle sue cascioni.* Critical ed. Edited by Alberto Morino. Firenze: Accademia della Crusca, 1976.

Reyna, Ruth. "On the Soul: A Philosophical Exploration of the Active Intellect in Averroes, Aristotle, and Aquinas." *Thomist* 36, no. 1 (January 1972): 131–149.

Richard of Middleton. *Super quatuor libros Sententiarum Petri Lombardi questiones subtilissimae.* Brixiae [Brescia], 1591. 4 vols. Facsimile ed., Frankfurt: Minerva, 1963.

Richard of Saint Victor. *De gratia contemplationis seu Beniamin maior.* In *PL*, vol. 196.

———. *De Praeparatione animi ad contemplationem Libri, dictus Beniamin minor.* In *PL*, vol. 196.

———. *Richard of St. Victor: The Twelve Patriarchs, the Mystical Ark, Book Three of the Trinity.* Translated by Grover A. Zinn. Classics of Western Spirituality. New York: Paulist Press, 1979.

———. *Selected Writings on Contemplation.* Translated by Clare Kirchberger. Classics of the Contemplative Life. London: Faber and Faber, 1957.

Rist, John M. *Augustine: Ancient Thought Baptized.* Cambridge: Cambridge University Press, 1994.

———. "Notes on Aristotle *De Anima* 3.5." *Classical Philology* 41, no. 1 (January 1966): 8–20.

———. "Plotinus and Christian Philosophy." In *The Cambridge Companion to Plotinus*, edited by Lloyd P. Gerson, 386–413. Cambridge: Cambridge University Press, 1996.

Ritacco-Gayoso, Graciela. "Intelligible Light and Love: A Note on Dionysius and Saint Thomas." *New Scholasticism* 63, no. 2 (Spring 1989): 156–172.

Robinson, Howard M. "Aristotelian Dualism." *Oxford Studies in Ancient Philosophy* 1 (1983): 123–144.

———. "Form and the Immateriality of the Intellect from Aristotle to Aquinas." In *Aristotle and the Later Tradition*, edited by Henry Blumenthal and Howard Robinson, Oxford Studies in Ancient Philosophy: Supplementary vol., 207–226. Oxford: Oxford University Press, Clarendon, 1991.

———. "Mind and Body in Aristotle." *Classical Quarterly* 28, no. 1 (1978): 105–124.

———. "Prime Matter in Aristotle." *Phronesis* 19, no. 2 (1974): 168–188.

Robson, C. A. "Dante's Use in the *Divina Commedia* of the Medieval Allegories on Ovid." In *Centenary Essays on Dante*, by members of the Oxford Dante Society, 1–38. Oxford: Clarendon Press, 1965.

Rodier, Georges. *Traité de l'âme: commentaire.* Commentary to Aristotle's *De anima.* Paris: Librairie Philosophique J. Vrin, 1985.

Rorem, Paul. *Pseudo-Dionysius: A Commentary on the Texts and an Introduction to Their Influence.* Oxford: Oxford University Press, 1993.

Rorty, Richard. *Philosophy and the Mirror of Nature.* Princeton: Princeton University Press, 1979.

Ross, James F. "Creation II." In *The Existence and Nature of God*, edited by Alfred J. Freddoso, 115–141. Notre Dame, Ind.: University of Notre Dame Press, 1983.

Ross, William David. *Aristotle.* 6th ed. New York and London: Routledge, 1995.

Russell, Jeffrey Burton. *A History of Heaven: The Singing Silence.* Princeton: Princeton University Press, 1997.

Russell, Robert John, Nancey Murphy, and C. J. Isham, eds. *Quantum Cosmology and the Laws of Nature: Scientific Perspectives on Divine Action.* 2d ed. Vatican City: Vatican Observatory, 1996.

Sacrobosco [Holy Wood], John of. *De Spera.* Edited and translated by Lynn Thorndike, 76–246. Chicago: University of Chicago Press, 1949.

Salmona, Bruno. "L'atto di Aristotele nell'ermeneutica Plotiniana." In *L'atto aristotelico e le sue ermeneutiche*, edited by Marcello Sánchez Sorondo, 95–105. Roma: Herder, 1990.

Sandweiss, Samuel. *Sai Baba: The Holyman . . . and the Psychiatrist.* San Diego, Calif.: Birth Day Publishing, 1975.

Sansone, Mario. "Il canto XXVII del *Purgatorio.*" In *Letture e studi danteschi*, 165–184. Bari: De Donato, 1975.

———. *Paradiso* 27. In *Lectura Dantis Scaligera: Paradiso*, edited by Mario Marcazzan, 961–998. Firenze: Felice Le Monnier, 1968.

Santi, Antonio. "La questione della creazione nelle dottrine di Dante e del tempo suo." *Giornale dantesco* 23 (1915): 197–207.

Sapegno, Natalino, ed. *La Divina Commedia*, by Dante Alighieri. 1956. Firenze: La Nuova Italia, 1985. 3 vols.

Sarolli, Gian Roberto. "Dante 'scriba Dei.' " *Convivium* 31 (1963): 385–422, 513–544, 641–671.

———. *Prolegomena alla* Divina Commedia. Firenze: Olschki, 1971.

Sasso, Gennaro. "*Se la materia delli elementi era da Dio intesa.*" *La cultura* 39, no. 3: 365–393.

Scaglione, Aldo. "(Christian) Theologians vs. (Pagan) Philosophers: Another Look at Dante's Allegory." *Mediaevalia* 12 (1989): 115–126.

Scartazzini, G. A., ed. *La Divina Commedia di Dante Alighieri riveduta nel testo e commentata da G. A. Scartazzini.* 3d ed. Milano: Ulrico Hoepli, 1899.

Schiller, Jerome. "Aristotle and the Concept of Awareness in Sense Perception." *Journal of the History of Philosophy* 13, no. 3 (1975): 283–296.

Schmitt-von Mühlenfels, Franz. *Pyramus und Thisbe: Rezeptionstypen eines Ovidischen Stoffes in Literatur, Kunst und Musik.* Heidelberg: Carl Winter Universitätsverlag, 1972.

Schnapp, Jeffrey T. *The Transfiguration of History at the Center of Dante's Paradise.* Princeton: Princeton University Press, 1986.

Schrödinger, Erwin. *Mind and Matter.* The Tarner Lectures, Trinity College, Cambridge, October 1956. Cambridge: Cambridge University Press, 1958.

_____. *My View of the World*. Translated by Cecily Hastings. Cambridge: Cambridge University Press, 1964.

_____. *Nature and the Greeks* and *Science and Humanism*. Cambridge: Cambridge University Press, 1996.

_____. *What Is Life? The Physical Aspect of the Living Cell* and *Mind and Matter*. Cambridge: Cambridge University Press, 1967.

Scott, John A. "Beatrice's Reproaches in Eden: Which 'School' Had Dante Followed?" *Dante Studies* 109 (1991): 1–23.

_____. "Dante and Philosophy." *Annali d'italianistica* 8 (1990): 258–277.

_____. "Dante's Allegory." *Romance Philology* 26, no. 3 (February 1973): 558–591.

_____. "Dante's Sweet New Style and the *Vita Nuova*." *Italica* 42 (1965): 98–107.

_____. "Dante's Use of the Word *Intelletto*." *Italica* 40, no. 3 (September 1963): 215–224.

_____. "Imagery in *Paradiso* XXVII." *Italian Studies* 25 (1970): 6–29. Revised and reprinted as "Su alcune immagini tematiche di *Paradiso* XXVII" in *Dante magnanimo*, 195–237. Firenze: Olschki, 1977.

_____. "The Unfinished *Convivio* as a Pathway to the *Comedy*." *Dante Studies* 113 (1995): 31–56.

_____. " 'Veramente li teologi questo senso prendono altrimenti che li poeti' (Conv. II i 5)." In *Sotto il segno di Dante: scritti in onore di Francesco Mazzoni*, edited by Leonella Coglievina and Domenico De Robertis, 299–309. Firenze: Le Lettere, 1998.

Scrivano, Riccardo. "*Paradiso* 28." *Quaderni d'italianistica* 10, no. 1–2 (1989): 269–285.

Sebastio, Leonardo. "La poesia come unità del cosmo e del sapere: *Paradiso* XXVIII." In *Saggi danteschi*, vol. 2 of *Bibliologia e critica dantesca: saggi dedicati a Enzo Esposito*, edited by Vincenzo De Gregorio. 2 vols. Ravenna: Longo.

_____. *Strutture narrative e dinamiche culturali in Dante e nel Fiore*. Firenze: Olschki, 1990.

Segre, Cesare. "L'itinerarium animae' nel Duecento e Dante." In *Letture classensi*, vol. 13, edited by Maria Corti, 9–32. Ravenna: A. Longo, 1984.

Sellars, Wilfrid. "Substance and Form in Aristotle." *Journal of Philosophy* 54, no. 22 (October 1957): 688–699.

Selvaggi, Filippo, S. J. *Filosofia del mondo: cosmologia filosofica*. Roma: Università Gregoriana Editrice, 1985.

_____. "Hylomorphism." In *Encyclopedia Britannica*, 14th ed., vol. 11, 983–984. Chicago: William Benton, 1973.

Serravalle, Giovanni Bertoldo da. *Fratris Johannis de Serravalle translatio et comentum totius libri Dantis Aldigherii*. 1417. Edited by Marcellino Da Civezza and Teofilo Domenichelli. Prato: Giacchetti, 1891. 2 vols. In *DDP*.

Seung, T. K. *The Fragile Leaves of the Sibyl: Dante's Master Plan*. Westminster, Md.: Newman Press, 1962.

_____. "The Metaphysics of the *Commedia*." In *The Divine Comedy and the Encyclopedia of Arts and Sciences*, edited by Giuseppe Di Scipio and Aldo Scaglione, 181–222. Philadelphia: John Benjamins, 1988.

Shapiro, Marianne. *Dante and the Knot of Body and Soul*. New York: St. Martin's Press, 1998.

Shields, Christopher. "The Generation of Form in Aristotle." *History of Philosophy Quarterly* 7, no. 4 (October 1990): 367–390.

_____. "Some Recent Approaches to Aristotle's *De anima*." In *De anima: Books II and III*, translated by D. W. Hamlyn, 157–181. Oxford: Oxford University Press, Clarendon, 1993.

———. "Soul and Body in Aristotle." *Oxford Studies in Ancient Philosophy* 6 (1988): 103–137.

———. "Soul as Subject in Aristotle's *De Anima*." *Classical Quarterly* 38, no. 1 (1988): 140–149.

Shoaf, Richard Allen. " 'Auri sacra fames' and the Age of Gold (*Purg.* XXII, 40–41 and 148–150)." *Dante Studies* 96 (1978): 195–199.

———. *Dante, Chaucer, and the Currency of the Word: Money, Images, and Reference in Late Medieval Poetry*. Norman, Okla.: Pilgrim Books, 1983.

Silverstein, H. Theodore. "Dante and Vergil the Mystic." *Harvard Studies and Notes in Philology and Literature* 14 (1932): 51–82.

Simonelli, Maria Picchio. "Convivio." In *ED*, 2: 193–204.

———. "L'Inquisizione e Dante: alcune osservazioni." *Dante Studies* 97 (1979): 129–149.

Simplicius. *In Aristotelis Physicorum libros quattuor priores commentaria*. Edited by H. Diels. Commentaria in Aristotelem Graeca, vol. 9. Berlin: Reimeri, 1882–1909.

———. *In De anima commentaria*. Edited by M. Hayduck. Commentaria in Aristotelem Graeca, vol. 11. Berlin: Reimeri, 1882–1909.

———. *In De Caelo commentaria*. Edited by P. Hoffmann. Commentaria in Aristotelem Graeca, vol. 9. Berlin: Reimeri, 1882–1909.

Singleton, Charles S. *Dante's* Commedia: *Elements of Structure*. 1954. Baltimore: Johns Hopkins University Press, 1977.

———. "The Irreducible Dove." *Comparative Literature* 9 (1957): 129–135.

———. *Journey to Beatrice*. Baltimore: Johns Hopkins University Press, 1958.

———. "The Poet's Number at the Center." *MLN* 80 (1965): 1–10.

———. "The Vistas in Retrospect." *Modern Language Notes* 81 (1966): 55–80.

Skemp, J. B. "*Hule* and *Upodoxe*." In *Aristotle and Plato in the Mid-Fourth Century*, edited by I. Düring and G. E. L. Owen, 201–212. Göteborg: Elanders Boktryckeri Aktiebolag, 1960.

Sklar, Lawrence. *Space, Time, and Spacetime*. Berkeley: University of California Press, 1976.

Skousgaard, Stephen. "Wisdom and Being in Aristotle's First Philosophy." *Thomist* 40, no. 3 (July 1976): 444–474.

Smalley, Beryl. *The Study of the Bible in the Middle Ages*. 1952. Notre Dame, Ind.: University of Notre Dame Press, 1964.

Smith, E. Lester, ed. *Intelligence Came First*. Wheaton, Ill.: Theosophical Publishing House, 1975.

Smith, Margaret. *An Introduction to Mysticism*. New York: Oxford University Press, 1977.

Smith, Wolfgang. *The Quantum Enigma: Finding the Hidden Key*. Peru, Ill.: Sherwoood Sugden, 1995.

Sokolowski, Robert. "Creation and Christian Understanding." In *God and Creation: An Ecumenical Symposium*, edited by David B. Burrell, C.S.C., and Bernard McGinn, 179–192. Notre Dame, Ind.: University of Notre Dame Press, 1990.

———. *The God of Faith and Reason: Foundations of Christian Theology*. 1982. Washington, D.C.: Catholic University of America Press, 1995.

———. "Matter, Elements and Substance in Aristotle." In *Substances and Things: Aristotle's Doctrine of Physical Substance in Recent Essays*, M. L. O'Hara, 91–116. Washington, D.C.: University Press of America, 1982.

Solmsen, Friedrich. "Antecedents of Aristotle's Psychology and Scale of Beings." *American Journal of Philology* 76 (1955): 148–164.

_____. "Aristotle and Prime Matter: A Reply to Hugh R. King." *Journal of the History of Ideas* 19, no. 1 (January 1958): 243–252.

_____. *Aristotle's System of the Physical World*. Ithaca: Cornell University Press, 1960.

_____. "Platonic Influences in the Formation of Aristotle's Physical System." In *Aristotle and Plato in the Mid-Fourth Century*, edited by I. Düring and G. E. L. Owen, 213–235. Göteborg: Elanders Boktryckeri Aktiebolag, 1960.

Sorabji, Richard. "The Ancient Commentators on Aristotle." In *Aristotle Transformed: The Ancient Commentators and Their Influence*, edited by Richard Sorabji, 1–30. Ithaca: Cornell University Press, 1990.

_____. "Body and Soul in Aristotle." In *Articles on Aristotle*, Vol. 4, *Psychology and Aesthetics*, edited by Jonathan Barnes, Malcolm Schofield, and Richard Sorabji, 80–87. New York: St. Martin's Press, 1978.

_____. "Infinite Power Impressed: The Transformation of Aristotle's Physics and Theology." In *Aristotle Transformed: The Ancient Commentators and Their Influence*, edited by Richard Sorabji, 181–198. Ithaca: Cornell University Press, 1990.

_____. *Matter, Space and Motion: Theories in Antiquity and Their Sequel*. Ithaca: Cornell University Press, 1988.

_____. *Time, Creation and the Continuum: Theories in Antiquity and the Early Middle Ages*. Ithaca: Cornell University Press, 1983.

Speer, Andreas. "Bonaventure and the Question of a Medieval Philosophy." *Medieval Philosophy and Theology* 6 (1997): 25–46.

_____. "Physics or Metaphysics? Some Remarks on Theory of Science and Light in Robert Grosseteste." In *Aristotle in Britain During the Middle Ages: Proceedings of the International Conference at Cambridge, 8–11 April, 1994*, 73–90. Turnhout: Brepols, 1996.

Spencer, Sidney. *Mysticism in World Religion*. 1963. Gloucester, Mass.: Peter Smith, 1971.

Spera, Francesco. "La poesia degli angeli: lettura del canto XXVIII del *Paradiso*." *Lettere italiane* 42, no. 4 (October–December 1990): 538–552.

Spitzer, Leo. "Note on the Poetic and Empirical 'I' in the Medieval Authors." In *Romanische Literatur-Studien: 1936–56*, 100–112. Tübingen: M. Niemeyer, 1959.

Sprague, Rosamond Kent. "A Parallel with *de Anima* III, 5." *Phronesis* 17, no. 3 (1972): 250–251.

Stabile, Giorgio. "Navigazione celeste e simbolismo lunare in *Paradiso* II." *Studi medievali* 21 (1980): 97–140.

_____. "Teologia e cosmologia nella *Commedia*." In *Letture classensi*, vol. 12, 139–173. Ravenna: Longo, 1983.

Stahl, Donald E. "Stripped Away: Some Contemporary Obscurities Surrounding *Metaphysics* Z3 (1029a10–26)." *Phronesis* 26, no. 2 (1981): 177–180.

Stapp, Henry P. "Mind, Matter, and Quantum Mechanics." *Foundations of Physics* 12, no. 4 (April 1982): 363–399.

Steel, Carlos. "Medieval Philosophy: An Impossible Project? Thomas Aquinas and the 'Averroistic' Ideal of Happiness." In *Was ist Philosophie im Mittelalter?*, edited by Jan A. Aertsen and Andreas Speer, Miscellanea Mediaevalia, vol. 26, 152–174. Berlin: De Gruyter, 1998.

Stephany, William A. "Biblical Allusions to Conversion in *Purgatorio* XXI." *Stanford Italian Review* 3 (1983): 141–162.

Stewart, David. "Aristotle's Doctrine of the Unmoved Mover." *Thomist* 37, no. 3 (July 1973): 522–547.

Stormon, E. J. "Problems of the 'Empyrean Heaven' in Dante." *Spunti e ricerche* 3 (1987): 23–33.

Stow, Sandra Debenedetti. *Dante e la mistica ebraica.* Firenze: Giuntina, 2004.

Strohmaier, Gotthard. *Von Demokrit bis Dante: die Bewahrung antiken Erbes in der arabischen Kultur.* Hildesheim: Olms, 1996.

Suppes, Patrick. "Aristotle's Concept of Matter and Its Relation to Modern Concepts of Matter." *Synthese* 28 (Spring 1974): 27–50.

Sweeney, Leo. "Existence/Essence in Thomas Aquinas's Early Writings." *Proceedings of the American Catholic Philosophical Association* 37 (1963): 97–131.

Sykes, R. D. "Form in Aristotle: Universal or Particular?" *Philosophy* 50, no. 193 (1975): 311–331.

Tagore, Rabindranath. *Fireflies.* New York: Macmillan, 1928.

Talbot, Michael. *Beyond the Quantum.* 1986. Toronto: Bantam Books, 1988.

———. *Mysticism and the New Physics.* London: Routledge and Kegan Paul, 1981.

Tateo, Francesco. "Percorsi agostiniani in Dante." *Deutsches Dante-Jahrbuch* 76 (2001): 43–56.

Taylor, A. E. *Aristotle.* 1919. New York: Dover, 1955.

Te Velde, Rudi A. *Participation and Substantiality in Thomas Aquinas.* Leiden: E. J. Brill, 1995.

Themistius. *On Aristotle's On the Soul.* Translated by Robert B. Todd. Ithaca: Cornell University Press, 1996.

———. *Commentaire sur le* Traité de l'âme *d'Aristote: traduction de Guillaume de Moerbeke.* Edited by G. Verbeke. Louvain: Publications Universitaires de Louvain, 1957.

———. *In De anima.* Edited by Richard Heinze. Commentaria in Aristotelem Graeca, vol. 5. Berlin: Academiae Litterarum Regiae Borussicae, 1899.

Thomas Cantimpratensis [Thomas de Cantimpré]. *Liber de natura rerum.* Editio princeps secundum codices manuscriptos. Berlin: Walter de Gruyter, 1973.

Thompson, David. "Dante and Bernard Silvestris." *Viator* 1 (1970): 201–206.

Thorndike, Lynn, ed. and trans. *The Sphere of Sacrobosco and Its Commentators.* Chicago: University of Chicago Press, 1949.

Tommaseo, Niccolò, ed. *La Commedia di Dante Allighieri, con ragionamenti e note di Niccolò Tommaseo.* 1865. Firenze: Lucio Pugliese, 1983. In *DDP.*

Tonquédec, Joseph de. *Questions de cosmologie et de physique chez Aristote et Saint Thomas.* Paris: Librairie Philosophique J. Vrin, 1950.

Torraca, Francesco. *La Divina Commedia di Dante Alighieri nuovamente commentata da Francesco Torraca.* 1905. 4th ed. Milano–Roma–Napoli: Albrighi Segati, 1920. In *DDP.*

Torrell, Jean-Pierre. O.P. *Saint Thomas Aquinas,* vol. 1, *The Person and His Work.* Translated by Robert Royal. Washington, D.C.: Catholic University of America Press, 1996.

Toulmin, Stephen, and June Goodfield. *The Fabric of the Heavens: The Development of Astronomy and Dynamics.* New York: Harper & Brothers, 1961.

Trovato, Mario. "Due elementi di filosofia psicologica dantesca: l'anima e l'intelligenza." *Forum Italicum* 4, no. 1 (March 1970): 185–202.

Truijen, Vincent. "Visione mistica." In *ED,* 6:1071–1073.

Underhill, Evelyn. *Mysticism: A Study in the Nature and Development of Man's Spiritual Consciousness.* 1930. Cleveland: World, Meridian, 1963.

The Upanishads. Translated by Swami Nikhilananda. 4 vols. New York: Bonanza/Harper, 1949–1959.

Vallese, Giulio. "Il canto decimo del *Paradiso* e il cielo della Sapienza." *Le parole e le idee* 11, no. 3–4 (1969): 219–241.

Van Emden, W. G. "Shakespeare and the French Pyramus and Thisbe Tradition, or Whatever Happened to Robin Starveling's Part?" *Forum for Modern Language Studies* 11, no. 3 (July 1975): 193–204.

Van Steenberghen, Fernand. *Histoire de la philosophie: période chrétienne.* Louvain: Publications Universitaires, 1964.

————. *Introduction à l'étude de la philosophie médiévale.* Louvain: Publications Universitaires, 1974.

Vance, Eugene. *Mervelous Signals: Poetics and Sign Theory in the Middle Ages.* Lincoln: University of Nebraska Press, 1986.

Vandelli, Giuseppe. "*Paradiso* 28." In *Letture dantesche,* edited by Giovanni Getto, 1915–1944. Firenze: Sansoni, 1964.

Vander Weele, Michael. "Mother and Child in *Paradiso* 27." *Religion and Literature* 26, no. 3 (Autumn 1994): 1–17.

Vasoli, Cesare. "Averroè." In *ED,* 1:473–479.

————. "La Bibbia nel *Convivio* e nella *Monarchia.*" In *Otto saggi per Dante,* 65–81. Firenze: Le Lettere, 1995.

————. "Il canto II del *Paradiso.*" In *Lectura Dantis Metelliana,* 27–51. Roma: Bulzoni, 1992.

————. "Dante, Alberto Magno e la scienza dei 'peripatetici'." In *Dante e la scienza,* edited by Patrick Boyde and Vittorio Russo, 55–70. Ravenna: Longo, 1995.

————. "Filosofia e teologia in Dante." In *Otto saggi per Dante,* 13–40. Firenze: Le Lettere, 1995.

————. "L'immagine 'enciclopedica' del mondo nel *Convivio.*" In *Otto saggi per Dante,* 83–102. Firenze: Le Lettere, 1995.

————. "Intelletto possibile." In *ED,* 3:469–472.

————. "Intelletto." In *ED,* 3:464–468.

————. "Materia." In *ED,* 4:861–864.

————. "Sillogismo." In *ED,* 5:249.

————. "Tempo." In *ED,* 5:546–551.

Venturi, Pompeo. *La Divina Commedia di Dante Alighieri già ridotta a miglior lezione dagli Accademici della Crusca. . . . 1732.* Firenze: L. Ciardetti, 1821. In *DDP.*

Vergineo, Gianni. "Il misticismo di S. Bonaventura nel *Paradiso* dantesco." In *Incontri bonaventuriani: aspetti della cristologia in S. Bonaventura,* vol. 3, 15–36. Montecalvo Irpino: Oasi Maria Immacolata, 1967.

Vincent of Beauvais. *Speculum naturale.* Vol. 1 of *Speculum quadruplex sive Speculum maius.* 1624. Facsimile ed., Graz, Austria: Akademische Druck-u. Verlagsanstalt, 1964.

Von Leyden, Wolfgang. "Time, Number, and Eternity in Plato and Aristotle." *Philosophical Quarterly* 14, no. 4 (January 1964): 35–52.

Von Richthofen, Erich. "The Twins of Latona, and Other Symmetrical Symbols for Justice in Dante." In *The World of Dante: Six Studies in Language and Thought,* edited by S. Bernard Chandler and J. A. Molinaro, 117–127. Toronto: University of Toronto Press, 1966.

Wallace, William A. "Thomism and the Quantum Enigma." *Thomist* 61, no. 3 (July 1997): 455–467.

Watts, Alan. *The Supreme Identity: An Essay on Oriental Metaphysic and the Christian Religion.* 1950. New York: Random House, Vintage Books, 1972.

Weisheipl, James A., O. P. "The Celestial Movers in Medieval Physics." In *The Dignity of Science: Studies in the Philosophy of Science Presented to William Humbert Kane, O. P.*, edited by James A. Weisheipl, 150–190. Thomist Press, 1961.

———. *Friar Thomas d'Aquino: His Life, Thought, and Work.* Garden City, N.Y.: Doubleday, 1974.

Werge, Thomas. "The Race to Death and the Race for Salvation in Dante's *Commedia.*" *Dante Studies* 97 (1979): 1–21.

Wilber, Ken, ed. *Quantum Questions: Mystical Writings of the World's Great Physicists.* Boston: Shambhala, 1985.

Wilkes, K. V. "*Psuche* versus the Mind." In *Essays on Aristotle's* De anima, edited by Martha C. Nussbaum and Amélie Oksenberg Rorty, 109–127. Oxford: Oxford University Press, Clarendon, 1992.

Wilkinson, L. P. *Ovid Recalled.* Cambridge: Cambridge University Press, 1955.

Williams, A. N. "Deification in the *Summa Theologiae*: A Structural Interpretation of the *Prima Pars.*" *Thomist* 61, no. 2 (April 1997): 219–255.

Williams, Bernard. "Hylomorphism." *Oxford Studies in Ancient Philosophy* 4 (1986): 189–199.

Williams, C. J. F. "Prime Matter in *De Generatione et Corruptione.*" Appendix to *Aristotle's De Generatione et Corruptione*, translated by C. J. F. Williams, 211–219. Oxford: Clarendon Press, 1982.

Williams, C. J. F., and R. J. Hirst. "Form and Sensation." In *Aristotelian Society*, Supplementary vol. 39 (1965): 139–172.

Wippel, John F. "Essence and Existence." In *The Cambridge History of Later Medieval Philosophy*, edited by Norman Kretzmann, Anthony Kenny, and Jan Pinborg, 385–410. Cambridge: Cambridge University Press, 1982.

———. *Metaphysical Themes in Thomas Aquinas.* Washington, D.C.: Catholic University of America Press, 1984.

———. *The Metaphysical Thought of Thomas Aquinas: From Finite Being to Uncreated Being.* Washington, D.C.: Catholic University of America Press, 2000.

———. "Thomas Aquinas and the Condemnation of 1277." *Modern Schoolman* 72, no. 2–3 (January–March 1995): 233–272.

Witt, Charlotte. *Substance and Essence in Aristotle: An Interpretation of* Metaphysics *VII–IX.* Ithaca: Cornell University Press, 1989.

Wittgenstein, Ludwig. *Culture and Value.* Edited by G. H. von Wright. Translated by Peter Winch. 1977. Chicago: University of Chicago Press, 1980.

———. *Diari segreti.* Edited and translated by Fabrizio Funtò. Roma-Bari: Laterza, 1987.

———. *Philosophical Investigations.* 3d ed. Translated by G. E. M. Anscombe. New York: Macmillan, 1958.

———. *Tractatus Logico-Philosophicus.* Translated by D. F. Pears and B. F. McGuinness. London: Routledge & Kegan Paul, 1961.

Woods, Michael. "Particular Forms Revisited." *Phronesis* 36, no. 1 (1991): 75–87.

———. "Universal and Particular Forms in Aristotle's *Metaphysics.*" In *Aristotle and the Later Tradition.* Oxford Studies in Ancient Philosophy, Supplementary vol., edited by Henry Blumenthal and Howard Robinson, 41–56. Oxford: Oxford University Press, Clarendon, 1991.

Woods, Richard, O. P. "Meister Eckhart and the Neoplatonic Heritage: The Thinker's Way to God." *Thomist* 54, no. 4 (October 1990): 609–639.

Yogananda, Paramahansa. *Autobiography of a Yogi*. Los Angeles: Self-Realization Fellowship, 1981.

Yu, Jiyuan. "Two Conceptions of Hylomorphism in *Metaphysics* ZHΘ." *Oxford Studies in Ancient Philosophy* 15 (1997): 119–145.

Yusa, Michiko. "Contemporary Buddhist Philosophy." In *A Companion to World Philosophies*, edited by Eliot Deutsch and Ron Bontekoe, 564–572. Malden, Mass.: Blackwell, 1999.

Zaehner, Robert Charles. *Mysticism Sacred and Profane: An Inquiry into Some Varieties of Praeternatural Experience*. New York: Oxford, 1961.

Zukav, Gary. *The Dancing Wu Li Masters: An Overview of the New Physics*. New York: William Morrow, Quill, 1979.

Zupan, Patricia. "The New Dantean *Alba*: a Note on *Paradiso* X, 139–148." *Lectura Dantis* 6 (Spring 1990): 92–99.

CPSIA information can be obtained
at www.ICGtesting.com
Printed in the USA
BVHW050844130723
667177BV00008B/241